Ruth A. Johnston

Grade level recommendation: This curriculum has a variety of information and activities designed to appeal to general readers as well as students of varying interest and ability. It is intended for grades 10-12 but could also be used with very motivated younger students.

Copyright 2019 Ruth A. Johnston. All rights reserved.

No part of this book may be reproduced, scanned or distributed in any printed or electronic form without permission. Please do not participate in or encourage piracy of copyrighted materials in violation of an author's rights. Thank you for respecting the hard work of this author. Contact editor@pannebakerpress.com for permissions.

ISBN: 978-0-9831810-3-3

With thanks to these contemporary poets, whose work is used by permission: "Higgledy-piggledy Thomas A. Edison," Anthony Harrington; the poem appears in Harrington's collection From the Attic: Selected Verse 1965-2015 (Kudzu Editions, 2015). "Higgledy-Piggledy T. Intermedia," Robin Pemantle. "Circe turned Odysseus' men to swine," Robert C. Crutchfield. "My Father's Watch," William G. Salter. "Elegy for a Woman Unknown," Lidia Wolanskyj. "Terzanelle in Blonde," Chryss Yost; the poem first appeared in Quarterly West, #45, Autumn/Winter 1997-98, and it also appears in Yost's collection Mouth & Fruit (Gunpowder Press, 2014)

In Chapter 11, quotation from Stéphane Mallarmé: Un coup de dés jamais n'abolira le hazard, translated by A. S. Kline, Copyright © 2007.

Illustration credits: New England stone wall photograph appears by permission of Curtiss Clark, The Field Notebook. "Symphony in White, No. 2: The Little White Girl," by James Abbott McNeill Whistler, appears by permission of the Tate Gallery, London. "Landscape with the Fall of Icarus," by Pieter Breughel, appears by permission of Musées Royaux des Beaux-Arts de Belgique, Brussels, Belgium/Bridgeman Images. Photograph of Bacchus mosaic at Paphos appears by permission of the Sonia Halliday Photo Library, Oxfordshire, UK.

Cover design by Streetlight Graphics, LLC.

Published by Pannebaker Press, in cooperation with Ellen McHenry's Basement Workshop.

Table of Contents

How To Use This Book vii

Speak Like Rain! 9

One: Art with Words 10
    1. Why do we make art? 10
    2. Word sounds 12
    3. Word images 14
    4. Learning to understand art 14
    Summary and Definitions 15
    Exercises 1 15

Two: Word Stress 19
    1. Word stress patterns 19
    2. Scanning lines for word stress patterns 21
    Summary and Definitions 23
    Exercises 2 23

Three: Accentual Meter 26
    1. Old English verse 26
    2. Nursery rhymes 28
    3. Romantic accentual verse 29
    Summary and Definitions 30
    Exercises 3 30

Four: Metrical Feet 38
    1. English metrical patterns 38
    2. Identifying the meter in a poem 39
    3. Irregular metrical feet 41
    Summary and Definitions 41
    Exercises 4 42

Five: Line Lengths and Blank Verse 50
    1. Naming metrical lines 50
    2. Line endings 52
    3. Blank Verse 54
    Summary and Definitions 54
    Exercises 5 54

Review 1 ... 63

Six: Rhyme ... 66
- 1. Types of rhymes ... 66
- 2. Placing rhymes ... 68
- Summary and Definitions ... 70
- Exercises 6 ... 70

Seven: Rhyme Schemes ... 80
- 1. Naming rhyming patterns ... 80
- 2. Couplets ... 82
- 3. Kinds of Stanzas ... 84
- Summary and Definitions ... 88
- Exercises 7 ... 89

Eight: Sonnets ... 98
- 1. The Sonnet's history ... 98
- 2. The English Sonnet form ... 99
- 3. The Italian Sonnet form ... 100
- 4. Modern variations on the sonnet ... 102
- Summary and Definitions ... 104
- Exercises 8 ... 105

Review 2 ... 115

Nine: Repetition and Variation of Sound ... 118
- 1. Alliteration ... 118
- 2. Assonance and Consonance ... 119
- 3. Repetition of words and phrase structure ... 121
- Summary and Definitions ... 123
- Exercises 9 ... 124

Ten: Repetition of Lines ... 132
- 1. Triolet, Rondeau, and Villanelle ... 133
- 2. Sestina ... 139
- Summary and Definitions ... 141
- Exercises 10 ... 141

Eleven: Free Verse ... 151
- 1. The grand gesture of long lines ... 152
- 2. The cut gemstone of a haiku ... 154
- 3. Pictures on the Page: Using White Space ... 157
- Exercises 11 ... 162

Review 3 ... 173

Twelve: Image in Description ... 176
- 1. Traditional descriptive poetry ... 176

    2. Ekphrasis: Word art describing visual art ... 181
    3. Imagist description ... 183
    Summary and Definitions ... 185
    Exercises 12 ... 186

Thirteen: Image as Analogy ... 195
    1. Simile: Keeping the images separate ... 195
    2. Metaphor: blurring the boundaries ... 198
    Summary and Definitions ... 202
    Exercises 13 ... 203

Fourteen: Image as Symbol ... 210
    1. Real objects with meaning ... 210
    2. Archetypes: universal symbols ... 213
    3. Interpreting symbols in poetry ... 217
    Exercises 14 ... 220

Fifteen: Image as Myth ... 228
    1. Myth as allusion, reference or symbol ... 229
    2. Myth as dramatic situation ... 232
    3. Poetry to create myths ... 236
    Summary and Definitions ... 238
    Exercises 15 ... 238

Last Review ... 251

Sixteen: Image as Story ... 255
    Summary and Definitions ... 261
    Exercises 16 ... 261

Seventeen: Voice as Image ... 280
    1. Voice presented as the image ... 280
    2. Spoken word art ... 285

After this book: ... 290

Answer Key ... 292

Index ... 325

About the Author ... 333

How To Use This Book

Speak Like Rain is designed primarily for students in a formal program with homework and tests, so exercises and reviews are built in. But general readers should also enjoy the book, and they should read the homework questions thoughtfully, at least answering in their minds. Skipping them over entirely would mean missing the wonderful poems and some additional teaching insights. The book is intended to be used as a consumable workbook: please write in it and make your own notes!

For students, the homework is designed to suit a range of study modes. It is perfect for self-teaching, either as homeschool or in an individualized learning setting. Teachers should find plenty of material for classroom use and as a springboard for their own ideas.

If you find poetry difficult or unappealing, you might find the homework sets long. The first one is always some kind of activity; it's usually analytical but often light-hearted as well. When the questions turn to studying famous poems, they are intended to grow more challenging as the set moves on. Still, the questions aim to ask concrete, objective things that even a poetry-nonlover can observe and know. Students who find poetry difficult might aim to answer the first four, and then just read the last questions, using the answer key as a tutorial conversation instead of a "right or wrong?" check.

The book is also designed for students and other readers who *like* poetry. If some of the homework questions seem easy, none of them will waste your time, and the poems will always challenge you beyond the basic level presented here. The text is full of ideas that the homework may not demand you to master, but which will let you move ahead on your own. Every homework set closes with suggestions for further study.

The "Summary and Definitions" section is there to tell you which terms and ideas might be on a test. Teachers can use the section for that purpose, too. The four Reviews included in this book are not intended to be tests, but they can measure your retention and ability to integrate concepts. They're also meant to be interesting to read.

The Answer Key at the back of the book tries to provide short answers to most of the homework questions, but in some cases, the only answer is your own opinion. In those cases, the Key will share my opinions that you can use as conversations with your thoughts.

Inclusion of contemporary poems is a special problem for an independent publishing project, because copyright holders require licensing fees that add up fast. I've tried to solve this in three ways: first, most of the poems are in the public domain; second, in a few places I use short passages as "fair use" illustration or provide titles so the reader can locate the full poems; third, I have used my poems (which I own, of course) and the work of a few contemporary poets who gave me direct permission. There are many great poems written between 1930 and the present; I hope you will find them.

Speak Like Rain!

Why "Speak Like Rain"?

In 1914, Danish-born Baroness Karen Blixen went to Kenya. She lived on a coffee farm near Nairobi until 1931. She learned local languages so that she could talk with her Kikuyu, Somali, and Masai neighbors. Later, after the farm failed and she returned to Denmark, she wrote about the people and events of those years in her memoir, *Out of Africa.*

Blixen hired many local people to work on her farm, sometimes working side by side with them. One evening they were harvesting maize, tossing the cobs into an ox-cart. To practice her Swahili vocabulary, she started making up nonsense rhymes, such as "The oxen like salt," because *ngumbe* (oxen) rhymed with *chumbe* (salt). The teenage boys working with her were delighted. They paused in their work and stood around her in a ring, hearing the first words and then waiting to hear the rhyme.

Each time the rhyme came, they laughed. "The *Wakamba* eat snakes (*mamba*)!" They were not interested in helping complete the rhymes, preferring the role of surprised listeners. But they wanted to hear more:

As they had become used to the idea of poetry, they begged: "Speak like rain. Speak like rain."

Why they should feel verse to be like rain I do not know. It must have been, however, an expression of applause, since in Africa rain is always longed for and welcome.

In an arid climate, the seasonal rain is never an annoyance. The air begins to feel different; the clouds on the horizon look different. A change in the wind, or an early rumble of thunder, may announce the coming rain. But there's a waiting period until finally the first drops splash down, then more and more, until the ground is running over with water. The sound of those first drops is the most welcome thing in the world.

Sounds that are like rain, anticipated and then welcomed: that's what poetry is made of. As you go through this book, I want you to hear how language sounds and ideas can work together to bring joy. Poetry began by being popular, not by being a high art that must be studied. Although we study it now, we can still hear it like rain.

ONE:

Art with Words

What is poetry?
Poetry is art made with words. The rest of this book is about what that means.

1. Why do we make art?

Humans have a philosophical problem: our lives are relatively short, but our minds can perceive expanses of space, time, and ideas that are much larger. When we study the science of our world, we can't help being impressed by how small we are compared to the galaxy or how little we see and hear, compared to molecular realities. When we study history, we realize how short even a very long life is compared to the many lifetimes that make up even a short span of history. Looking out at the world, we see how small our parts are compared to the millions of other people whose lives are just as important to them, but completely unknown to us. We can understand connections between space and time, or between kinds of people. We may understand even larger connections about spiritual and divine realities.

Most people have days and moments when we suddenly feel connected to part of the larger reality. We may have an idea that could be put into words, or we might feel a wordless idea or an emotion. We *see* or *hear* something with spiritual perception. The insight often comes when experiencing some kind of extreme: like seeing an extremely large ocean or an extremely small particle; or feeling either extreme isolation or extreme crowdedness. But insights can also come in the little moments of daily life, when nobody watching us could tell that something has changed.

Almost everyone wants to mark our transcendent moments in some way. We may turn to someone and point to what we see, but it may come out only as, "how enormous the sun is on the horizon!" or "see that great flock of birds!" Later, we may find ourselves trying to explain an idea about truth or even what the feeling of connection was like. We want to hold onto it. It feels like we touched something permanent, and we want to put up a marker to remember it.

That impulse, to hold onto the moment of feeling or insight, is what prompts us to create art. The art we make often outlasts not just the moment or day, but also our individual lives. Some art lasts for centuries or millennia. Ancient people painted animals and spirits on cave walls, signing their drawings by a hand print. While other art made at the same time didn't last, the cave drawings did.

We don't understand what story, idea, or insight the cave artists were remembering, but seeing them in our own time, we experience a sense of connection to the distant past. We are amazed to see that not only were the drawings accurate enough for us to recognize the animals, but they clearly also convey the beauty of the animals. The rhinoceros's outline is graceful, probably more graceful than the actual animal was, because the artist was showing us his feeling about it. The hand prints not only sign the work, they play with color and shape to represent human spirits, overlapping and reaching upward together.

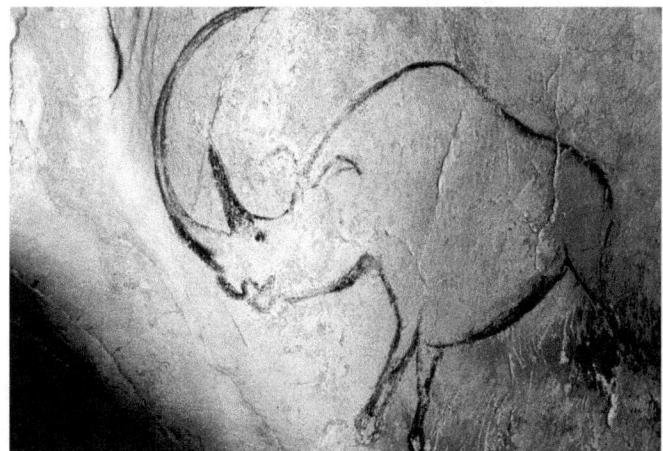 

Art creates connections between people by representing both what is shared, and what is unique or even isolating. We may commemorate a community experience like worship or hunting, and it seems that much early art served this shared purpose. But even in ancient times, and more in modern times, art also tried to preserve the deeply individual moment that could not be shared directly. Making art that speaks to an isolated moment is a way of bridging over the gap between us. Even if a feeling or experience is unique to me, you can experience some of it by hearing my song, seeing my painting, or reading my story.

The next step (the hard part!) is making the actual art. There's a new mandate at this stage: the art must be beautiful, even if the truth or insight it represents may have been painful or ugly. The artistic beauty can be conventional and easily seen by all, or it may be unconventional, valued only by trained eyes. Still, it must be there in some way. Beauty matters, because to our senses, it is a kind of absolute goodness. It's how we declare that all truth and insights are good, *even* when they're painful. It's beautiful to know truth about something ugly.

Art can be made with sound, movement, line, color, shape, and words: giving us music, dance, drawing, painting, sculpture, and poetry. Artists need some talent and training, so usually they work in only one medium.

Everyone has tried to draw a picture, so visual art is the one we understand most readily. We know that a good artist needs a steady hand, experience with materials, and good judgment. It's hard to get the colors mixed or chosen accurately, and even harder to reflect dimensional depth, such as shadows, or the change in color across wide spaces. Anyone who has studied either drawing or art history is also aware that shapes and colors are arranged according to principles of balance and beauty.

We make art with sound any time we perform or participate in music. Only original composers make musical art from scratch, and that process is mysterious to most of us. But since sound lasts only a brief moment, every time we sing or play a song or sonata, the art is re-created in a personal way. Both composers and performers are active in the musical art. Dance, art made with movement, is usually tied to music. Ballet gives us color, movement, and sound all in one package.

Visual and musical art usually connect easily with viewers and hearers. Even when we don't understand the insight or feeling that inspired a painting, we can still appreciate what we see (we like pictures!). As for music, everyone has a favorite song. It's only when visual and musical art are very abstract that it's a problem to appreciate them. Even then, as long as they have beautiful colors, lines, chords, and tones many people who aren't trained specialists can enjoy seeing and listening.

At first it's harder to see how words can be used for art, since we use them in daily speech. Words aren't special the way the elements of music, dance, and painting are. We can hear how music is different from daily sounds (thuds, bangs, dings, chimes and shouts); we can understand how dance movement is different from tying shoes or climbing into a truck. But there is no special set of words used only for art.

Additionally, we can define poetry as not only "art made with words," but art made with *nothing but* words. Song lyrics are *like* poems, but they aren't the same, because if you just read them without the melody, they lose half their artistry. Words that are placed into a mural or painting are part of the visual decoration. A true poem stands alone, separate from the paper or stone it was written on. You can recopy it, or you can give it to different people to read, and it still accomplishes its purpose.

2. Word sounds

Art made with words breaks into two parts: its sounds and its images. We use both sounds and images in daily speech, when we aren't trying to create art. They can have other purposes: grabbing attention, making us laugh, or helping us remember.

We start teaching young children about rhyming words because we want them to hear the sounds so they'll be ready to learn to read. All children's songs rhyme; I can't think of any exceptions. In the past, and sometimes still in our time, children also learned traditional rhymed poems, like, *"Baa, baa, black sheep, have you any wool? Yes sir, yes sir, three bags full."* In my 1960s nursery school, the teachers placed an unlit candle on the floor and each child had a turn jumping over it, while the class chanted, "Jack be nimble, Jack be quick, Jack jump over the candlestick!" We also teach children to remember the lengths of months with a rhyme coined so many years ago that it still preserves an outdated verb form: "Thirty days hath September, April, June, and November." At a little older age, children learn that "In fourteen hundred ninety-two, Columbus sailed the ocean blue."

Everyone likes the rhyming sound effect. Our minds feel pleasure in the cycle of setting up a sound for special notice, waiting to hear how the sound will be repeated, then getting the answering chime of the second rhyme. That's probably why the African boys thought rhyming was "like rain." When it's going to rain, we see lightning and wait to hear the thunder, or we hear thunder, feel the wind shift, and wait for the patter of water on our faces. We anticipate, then we get an answer. Like the African boys, we often laugh at rhymes. Children nearly always laugh, and adults, too, making up rhyming phrases as jokes (sometimes adding, "I'm a *poet* and don't *know it!*").

In mid-19th century London, Cockney dialect started using rhyming as a deliberately confusing slang. The phrase "apples and pears" rhymed with "stairs," so they would leave off the rhyming part ("pears") and say only "up the apples" to mean "upstairs." The listener had to complete the rhyme in his head to get the joke or know its meaning. The American use of "bread" to mean money probably came from Cockney "bread and honey" to rhyme with "money;" we also picked up their term "raspberry," originally "raspberry tart" to rhyme with "fart."

In the century since Londoners started using rhymes to create word substitutes, the pool of slang words kept changing. They came up with elaborate combinations of previous rhymes, puns, and names of current celebrities, always looking for a new, clever rhyme. While rhyming slang isn't as popular as it once was, you can still hear it. "Tony Blairs" rhymes with "flares" (wide-leg pants), and "Britney Spears" could stand for "beers." The rhyming part is always left for the listener to figure out. Someone could say, "He tossed back a few more Britneys than was good for him, put on his Tonys, and walked out on the frog." ("Frog," an old rhyming slang, stood for "frog and toad," to rhyme with "the main road.")

We also arrange words by their beginning sounds. This effect, too, is often comic. Family nicknames for children sometimes use repeated first sounds, like Silly Sammy or Pretty Patty. To make fun of someone, we may come up with a word that repeats the first sound of their name, like the old rhyme about Simple Simon (who met a pieman). Repeated sounds are memorable, so businesses like to use them: Bob's Big Boy, Ramblin' Roses, or Connie's Cards and Clutter. Some preachers use a sermon style organized around points that start with the same letter: Purpose, Prepare, Practice, Paradise!

Words have natural rhythm, too. We barely think about their rhythm until someone speaks a word in the wrong pattern. The error stands out clearly and may trip up listeners in their comprehension. American and British speakers of English use some different word stress patterns that sound very strange at first. Americans say "LAB'ratory," while the British say, "laBORat'ry. When I listen to audiobooks read by British narrators, I notice that where I would say "PRINcess, DUchess, AUthoress," the narrator consistently talks about the "prinCESS, duCHESS, and authoRESS."

We can use the rhythm built into phrases to coordinate people's movement. Soldiers on long marches need to walk at the same pace, close together, and keep their feet moving left and right like the others. Rhythmic chants called cadences make the effort less conscious, and therefore easier. Cheerleaders at football and basketball games also use rhythmic chants to coordinate their voices and encourage the crowd to join in. The rhythm has to be predictable and repeated so that people can join with confidence.

When people gather for a political protest, they pay a lot of attention to the rhythm of words. They want their many voices to sound like one very loud voice, so they need to chant the same words at the same time. Rhythm helps. The most common protest chant has a very simple outline: "hey HEY! (pause) ho HO! (pause) This bad thing has GOT to GO!" Chants of this kind have to be even simpler than army cadences or cheerleader slogans, because they can't depend on protesters having any previous practice. They have four strong beats and a very simple, obvious rhyme to close the phrase. Being clever gets no points at a protest; it only matters to keep it simple and loud.

At dance clubs in the 1980s, DJs talked a rhythmic patter between songs. With introductory drum measures playing in the background, they timed their words to go with, then against, the beat. Crowds loved it, and this style became rap music, or hip-hop. Both rhyme and rhythm matter tremendously in hip-hop style, since the melody of a traditional song is usually left out. Starting with the natural spoken rhythm of words and phrases, the rapper's "flow," or chanting style, can also manipulate phrases into unnatural patterns that are spoken too fast or use the strong beat on words that we don't expect. Clever words and unexpected rhymes win points, since the rapper wants to stand out, not blend into a group the way chanting protesters do.

Rhythm and rhyme both help when we have to memorize things. Before the spread of papermaking technology in the late Middle Ages, stories and information had to be memorized. Singers learned long story-songs that always used rhyme, first-sound repetition, or a set rhythm to prompt the memory. Students learned rhymes with information, such as the one about "Thirty days hath September."

One of the most colorful examples of rhyme used for memory comes from the Mongol hordes of Genghis Khan, in the 1200s. The armies were very large, and they had many non-Mongol men who had only recently joined up. Everyone was assigned to a group of 10, 100, and 1000; those units used marching cadences to teach the laws of the Mongol empire. They also learned rhymed chants to remember phrases that were likely to be used in messages. When a man was pulled out of the ranks and told to take a message to another unit some miles away, he received it as a rhyme using these familiar phrases. He only had to remember the new information that was mixed in; the rest came to him like song lyrics.

3. Word images

The sound of words (rhyme, alliteration, and rhythm) fills the first half of poetry's artistic tool box. The other side of the box is filled with images that can be used in various ways. Here too, we can raise our awareness of images in everyday speech, where they are used for explanations or dramatic effect. Poetry uses them in distinctive ways, but like all words, images have practical uses.

We use simple images in some figures of speech. "I'm sorry to burst your bubble" brings the vivid image of bubbles made of gum or soap, pricked and suddenly vanishing. We can also say, "I'm sorry to rain on your parade," and anyone who has participated in a local parade can feel how dismal it is when the float gets soaked and most watchers have been driven indoors. Some of the sayings use *like* or *as*, for example, "busy as a bee," or "working like a dog." When the comparison is unexpected but created with a well-known experience, the impression is stronger.

When we need to explain an unusual experience, we go for this stronger impression. If you live through a natural disaster, you may not have a standard set of descriptions to lean on. How do you explain a tornado to people who live outside twister zones? Tornados are often compared to the loud, ongoing noise of a train passing close by, on the assumption that most places still have trains. When a tornado approaches, the air pressure suddenly drops, leading some people to describe popping eardrums "like when you're in an airplane taking off." Other images are needed to describe the flying debris, bizarre destructive patterns afterward, and especially the serious fear that the tornado provokes. "It was like…" we say, reaching for any image that can lend part of an idea.

Advertisers use images to tell us how to feel about their products. They borrow how we already think or feel about, for example, a large boulder: we know that it's likely to be in the same place for many years, unchanged, because stone isn't easily broken down. We feel that a boulder is a reliable landmark, so the idea is more comforting than threatening. For many years, Chevrolet ran an ad campaign that constantly reminded people that Chevy trucks and cars were "like a rock." They chose their words carefully, not saying "our trucks are *like rocks*," since we don't have a positive feeling about "rocks" (they break lawnmower blades, hit windshields, and make us stumble). All of the trucks together are *like a rock*: like a big boulder that is reliably always the same.

Product names are also carefully chosen for the images (and feelings) they give us. "Galaxy" is a good name for a computerized cell phone, because it gives you a sense of reaching across distances. "Android," another phone product name, evokes the character of a robot that's so good it seems human. Cars and trucks may have the most carefully chosen names. Mountain ranges are good for trucks: Tahoe, Tacoma, Sierra, Denali. Other geographical words are good, if they suggest speed, size or strength: Frontier, Avalanche, Tundra, Canyon, Ridgeline. Some use a fierce but fast animal: Ram, Charger. Heroic human figures also work: Raider, Titan, Ranger. For every product that gets named, there are dozens of words that are considered and then discarded, because some aspect of that image isn't going to be positive.

4. Learning to understand art

Every kind of art has techniques and terms. Music has major and minor, arpeggios and crescendos, riffs and bridges. Painting has positive and negative space, chiaroscuro and diptychs, pastels and oils. Dance has pointe and par terre, swing and tango, lifts and drops. Anyone who learns an art, either to do it or to understand it, has to learn the terms so they can talk about the individual pieces and techniques of the art.

Poetry has its own set of words to describe all of the ways that art can be made from words. The first is the core word, "poem." It is a shortened, Anglicized form of Greek *poiema*, "the result of making." With most words, we just say things, but when we arrange them as art, we have *made* something: a poem.

Studying poetry means learning to see each feature of artistry and know its special term. Additionally, it means understanding how the artistic features of sound and image work together. In every art, its separate features and techniques don't mean much on their own, but rather the artist uses these tools to craft something out of the whole. When you can understand how the whole piece of art is made (even if you aren't able to make it yourself), you understand the art.

There are people whose emotion about art makes them reluctant to study it, since analysis may destroy naive but precious first impressions. But most of the time, we like art better after studying it. The art form for which I have the least natural feeling is dance, especially classical ballet. However, I watched a YouTube tutorial on how some dance motions are pantomime for words. These motions aren't as clear and grammatical as Sign Language, but they're similar. In the tutorial, two dancers explained the signs as they are traditionally used in the ballet "Swan Lake." Once I saw that apparently random arm movements were actually a sign language conversation, I could watch a short performance with a lot more interest and appreciation. I think every art has features like this, hidden until we're trained to see or hear them.

This book starts with the sound features of word art, then talks about images. In some of the lessons, I use my poems as illustrations (and in a few special cases, poems by other contemporary poets). Sometimes students feel concerned that literature textbooks are putting thoughts into the writers' heads that may not have been there, but with a living writer, this isn't a problem. I always find it very interesting to know what was in an artist's mind, and why he chose this technique instead of another one, and how he thinks it works to commemorate and illustrate his original idea. This is not to say that the meaning of art is restricted to what the maker had in mind, but it's a place to start.

Summary and Definitions

Poetry is art made only with words.

To create art, poetry uses sound effects, like rhyme and rhythm, and images.

We understand and even like a form of art more when we understand its techniques and terms. This is why we study poetry.

Exercises 1

1. Have you had some experience that made you wish you could commemorate it in a picture, song, or piece of writing?

2. For each poem, note four things:

    a) What is your impression of the insight that prompted someone to create this piece of word art? Even if you don't feel you fully understand the poem, say what you can, not overlooking the obvious. ("La Figlia Chè Piange" means "The Girl Who Weeps.")

    b) In what ways are the words used as art? Look for *sound* effects: words beginning with the same sound; rhymes; rhythm patterns. Also consider any other ways the words call attention to themselves: repetition, unusual word choice, odd spelling, and arrangement in lines. Try circling or underlining the sound elements so you can see them at a glance.

    c) What visual *images* does each poem portray?

    d) When you read the poem again, after noticing the sounds and images, does it change your impression of the poem as art?

A Poison Tree

I was angry with my friend:
I told my wrath, my wrath did end.
I was angry with my foe:
I told it not, my wrath did grow.

And I watered it in fears,
Night and morning with my tears;
And I sunnèd it with smiles,
And with soft deceitful wiles.

And it grew both day and night,
Till it bore an apple bright;
And my foe beheld it shine,
And he knew that it was mine,

And into my garden stole
When the night had veiled the pole:
In the morning glad I see
My foe outstretched beneath the tree.

William Blake, 1757-1827

The Eagle

He clasps the crag with crooked hands;
Close to the sun in lonely lands,
Ringed with the azure world, he stands.

The wrinkled sea beneath him crawls:
He watches from his mountain walls,
And like a thunderbolt he falls.

Alfred Lord Tennyson, 1809-1892

La Figlia Che Piange

Stand on the highest pavement of the stair—
Lean on a garden urn—
Weave, weave the sunlight in your hair—
Clasp your flowers to you with a pained surprise—
Fling them to the ground and turn
With a fugitive resentment in your eyes:
But weave, weave the sunlight in your hair.

So I would have had him leave,
So I would have had her stand and grieve,
So he would have left
As the soul leaves the body torn and bruised,
As the mind deserts the body it has used.
I should find
Some way incomparably light and deft,
Some way we both should understand,
Simple and faithless as a smile and shake of the hand.

She turned away, but with the autumn weather
Compelled my imagination many days,
Many days and many hours:
Her hair over her arms and her arms full of flowers.
And I wonder how they should have been together!
I should have lost a gesture and a pose.
Sometimes these cogitations still amaze
The troubled midnight and the noon's repose.

T. S. Eliot, 1888-1965

Morning lyric

The soul wakes in a clean white shift
and blinks in generic sunshine.
It could be any of a million days.

At arm's reach, wrinkled, is today:
the recollected schedule, leg by leg,
belted with a string of have-to's—

Attitudes de rigueur slipped
over the head, pulled smooth—
a quick brush through vanity—

Habits laced against sudden
shocks, cushioned in self-pity:
Ready to go out, two inches shorter.

Ruth Johnston

The last poem is from my own collection, so I can explain directly the insight that prompted it. I was thinking about how there are usually a few minutes of waking up when we are still lying in bed and sleepy, while we collect our thoughts for the day. In the state of waking up, we feel like a simple, eternal soul who could be the same being in any place or time. But after we've remembered what today is with its schedule, the worries from yesterday, the anxieties of later today, the jealousies and fears we carry about in the daytime, we seem much less simple and eternal. I chose to make phrases about attitudes with the language of getting dressed, so that both ideas are present in each line. Today = clothing, obligations = belt, vanity = hair, habits = shoes, self-pity = socks. When we are all "dressed," the poem says, ready to compete with other people and protect our egos, we have shrunk to something smaller than the natural, simple heart we had on waking.

Two:

Word Stress

When we speak English, we shift from louder to softer tones within each sentence and word. For all words with two or more syllables, one of the syllables must be said a little bit louder and more clearly than the others. This feature of English is called word stress; the louder, clearer syllable is *stressed*.

We rarely think about the fact that we're altering our voices to be louder and softer many times within a second. Perhaps it's most obvious if we're angry: "You ALways exAGgerate!" People who never stop to think about syllables still know exactly which one to say louder when they're angry. If someone says the wrong part louder, the word doesn't sound right: "You alWAYS exaggerATE!" Nobody would say that. So while we rarely think about it while speaking, we actually know these patterns very well. The only hard part is learning to think about how we speak.

Making art with words means thinking *very* carefully about how we speak; every sound becomes a tool. Word stress is always, always part of poetry. Other artistic sounds like rhyme may be skipped, but English words can't just "skip" word stress, so it's always there. Most poetry uses the stress to make patterns that please our ears. But even when a poem doesn't use stress in a patterned way, we need to keep listening and hearing it. It's like listening to the bass line of a song; anyone with ears trained for music can't stop hearing it, even when it's very low or quiet.

1. Word stress patterns

In English words, syllables can be spelled in a lot of different ways; it's not easy to see them in writing, and we may handle the syllables differently at times. Dictionary entries always break each word into syllables and provide a guide to word stress. The most common stress pattern is shown first, and if there is an acceptable alternative, it's also given. Dictionary entries and many poetry books show the stressed syllable marked with a little slash mark pointing at it, or just before it (poetry book: blánket; dictionary: ˈblaŋ kət). However, in this text, it's easier to see stressed syllables if I spell them in all capital letters: BLANket.

In general, every time your mouth opens, dropping the chin, you're saying a syllable. The word "syllable" itself has three syllables, each one centered around a sound that could be sustained like a musical note, if we had to: y, a, and l. Officially, vowels are the sounds that can be sustained: aaaah, eeee, ooo, and so on. But R, L, M, and N can also be sustained, forming the heft of a syllable (L forms the main sound of the third syllable of "syllable").

In words of two syllables, one of them carries the stress, while the other is de-emphasized. However, sometimes we stress both syllables, usually because it's a compound word and we feel that both parts are important. Here are all three cases (be sure to read these examples out loud):

| BLANket | withOUT | GALL-STONE |
| WONder | reSENT | SNOW-MAN |

In three-syllable words, usually just one syllable is stressed, and it's normally one of the first two. We see stress at the end mostly in words borrowed from French. These three patterns are shown below:

ELephant	apPROAches	personNEL
WONderful	reSENTful	majorETTE

Three-syllable words sometimes have a secondary stress. If I say "restaurant" and I'm careful to say all three syllables, I put some stress on the "rant" part. I could write it as REStauRANT, using boldface letters to show where the main stress goes. Foreign words often go into this pattern: SMORgasBORD, FAHRenHEIT. Words we don't use very often may also go like this, because it's important to hear every syllable clearly: PERiGEE, PINaFORE, ANoDYNE. Some final syllables matter because they define a profession or type: AUCtionEER, REFerEE, MUSketEER, SIamESE, TANgerINE. Some two-stress words are compound, so that the last syllable feels a bit like its own word: APpleSAUCE, WINterGREEN, BUTtonHOLE. And there are just some three-syllable words that need a second stress: ATtiTUDE, ENveLOPE, TELePORT.

If we had to simplify these words to show just one stressed syllable, we'd choose the heavier stress, on the first syllable. Some dictionaries will show you both stresses, some just one. When you see words like this used in poetry, in the following chapters, sometimes the second word stress will matter, while other times it won't. (Choosing when to make something matter is part of making art.)

Four-syllable words usually break into two's, following the pattern of two shorter words like "HURry FASter," *DUM da DUM da*.

    DICtionARy
    SUperVIsor

They can also follow a pattern like the phrase "an ELephant," *da DUM da da*.

    specTACular
    inSENsitive

Sometimes, four syllables are handled differently in American and British dialects. Americans are comfortable with one word having two stresses, but British speech tends to avoid this. Four-syllable words may be pressed into three-syllable patterns. Here is how Americans and British would stress a word like "dormitory."

    DORmiTORy (American)
    DORmit'ry (British)

"Laboratory" has five syllables, but it gets reduced to four by both Americans and British. They don't do it the same, though:

    LAB'raTORy (American)
    laBORat'ry (British)

Longer words usually fall into patterns of alternating stress and non-stress, breaking the word into smaller sets of two and three syllables:

UniVERsity
inCENdiARy
susCEPtiBILity
DIFFerENtiAtion

What about words with just one syllable? On their own, they have no pattern; when we read them in a list, we usually give each one a strong stress: RED, BLACK, LOSS, GAIN, ME, YOU, NOW, THEN, A, THE, AND. But when these short words occur in clusters, only some of them are stressed. The nouns, verbs and adjectives are usually stressed (loss, gain, red, black). However, it's normal not to put any emphasis on an article unless we really want to single out its meaning. Normally, we stress the noun:

the END
a TREE
the CAR

We also don't usually stress conjunctions or prepositions:

CARS and TRUCKS
but NOW
for ONCE
by ME

Most prepositional phrases turn into clusters of three or four syllables:

in the END
up on TOP
by the SEA
aROUND the BEND
inSIDE my HEAD

However, there's a lot of interpretive leeway in these matters. We could say "in the end" with a second stress on the preposition: "IN the END." And in many of these phrases, we could use unusual word stress if we really wanted a meaning to stand out. "I said to come stand BY me, not beHIND me." The variations that we use for shades of meaning play into the language's musicality, so they are part of the artist's tool kit, like shades of color.

2. Scanning lines for word stress patterns

Here are three sentences with very similar meaning, but noticeably different word stress patterns:

The CAR is in the STREET.
The RED CAR is at the END of the STREET.
My NEW red CAR is PARKED outSIDE your HOUSE.

The first two are ordinary things anyone might say. So is the third sentence, but it falls into a pattern: *da DUM da DUM da DUM da DUM da DUM*. I could push the first sentence into this kind of one two, one two pattern, but it would sound a little strained, "the CAR is IN the STREET." It would sound like either I wanted to say it wasn't *next to* the street, or else like I was pushing the words into a regular pattern, like poetry.

When we notice and mark a regular pattern in a line, it is called *scanning* the line. The study of stress patterns in speech is called *scansion* or *prosody*, but I will not be emphasizing these terms.

When we scan a line of words by hand, we mark the stressed words and syllables with a little slash or accent: The cár is in the stréet. Written by hand, the accent marks are usually bigger and easier to see. Additionally, there's a symbol for unstressed syllables and words, a little ˘ like the marking for a short vowel. da DUM would be marked: ˘ ´ In the text, I will continue to use ALL CAPS to show stressed syllables, but working with a pencil, you should expect to show stresses with the accent mark.

Going back to the lines about the new red car parked in the street, I can change the words a little and form a new pattern. Now I want the pattern to run *DUM da DUM da* (not *da DUM da DUM*). By taking out the color word "red," I remove one syllable and shift stress to "my." The whole pattern changes:

MY new CAR is PARKED outSIDE your HOUSE.

I can change one more word and get a perfect pattern of five "*DUM da*" pairs:

MY new CAR is PARKED outSIDE your CAbin.

If you compare the two lines, you'll see that their word stress patterns are exactly reversed:

My NEW red CAR is PARKED outSIDE your HOUSE.
MY new CAR is PARKED outSIDE your CAbin.

Those are the two patterns that English falls into naturally; both are made of pairs. Sometimes, words fall into patterns of threes. They're either *da da DUM*, or *DUM da da*. Here is one of each, and both still sound like natural sentences from daily life.

In the END, what you BOUGHT is a CAR.
CARS like this GO just too FAST for me.

I've been forming these patterned sentences with very short words, to keep them very clear. But of course, longer words fall into the same patterns: The LAB'raTORy's DOOR was LOCKED.

(I can use the British way of pronouncing "laboratory," but I must organize words around it in a very different way: then i SAW my laBORat'ry's DOOR was unHINGED.)

There's one more twist on word stress. A small set of words can have the stress on the first or the second syllable, but the meaning changes in each case. There are about 25 variable words; most form a noun/verb pair. They include address, combine, construct, contrast, increase, decrease, import, export, insult, object, perfect, project, and record. One variable-stress word that does not form a noun-verb pair is "content." When its stress is on CON, it is a noun, but when the stress falls on TENT, it's an adjective.

Variable words can be fitted into patterns, but we have to be sure we're using the form we want. If the line's stress pattern forces the reader toward reading "conTENT" when you intended the meaning of "CONtent," you may have a problem. Either that, or you're playing a trick on your reader by importing both meanings, one through stress pattern and the other through context.

In the next lessons, we'll look at the ways word stress patterns create art in poetry. For this lesson, we focus only on being able to hear and mark word stress patterns. Early childhood knowledge of nursery rhymes and songs usually helps, but lots of exposure to hiphop music may make it harder for a student to hear normal word stress. Hiphop uses word stress, but often it deliberately *changes* normal stress, distorting the words. Whether or not this is the cause, it seems that students who grew up during the hiphop era have a lot of trouble marking word stress.

If you find scanning lines difficult, know at least that you're not alone. With practice, you'll get it. Everyone who speaks English actually does know, and therefore at some level can *hear*, word stress. The only challenge is making it into conscious knowledge.

Summary and Definitions

Every English word has one syllable that receives a strong stress, pronounced a little bit louder and more distinctly. One-syllable words can be stressed or unstressed, depending on the phrase they appear in. In words of two or more syllables, native English speakers know the correct stress pattern; the dictionary also provides it. American and British habits may be different.

Word stress is one of the main artistic tools used to create poetry, because it forms patterns. When we mark these patterns, we scan the line.

Exercises 2

Review:

a) What is poetry?

b) Why do we study arts like dance and music, if we can't do them?

1. Match the words in each group that have the same word-stress patterns. (Words with variable stress are matched only to other variable-stress words.)

tiger	believe	fortunate	Italian
giraffe	impressive	oppose	balcony
banana	hurry	cathedral	garage
record	project	majorette	address
license	balloon	object	personnel
approach	football	thankless	saddle
fantastic	elephant	simplify	exercise
simple	menu	approval	lingerie
triangle	appalling	musketeer	ballistic

2. Using a pencil or pen, scan these words and phrases (that is, mark ' for stressed syllables).

Fortunate	garbanzo	referee	somber	delighted	refer
Delight	appreciate	in the dark	theater	balloon	September
A bird	the house	this and that	this one	you see?	who's there?

3. Choose the word or phrase that will continue the same word-stress pattern begun by the first words. The phrases won't make sense or rhyme. Just listen to the sounds of the word stress.

Fortunate, exercise,	a. triangle b. muffler c. in the house	giraffe, my car	a. the tree b. balcony c. dump truck
Somber, this one,	a. degree b. lion c. multiply	Who's there? It's me	a. Italian b. tiger c. a dog
garbanzo, approval,	a. graduate b. window c. Norwegian	referee, in the rain,	a. around the bend b. daredevil c. balconette

4. In these sentences, words and phrases have been arranged to form a consistent pattern. Scan the patterns, using 'marks. There may be some words, like "is" or "in," that would not be stressed if they were in isolation, but they do get stress to make the pattern right. Underline these words, for example:

   I took my question to the seer: i TOOK my QUEStion TO the SEER (in isolation: to the SEER)

   a) But soft! what light through yonder window breaks?
   b) A little learning is a dangerous thing.
   c) The sea is calm tonight. The moon shines full.
   d) Can you come over here to eat tonight?
   e) Shall I compare thee to a summer's day?

6. Scan these sets of words and mark the one whose stress pattern doesn't match the other two. (Remember that words over three syllables have a secondary stress.) If English isn't your native language, or if you're struggling, try checking what a dictionary can tell you about each word's stress.

Teleport	alphabetize	electricity	absolutely	incarcerate	determination
Appreciate	incinerate	arbitrary	community	collaborate	counterfactual
Bombardier	meridian	university	alligator	sentimental	impermissible

Word Stress

7. Challenge Question. Some phrases can be used to answer different questions, but we vary the word stress in each case. Mark the word that gets the stress for each answer, and think of a word with the same pattern.

   Ex. What should I do? GIVE me one. (like STRAWberry)

   How many do you want? Give me one. like _____
   Okay, I gave one to him, now what? Give me one. like _____

   Where are you? I'm right here. like _____
   Is my sister right here? I'm right here. like _____

   Do you agree? I do. like _____
   Who says it's so? I do. like _____

   Is this your cat? This is my dog. like _____ (finding a word may be tough)
   Is he the policeman's dog? This is my dog. like _____
   Which one is your dog? This is my dog. like _____

8. For further reading: T. S. Eliot (1888-1965) wrote a short book of poems about cats, called *Old Possum's Book of Practical Cats*. It became the basis for the lyrics of the Broadway musical CATS. Whether or not you like the musical, find the *Book of Practical Cats* online or in the library, and read three of the poems out loud. While Eliot is best known for writing very formal, modern free verse, his cat poems use word stress patterns that are informal, strong, and easy to hear. "Skimbleshanks the Railway Cat" has a special pattern that imitates the sound of the train for some of the stanzas. (A stanza is the visual and metrical grouping of some lines, usually with blank lines to separate them from other stanzas.) Several of the poems allow the stress patterns to shift (in an effect that's similar to how some songs change key), including "The Old Gumbie Cat," "The Rum Tum Tugger," and "Skimbleshanks." Be sure to include at least one of these poems with shifting meter. Also, notice that the last poem, "The Ad-dressing of Cats," makes a point of using a variable-stress word, "address;" the pattern tells you clearly which variation to use.

Three:

Accentual Meter

There are two standard ways to make word stress patterns in English. The first is called accentual meter; it counts how many strong stresses are in a line, but it doesn't count or regulate weak stresses. The second is qualitative meter (also called accentual-syllabic meter), which measures out all word stresses, both strong and weak, to create patterns. Both kinds of meter have been part of English poetry since the late Middle Ages, but accentual meter is the older one. Its use goes back into the Dark Ages of oral poetry in Old English, Old German, Old Danish, and Icelandic.

Accentual meter is the natural rhythm of English and the other Germanic languages, while qualitative meter was originally a way of imitating Latin verse, which had itself imitated Greek verse. When the Greek language became a standard part of higher education during the Renaissance, imitating its patterns became fashionable. Shakespeare used qualitative meter in all of his sonnets and plays, and so did everyone of his time. It was the standard sound of all poetry during the 1600s and 1700s. Accentual meter was preserved only in antiquated rhymes, folk sayings, and nursery songs.

At the start of the 1800s, poets were looking for a fresh sound. The poets of the previous decades had created verses so polished and formal that the younger generation felt nothing new could be done without disruption. Between 1805 and 1837, the first transcriptions and translations of *Beowulf* were published, and this revived interest in the older poetic traditions. What seemed primitive to one generation felt fresh to the next. Because accentual meter was still extremely familiar in the form of nursery rhymes, it was easy for poets to adapt it for higher artistic purposes.

During the rest of the century, poets played with accentual meter as an alternative to formal qualitative meter. Alfred Tennyson and Robert Browning used it for song lyrics that interrupted and lightened the long, formal narratives of their story-poems. Browning also used it as the main meter for some of his poems, stepping away from the sing-song of nursery chants and making the accentual meter feel both artistic and natural in English. In the next century, American Robert Frost sometimes used accentual meter. Finally, it's worth mentioning that early rap music started with accentual meter phrases that were a lot like nursery rhymes.

1. Old English verse

The language we speak is a blend of French and a German-like language that is called either Old English or Anglo-Saxon. Before about 1150, Old English did not include any French infusion. (If you're interested in learning more about how Old English blended with French to create modern English, check out my book *Excavating English*. It tells the historical story and gives many examples of how the language changed.) From the 700s through about 1100, poetry in Old English did not have any rhyme. Instead, each line had four strong word stresses. We don't know if there was a musical accompaniment, but there probably was. The harp may have been strummed with each stressed word; it may have been a foot-tapping experience for listeners, but we really don't know.

Let's look at two examples; both are famous first lines. The earliest Christian hymn in English may have been composed as early as 680. Its author, Caedmon, was an illiterate cow-herder who knew nothing about Latin verse. He couldn't write, but using the traditional verse forms, he could make up poetry out loud for someone else to write down. He began like this:

> Nu scúlon hérian héofon-rices Weárd

It's pronounced something like "Nu shulon heryan heaven-riches Ward," and it means, "Now we must praise the heaven-kingdom's guardian." I've placed a stress mark on each of the four accented syllables. Caedmon probably chanted it with a heavy stress, or perhaps even a drum beat, at each of these points. The rest of the hymn went on in the same pattern: one-two-three-four.

The first line of *Beowulf,* which is now the most famous poem of that period, has the same pattern:

> We Gár-Déna in geár-dágum

This is pronounced something like "We Gar-Dayna in yar-dagum," and it means, "We Spear-Danes in olden days..." There are four strong stresses. We don't know if there was any sort of melody accompanying the chanted verse. But we can see that all through the long poem, the one-two-three-four pattern came through in each line. Sometimes the first strong beat was on the first word, while other times it was not. Sometimes, as in "Gar-Dena" and "gear-dagum," two strong stresses were next to each other, while other times they were not. These pattern variations were interesting to listen to. The audience found artistic beauty in the way the singer/poet delivered them.

J. R. R. Tolkien, author of *The Lord of the Rings*, was a scholar of Old English poetry. He used the Old English form of verse for the songs of Rohan, whose culture was modeled after the Anglo-Saxons. It's easier for us to read his imitations than to read more lines of *Beowulf*, since Tolkien used modern English. We can see and hear the patterns, as if we were an Old English audience.

Tap your foot or finger as each line delivers its one-two-three-four pattern. Notice how each line forms a different pattern. "SPEAR shall be SHAKen" is different from "RIDE now, RIDE now," and both are different from the first line, "aRISE, aRISE." What other patterns do you see?

> Arise, arise, Riders of Theoden!
> Fell deeds awake: fire and slaughter!
> spear shall be shaken, shield be splintered,
> a sword-day, a red day, ere the sun rises!
> Ride now, ride now! Ride to Gondor!

We could describe the way unstressed syllables are handled with simple musical notes. "Ride now, ride now!" could be represented by four quarter-notes, a full measure in 4/4 time. "Spear shall be shaken" is the same full measure, but the two unstressed syllables would be shown as eighth-notes: quarter, two eighths, quarter, quarter. That's why accentual meter feels more musical and fits easily into melodies, because like music, it can fit a different number of notes into one measure.

2. Nursery rhymes

Before children's books, mothers and nannies entertained children with stories and songs that they had memorized when they were children. The stories and songs were handed down, usually without any updating, so that some very old verse forms and words were preserved. Little children don't care much if a song makes sense, since everything in their world is a bit surprising and nonsensical. In my 1970s childhood (when traditional nursery rhymes were less popular than in the 1940s or 50s) we still passed on hand-clapping and rope-skipping songs from child to child. Sometimes, these chants had lines that we didn't understand at all, but we repeated them anyway.

Nursery songs and chants are meant to be foot-tapping and hand-clapping; they're said or sung with emphasis on the accented syllables. They may have tunes, but if not, they are easily set to music. Accentual verse like this is identical with song lyrics, and we hear it with a musical sense.

> to MARket, to MARket
> to BUY a fat PIG
> then HOME again, HOME again,
> JIGetty JIG.

> OLD king COLE
> was a MERry old SOUL
> and a MERry old SOUL was HE.
> he CALL'd for his PIPE
> and he CALL'd for his BOWL
> and he CALL'd for his FIDdlers THREE.

"To Market, to Market" has two strong beats per line, with sometimes one, sometimes two unstressed syllables between. It doesn't matter for the sound whether it's one or two. When there are two unstressed syllables, we just tuck them in quickly to keep the beat. "Old King Cole" also varies its line lengths: two beats, two beats, then three beats. This kind of variation is typical of accentual verse (as it's also typical of song lyrics). It sounds right in a musical way.

"Old King Cole" is not much different from the famous hiphop lyrics from 1990's "The Fresh Prince of Bel Air." "Bel Air" is accompanied by a drum beat that gives us four strong beats per line, and the unstressed words and syllables get turned into eighth notes and quarter notes to fit into the rhythm. Most of the lines use one or two unstressed syllables between strong stresses, but in two cases, three words have to be spoken in the same rhythm as one.

> On the PLAYground was WHERE I spent MOST of my DAYS
> CHILlin' out MAXin' reLAXin' all COOL
> And all SHOOTin some B-ball outSIDE of the SCHOOL
> When a COUPle of GUYS who were UP to no GOOD
> STARTed making TROUble in my NEIGHborHOOD
> I got in ONE little FIGHT and my MOM got SCARED
> She said 'You're MOVin' with your AUNTie and UNcle in Bel AIR.'

Early hiphop rhythms were very close to nursery rhymes, using the natural stress patterns of English. Later rappers have moved away from straightforward accentual meter, so much of hiphop is not a good guide to accentual meter.

3. Romantic accentual verse

The poets who grew tired of the carefully-measured, formal verse of the 1700s had all been raised with nursery rhymes, probably including some that we've lost now. In the early 1800s, there was generally a movement toward whatever seemed natural, primitive, and emotional. Formal, symmetrical gardens were torn out, replaced with wild-looking (though not actually wild) landscapes (and sometimes newly-built "ruins"). Beethoven's greatest symphonies were written during this period. When we compare them with the great music of the previous decades, such as Handel or Bach, we can hear how much less mathematical, formal and regular they are.

The Romantic poets' challenge was to use the "vulgar" folk rhythm of nursery rhymes while creating *art* that everyone could appreciate. They wanted to write about elevated subjects with beautiful words, but with accentual meter. Sometimes, they used accentual meter specifically as songs (though as far as I know, without actual music) within longer narrative poems that used a more formal style for the main body.

Here is the first stanza of a song in one of Tennyson's long poems, "Maud." (As noted in the last exercise of Lesson One, the *stanza* is a group of lines that belong together, usually separated from other stanzas by a blank line.) I have put the stressed syllables in all capital letters so that you can easily see and hear the pattern. Try tapping your finger along with the stressed syllables as you read it out loud.

> SEE what a LOVEly SHELL,
> SMALL and PURE as a PEARL,
> LYing CLOSE to my FOOT,
> FRAIL, but a WORK diVINE,
> MADE so FAIRily WELL
> With DELicate SPIRE and WHORL,
> How exQUISitely miNUTE,
> a MIRacle of deSIGN!

Notice that between the stressed syllables and words there can be one, two or three unstressed syllables, as in the nursery rhymes. The first six lines all have three strong beats, but the last two lines seem to have two. We could make them have three beats, like the other lines, by stressing the normally unstressed syllables "ly" and "of":

> How exQUISiteLY miNUTE,
> a MIRacle OF deSIGN!

However, with accentual meter, we don't have to even things up. It's okay if the last two lines have two strong beats, as long as they sound natural to your own musical ear. In the next lesson, we'll start looking at qualitative meter, in which syllables do have to be evened up that way.

Let's look at another stanza of the same poem by Tennyson, where I haven't marked the stresses with capital letters. Try tapping along with your finger, hearing the three strong beats as though they are set to music.

Slight, to be crushed with a tap
Of my finger-nail on the sand,
Small, but a work divine,
Frail, but of force to withstand,
Year upon year, the shock
Of cataract seas that snap
The three-decker's oaken spine
Athwart the ledges of rock,
Here on the Breton Strand!

Accentual-meter verse is not as common as the qualitative meter that we'll study next, but it's important because it is truly the natural beat of the English language.

Summary and Definitions

Accentual meter counts the number of strong stresses in a line, not the number of syllables. A *stanza* is a group of lines that belong together, usually separated from other stanzas by a blank line.

Old English (Anglo-Saxon) poetry, like *Beowulf*, used accentual meter with four strong beats per line. Nursery rhymes preserved this old pattern for us when it fell out of fashion in the Middle Ages.

In the early 19th century, young poets were looking for a fresh way to write, something more primitive and natural. They used accentual meter, so that it came back into formal English poetry as an option.

Exercises 3

Review:

a) Why do we make art?

b) Scan these words and phrases, marking the stressed syllable(s):

in sunshine	cold grey stones	a gallant knight
had journeyed	from the dying moon	in England
shaven and shorn	of the shadow	across the lakes

c) The first two words or phrases set a word-stress pattern (but make no sense). Choose a word or phrase from the parentheses that matches and continues the pattern.

You came back, in the dark… (perspective, personnel)
Simplify, algebra… (pineapple, gorilla)
The last one, I can't wait… (about you, a big deal)
Abracadabra… (why did you say that, give it to me)
Circumvent, tell me now!… (smorgasbord, banana)

1. "The House that Jack Built" was a story where each stanza built on each preceding stanza. We have it in one set form, in which it talks about the house with its malt, rat, cat, dog, cow, maiden, man, priest, rooster, and farmer. But we could tell other stories this way.

    a) Read the rhyme out loud and clap your hands with the steady two-beats-per-line rhythm.

To save space, I've provided the first and second stanzas, and the last one. Begin the next stanza, "This is the rat that ate the malt," and continue to re-create the stanzas in order. If you aren't familiar with the rhyme and find it difficult to reconstruct, just look it up.

(1) This is the house
that Jack built.

(2) This is the malt
that lay in the house
that Jack built.

(3) This is the rat
That ate the malt
That lay in the house
That Jack built.
.
.
.

(11) This is the farmer sowing the corn,
That kept the cock that crowed in the morn.
That waked the priest all shaven and shorn,
That married the man all tattered and torn,
That kissed the maiden all forlorn,
That milked the cow with the crumpled horn,
That tossed the dog,
That worried the cat,
That killed the rat,
That ate the malt
That lay in the house that Jack built!

b) Try to complete a rhyme-story of your own, using a familiar modern scenario. For example: "This is the app that Jack made," or "This is the book that Ruth wrote." Can you carry it out to 11 or 12 places like the traditional nursery rhyme?

2. "El Dorado" was the name of a legendary place in South America that was very rich in gold. Conquistadors tried to find it for years, mapping much of the Amazon River while doing so. Poe wrote about it in a short lyrical poem with accentual meter, like a song.

The first stanza's word stresses go like this:

GAily beDIGHT,
A GALLant KNIGHT,
In SUNshine AND in SHAdow,
Had JOURneyed LONG,

SINGing a SONG,
In SEARCH of ELdorAdo.

a) In the first stanza, how many stresses are in each line? Do you see the same pattern in the rest of the stanzas? Does the rhythm feel natural? Are there lines when the accentual pattern forces you to stress a word or syllable that you probably would not stress in normal speech?

b) Because this is about a "knight," we know it's set in the past, so he might be one of the literal Conquistadors. But when he poses questions to a "shade," this suggests that the meaning isn't literal. What might the poet mean "El Dorado" to stand for?

Eldorado

Gaily bedight,
A gallant knight,
In sunshine and in shadow,
Had journeyed long,
Singing a song,
In search of Eldorado.

But he grew old—
This knight so bold—
And o'er his heart a shadow
Fell as he found
No spot of ground
That looked like Eldorado.

And, as his strength
Failed him at length,
He met a pilgrim shadow—
"Shadow," said he,
"Where can it be—
The land of Eldorado?"

"Over the Mountains
Of the Moon,
Down the Valley of the Shadow,
Ride, boldly ride,"
The shade replied,—
"If you seek for Eldorado!"

Edgar Allen Poe, 1809-1849

3. Alfred Tennyson's narrative poems were popular during his own time, but as our time prefers stories in prose, he is now best remembered for lyrical poems that are somewhat like song lyrics.

a) For each poem, count the number of strong stresses in the lines of one stanza, to find the pattern; check your count with another stanza. Do any stanzas have lines that don't match? Notice how the number of words and letters does not well predict the number of beats in the line.

b) Contrast the mood and tone of each song. See if you can put words to the feeling that the poem is trying to memorialize.

c) Notice, too, the role of repeated words in these songs. When a word or phrase appears a second time, is it exactly the same?

Sweet and Low

Sweet and low, sweet and low,
Wind of the western sea,
Low, low, breathe and blow,
Wind of the western sea!
Over the rolling waters go,
Come from the dying moon, and blow,
Blow him again to me;
While my little one, while my pretty one, sleeps.

Sleep and rest, sleep and rest,
Father will come to thee soon;
Rest, rest, on mother's breast,
Father will come to thee soon;
Father will come to his babe in the nest,
Silver sails all out of the west
Under the silver moon;
Sleep, my little one, sleep, my pretty one, sleep.

Break, Break, Break

Break, break, break
On thy cold grey stones, O Sea!
And I would that my tongue could utter
The thoughts that arise in me.

O, well for the fisherman's boy,
That he shouts with his sister at play!
O, well for the sailor lad,
That he sings in his boat on the bay!

And the stately ships go on
To their haven under the hill;
But O for the touch of a vanished hand,
And the sound of a voice that is still!

Break, break, break,
At the foot of thy crags, O Sea!
But the tender grace of a day that is dead

Will never come back to me.

THE SPLENDOUR FALLS

The splendour falls on castle walls
And snowy summits old in story;
The long light shakes across the lakes,
And the wild cataract leaps in glory.
Blow, bugle, blow, set the wild echoes flying,
Blow, bugle; answer, echoes, dying, dying, dying.

O, hark, O, hear! how thin and clear,
And thinner, clearer, farther going!
O, sweet and far from cliff and scar
The horns of Elfland faintly blowing!
Blow, let us hear the purple glens replying,
Blow, bugle; answer, echoes, dying, dying, dying.

O love, they die in yon rich sky,
They faint on hill or field or river;
Our echoes roll from soul to soul,
And grow forever and forever.
Blow, bugle, blow, set the wild echoes flying,
And answer, echoes, answer, dying, dying, dying.

Alfred, Lord Tennyson, 1809-1892

4. Two lyrical poems by Robert Browning: The first is a short song, which appears in a story-poem as, literally, the naive, innocent song of a young girl walking through the town. The second is a sentimental memory of England by a traveler who may be in Italy or Spain.

For both poems, count the strong beats in each line. "Pippa's Song" has no irregularities; it just bounces along like a song. How many strong beats per line? "Home Thoughts, From Abroad," is much less regular. Its first stanza is more song-like; count how many strong beats are in each line, so that you can see the pattern formed over its 8 lines. The second stanza's accentual meter will probably be much more difficult to hear, because Browning did not limit himself to making sure the lines all matched. After "all the swallows," he lets the lines wander out to the length of five strong beats, stopping the song-like rhythm. In the second stanza, would you stress "when" or "May"?

PIPPA'S SONG, FROM PIPPA PASSES

The year's at the spring,
And day's at the morn;
Morning's at seven;
The hill-side's dew-pearl'd;
The lark's on the wing;
The snail's on the thorn;
God's in His heaven—

ACCENTUAL METER

All's right with the world!

Home Thoughts, from Abroad

Oh, to be in England
Now that April's there,
And whoever wakes in England
Sees, some morning, unaware,
That the lowest boughs and the brushwood sheaf
Round the elm-tree bole are in tiny leaf,
While the chaffinch sings on the orchard bough
In England—now!

And after April, when May follows,
And the whitethroat builds, and all the swallows!
Hark, where my blossomed pear-tree in the hedge
Leans to the field and scatters on the clover
Blossoms and dewdrops—at the bent spray's edge—
That's the wise thrush; he sings each song twice over,
Lest you should think he never could recapture
The first fine careless rapture!
And though the fields look rough with hoary dew,
All will be gay when noontide wakes anew
The buttercups, the little children's dower
—Far brighter than this gaudy melon-flower!

Robert Browning, 1812-1889

5. Robert Frost, an American poet, used accentual verse for this famous meditation on roads and choices. While his meter is accentual and his theme is very down to earth, the style is still much more formal and less song-like than other poems presented in this lesson.

   a) For at least one stanza, mark the strong stresses and see if the weak stresses between them vary in number or pattern. How easy or hard is it for you to "hear" the accentual rhythm of this poem, compared to "Sweet and Low" or "Pippa's Song"?

   b) The poet appears to be talking in a literal way about a walk (or perhaps horseback ride) that he took through the woods. The "roads" he takes aren't paved, and the less-traveled one has some grass growing on it. The poem seems to be entirely straight-forward, about a walk in the wood, until late in the poem. Can you identify a line (numbering them from 1 to 20) where the poem seems to turn away from the literal path story? What does the last stanza seem to be talking about, and does this change your view of the early stanzas?

   c) In the last stanza, he makes two "I" statements, "I shall" and "I took." Do you feel that they would scan in the same pattern? How does the line ending "and I—" influence the next line? How does it alter the meaning if you read these lines with or without stress on "I"?

The Road Not Taken

Two roads diverged in a yellow wood,
And sorry I could not travel both
And be one traveler, long I stood
And looked down one as far as I could
To where it bent in the undergrowth;

Then took the other, as just as fair,
And having perhaps the better claim,
Because it was grassy and wanted wear;
Though as for that the passing there
Had worn them really about the same,

And both that morning equally lay
In leaves no step had trodden black.
Oh, I kept the first for another day!
Yet knowing how way leads on to way,
I doubted if I should ever come back.
I shall be telling this with a sigh
Somewhere ages and ages hence:
Two roads diverged in a wood, and I—
I took the one less traveled by,
And that has made all the difference.

Robert Frost, 1874-1963

6. For further reading, try looking at some of the poems Tolkien put into *The Hobbit* and *The Lord of the Rings*. Some of the hobbits' informal poems and all of the verses chanted in Rohan follow accentual patterns. The poetry of Rohan is, of course, directly imitating Old English verse. More surprisingly, hearing an audiobook (narrated by Rob Inglis) of *The Fellowship of the Ring* made me realize that when Tom Bombadil speaks, his sentences nearly always fall into lines of three or four strong stresses. They are written as ordinary sentences, but as an example, here is one early speech broken down into accentual-verse lines:

> "Here's my pretty lady!
> Here's my Goldberry
> clothed all in silver-green
> with flowers in her girdle!
> Is the table laden? I see
> yellow cream and honeycomb,
> and white bread, and butter;
> milk, cheese and green herbs
> and ripe berries gathered.
> Is that enough for us?
> Is the supper ready?"

Four:

Metrical Feet

Every language has its own traditions of how words are used artistically, depending on how the language works. English uses word stress, but not all languages have that trait. In French and Japanese poetry, syllables are counted, not stresses. Some languages hold certain syllables a fraction of a second longer than others, and this trait becomes part of its poetic artistry. Ancient Greek and Latin both had this system.

Latin study became universal during the Middle Ages, at the same time that the French language, a form of Latin, loaned many words to English. In medieval poetry such as Chaucer's *Canterbury Tales*, we start to see two poetic traits new to English verse: rhyme at the ends of lines, and equal metrical feet. Latin didn't use rhyme, but it did use metrical feet. The transition to using the Latin system in English became more complete in Shakespeare's time, when advanced students learned Greek poetry as well.

The types of metrical feet, and their names, are all borrowed from Greek. Greek poetry was often recited out loud, perhaps with music, on a stage. There were dancers who moved left to right, then right to left, beating their feet in time to the meter. Some Greek vowels were held longer than others, and in poetry, this difference was exaggerated. The rhythm of Homer's epic poems goes "long, short, short; long, short, short," and sometimes it varies with "long, long." They may have been recited to a harp or drum beat that kept time.

Each pattern of repetition is called a foot; "long, short, short" is one foot. That Homeric foot is called a *dactyl* in Greek; it means "finger" (compare to pterodactyl, the feather-finger dinosaur). It might be named the "finger" because the first finger bone, from knuckle to knuckle, is longer than the next two (long, short, short). In any case, we call each unit of repetition a foot, while they called it a finger. The line was measured by how many fingers/feet it had, usually six in Homer's epic poems. Because the words were measured like distances, the Greek system is called "quantitative" meter. Adapted into English's system of word stress, it is called "qualitative" or "accentual-syllabic" meter. In daily use in literature classes, it is just called *meter*.

1. English metrical patterns

There are five kinds of English metrical foot, called by their Greek names. You have already practiced seeing them in word stress patterns, so only their names are new.

Two syllables:
iamb (long i, silent b): aMAZE, withOUT, reGRET
trochee (hard k sound in middle): TIger, LOUDer, HUNter
spondee: SKY-BLUE, GALL-STONE, STOP SIGN

Three syllables:
dactyl (rhymes with pencil): EXercise, UNderwear, SPIderman
anapest: overSEAS, personNEL, majorETTE

Of these, iambs are by far the most common. English tends to fall into iambic patterns easily, whereas other patterns feel much more unnatural. Spondees are natural enough, but they don't form whole lines. They show up among trochees and iambs, giving some variation. But the three-syllable patterns, especially dactyls, can be very hard to sustain in English.

2. Identifying the meter in a poem

To identify the metrical pattern of a line, first try to read it and see if you can hear the pattern. If you aren't sure, you can try building it this way. Start by identifying some two-syllable words that have one syllable clearly stressed (like TIger or girAFFE). Next, look at short phrases that suggest a typical stress pattern (like a TREE, or in the DARK). When you have these marked, does it suggest a pattern?

Here are four lines from different poems:

a) He clasps the crag with crooked hands

b) The lads in their hundreds to Ludlow come in for the fair

c) This is the forest primeval. The murmuring pine and the hemlock

d) I was angry with my friend

Two-syllable words: crooked, hundreds, Ludlow, forest, hemlock, angry. There are a few three-syllable words also: primeval and murmuring. Additionally, I can group some words into phrases, like nouns with "the," or phrases with a preposition: the crag, with crooked hands, the lads, in their hundreds, to Ludlow, for the fair, the forest, the murmuring pine, the hemlock, with my friend. In these phrases, the stress is normally on the noun. When I put all of these observations together, I can see:

a) he clasps the CRAG with CROOKed HANDS

b) the LADS in their HUNdreds to LUDlow come in for the FAIR

c) this is the FORest priMEval. the MURmuring PINE and the HEMlock

d) i was ANgry with my FRIEND

We can look for patterns now. Line a) suggests iambs: "...the CRAG with CROOK-ed HANDS." Can we complete the remaining phrase that way? Yes, "he CLASPS" is perfectly normal speech: "He CLASPS the CRAG with CROOKed HANDS."

The second and third lines each have only one foot that isn't already marked, "come in" and "this is." In normal speech, we can say COME in, or come IN; we can say THIS is, or this IS. It depends on what we mean to emphasize.

In Line b), if we put the stress on "in," we create a regular metrical pattern: "the LADS in their HUNdreds to LUDlow come IN for the FAIR." It's based on three syllables, not two, so it's either dactyls or anapests. Anapests go like this: da da DUM, da da DUM. That's the basic rhythm of the line, and it fits if we don't mind the first foot being irregular: da DUM da da DUM da da DUM da da DUM da da DUM. Let's check by adding the next line:

> the LADS in their HUNdreds to LUDlow come IN for the FAIR
> There's MEN from the BARN and the FORGE and the MILL and the FOLD

The repeated phrases like "from the barn" create such a strong anapestic pattern that we can't be mistaken. The first foot of each line is irregular: "the LADS" or "there's MEN". We could rewrite them to say, "see the LADS" or "look there's MEN". If we changed the first foot in each line to have two weak stresses, not one, would it make the pattern sound better to your ear, or worse?

In Line c), we can only make a regular pattern for "this is" by stressing THIS, not "is." In normal speech, if we say "THIS is the one," we intend an emphasis: this one, not another. The meaning fits well into the line: "THIS is the FORest priMEval. (This forest, not another one.) the MURmuring PINE and the HEMlock…" The pattern here, also based on threes, seems like dactyls because of its opening stress on THIS: DUM da da DUM da da. So while both of the lines are based on threes, one gives us anapests, the other dactyls.

Longfellow's line about the "forest primeval" is the best-known line of dactyls, but even he found it hard to sustain them. By the second line, the dactyls are only clear if we put a pause like a musical rest in the middle of the line:

> THIS is the FORest priMEval. the MURmuring PINES and the HEMlocks
> BEARded with MOSS, and in GARments [pause] GREEN, indisTINCT in the TWIlight…

The lines open a long, book-length story in verse about the expulsion of French speakers from Canada around 1760. Having begun so strongly in dactyls, Longfellow only sometimes uses any regular meter at all. He seems to have chosen this opening to capture attention, but he had no intention of keeping it up for long.

Line d) presents some uncertainty. "i was ANgry with my FRIEND." That's how it would sound in daily speech, and it would be odd to stress any of the other words. However, we can include the next line to check if the sample seems to be in a regular meter or not:

> i was ANgry with my FRIEND
> i told my wrath, my wrath did end.

In the case of its next line, each phrase has a normal stress pattern. In a phrase like "I was" or "I told," normally we stress the verb: i TOLD you already! And it would sound like arguing to say "MY wrath!" The normal daily speech pattern would be "my WRATH," like "my CAR," "my SON," and so on. The compound verb "did end" could go either way, "DID end," or "did END." The first one is what we use when we're arguing, "yes it DID!" but it's more in normal speech not to stress the helping verb "did." So "did END" is better here.

When we read the two lines together, it's clear that we should stress "with" in the first line, even if it wouldn't carry much stress in daily speech. The lines then fall into a clear pattern of iambs, and this pattern is carried throughout the rest of the poem.

However, there is an irregularity in the first line, which I'll show by putting each foot, each unit of two syllables, into brackets:

> [I] [was AN]-[gry WITH] [my FRIEND]
> [i TOLD] [my WRATH], [my WRATH] [did END]

In the very first foot of the first line, the meter is wrong. Every iambic foot is da DUM, except for this first foot, which is just DUM. It's missing the "da." There's no way around it, half of the foot *is* missing. It is not an iamb. But we don't really mind when we read the lines; perhaps the missing upbeat makes us hold "I" a little longer and more insistently. Who was angry? I was!

3. Irregular metrical feet

Lines are allowed to have irregularities because they are part of the artistry of sound. In the lines above, because Blake left out the weak stress before "I," the pronoun carries the weight of the whole foot. That's what the poem is about: it is about how I handle my anger, how I take revenge, and how I feel about the outcome.

Sometimes, an irregular metrical foot tempts us to read it as it were like the other feet, except that this unusual stress would slightly change the meaning. Which way should we read it? Should we allow the meter to impose word stress where we don't expect it? Or should we read that phrase in a natural way and hear a little blip in the tick-tock-tick of the metrical stress? There is no single right answer, just as there is no one right way to play a song.

In schools before about 1970, students had to memorize and recite famous old poems. They usually read the lines with the meter stressed to be pretty obvious, and most kids probably recited words to make the meter very regular. The virtue of reading this way is that our ears learn to hear the meter very clearly. If the classroom teacher then read the poems out loud, but used a more natural speech pattern so that some lines didn't sound as clearly metrical, the students could still hear the underlying "da DUM da DUM" that they had memorized.

Metrical irregularity becomes a bit like syncopation in jazz and rock music, where the notes don't begin and end on the 1-2-3-4 beats of each measure. We can appreciate syncopation because, underlying the complicated rhythm, we can still hear the beat. Even more like syncopation are the free verse lines that began with the Jazz Age. There's no regular pattern, but a poetry-trained ear can't help still hearing some patterns that come and go.

When I read a poem for the first time, I often tap my fingers to the beat, as if to music. I count out the stressed syllables, usually starting with the thumb of my right hand, and then the fingers in order. When I do this, I know by my fingers how many feet are in the line. I can tell easily whether the lines are all the same length or not. It's very common to use five metrical feet in English verse, so most of the time I tap from my thumb to my pinky finger, then start over at the next line.

Once I have the pattern established, I can notice when the way I would read a phrase or sentence doesn't match what my next finger-tap expects. I may stop and look at it, go back and see if I read it right. Once I know that it's irregular, I can read the line with a mismatch between voice and finger-taps and just keep moving.

When the sound helps us understand the meaning, it's part of making art with words. When one sound rule (the way daily English is spoken) and another sound rule (the metrical pattern of a line) clash, it creates artistic tension between the two. We don't need to resolve the tension clearly in favor of natural speech or decorative meter. We just need to notice the way these two separate things play with and against each other.

Summary and Definitions

Word stress can be repeated in regular patterns of two or three syllables. This is called *qualitative* or *accentual-syllabic meter*. Most people just refer to it as meter, forgetting about the accentual option.

The patterns are named for similar ones in Greek poetry, although ours are adapted for word stress, not syllable length. Two-syllable patterns are *iambs* (da DUM), *trochees* (DUM da), and *spondees* (DUM DUM). Three-syllable patterns are *dactyls* (DUM da da) and *anapests* (da da DUM).

Each repeated unit is called a *foot*. We can measure the line by how many feet it has.

Irregular feet can be part of a line of meter without changing our idea of what the overall meter is. We determine the meter by looking at more than one line.

Exercises 4

Review:

a) Which word matches the stress pattern of the first word?

    Lollapalooza… (opportunity, abracadabra)
    Opportunity… (Deuteronomy, determination)
    Counterfactual… (extravaganza, sanctimonious)
    Determination… (extravaganza, electricity)

b) Name two forms of verse that used accentual meter.

c) Which line matches the same number of accentual beats as the first one given?

Break, break, break… (Oh, to be in England; The year's at the spring)

Then took the other as just as fair… (O, sweet and far from cliff and scar; Now that April's there)

He met a pilgrim shadow… (Wind of the western sea; All's right with the world!)

All's right with the world… (In search of Eldorado; In England—now!)

1. Compose nonsense lines for these metrical patterns.

   For example:

   (x) 2 dactyls: triangle multiply

       a) 4 iambs: _____
       b) 4 trochees: _____
       c) 4 dactyls: _____
       d) 4 anapests: _____

For each line you composed, write a second one that matches its meter but uses words differently. If your first line a) used 4 two-syllable words like "tiger" or "hurry," your second line to match it should use at least one phrase and a longer word. For example:

    (x) 2 dactyls: triangle multiply
　　　　　　　　　　　　Give me the exercise
    (or)   my opportunity

If you find this exercise very difficult, try checking the answer key to see my examples. Use past homework or review sets as a "word bank" for longer words.

    a) 4 iambs: _____

    _____

b) 4 trochees: _____

_____

c) 4 dactyls: _____

_____

d) 4 anapests: _____

_____

2. "The Lads in their Hundreds" was written shortly after World War I. It has a perfectly regular metrical pattern. da DUM is the first foot, then it settles into regular anapests: da da DUM, da da DUM...

   a) First, read it through, tapping your fingers to the stressed words.

   b) Choose a line that you can tinker with, to make one of the metrical feet irregular. For example, I could throw the first line off like this: "The lads in their hundreds to Ludlow come to the fair." The meaning is the same, but now, the meter stumbles after "Ludlow." Try making a similarly stumbling line by altering one or two words.

   c) What is the poem's meaning, and what feeling moved the poet to create this art? How would you feel about his message if he just wrote it out in ordinary speech, instead of in an artistic way? Does the meter add an emotional message to the plain sense of the words?

THE LADS IN THEIR HUNDREDS

The lads in their hundreds to Ludlow come in for the fair,
There's men from the barn and the forge and the mill and the fold,
The lads for the girls and the lads for the liquor are there,
And there with the rest are the lads that will never be old.

There's chaps from the town and the field and the till and the cart,
And many to count are the stalwart, and many the brave,
And many the handsome of face and the handsome of heart,
And few that will carry their looks or their truth to the grave.

I wish one could know them, I wish there were tokens to tell
The fortunate fellows that now you can never discern;
And then one could talk with them friendly and wish them farewell
And watch them depart on the way that they will not return.

But now you may stare as you like and there's nothing to scan;
And brushing your elbow unguessed-at and not to be told
They carry back bright to the coiner the mintage of man,
The lads that will die in their glory and never be old.

A. E. Housman, 1859-1936

3. William Blake was an artist who illustrated many of his poems. The picture shows the engraving Blake printed with "The Tyger" in 1794. This poem is famous partly because it's concrete and colorful, and partly because it has an insistent, hammering meter made of trochees (DUM da). The trochees are so militant that they easily push us to put stress where we normally would not, on words like "in" and "and."

   a) Using your fingers to tap through the strong stresses, read the poem out loud. There are six irregular lines, in which the first words can't be read as trochees without really violating normal English. Which are these lines? If these lines formed their own poem, what would its meter be?

   b) The trochaic meter makes some words stand out, especially if they are the start of a line, such as "IN what distant," "ON what wings," "WHAT the hand," and "WHAT the anvil?" How does this strange emphasis influence a phrase's meaning?

   c) At the end of the 5th stanza, the meter shifts the stress from "DID he SMILE his WORK to SEE" to "did HE who MADE the LAMB make THEE?" How does this changing emphasis in the phrase "did he" shape the meaning?

   d) what is the effect of Blake's choice to repeat the first stanza as the closing stanza? If the poem omitted it, how would it be changed?

THE TYGER

Tyger! Tyger! burning bright
In the forests of the night,
What immortal hand or eye
Could frame thy fearful symmetry?

In what distant deeps or skies
Burnt the fire of thine eyes?
On what wings dare he aspire?
What the hand dare seize the fire?

And what shoulder, and what art,
Could twist the sinews of thy heart?
And when thy heart began to beat,
What dread hand? and what dread feet?

What the hammer? what the chain?
In what furnace was thy brain?
What the anvil? what dread grasp
Dare its deadly terrors clasp?

When the stars threw down their spears,
And watered heaven with their tears,
Did he smile his work to see?
Did he who made the Lamb make thee?

Tyger! Tyger! burning bright
In the forests of the night,
What immortal hand or eye
Dare frame thy fearful symmetry?

William Blake, 1757-1827

4. Longfellow, the first American poet to achieve real popularity, grew up in Portland, Maine near the Atlantic coast. His boyhood hours on the beach provided him a way to capture his insight about the process of making poetry.

   a) What is the prevailing type of meter? In the first stanza, there are a few irregular feet. First, notice that while "storm-wind" could be said with little stress on "wind," it can also be read as a spondee, with equal emphasis on both "storm" and "wind." Second, in the last line of the first stanza, the first word "Laden" adds an extra syllable so that the meter stumbles. (If you can't hear this, try changing the line to "Thick with seaweed from the rocks." Do you hear the difference?) Do you think the altered foot in this line makes the meter weaker? Does it make the poem weaker?

   b) Count the number of feet in each line. Do the later stanzas follow the number pattern set by the first? Also, notice that some lines end in a strong downbeat: DUM. Others don't, they end with a weak upbeat: DUM da. Contrast "Atlantic" and "gigantic" with "equinox." The strong ending is more typical in English poetry. Do you think that one or the other way seems better?

   c) Longfellow paints a picture of the sea, but then he starts to interpret it in the 5th stanza; he's really speaking about how and why a poet writes a poem. What is the ocean, in this analogy? What is a storm, the beach/reef, the seaweed itself?

Seaweed

When descends on the Atlantic
    The gigantic
Storm-wind of the equinox,
Landward in his wrath he scourges
    The toiling surges,
Laden with seaweed from the rocks:

From Bermuda's reefs; from edges
    Of sunken ledges,
In some far-off, bright Azore;
From Bahama, and the dashing,
    Silver-flashing
Surges of San Salvador;

From the tumbling surf, that buries
    The Orkneyan skerries,
Answering the hoarse Hebrides;
And from wrecks of ships, and drifting
    Spars, uplifting
On the desolate, rainy seas;—

Ever drifting, drifting, drifting
    On the shifting
Currents of the restless main;
Till in sheltered coves, and reaches
    Of sandy beaches,
All have found repose again.

So when storms of wild emotion
    Strike the ocean
Of the poet's soul, erelong
From each cave and rocky fastness,
    In its vastness,
Floats some fragment of a song:

From the far-off isles enchanted,
    Heaven has planted
With the golden fruit of Truth;
From the flashing surf, whose vision
    Gleams Elysian
In the tropic clime of Youth;

From the strong Will, and the Endeavor
    That forever
Wrestle with the tides of Fate;
From the wreck of Hopes far-scattered,
    Tempest-shattered,
Floating waste and desolate;—

Ever drifting, drifting, drifting
    On the shifting
Currents of the restless heart;
Till at length in books recorded,
    They, like hoarded
Household words, no more depart.

Henry Wadsworth Longfellow, 1807-1882

Metrical Feet

5. If you judged the meter of Frost's "Mending Wall" by its first line, you would have difficulty. No native speaker of English can read the first word "Something" without a heavy stress on the first syllable, but if you try to keep that pattern (DUM da, DUM da) going, it won't work. (SOMEthing THERE is THAT does NOT...nah this isn't working.)

    a) Looking at the first four lines, what is the prevailing meter? How many feet are in each line? If we change the first line to read, "A thing there is that does not love a wall," the metrical irregularity goes away. Does this improve the poem or not? Are there other lines with irregular feet that make some words stand out?

    b) The poem is a short story about annually fixing up a boundary wall in New England. The illustration shows you one of these typical walls, made long ago by removing stones from fields and just piling them at the edges. In the natural world, what makes stones fall off the wall? What does this suggest to the poet about the world; why "elves"? When he says his neighbor walks in darkness, what do you think he means?

Mending Wall

Something there is that doesn't love a wall,
That sends the frozen-ground-swell under it,
And spills the upper boulders in the sun;
And makes gaps even two can pass abreast.
The work of hunters is another thing:
I have come after them and made repair
Where they have left not one stone on a stone,
But they would have the rabbit out of hiding,
To please the yelping dogs. The gaps I mean,
No one has seen them made or heard them made,
But at spring mending-time we find them there.
I let my neighbor know beyond the hill;
And on a day we meet to walk the line
And set the wall between us once again.
We keep the wall between us as we go.
To each the boulders that have fallen to each.
And some are loaves and some so nearly balls
We have to use a spell to make them balance:
"Stay where you are until our backs are turned!"
We wear our fingers rough with handling them.
Oh, just another kind of out-door game,
One on a side. It comes to little more:
There where it is we do not need the wall:
He is all pine and I am apple orchard.
My apple trees will never get across
And eat the cones under his pines, I tell him.
He only says, "Good fences make good neighbours."
Spring is the mischief in me, and I wonder

If I could put a notion in his head:
"*Why* do they make good neighbours? Isn't it
Where there are cows? But here there are no cows.
Before I built a wall I'd ask to know
What I was walling in or walling out,
And to whom I was like to give offence.
Something there is that doesn't love a wall,
That wants it down." I could say "Elves" to him,
But it's not elves exactly, and I'd rather
He said it for himself. I see him there
Bringing a stone grasped firmly by the top
In each hand, like an old-stone savage armed.
He moves in darkness as it seems to me,
Not of woods only and the shade of trees.
He will not go behind his father's saying,
And he likes having thought of it so well
He says again, "Good fences make good neighbours."

Robert Frost, 1874-1963

6. Just for fun: dactyls and anapests are not common in formal verse, but they show up in comic forms like these: the limerick and the "double-dactyl." These short, funny verse forms are generally called "light verse." You're probably familiar with the limerick form that has two long lines, then two shorts, and a final longer line that rhymes with the first two. How many feet are in each anapestic line? Have you ever made up a limerick, or do you know any to share? The first famous collection was made by Edward Lear, and they've remained popular ever since.

There was an Old Man with a beard,	There was a young lady named Bright
Who said, 'It is just as I feared!	Whose speed was far faster than light
Two Owls and a Hen,	She set out one day
Four Larks and a Wren,	In a relative way
Have all built their nests in my beard!'	And returned the previous night.
Edward Lear, 1846	*A. H. Reginald Buller,* 1923

The doubledactyl was invented in the 1950s; it contains two stanzas made of dactyls. The first line has to be a nonsense word like "Higgledy-piggledy," and the second line has to be a name that takes up the whole line; the second stanza requires a single word that takes up a whole line. Names are among the few English items that do often fall into dactyls. This form of light verse is at its funniest when it's making use of an unusual word or a quirky fact:

Higgledy Piggledy	Higgledy Piggledy
Thomas A. Edison	*T. Intermedia*
Dreamed up the phono	genuine blue-tongued Tas-
As well as the light.	manian skink:
Thanks to his genius e-	Vomero-nasally
Lectromechanical	he can identify
We can read labels	olefactorily
Of records at night.	more than you think.
Anthony Harrington, 1992	*Robin Pemantle*, 1995

7. For further reading, I recommend the little book Rhyme's Reason by John Hollander (one of the inventers of the doubledactyl). If you are mostly familiar with what these first lessons have been talking about, you may want the further challenge of the way Hollander's book illustrates techniques and terms of poetry while using them. For example, he illustrates dactyls with the line, "Listen, my typewriter clatters in dactyls along with my prose!" As we look at more advanced forms, Hollander's clever, often funny, examples may bring the study of poetry alive. Hollander's first ten pages cover the metrical forms in this lesson. If you turn to pages 21, 22 and 23, you can find his discussion of the previous lesson's accentual meter. On pages 34-36, he discusses how Greek quantitative verse was adapted for English.

Five:

Line Lengths and Blank Verse

Many poems can be described by *how many* metrical feet are in each line, because every line is the same. Since the time when meters that imitate Greek became dominant in English, we've used Greek-based adjectives and nouns to describe the types of lines. There is one kind of English verse that's defined only by its metrical lines.

1. Naming metrical lines

The name of a metrical line describes its type of meter and number of feet. The first word is an adjectival form of the type of foot. Here are the adjectival forms:

iamb	iambic
trochee	trochaic
dactyl	dactylic
spondee	spondaic
anapest	anapestic

You need to know all these words, but there's one that gets the most use. English falls easily into the patterns of iambs, so that it has become the day-to-day working meter of most poetry. We will talk about "iambic" very often.

The second word counts the number of feet. Here are the Greek prefixes for number, which are then attached to the word "meter":

2	di-
3	tri-
4	tetra-
5	penta-
6	hexa-
7	hepta-

There isn't an official word for a line with only one foot in it, but we could call it monometer (*monos* is Greek for "only," often used for "one"). It's too rarely used to need a term. Instead, we start with dimeter and trimeter as the shortest line forms. Tetrameter and pentameter are the most common line lengths in English poetry. Hexameter has only been occasionally used, and mainly in the very formal 1700s, while heptameter is as much a curiosity as monometer would be.

We've seen *dimeter* twice, although it was using accentual meter, not one of the Greek-named forms. (In the lines below, I've only lightly marked the stressed syllables to make the count clearer, using the little accent.)

(A) Gaíly bedíght,
A gállant kníght,

(B) The yeár's at the spríng,
And dáy's at the mórn;

We've seen *trimeter*, also with accentual meter:

(C) Seé what a lóvely shéll
Smáll and púre as a peárl.

(D) Breák, breák, breák
On thy cóld grey stónes, O Seá!

Moving to four feet, samples (E) and (F) are accentual tetrameter:

(E) And áfter ápril, when Máy fóllows

(F) Two roáds divérged in a yéllow woód

Next, samples (G) and (H) are both *iambic tetrameter*, so here we can start using the meter-type adjectives. Remember that the very first foot of (H) is irregular, so that it doesn't seem iambic at first; but its pattern overall is clear. If I put the feet in brackets, we can see the number of feet clearly:

(G) [He clásps] [the crág] [with croók]- [ed hnds;]

(H)) [Í] [was án] [gry wíth] [my fríend:]
[I tóld] [my wráth,] [my wráth] [did énd.]

"The Tyger" is also tetrameter, but its meter is made of trochees. So it is *trochaic tetrameter*:

(I) [Týger!] [Týger!] [búrning] [bríght]
[ín the] [shádows] [óf the] [níght]

The most common meter in English is *iambic pentameter*. It sounds like just walking along, making it the perfect meter for "Mending Wall," the story of taking a walk along a wall.

(J) [Sómething] [there ís] [that dóes] [n't lóve] [a wáll,]
[That sénds] [the fró] [zen-gróund] [-swell ún] [der ít.]

We've also had pentameter that isn't iambic. "The Lads in their Hundreds" uses anapestic meter, but the feet give us a full count to five. So it is *anapestic pentameter*.

(K) [The láds] [in their hún] [dreds to Lúd] [low come ín] [for the faír]
[There's mén] [from the bárn] [and the fórge] [and the míll] [and the fóld,]

Longfellow's first lines of *Evangeline* are unusual not only for being in dactyls, but also for the number of feet. It is *dactylic hexameter*.

(L) [Thís is the] [fórest pri] [méval. The] [múrmuring] [pínes and the] [hémlock]
[Béarded with] [móss, and in] [gárments] [gréen, indis] [tínct in the] [twílight]

Finally, we've also seen a poem that varied its line lengths. In "Seaweed," there is trochaic tetrameter in the first line, then trochaic dimeter; two more trochaic tetrameter lines follow, another of dimeter, then last tetrameter again. We can't describe this poem with one label; writing about it, we'd have to say that its lines vary, with a pattern that each stanza follows. There's no name for the pattern.

(M) Whén descénds on thé Atlántic
    Thé gigántic
Stórm-wind óf the équinóx,
Lándward ín his wráth he scoúrges
    The tóiling súrges,
Láden with seáweed fróm the rócks.

2. Line endings

Lines most often end with a strong stress. This custom probably comes from singing; the lyrics give a singer a quick upbeat rest to take a breath between lines. When lines end this way, we feel it as normal, natural, and unremarkable. However, as part of using word stress for artistic decoration and emphasis, lines can also end with an unstressed syllable.

In languages descended from Latin, nouns with masculine gender often end in a consonant, while nouns with feminine gender often end with a vowel (e or a). This pattern led literary critics to name the lines that end with a little upbeat *"feminine,"* while the ones that end in a strong stress are *"masculine."*

We see both kinds of line in "Mending Wall." Compare lines 7 and 8, measured in iambs:

Where THEY have LEFT not ONE stone ON a STONE, (masculine)
But THEY would HAVE the RABbit OUT of HIDing, (feminine)

If line 8 ended in a masculine way like the preceding lines, it would say something like "But they would have the rabbit at all cost." "Cost" would end the line with a strong stress, whereas "hiding" tags on the unstressed "ing." There are some other pairs like this in "Mending Wall," including the last line:

he SAYS aGAIN, "good FENces MAKE good NEIGHbours." (feminine)

Out of this poem's 45 lines, 9 of them have feminine endings. In a few cases, it would have been very easy for Frost to make them masculine, as for example when one feminine ending is, "I tell him," where he could have written, "I say." Frost's 80% masculine endings, 20% feminine ones, may be close to the proportions in English verse as a whole. Those who are mathematically inclined might like to keep count.

There isn't any one settled meaning or effect of using this slight line variation. Often, it serves to bring the words or line to our attention. Sometimes, it leaves the line's thought feeling tentative, without that determined stamp of the foot that characterizes the masculine ending.

Line endings can also be named by how they cooperate with punctuation. When the line ends with a period, comma, colon or semi-colon, it is sensibly called *end-stopped*. When we read a line of poetry out loud, we tend to pause at the end of a line, and in these cases, the punctuation agrees. Poets may ignore punctuation, though, and come to the end of a line while in the middle of a sentence or phrase. Literary critics gave this a less sensible name; instead of "run-on," they call the line *enjambed* (or *enjambment*, as a noun). They were borrowing a French word for stepping over something (*jambe* means leg), at a time when most literate people knew some French. There is one more interaction between lines and punctuation, named this time in Latin: *caesura*. It means a pause, a place where the line is broken in half by punctuation.

In "Mending Wall," line after line is end-stopped by some kind of punctuation or even just the end of a phrase. But when the poet introduces some uncertainty (why do we make walls, when there is no purpose?), he begins to work against the punctuation. Three clear caesurae (or caesuras, both plurals are now acceptable) are marked below by a double vertical line:

> Spring is the mischief in me, and I wonder
> If I could put a notion in his head:
> "*Why* do they make good neighbours? Isn't it
> Where there are cows? || But here there are no cows.
> Before I built a wall I'd ask to know
> What I was walling in or walling out,
> And to whom I was like to give offence.
> Something there is that doesn't love a wall,
> That wants it down." || I could say "Elves" to him,
> But it's not elves exactly, and I'd rather
> He said it for himself. || I see him there
> Bringing a stone grasped firmly by the top
> In each hand, like an old-stone savage armed.

Each of the full stops, mid-line, are more noticeable than if they came at the end of a line: "...cows?" "...down." "...himself." They contrast even more strongly with the tumbling-on effect of the many enjambed lines: "wonder/ if," "isn't it/ where," or "rather/he." In this passage, six phrases "step over" the boundary of the enjambed line. For this reason, the lines flow on rapidly, sometimes stopping in the middle and then picking up the flow. They only come to a conclusion when the neighbor is again the focus, armed with stones like a savage. The neighbor's unwillingness to think creatively about walls seems emphasized by the return to end-stopped lines:

> He moves in darkness as it seems to me,
> Not of woods only and the shade of trees.
> He will not go behind his father's saying,
> And he likes having thought of it so well
> He says again, "Good fences make good neighbours."

3. Blank verse

During the centuries when stage dramas were seen as poems enacted out loud, all scripts were written in verse. Sometimes the results were formal, decorative and unnatural, but in, for example, the plays of Shakespeare, the verse can be said in a natural, conversational way. One thing that made this possible was the acceptance of an extremely minimal kind of poetry. Every line had five feet, and as a rule, they were organized in iambs. It wasn't hard to write this way in English, which naturally falls into the iambic form as a strolling-along kind of rhythm.

We call this minimal verse with iambic pentameter *blank verse*. It is not rhymed, unless at times there are rhymed pairs to make a passage feel finished. If it were all rhymed, it would just be rhyming iambic pentameter. We only call it blank verse when it does not rhyme.

After the time of Shakespeare's blank verse plays, blank verse was the most accepted formal poetic style. John Milton used it to write his Biblical epic, *Paradise Lost*. Stage plays used blank verse all through the 1700s and well into the 1800s. Narrative poems, used to tell stories the way novels do now, also often used blank verse.

Blank verse is no longer used for any of these purposes; its verse aspect may be minimal, but just using meter now disqualifies it from telling long stories, when normal prose is so much more flexible. However, poets can and do still use it when they want to write an extended thought, or even a short story, without distracting the reader's attention from the content. Robert Frost told several short stories this way, including "Mending Wall." If you like this style, look up "The Death of the Hired Man."

Summary and Definitions

Lines of verse are described by the type and number of feet. Adjectives for the kinds of feet: *iambic, trochaic, spondaic, dactylic, anapestic*. Nouns for the number of feet in the line: *dimeter, trimeter, tetrameter, pentameter, hexameter, heptameter*. The combination most commonly used is "iambic pentameter."

Lines may be described as iambic, trochaic, etc. even if some feet in the line do not match that pattern. We look at the predominant pattern in the line, stanza, and poem to determine the meter.

Lines that end with a strong stressed syllable are called *masculine*; lines that end with an unstressed syllable are called *feminine*. Lines can also work with or against punctuation. When the line ending matches a period, comma, or other kind of punctuation, it is *end-stopped*. When the phrase goes past the line ending, wrapping into the next line before punctuation makes it pause, it is called *enjambed* (adj.) or *enjambment* (noun). Punctuation can create a *caesura*, a pause, in the middle of a line.

Poetry written in iambic pentameter without rhymes is called *blank verse*. It is the format that Shakespeare used for his plays.

Exercises 5

Review

a) Which type of meter has the same number of syllables per line? (Accentual; qualitative)

b) Choose the line with the same number of accentual beats:

- o Two roads diverged in a yellow wood... (But the tender grace of a day that is dead; Will never come back to me.)

- o Slight, to be crushed with a tap... (Shootin' some b-ball after school; And whoever wakes in England)

- o Sleep, my little one, sleep, my pretty one, sleep... (That's the wise thrush; he sings each song twice over; And that has made all the difference.)

c) Name the type of metrical foot each nonsense line uses:

Good job, stop sign blindsides. _____

He sings between balloons, imagine that. _____

Wait for a simplified good opportunity. _____

Do you like Norwegian traffic? _____

Pepperoni identical three musketeers. _____

1. In a poem, I used blank verse to describe an experience of grief that isolates us from others, symbolized by a watershed (the point that separates where rainwater will flow when falling on a mountain). I've used a thesaurus to find synonyms for one word in each line in the first stanza. In each parenthesis set, choose the one word that fits into iambic pentameter.

   > There is a region past the {line, boundary, frontier} of tears
   > That few men {intrude, appropriate, trespass} and unwillingly.
   > None find it save they {clamber up, scale, ascend} the watershed
   > And {survey, look upon, glimpse} the rainless, grassy plains.
   > There shadows {stretch, extend, deepen} too long and colors are
   > Too bright, too dark, or any way but {factual, existing, real}.
   > The {looker, spectator, beholder}, panting, rests and feels a wave
   > Of longing {for, about, concerning} the land he left behind.
   > He turns his {head, shoulder, abdomen}, but the watershed
   > Here has no fingerholds: {granite, obsidian, pure glass}.
   > Look {ahead, straight, forward}, stranger: lean into the air.
   > {Remove, eliminate, shed} your eyes; you will not need them there.

2. "My Picture Left in Scotland" was written in the time of Shakespeare; in order to understand it, you have to imagine a man writing letters to a younger lady in far-off Scotland. He is a gifted writer, and his letters are winning her over to the idea of marrying him, but they have never met. Then someone passes to her a "miniature," a small painted picture of him. Now she can see his aging appearance, and her attitude starts to change. (Note: the Greek god Apollo was the patron of poets.)

   College classes may assign students to write about poems without much explanation of what they're looking for. This can be a daunting task unless you've learned how to build an essay in stages, so from this point on, you will have assignments to write incrementally longer and more complex observations about some poems. In this first assignment, write two paragraphs about "My Picture Left in Scotland." In the first, describe the meter and line lengths, and how they vary to help express the poet's thought. In the second, explain the poet's message. What is his attitude to himself? Why is Love deaf?

My Picture Left in Scotland

I now think Love is rather deaf than blind;
    For else it could not be
        That she
Whom I adore so much, should so slight me,
And cast my love behind.
I'm sure my language to her was as sweet,
    And every close did meet
In sentence, of as subtle feet,
        As hath the youngest he
That sits in shadow of Apollo's tree.

Oh, but my constant fears,
That fly my thoughts between,
Tell me that she hath seen
My hundreds of gray hairs,
Told seven and forty years,
Read so much waist, as she cannot embrace,
My mountain belly, and my rocky face,
    And all these, through her eyes, have stopped her ears.

Ben Jonson, 1573-1637

3. William Cowper (pronounced "cooper") was a popular poet during his lifetime, in the late 1700s. Some of his poems became hymns, as he was close friends with John Newton, a hymn writer and minister. "Light Shining Out of Darkness" is one of his most famous poem/hymns. It follows a certain pattern of line lengths which is one component of a poem form called "ballad form." We'll talk more about this form in later lessons, too.

As in the last exercise, write two paragraphs, one to describe the metrical pattern, including commenting on any irregular lines you find, the second to describe the way you understand the poet's message. What images and pictures does he use? Do you think his metrical style contributes to the meaning of the poem? How would you feel differently about the poem's message if it had no meter? (If you would not feel differently about it, it's okay to say so.)

Light Shining Out Of Darkness

God moves in a mysterious way,
His wonders to perform;
He plants his footsteps in the sea,
And rides upon the storm.

Deep in unfathomable mines
Of never failing skill,
He treasures up his bright designs,
And works his sov'reign will.

Ye fearful saints, fresh courage take;
The clouds ye so much dread
Are big with mercy, and shall break
In blessings on your head.

Judge not the Lord by feeble sense,
But trust him for his grace;
Behind a frowning providence
He hides a smiling face.

His purposes will ripen fast,
Unfolding every hour;
The bud may have a bitter taste,
But sweet will be the flower.

Blind unbelief is sure to err,
And scan his work in vain:
God is his own interpreter,
And he will make it plain.

William Cowper, 1731-1800

4. Percy Bysshe Shelley was one of the first poets to rebel against the previous generation's highly-regular meter. He wrote less formal, more exploratory poems but still often used iambic pentameter. Here, compare and contrast two of his best-known short poems in iambic pentameter. "Ozymandias" is describing the ruins of an ancient statue with an inscription. What do you think of Ozymandias' inscription, paired with the remains of his statue?

"Mutability" is a meditation on human nature; "mutability" means the quality of being changeable. Granite is not very mutable, but easily-melted lead is. What does Shelley say about mankind's mutability? What comparisons does he make?

Write a few paragraphs discussing the similarities and differences between the two poems in tone, message and use of iambic pentameter. Don't forget to note irregularities or anything else that stands out to you. (Why does Shelley skip the middle letter of "never"?)

Ozymandias

I met a traveller from an antique land,
Who said—"Two vast and trunkless legs of stone
Stand in the desert.... Near them, on the sand,
Half sunk a shattered visage lies, whose frown,
And wrinkled lip, and sneer of cold command,
Tell that its sculptor well those passions read
Which yet survive, stamped on these lifeless things,
The hand that mocked them, and the heart that fed;
And on the pedestal, these words appear:
My name is Ozymandias, King of Kings,
Look on my Works, ye Mighty, and despair!
Nothing beside remains. Round the decay
Of that colossal Wreck, boundless and bare
The lone and level sands stretch far away."

Mutability

We are as clouds that veil the midnight moon;
How restlessly they speed, and gleam, and quiver,
Streaking the darkness radiantly!—yet soon
Night closes round, and they are lost for ever:

Or like forgotten lyres, whose dissonant strings
Give various response to each varying blast,
To whose frail frame no second motion brings
One mood or modulation like the last.

We rest.—A dream has power to poison sleep;
We rise.—One wandering thought pollutes the day;
We feel, conceive or reason, laugh or weep;
Embrace fond woe, or cast our cares away:

It is the same!—For, be it joy or sorrow,
The path of its departure still is free:
Man's yesterday may ne'er be like his morrow;
Nought may endure but Mutability.

Percy Bysshe Shelley, 1792-1822

5. Here are two famous passages of blank verse to compare. First, Hamlet's "To be or not to be" speech; second, the prologue to Milton's long epic poem *Paradise Lost*.

When you read these passages of blank verse, count out the metrical feet carefully. You will find many irregularities, especially in Hamlet's speech. For example, the first line has a feminine ending; the second line's first foot is a trochee; the foot right before the caesura in line 5 has an extra syllable; line 13 doesn't have five feet. Perhaps using a color code, trying noting a) feminine line endings, b) lines that aren't pentameter, and c) feet that aren't iambic. On the other hand, there are places where unusual, archaic words (such as contumely, quietus and fardel) give us cues for pronunciation by where they are placed in the meter. Underline or circle words like this; look also for words that have been abbreviated to fit the meter (like th' or ne'er).

In which poem do you find more regular meter? How would you compare the styles? Both are (to modern ears) formal and archaic, but they have many differences. Write a paragraph that discusses the different ways they use blank verse. Further, how would you compare them to "Mending Wall," which was also blank verse?

Hamlet's Soliloquy

To be, or not to be—that is the question:
Whether 'tis nobler in the mind to suffer
The slings and arrows of outrageous fortune
Or to take arms against a sea of troubles
And by opposing end them. To die, to sleep—
No more—and by a sleep to say we end
The heartache, and the thousand natural shocks
That flesh is heir to. 'Tis a consummation
Devoutly to be wished. To die, to sleep—
To sleep—perchance to dream: ay, there's the rub,
For in that sleep of death what dreams may come
When we have shuffled off this mortal coil,
Must give us pause. There's the respect
That makes calamity of so long life.
For who would bear the whips and scorns of time,
Th' oppressor's wrong, the proud man's contumely
The pangs of despised love, the law's delay,
The insolence of office, and the spurns
That patient merit of th' unworthy takes,
When he himself might his quietus make
With a bare bodkin? Who would fardels bear,
To grunt and sweat under a weary life,
But that the dread of something after death,
The undiscovered country, from whose bourn
No traveller returns, puzzles the will,
And makes us rather bear those ills we have
Than fly to others that we know not of?
Thus conscience does make cowards of us all,
And thus the native hue of resolution
Is sicklied o'er with the pale cast of thought,
And enterprise of great pitch and moment
With this regard their currents turn awry
And lose the name of action. — Soft you now,
The fair Ophelia! — Nymph, in thy orisons
Be all my sins remembered.

Shakespeare, 1564-1616 (?)

Paradise Lost, Book I, lines 1-26

Of man's first disobedience, and the fruit
Of that forbidden tree whose mortal taste
Brought death into the world, and all our woe,
With loss of Eden, till one greater Man
Restore us, and regain the blissful seat,
Sing, Heavenly Muse, that, on the secret top
Of Oreb, or of Sinai, didst inspire
That shepherd who first taught the chosen seed
In the beginning how the Heavens and Earth
Rose out of Chaos: or, if Sion hill
Delight thee more, and Siloa's brook that flowed
Fast by the oracle of God, I thence
Invoke thy aid to my adventurous song,
That with no middle flight intends to soar
Above th' Aonian mount, while it pursues
Things unattempted yet in prose or rhyme.
And chiefly thou, O Spirit, that dost prefer
Before all temples th' upright heart and pure,
Instruct me, for thou know'st; thou from the first
Wast present, and, with mighty wings outspread,
Dovelike sat'st brooding on the vast abyss,
And mad'st it pregnant: what in me is dark
Illumine; what is low, raise and support;
That, to the height of this great argument,
I may assert Eternal Providence,
And justify the ways of God to man.

John Milton, 1608-1674

6. Challenge Question. During Britain's war (1853-6) against Russians and Turks in Crimea, a front line miscommunication sent a brigade of lightly-armed horsemen against an artillery battery. The nation was shocked by the high casualties caused by the mistake, but Tennyson wrote a lyrical poem to encourage people to focus on their courage rather than the outcome.

   a) What is the meter he uses? How does it differ from the meter in "The Lads in their Hundreds"? What is the pattern of feet per line? How regular is the meter?

   b) How does Tennyson's attitude to the dead compare to Housman's?

THE CHARGE OF THE LIGHT BRIGADE

I
Half a league, half a league,
Half a league onward,
All in the valley of Death
Rode the six hundred.
"Forward, the Light Brigade!
Charge for the guns!" he said.
Into the valley of Death
Rode the six hundred.

II
"Forward, the Light Brigade!"
Was there a man dismayed?
Not though the soldier knew
Someone had blundered.
Theirs not to make reply,
Theirs not to reason why,
Theirs but to do and die.
Into the valley of Death
Rode the six hundred.

III
Cannon to right of them,
Cannon to left of them,
Cannon in front of them
Volleyed and thundered;
Stormed at with shot and shell,
Boldly they rode and well,
Into the jaws of Death,
Into the mouth of hell
Rode the six hundred.

IV
Flashed all their sabres bare,
Flashed as they turned in air
Sabring the gunners there,
Charging an army, while
All the world wondered.
Plunged in the battery-smoke
Right through the line they broke;
Cossack and Russian
Reeled from the sabre stroke
Shattered and sundered.
Then they rode back, but not
Not the six hundred.

V
Cannon to right of them,
Cannon to left of them,
Cannon behind them
Volleyed and thundered;
Stormed at with shot and shell,
While horse and hero fell.
They that had fought so well
Came through the jaws of Death,
Back from the mouth of hell,
All that was left of them,
Left of six hundred.

VI
When can their glory fade?
O the wild charge they made!
All the world wondered.
Honour the charge they made!
Honour the Light Brigade,
Noble six hundred!

Alfred, Lord Tennyson, 1809-1892

7. For further reading, pick up a Dr. Seuss rhyming book like *Horton Hears a Who* or *The Cat in the Hat*. What meter is he using? If you go back to T. S. Eliot's *Book of Practical Cats*, can you identify the metrical lines? (hint: some of them don't use these standard meters)

Review 1

Try to complete the whole review without turning pages back. When you've seen what you can remember, you can use the text to check.

1. What is poetry? It is _____ made with _____

2. Write the number of feet that each type of line has:

   pentameter _____   tetrameter _____

   heptameter _____   dimeter _____

   trimeter _____   hexameter _____

   (Bonus: Alexandrine _____   Fourteener _____)

3. The difference between pure accentual meter and accentual-syllabic meter is that:
   a) only one of them can be measured in feet
   b) pure accentual meter doesn't care how many total syllables it has
   c) accentual-syllabic meter is more like normal speech
   d) only pure accentual meter pays attention to word stress

4. Poetry, as art, is made with two basic elements:
   a) light and shadow
   b) letters and colors
   c) sound elements and images
   d) key signature and barre positions

5. For each type of metrical foot, write the corresponding noun or adjective.

   a) _____, trochaic   b) iamb, _____

   c) spondee, _____   d) _____, anapestic

   e) dactyl, _____

6. Name the type of metrical foot shown in each example, using the terms in #5.

   a) Austrian _____   b) Finland _____

   c) Japanese _____   d) Brazil _____

   e) Ecuador _____   f) Hong Kong _____

63

7. Sort these 20 place names by their type of meter in American English; there will be an equal number in each column: Norway, Taiwan, Mumbai, Hungary, Peru, Canada, Sweden, Shanghai, Ukraine, Vietnam, Cape Town, Yemen, Sudan, Latvia, San Juan, Turkey, China, Key West, Pakistan, Germany.

Iamb	Trochee	Dactyl	Spondee

8. At the points marked in these lines, what kind of relationship does the punctuation have to the line ending? Circle the right choice below.

   Two roads diverged in a yellow wood, (a)
   And sorry I could not travel both (b)
   And be one traveler, (c) long I stood
   And looked down one as far as I could (d)
   To where it bent in the undergrowth; (e)

   a) end-stopped, enjambed, caesura
   b) end-stopped, enjambed, caesura
   c) end-stopped, enjambed, caesura
   d) end-stopped, enjambed, caesura
   e) end-stopped, enjambed, caesura

9. Match the type of verse to its example. Possible answers: limerick, blank verse, accentual verse, double-dactyl.

   a) _____

   Hippity hoppity
   Alfred Lord Tennyson
   Wrote little songs in
   Accentual verse.

   Without them his lengthy
   Syllabic-accentual
   Stories would sound to us
   Drier and worse.

b) _____

An Englishman named Edward Lear
Thought Victorian poetry drear.
He surmised anapests
Would pass giggle tests
And with levity make his career.

c) _____

See how informal verse
Can be fresher and light as a song
Like a window opened on spring
In a narrative formal and long.

Tennyson, Browning and Poe
And others about the same age
Used the nursery's lyrical jig
To break out of their elders' cage.

d) _____

To tell a tale in verse requires some work,
But there are ways to make it easier.
First choose a walking step that isn't hard
To fit to daily speech; then count to five.
You'll find your story grows quite easily,
Which lets you focus on the narrative.

10. Match the first line to the poet. Possible answers: Blake, Browning, Frost, Poe, Tennyson

    a) Two roads diverged in a yellow wood…

    b) He clasps the crag with crooked hands…

    c) Gaily bedight…

    d) Tyger! Tyger! burning bright…

    e) Oh to be in England…

Six:

Rhyme

Rhyme is the sound element of poetry that people are most familiar with. We use rhyme a great deal with children, because we want them to become aware of the sounds in words. It's helpful to hear how the ends of words can be the same when you learn to read. Dr. Seuss's books are read out loud to young children now, but they were written to help early readers by using the same spellings over and over: Hop on Pop!

1. Types of rhymes

The ordinary meaning of "rhyme" is that two words end in syllables with the same vowels and consonants. With the beginning sound struck off, they would be identical. Of course, there are many English rhymes that are identically-spelled, "word families" used to teach children early spelling. Tennyson's "The Eagle" used three: hands, lands, stands.

The second stanza of "The Eagle" has three perfect rhymes, but they don't employ the same letters: crawls, walls, falls. Because English has many oddly-spelled words, poets can find rhyming sets that use quite different letters. William Blake rhymed "foe" with "grow"; we could also rhyme it with "although," "so," and even the borrowed French word "beau." Poets like using surprisingly-spelled rhymes; it's like getting a high-scoring word in "Scrabble."

When a word ends in a vowel, like "ee," "ay," or "o," the rhyme is usually just with this sound. "Melody" and "memory" rhyme in this basic way, both ending in -y (ee). However, if the whole syllable is included, then the consonant would need to match, too. Then "melody" would rhyme with "lady," and "memory" with "Mary." The choice to rhyme with more or fewer sounds is up to the artist.

The simplest kind of rhyme matches only the last sound or syllable, but poets can also choose words that match consonants and vowels for two syllables. This *double rhyme* is most often found in feminine-ending lines, because the rhyme is stronger if it includes the stressed syllable. So while "ending" technically rhymes in the last syllable with "sledding," it doesn't feel like a good rhyme. "Spending" and "pretending" make more satisfying rhymes, since the rhyme includes the stressed syllable.

There are many words that end in dactyls: cómedy (the whole word is a dactyl), ecólogy, anónymous, estáblishment. Many of these words have Greek endings like -ology or -onomy, where the stress goes on the syllable "ól" or "ón." It isn't hard to find rhymes for words like theology or astronomy, but if we want the stressed syllable to be included, we end up with similarly-formed words: apology, neurology; gastronomy, autonomy. When we rhyme a pair of words by matching three syllables, it can be called a *triple rhyme* or, if it forms a dactyl, a *dactyl rhyme*.

If you're setting out to rhyme a complicated word, you can choose to rhyme it at any of these levels. Let's say the word is "velocity." At the simplest level, anything that ends in an "ee" sound is good enough.

"Velocity" could rhyme with "me," but to come closer to matching sounds, it might do better with "tea," which includes a consonant. You could also choose to match two syllables, rhyming it with "city," "pity" or "quality." However, if you can match the rhymes to the stressed middle "o" in velocity, it's considered stronger. So you could go for a dactyl-rhyme like "ferocity", "paucity," or "animosity." You could also create a dactyl-rhyme out of shorter words, making a phrase like "cross it he" somehow fit into the lines:

> He charged at high velocity
> but the river was deep,
> so to cross it he
> suddenly sprouted wings.

Clever rhymes like that are more typical of light-hearted poetry, because they call attention to themselves and away from any serious feeling or message. In 1818, George Gordon Byron (usually called Lord Byron, since he was an English baron) wrote a long satirical poem filled with complicated, clever rhymes. It opens this way:

> I want a hero: an uncommon want,
> When every year and month sends forth a new one,
> Till, after cloying the gazettes with cant,
> The age discovers he is not the true one;
> Of such as these I should not care to vaunt,
> I'll therefore take our ancient friend Don Juan—
> We all have seen him, in the pantomime,
> Sent to the Devil somewhat ere his time.

In a country with a high Spanish-speaking population, Americans automatically pronounce the name "Juan" as "wan." But Byron's rhymes make it clear that he said Ju-an, to rhyme with "new one" and "true one." We can also tell that he said "cant" to rhyme with vaunt and want.

Poems sometimes use *sight rhymes*; if an American rhymed "cant" and "want," it would be only a rhyme in using the same letters. We find a lot of sight rhymes in Shakespeare today, but it's likely that the rhymes were normal sound matches when the poet chose them, but the language changed.

Rhyming words are among our most important clues about how words were pronounced in the past. Chaucer's *Canterbury Tales* open with rhyming "soote" (sweet) and "roote" (root), so that we can guess that in the 1300s, he rhymed both of them with our modern "boat." In the next lines, "licour" (liquor, meaning liquid) and "flour" (flower) almost certainly rhymed with modern "moor" (or, borrowed from French, modern "liqueur").

Poets can choose to use sight rhymes, also called *visual rhyme*s or *eye rhymes*. They could pair "have" with "grave," or "enough" with "bough." It's not a common practice, because it subverts the core sound-charm of rhymes. Deliberate sight rhymes are like songs that end on the wrong note. There's no rule against doing it that way, but the artist should have a very good reason for calling attention to the word pair, then leaving the reader flat. It's like summer thunder without rain.

The other important type of rhyme uses a near match, but not an exact match, of ending sounds. We call this *off-rhyme, half rhyme, near rhyme* or *slant rhyme*. A good slant rhyme might use the same vowel, with a consonant that is similar but not the same. N and M are both nasal sounds, so a slant rhyme might pair "rhyme" with "fine." Instead of rhyming "moon" with "June," the poet could pair it with "assume." Another slant rhyme might keep the ending consonant but alter the vowel, pairing "keep" with "cape" or "lip."

Slant rhymes are normally used in serious poetry, so they don't tend to have multi-syllabic cleverness like Byron's. They signal that a word is chosen for its meaning, even if the rhyme is only half right, instead of searching for other ways to say not quite the right thing but with a perfect rhyme. However, when I was generating different matches for "velocity," it occurred to me that one kind of slant rhyme could maintain the dactyl pattern and some vowels, while altering consonants: "prophecy" and "audacity" might work as slant rhymes.

Slant rhyme is most associated with the American poetess Emily Dickinson, whose minimalist, philosophical verses did not have room for creating elaborate perfect rhymes the way Lord Byron did. She used them in combination with perfect rhymes, tacitly daring us to accept that there is really no difference. Her poems usually did not have titles, either, so we can only refer to this poem as "Hope is the thing with feathers." I've put the rhymes in italics:

Hope is the Thing with Feathers

Hope is the thing with feathers
That perches in the *soul*,
And sings the tune without the words,
And never stops at *all*,

And sweetest in the gale is heard;
And sore must be the *storm*
That could abash the little bird
That kept so many *warm*.

I've heard it in the chilliest land,
And on the strangest *sea*;
Yet, never, in extremity,
It asked a crumb of *me*.

"Soul" and "all" are very good slant rhymes. Their final consonant is the same, and their vowels, while different, are similar (they are both pronounced with the tongue low in the mouth). I don't think the slant rhyme would have felt as right if she had written, "and never stops to *feel*." Similarly, "storm" and "warm" are nearly identical in some American dialects, but Emily probably pronounced them a little differently. However, instead of making it a rule for herself to use slant rhymes, she closed the poem with a simple, perfect rhyme. Her use of slant rhymes seems to say "I only care what it is that I want to say, and I will go to just a *little* trouble to fit it into what you expect, but no more. Deal with it."

2. Placing rhymes

We commonly think about rhymes that are placed at the ends of lines; they are *end rhymes* or *end-stopped*, using the same term we use for punctuation at a line's end. However, rhymes can be placed close within the same line or across the distance of several lines.

Rhymes within a line are called *internal rhyme*. If they are placed at a mid-point and at the end, they sound like two shorter lines with end rhymes:

> Once upon a midnight *dreary*, while I pondered, weak and *weary*
> Over many a quaint and curious volume of forgotten lore—
> While I nodded, nearly *napping*, suddenly there came a *tapping*,
> As of some one gently *rapping, rapping* at my chamber door.
> "'Tis some visitor," I muttered, "*tapping* at my chamber door—
> Only this and nothing more."

Edgar Allen Poe's famous "The Raven" uses internal rhyme as an organizing device, since its lines are unusually long. There are eight metrical feet (octameter) in each of these lines, except for the last, which has four. The rhymes make us hear the lines of eight as two lines of four:

> Once upon a midnight dreary,
> while I pondered, weak and weary

However, the overall composition shows that Poe intended the primary rhymes to be lore, door, and more, which are all end-stopped. If he had organized the poem in lines of four feet, this pattern would have been harder to spot. So instead, he used internal rhyme to break up some of the long lines, but not others. By using "napping" and "tapping" as internal rhymes, then repeating "rapping" and "tapping" in less-expected feet in the next two lines, he creates a lot of variation in his rhyme pattern. So many rhymes could become dull, but because of the way he varies their placement, they are welcome each time they come around again (like rain).

Rhymes can also help connect phrases that are not close to each other. Our mind's ears are very attuned to noticing similarities, so we usually remember what sounds we have heard for a short period of time, then we forget. A poem can play with this short-term memory by springing a rhyme just when we've almost begun to forget that we heard this sound before.

In the first lesson, you looked at T. S. Eliot's "La Figlia Chè Piange". Rhyme is a prominent part of this poem's beauty, but Eliot places rhyming pairs as far apart as five lines:

> So he would have *left*
> As the soul leaves the body torn and bruised,
> As the mind deserts the body it has used.
> I should find
> Some way incomparably light and *deft*,

Partly because "bruised" and "used" are placed in adjacent lines, our ears start to forget about the sound of "left." The word "find," which has many possible rhymes, sets up an expectation that we might see its rhyme placed next, like bruised and used; perhaps he will rhyme "find" with "mind" or "kind." But instead, Eliot gives us "deft." It's a little bit unexpected, which is often an artistic way to enhance beauty. It also helps keep the lines together in our minds, connecting ideas so that we unify the passage. If you look back at the poem, you'll see that Eliot does this in more than one place.

How far away can you place a rhyme, internally or end-stopped, and still have it work? That's a question of judgment and one of the artistic choices. If you are writing blank verse and don't want anything to rhyme, "how long do people remember sounds?" is also relevant. In the blank verse of "Mending Wall," I am sure Frost expected us to ignore the rhyme between "spell," which comes in the middle of a line, and "well," many lines later. He was right; the ear has long since forgotten to keep "-ell" in mind.

Summary and Definitions

Two words *rhyme* if they share the same final vowel and consonant sounds, regardless of how they're spelled. Rhymes can involve only one syllable, or they may be *double rhymes* (two syllables), *triple rhymes* (three syllables), or *dactyl rhymes* (three syllables in a dactyl stress pattern). Rhymes sound strongest if they match in stressed syllables. Multiple words, taken as a group, may also be rhymed with single words.

When two words almost rhyme, they are the same in the vowel or the consonant sound, but not in both. This has various names, including *slant rhyme*, *off-rhyme*, *half-rhyme*, and *near rhyme*.

Words that are spelled the same, but do not sound the same, are *sight rhymes*, *visual rhymes*, or *eye rhymes*. They are usually a sign that the language has changed, since rhyming appeals to hearing, not to sight.

Rhymes are most commonly placed at the end of a line, where they can be described as *end rhymes* or *end-stopped*. A pair of rhyming words can also share the same line, as *internal rhymes*.

Exercises 6

Review

a) Choose the word that matches the line's stress pattern:

  Give it back to me! (extravaganza, counterfactual, lollapalooza)

  When can you tell me? (Deuteronomy, determination, abracadabra)

  It's just my size. (incarcerate, meridian, watermelon)

b) Choose the line that's accentual meter:

  I've heard it in the chilliest land; Sit and watch by her side an hour

  While the one eludes, must the other pursue; Once upon a midnight dreary

  I crossed a moor, with a name of its own; Charging an army, while all the world wondered.

c) Blank verse is (unrhymed trochaic pentameter; rhymed iambic tetrameter; unrhymed iambic pentameter)

1. In 1905, E. Clerihew Bentley published a book of light verse called *Biography for Beginners*. As a schoolboy, he had amused his friends (one of them was G. K. Chesterton, later a famous writer) with little unmetered four-line verses about famous people. In a "clerihew," the first line is entirely, or mainly, the person's name. Here are some of Bentley's clerihews for you to complete. The first two lines rhyme, and the next two as well; you may notice that the meter's all over the place.

a) The novels of Jane _____
Are the ones to get lost in.
Who has the ability
to put down Sense and _____ ?

b) When their lordships asked Bacon
How many bribes he had _____
At least he had the grace
To get red in the _____

c) On one occasion when Browning
Saved a debutante from _____
She inquired faintly what he _____
By that stuff about good news from Ghent.

d) King George the _____
Ought never to have occurred.
One can only wonder
At so grotesque a _____

e) "The moustache of _____
Could hardly be littler,"
Was the thought that kept _____
To Field-Marshal Goering.

f) It was a pity about _____
Insane jealousy of chickens;
And one could almost weep
At his morbid distrust of _____

g) Although Machiavelli
Was extremely fond of _____,
He stuck religiously to mince
While he was writing The _____

h) How many times, mused Hugo,
Does four into 372 go?
Come now, let me see:
I have it! _____

i) Peter the _____
Neglected to apply for a permit
When raising his mixed brigade
For the _____

j) Sir Humphrey Davy
Detested _____
He lived in the odium
Of having discovered _____

2. In this nature poem by Emily Dickinson, the rhymes vary widely. There is one perfect rhyme and several slant rhymes, with a few that may not strike you as rhymes at all. We can tell when Emily intended a set of words to rhyme, because she usually followed the rhyming pattern set by hymns, in which the second and fourth lines rhyme. This form is so typical of old songs that it's called the hymn or ballad form.

   a) perfect rhyme:

   b) slant rhyme:

   c) intended slant rhyme; what do you think, do these sets rhyme in your ear? What do the word endings have in common?

   d) what does the last line mean, "its sea"? Who is "its"?

From Cocoon Forth a Butterfly

From cocoon forth a butterfly
As lady from her door
Emerged—a summer afternoon—
Repairing everywhere,

Without design, that I could trace,
Except to stray abroad
On miscellaneous enterprise
The clovers understood.

Her pretty parasol was seen
Contracting in a field
Where men made hay, then struggling hard
With an opposing cloud,

Where parties, phantom as herself,
To Nowhere seemed to go
In purposeless circumference,
As 't were a tropic show.

And notwithstanding bee that worked,
And flower that zealous blew,
This audience of idleness
Disdained them, from the sky,

Till sundown crept, a steady tide,
And men that made the hay,
And afternoon, and butterfly,
Extinguished in its sea.

Emily Dickinson, 1830-1886

3. In these eight early stanzas of *Don Juan*, you can see how cleverly Lord Byron handled rhymes. He describes the young Don's mother here, with praise that is so overblown it's clear we are not supposed to take it seriously. He is satirizing the way young women in England were educated, while appearing to talk about a young lady in Spain. Many of the things he mentions will be unknown to you, but imagine that they are the equivalent of pop culture references: movies, books, actors and singers who will soon be forgotten. In the very last line, there's a satirical reference to advertising in 1818; Macassar Oil was a hair oil that advertised itself as "incomparable." Byron jests by taking this seriously; if Macassar Oil is the best thing ever, then surely it's even better than Dona Inez. He also lassoes a clever rhyme this way.

Look for rhyming sets that include:

    a) identical sounds spelled different ways:

    b) double (two syllable) rhymes:

    c) triple (three syllable) rhymes:

    d) rhymes that cross word-boundaries:

    e) rhymes that seem to you a bit forced:

    f) rhyming clues for how Byron pronounced the names Inez and Lopé:

Don Juan, Canto I, Stanzas 10-17

His mother was a learnèd lady, famed
For every branch of every science known—
In every Christian language ever named,
With virtues equalled by her wit alone:
She made the cleverest people quite ashamed,
And even the good with inward envy groan,
Finding themselves so very much exceeded,
In their own way, by all the things that she did.

XI.

Her memory was a mine: she knew by heart
All Calderon and greater part of Lopé;
So, that if any actor missed his part,
She could have served him for the prompter's copy;
For her Feinagle's were an useless art,
And he himself obliged to shut up shop—he
Could never make a memory so fine as
That which adorned the brain of Donna Inez.

XII.

Her favourite science was the mathematical,
Her noblest virtue was her magnanimity,
Her wit (she sometimes tried at wit) was Attic all,
Her serious sayings darkened to sublimity;
In short, in all things she was fairly what I call
A prodigy—her morning dress was dimity,
Her evening silk, or, in the summer, muslin,
And other stuffs, with which I won't stay puzzling.

XIII.

She knew the Latin—that is, "the Lord's prayer,"
And Greek—the alphabet—I'm nearly sure;
She read some French romances here and there,
Although her mode of speaking was not pure;
For native Spanish she had no great care,
At least her conversation was obscure;
Her thoughts were theorems, her words a problem,
As if she deemed that mystery would ennoble 'em.

XIV.

She liked the English and the Hebrew tongue,
And said there was analogy between 'em;
She proved it somehow out of sacred song,
But I must leave the proofs to those who've seen 'em;
But this I heard her say, and can't be wrong,
And all may think which way their judgments lean 'em,
"'T is strange—the Hebrew noun which means 'I am,'
The English always use to govern d—n."

XV.

Some women use their tongues—she *looked* a lecture,
Each eye a sermon, and her brow a homily,
An all-in-all sufficient self-director,
Like the lamented late Sir Samuel Romilly,
The Law's expounder, and the State's corrector,
Whose suicide was almost an anomaly—
One sad example more, that "All is vanity,"—
(The jury brought their verdict in "Insanity!")

XVI.

In short, she was a walking calculation,
Miss Edgeworth's novels stepping from their covers,
Or Mrs. Trimmer's books on education,
Or "Coelebs' Wife" set out in quest of lovers,
Morality's prim personification,
In which not Envy's self a flaw discovers;
To others' share let "female errors fall,"
For she had not even one—the worst of all.

XVII.

Oh! she was perfect past all parallel—
Of any modern female saint's comparison;
So far above the cunning powers of Hell,
Her Guardian Angel had given up his garrison;
Even her minutest motions went as well
As those of the best time-piece made by Harrison:
In virtues nothing earthly could surpass her,
Save thine "incomparable oil," Macassar!

4. When he wrote "The Raven," Poe faced a challenge. He had decided, apparently, to keep the rhymes with "door" going through all 18 stanzas. This much of the same rhyme is generally too much of a good thing; it is monotonous and may bore (yes indeed too much may bore, words that always rhyme with door, piling up more and more). So Poe needed a way to keep the ear guessing with other patterns that appear to form, and then dissolve.

   a) Poe's main technique is the irregular use of internal rhyme. Every stanza has at least two sets of internal rhymes; in the first stanza, we see "dreary" and "weary," then "napping," "tapping," and "rapping," with "rapping" repeated three times. These two rhyming sets are also the ends of lines 1 and 3, the only lines that don't rhyme with "door." But within this pattern, there are many variations.

   Look at the first 5 stanzas, and in each, compare the 2nd line, which always rhymes at the end with "door." In which stanzas does it have other internal rhymes? Are they always rhymed within the line?

   b) In each set of lines 4 and 5, which always rhyme with "door," Poe achieves some variation by changing how much of the line is identical. In stanza 1, "-apping at my chamber door" is repeated, so in a sense, that whole section rhymes. In stanza 2, it's only the name "Lenore," while in 3, it's nearly the entire lines. Observe how these sets of lines 4 and 5 are managed in the rest of the stanzas. How many different kinds of repeated phrases and variations does he use? Give some examples.

   c) In most of the stanzas, there is one line that has no internal rhyme, usually line 2 (as in the 4th stanza). Sometimes it's line 5 (as in the 2nd stanza), and in some stanzas, both (as in the 8th). When you read through a group of stanzas, how do these lines feel to you? The ones with internal rhyme can feel like they are broken into halves; do the ones without feel longer? Look at stanza 5; in its 5th line are "whispered" and "murmured." Do they seem to you like internal rhymes?

   d) Odd rhyming pairs: In 6, what rhymes with lattice (there are two answers)? In 7, what rhymes with "stayed he" (again there are two answers)? Do you feel like these odd rhymes are successful or forced? When you just read the stanza out loud, do they sound like they rhyme?

   In stanzas 15 and 18, the second lines have sound pairs that don't quite rhyme, but may seem like rhymes. These are "Tempter" and "sent or," and "pallid" and "Pallas." What do you think?

   e) In 15 and 16, Poe repeats the first line. Does its meaning change between the stanzas? How do you feel about his artistic choice to repeat the line? Does it add or subtract to the emotional tone, to you?

THE RAVEN

(1) Once upon a midnight dreary, while I pondered, weak and weary,
Over many a quaint and curious volume of forgotten lore—
While I nodded, nearly napping, suddenly there came a tapping,
As of some one gently rapping, rapping at my chamber door.
"'Tis some visitor," I muttered, "tapping at my chamber door—
Only this and nothing more."

(2) Ah, distinctly I remember it was in the bleak December;
And each separate dying ember wrought its ghost upon the floor.
Eagerly I wished the morrow;—vainly I had sought to borrow
From my books surcease of sorrow—sorrow for the lost Lenore—
For the rare and radiant maiden whom the angels name Lenore—
Nameless here for evermore.

(3) And the silken, sad, uncertain rustling of each purple curtain

Thrilled me—filled me with fantastic terrors never felt before;
So that now, to still the beating of my heart, I stood repeating
"'Tis some visitor entreating entrance at my chamber door—
Some late visitor entreating entrance at my chamber door;—
This it is and nothing more."

(4) Presently my soul grew stronger; hesitating then no longer,
"Sir," said I, "or Madam, truly your forgiveness I implore;
But the fact is I was napping, and so gently you came rapping,
And so faintly you came tapping, tapping at my chamber door,
That I scarce was sure I heard you"—here I opened wide the door;—
Darkness there and nothing more.

(5) Deep into that darkness peering, long I stood there wondering, fearing,
Doubting, dreaming dreams no mortal ever dared to dream before;
But the silence was unbroken, and the stillness gave no token,

And the only word there spoken was the whispered word, "Lenore?"
This I whispered, and an echo murmured back the word, "Lenore!"—
Merely this and nothing more.

(6) Back into the chamber turning, all my soul within me burning,
Soon again I heard a tapping somewhat louder than before.
"Surely," said I, "surely that is something at my window lattice;
Let me see, then, what thereat is, and this mystery explore—
Let my heart be still a moment and this mystery explore;—
'Tis the wind and nothing more!"

(7) Open here I flung the shutter, when, with many a flirt and flutter,
In there stepped a stately Raven of the saintly days of yore;
Not the least obeisance made he; not a minute stopped or stayed he;
But, with mien of lord or lady, perched above my chamber door—
Perched upon a bust of Pallas just above my chamber door—
Perched, and sat, and nothing more.

(8) Then this ebony bird beguiling my sad fancy into smiling,
By the grave and stern decorum of the countenance it wore,
"Though thy crest be shorn and shaven, thou," I said, "art sure no craven,
Ghastly grim and ancient Raven wandering from the Nightly shore—
Tell me what thy lordly name is on the Night's Plutonian shore!"
Quoth the Raven "Nevermore."

(9) Much I marvelled this ungainly fowl to hear discourse so plainly,
Though its answer little meaning—little relevancy bore;
For we cannot help agreeing that no living human being
Ever yet was blessed with seeing bird above his chamber door—
Bird or beast upon the sculptured bust above his chamber door,
With such name as "Nevermore."

(10) But the Raven, sitting lonely on the placid bust, spoke only
That one word, as if his soul in that one word he did outpour.
Nothing farther then he uttered—not a feather then he fluttered—
Till I scarcely more than muttered "Other friends have flown before—
On the morrow he will leave me, as my Hopes have flown before."
Then the bird said "Nevermore."

(11) Startled at the stillness broken by reply so aptly spoken,
"Doubtless," said I, "what it utters is its only stock and store
Caught from some unhappy master whom unmerciful Disaster
Followed fast and followed faster till his songs one burden bore—
Till the dirges of his Hope that melancholy burden bore
Of 'Never—nevermore'."

(12) But the Raven still beguiling all my fancy into smiling,
Straight I wheeled a cushioned seat in front of bird, and bust and door;
Then, upon the velvet sinking, I betook myself to linking
Fancy unto fancy, thinking what this ominous bird of yore—
What this grim, ungainly, ghastly, gaunt, and ominous bird of yore
Meant in croaking "Nevermore."

(13) This I sat engaged in guessing, but no syllable expressing
To the fowl whose fiery eyes now burned into my bosom's core;
This and more I sat divining, with my head at ease reclining
On the cushion's velvet lining that the lamp-light gloated o'er,
But whose velvet-violet lining with the lamp-light gloating o'er,
She shall press, ah, nevermore!

(14) Then, methought, the air grew denser, perfumed from an unseen censer
Swung by Seraphim whose foot-falls tinkled on the tufted floor.
"Wretch," I cried, "thy God hath lent thee—by these angels he hath sent thee
Respite—respite and nepenthe from thy memories of Lenore;
Quaff, oh quaff this kind nepenthe and forget this lost Lenore!"
Quoth the Raven "Nevermore."

(15) "Prophet!" said I, "thing of evil!—prophet still, if bird or devil!—
Whether Tempter sent, or whether tempest tossed thee here ashore,
Desolate yet all undaunted, on this desert land enchanted—
On this home by Horror haunted—tell me truly, I implore—
Is there—is there balm in Gilead?—tell me—tell me, I implore!"
Quoth the Raven "Nevermore."

(16) "Prophet!" said I, "thing of evil!—prophet still, if bird or devil!
By that Heaven that bends above us—by that God we both adore—
Tell this soul with sorrow laden if, within the distant Aidenn,
It shall clasp a sainted maiden whom the angels name Lenore—
Clasp a rare and radiant maiden whom the angels name Lenore."
Quoth the Raven "Nevermore."

(17) "Be that word our sign of parting, bird or fiend!" I shrieked, upstarting—
"Get thee back into the tempest and the Night's Plutonian shore!
Leave no black plume as a token of that lie thy soul hath spoken!
Leave my loneliness unbroken!—quit the bust above my door!
Take thy beak from out my heart, and take thy form from off my door!"
Quoth the Raven "Nevermore."

(18) And the Raven, never flitting, still is sitting, still is sitting
On the pallid bust of Pallas just above my chamber door;
And his eyes have all the seeming of a demon's that is dreaming,
And the lamp-light o'er him streaming throws his shadow on the floor;
And my soul from out that shadow that lies floating on the floor
Shall be lifted—nevermore!

Edgar Allen Poe, 1809-1849

5. For further reading, if you have Hollander's *Rhyme's Reason*, start by reading page 14, observing the many terms and kinds of rhyme he works in. Then look at pages 54-56 on "Anomalous Rhymes." Look again at T. S. Eliot's *Book of Practical Cats*; in this light verse, he uses many clever rhymes.

Also for further reading, read a canto (section) of Byron's *Don Juan*.

Seven:

Rhyme Schemes

Poems often engage with our memories by setting up expectations. That's why rhyme is "like rain": we know the weather patterns that make us expect it, and then it arrives. Birds may fall silent; the wind picks up; we hear thunder; it grows darker. Then it begins to rain. Anticipation ends with fulfillment.

In poetry, anticipation is strongest when we're trained to expect a certain sound at a certain point. Blake's "A Poison Tree" set up an expectation for rhymes at fixed points and delivered them every time. Poe's "The Raven" played with our expectations, always delivering the doors and mores, but occasionally withholding other rhymes when expected or suddenly delivering extra rhymes without warning. Emily Dickinson wanted us to expect rhymes at fixed points, but sometimes her slant rhymes didn't deliver much "rain." All of these artistic choices are possible because our minds pick up patterns, remember them, and watch to confirm if they continue. We pay attention to patterns.

We call a poem's pattern of rhymes its *rhyme scheme*. The word "scheme" is most often used in daily conversation to suggest manipulation and secrecy, but at base it just means a systematic plan. To describe rhyme schemes, we need a way of naming the rhymes.

1. Naming rhyming patterns

We use the English alphabet to describe rhyming patterns. The first time we meet a word that will have a rhyme, we name it A. The letter stands for the sound, rather than the word or the line. When we see its rhyming companion, it is another A. If it occurs again, it is still A.

The next one we encounter is B, and its matches are all B. Each new rhyming sound is the next letter. To take a very simple example, Tennyson's "The Eagle" is labeled like this:

He clasps the crag with crooked hands;	A
Close to the sun in lonely lands,	A
Ringed with the azure world, he stands.	A
The wrinkled sea beneath him crawls:	B
He watches from his mountain walls,	B
And like a thunderbolt he falls.	B

So when writing about the poem, we can say that its rhyme scheme is AAA, BBB. If it continued to more stanzas, we would expect CCC and then DDD.

Rhyme Schemes

Blake's "A Poison Tree" presents a very steady, regular pattern. The rhyming sounds change from stanza to stanza, but they always follow the model of the first one. First, I'll name it by using a fresh letter for each rhyming sound.

I was angry with my friend:	A
I told my wrath, my wrath did end.	A
I was angry with my foe:	B
I told it not, my wrath did grow.	B
And I watered it in fears,	C
Night and morning with my tears;	C
And I sunnèd it with smiles,	D
And with soft deceitful wiles.	D
And it grew both day and night,	E
Till it bore an apple bright;	E
And my foe beheld it shine,	F
And he knew that it was mine,	F
And into my garden stole	G
When the night had veiled the pole:	G
In the morning glad I see	H
My foe outstretched beneath the tree.	H

Because it's so regular, we don't need to use all of these letters. Every single one follows the first model, AABB. When the stanza sets a model that is repeated in every other stanza, we only need to name the pattern in the model. In this case, you could say the rhyme scheme is AABB, and we'd assume that each stanza has its own A and B sounds.

Other poems need to use up more letters because there is no stanza model to follow. In "La Figlia Chè Piange," Eliot does not set up a regular pattern. Instead, the ear never knows what to expect next. I'll use a new letter each time I meet a new rhyming sound.

Stand on the highest pavement of the stair—	A
Lean on a garden urn—	B
Weave, weave the sunlight in your hair—	A
Clasp your flowers to you with a pained surprise—	C
Fling them to the ground and turn	B
With a fugitive resentment in your eyes:	C
But weave, weave the sunlight in your hair.	A
So I would have had him leave,	D
So I would have had her stand and grieve,	D
So he would have left	E
As the soul leaves the body torn and bruised,	F

As the mind deserts the body it has used.	F
I should find	X
Some way incomparably light and deft,	E
Some way we both should understand,	G
Simple and faithless as a smile and shake of the hand.	G
She turned away, but with the autumn weather	H
Compelled my imagination many days,	I
Many days and many hours:	J
Her hair over her arms and her arms full of flowers.	J
And I wonder how they should have been together!	H
I should have lost a gesture and a pose.	K
Sometimes these cogitations still amaze	I
The troubled midnight and the noon's repose.	K

Every letter has at least one match, which is why I gave it a letter. There's one line that has no true end-rhyme: "I should find..." (It does have internal and slant rhymes.) Because there is no other "-ind" end-rhyme, it can't be given a letter in the alphabet order. It is called X. Every line that stands alone is X. If there is more than one unrhymed line in a poem, they're still called X; the X lines don't have to rhyme.

The only way to describe the rhyme scheme of Eliot's poem would be to provide all of these letters, A through K, because there are no repeating patterns. It wouldn't be very helpful to write out a string of letters, so if we were writing about this poem, we'd be more likely to just describe it. We could write, "There are 11 different rhymes, and they can occur as far apart as 5 lines. In three places, however, the rhymes occur in succeeding lines. There is one non-rhymed line in almost the center of the poem, line 13 out of 25. This middle line, shorter than the rest and missing an end-rhyme, creates a kind of caesura in the middle of the poem, a brief pause in the rhythm. It does have a nearby internal rhyme."

Unrhymed X lines can be used to great artistic effect; they are another of the tools in the poet's paintbox. They can be used to disrupt expectation, or to set the reader's ear up not to expect more rhyming. In Eliot's poem, the X rhyme "find" serves to push the E rhyme "deft" out to five lines away from "left," where we have ceased to expect it.

2. Couplets

The simplest rhyme scheme pattern is two lines in succession, rhymed AA. This is called a *couplet*. We see them in Shakespeare's plays at times, where dialogue in blank verse closes with a rhymed couplet. After the ear has stopped listening for rhymes, a couplet has the effect that some chord sequences do in music, signaling to the ear that the melody has finished.

Byron's "Don Juan" closed each stanza with a couplet, too. For example:

> In virtues nothing earthly could surpass her,
> Save thine "incomparable oil," Macassar!

Couplets can close a stanza, as Byron did, or they can tumble along in succession. We describe such a poem as being rhymed AA, BB, CC, and so on. When rhymes come so close together, they can sound a little too much like artificial chatter. The form was very popular in the 18th century. It was often used to carry out a long story, so it became known as "heroic couplets."

William Cowper wrote some long poems in rhymed iambic pentameter (heroic couplets), including one, "Tirocinium," that gave his views on the destructiveness of sending young children away to boarding schools. Here is one passage:

> Would you your son should be a sot or dunce,
> Lascivious, headstrong, or all these at once,
> That in good time, the stripling's finish'd taste
> For loose expense and fashionable waste,
> Should prove your ruin, and his own at last,
> Train him in public with a mob of boys,
> Childish in mischief only and in noise,
> Else of a mannish growth, and five in ten
> In infidelity and lewdness, men.
> There shall he learn, ere sixteen winters old,
> That authors are most useful, pawn'd or sold,
> That pedantry is all that schools impart,
> But taverns teach the knowledge of the heart.

Most of the lines form couplet pairs, with one exception (taste-waste-last). When the reading ear has anticipation set up by an end-rhyme that is quickly matched, then another, then another, it can create a sense of emotional comfort and certainty. It's almost a persuasive technique, leading the reader to feel like "oh, of course," the message must be true, because anticipation and expectation are constantly soothed.

Emily Brontë, author of *Wuthering Heights*, includes this short poem among her works. With four trochaic feet, she creates a series of four couplets.

Fall, Leaves, Fall

> Fall, leaves, fall; die, flowers, away;
> Lengthen night and shorten day;
> Every leaf speaks bliss to me,
> Fluttering from the autumn tree.
> I shall smile when wreaths of snow
> Blossom where the rose should grow;
> I shall sing when night's decay
> Ushers in a drearier day.

I think Emily deliberately used successive couplets to bring an ironic note of certainty into her otherwise melancholy poem. If she had left it entirely unrhymed, it would have felt sadder. But she wanted to convey a sense of double feeling: in fall and winter, things are dying, which is naturally felt as sad; but on the other hand, for some private reason she says that it will make her happy. The rhyme scheme's comfort and closure support the mysterious theme of her private contentment in the face of wintry death.

Couplets are usually matched in meter and line length, because they are meant to feel complete and finished. However, they don't need to be matched. A poet may choose to mismatch them for some reason.

In this poem, "Prayer for Moving Day," I deliberately broke the couplets, making the second line pull up short as the rhyme chimes in. The other lines in each stanza do not rhyme, so each couplet stands out. I wanted to convey a sense of uncertainty; the poem was about the uncertainty and fear of moving away from people you know. The last lines form three rhymes, a sort of triple couplet, to suggest some resolution (anticipation is met twice!), but the final line still pulls up short.

Prayer for Moving Day

The first rays burn along Your shears. Wait
One moment and admire the tensile strength
And twisted beauty of my network home,
This dew-pearled web of friends; consider what
Those blades will cut.

All engineering laces weak and strong,
And some ties I love less and others more.
One thread from flower to branch, one ropes a thorn,
And some encircle, wander or hold all
Weight like a wall.

By nature, spiders drop and rise, but hearts
Were made to cling and hold. Cut free, You watch
Me fall, or drift, or scream and comb the air.
Throw down some rope! Be it of thought or song,
Or curling smoke of prayer, it must be long
And hold me strong.

3. Kinds of Stanzas

My early definition of a stanza was a group of lines, usually separated from each other by blank lines. In Italian, *stanza* means a room (I guess the blank space forms the walls). But in poetry, the stanza is usually more unified than just being separated by space. It is like the verse of a song; the melody stops at the end of the verse and repeats again for the next one. Poetry's original use of stanzas was the same as in song: providing a complete thought. It was easy to set such stanzas to music, to make songs or church hymns:

God moves in a mysterious way,
His wonders to perform;
He plants his footsteps in the sea,
And rides upon the storm.

These lines work as a complete thought in a poem, or as a verse in a song. A couplet could be a type of stanza if it stands alone. Usually couplets are part of a larger stanza, but a poet could make the choice to place the two rhymed lines alone.

Next is a three-line stanza, the *tercet*. "The Eagle" was made of two tercets. Rhymes helped to tie the tercets together, AAA and BBB. Tercets can be unrhymed, or they could rhyme in other ways, such as XAA or

ABA. Tercets feel like modified couplets sometimes. They're a couplet with an extra line at the beginning or end, or perhaps put into the middle.

Tercets were the organizing form in "Morning Lyric," my unmetered, unrhymed poem shown in the first lesson:

> The soul wakes in a clean white shift
> and blinks in generic sunshine.
> It could be any of a million days.

My unmetered, unrhymed sets of three still count as tercets. In that short poem, sets of three lines were the only structure imposed on the idea. Since tercets have usually been held together with rhyme, the *absence* of rhyme stands out more than it would if the poem presented its lines in a disorganized string.

Tercets have a special rhyme scheme, first used by Dante in his *Divine Comedy*. It is called *terza rima*, and you have to see several stanzas to observe the pattern of interlocking rhyme. If the first stanza is ABA, the second is BCB, then CDC, and so on. Shelley wrote a long poem, "Ode to the West Wind," which used four tercets in *terza rima*, then a couplet. Here's the first set:

O wild West Wind, thou breath of Autumn's being,	A
Thou, from whose unseen presence the leaves dead	B
Are driven, like ghosts from an enchanter fleeing,	A
Yellow, and black, and pale, and hectic red,	B
Pestilence-stricken multitudes: O thou,	C
Who chariotest to their dark wintry bed	B
The winged seeds, where they lie cold and low,	C
Each like a corpse within its grave, until	D
Thine azure sister of the Spring shall blow	C
Her clarion o'er the dreaming earth, and fill	D
(Driving sweet buds like flocks to feed in air)	E
With living hues and odours plain and hill:	D
Wild Spirit, which art moving everywhere;	E
Destroyer and preserver; hear, oh hear!	E

Four lines are a very common grouping; you have seen a number of them already. This type of stanza is called a *quatrain*. Both of Blake's poems presented here, "A Poison Tree" and "The Tyger," are made of quatrains rhymed AABB. When we call them quatrains, we are saying that each one follows the model of the first. We don't need to mention that the rhyming sounds change in other stanzas. "Quatrains of trochaic tetrameter, rhymed AABB," tells you everything.

There are four typical rhyme schemes for quatrains. In addition to AABB, they can be rhymed ABAB, or ABBA. Shelley's "Mutability" was made of quatrains rhymed ABAB:

We are as clouds that veil the midnight moon;	A
How restlessly they speed, and gleam, and quiver,	B
Streaking the darkness radiantly!—yet soon	A
Night closes round, and they are lost for ever.	B

Quatrains rhymed ABBA are very common in sonnets, which you'll see in the next lessons, but they are a little harder to find outside of the sonnet form. William Butler Yeats's "When You Are Old And Grey" provides one example of iambic pentameter lines ABBA:

When you are old and grey and full of sleep,	A
And nodding by the fire, take down this book,	B
And slowly read, and dream of the soft look	B
Your eyes had once, and of their shadows deep;	A

Thomas Hardy's short accentual-meter poem, "Neutral Tones," is made of ABBA quatrains. With Hardy's stanza set next to Yeats', you should be able to hear clear differences between the accentual meter and iambic pentameter. (If not, try to force Hardy's lines into iambs; does it work?)

We stood by a pond that winter day,	A
And the sun was white, as though children of God,	B
And a few leaves lay on the starving sod,	B
—They had fallen from an ash, and were grey.	A

In both cases, the ABBA rhyme scheme seems to unite the quatrain more, not permitting it to break into two couplets. The closing A rhyme connects the ending of the quatrain to its first line. When I read it, my eye has to glance back to the first A rhyme, and if I read it out loud, my voice intonation avoids sending signals that the sentence is over and the ideas have moved on. "No," the ABBA structure says, "wait for it, keep everything in mind…and…there it is. Done."

By far the most common quatrain rhyme scheme is XAXA; it is called *ballad form* or *hymn form*. We don't even hear its unrhymed lines as X. The rhymes, coming on the 2nd and 4th lines, seem to connect the unrhymed lines into super-lines, like this:

God moves in a mysterious way / his wonders to perform
He plants his footsteps in the sea, / and rides upon the storm.

It's like a couplet with seven, not five, iambic feet in each line. But it isn't meant to be heptameter, nor is it ever written that way. It's always written as four separate lines of three and four feet. It's the most familiar pattern for church music, the old hymn; it was also the old pattern for popular music (ballads) since the Middle Ages. One reason that the rhyming lines had only three feet was so that the last note could be held longer, to sound finished and to allow the singer to take a breath.

Emily Dickinson used this form for nearly all of her poems:

Hope is the thing with feathers	X
That perches in the soul,	A

And sings the tune without the words,	X
And never stops at all.	A

Tennyson's "Break, Break, Break" uses the ballad/hymn rhyme scheme, although he did not use iambs or measure out four feet. Each of his lines is three accentual feet; however, the rhyme scheme is again XAXA. By coming so close to the old ballad form, he conveyed the idea that his lines were meant to be heard as a song or set to music.

Break, break, break	X
On thy cold grey stones, O Sea!	A
And I would that my tongue could utter	X
The thoughts that arise in me.	A

There are less common, longer stanza forms. Five lines form a *quintet* (or perhaps a cinquain, though that term is usually reserved for an unrhymed poem counted in syllables). In metered, rhymed verse, they feel like quatrains with an extra line. Frost's five-line stanzas in "The Road Not Taken" were rhymed ABAAB:

Two roads diverged in a yellow wood,	A
And sorry I could not travel both	B
And be one traveler, long I stood	A
And looked down one as far as I could	A
To where it bent in the undergrowth;	B

One famous quintet form is the limerick. It's rhymed AABBA, though the lines are not of equal length. Its special comic feeling comes from the B lines being only two accentual feet long, while the final A rhyme returns to three feet. This sets up extra anticipation of the clever rhyme that should round out the joke.

Edgar Allen Poe's accentual poem "El Dorado" uses six-line stanzas, called *sestets*. He tied the lines together with the B rhyme. You could think of his sestet as two tercets that rhyme.

Gaily bedight,	A
A gallant knight,	A
In sunshine and in shadow,	B
Had journeyed long,	C
Singing a song,	C
In search of Eldorado.	B

Longfellow's "Seaweed" is another in sestets. It turns out to follow the same rhyme scheme as "El Dorado."

When descends on the Atlantic	A
The gigantic	A
Storm-wind of the equinox,	B
Landward in his wrath he scourges	C
The toiling surges,	C
Laden with seaweed from the rocks...	B

Sestets could also be rhymed ABCABC, ABBACC, or AABBCC. Of course, like any stanza, they can be unrhymed and only used to organize an idea with blank lines to separate it from the others.

A seven-line stanza is a *septet*. A. E. Housman wrote a poem in septets, and he rhymed them like the sestets above, but with an extra C line.

How clear, how lovely bright,	A
How beautiful to sight	A
Those beams of morning play;	B
How heaven laughs out with glee	C
Where, like a bird set free,	C
Up from the eastern sea	C
Soars the delightful day.	B

Thomas Wyatt, a Tudor-era poet, also wrote a poem with septets, but he rhymed them differently.

They flee from me that sometime did me seek	A
With naked foot, stalking in my chamber.	B
I have seen them gentle, tame, and meek,	A
That now are wild and do not remember	B
That sometime they put themself in danger	B
To take bread at my hand; and now they range,	C
Busily seeking with a continual change.	C

Wyatt's choice of B and C rhymes in this stanza gives us a choice of hearing which sounds are more similar: danger and remember? Or danger and range? Technically, the final -er is the true rhyme, so I've called it B. The near rhyme of "danger" with "range" and "change" ties the lines closer in sound.

Eight lines form the last kind of common stanza; they are called an *octave*. The number eight can be seen as 4+4, or 6+2, with rhyme schemes organized around these sets. Lord Byron used octaves in "Don Juan," each organized as a sestet rhymed ABABAB, and then a couplet, CC. The rhyme scheme had been pioneered by the medieval writer Boccaccio, and in Italy it was used for long heroic stories. Byron's choice to use *ottava rima*, the heroic form, was intentionally ironic:

I want a hero: an uncommon want,	A
When every year and month sends forth a new one,	B
Till, after cloying the gazettes with cant,	A
The age discovers he is not the true one;	B
Of such as these I should not care to vaunt,	A
I'll therefore take our ancient friend Don Juan—	B
We all have seen him, in the pantomime,	C
Sent to the Devil somewhat ere his time.	C

Summary and Definitions

Our minds appreciate rhyme more when we can predict and anticipate the sounds. A regular pattern of rhyming words is called a *rhyme scheme*. Some rhyming poems do not follow schemes.

We describe a rhyme scheme by labeling each rhyming sound with a successive letter. When every stanza follows the same model, such as ABAB, we don't need to describe more than one stanza's pattern.

A *couplet* is a pair of successive lines rhymed AA.

Stanzas are named for how many lines they have, not for their rhyme schemes. In each type of stanza, different patterns are possible. The stanza names can also be used to describe groups of unrhymed lines.

Rhyme Schemes

Three lines: *tercet*
Four lines: *quatrain*
Five lines: *quintet*
Six lines: *sestet*
Seven lines: *septet*
Eight lines: *octave*

Exercises 7

Review:

> To our theme.—The man who has stood on the Acropolis,
> And look'd down over Attica; or he
> Who has sail'd where picturesque Constantinople is,
> Or seen Timbuctoo, or hath taken tea
> In small-ey'd China's crockery-ware metropolis,
> Or sat amidst the bricks of Nineveh,
> May not think much of London's first appearance—
> But ask him what he thinks of it a year hence!

a) In these lines from Don Juan (Canto XI, stanza VII), match the special kinds of rhymes.

perfect rhyme	Acropolis, Constantinopole
slant rhyme	he, tea
double rhyme	tea, Nineveh
dactyl rhyme	appearance, year hence

b) Describe the meter. How does the meter improve the final pair of rhymes?

c) How can you make the long line about Constantinople fit into the same meter as the rest?

d) According to Byron, which syllable is stressed in "Timbuctoo"?

1. Choose words to fit the (nonsense) rhyme schemes, with follow-up questions. Feel free to consult a rhyming dictionary for ideas.

   a)

   He sings between balloons, imagine that.   A
   Before you go inside, spare me a dime.   B
   Abominable Snowman woolen _____   A
   　What is the type of metrical line? _____
   　What kind of stanza does this form? _____
   　Choose an alternative rhyming word for the pattern ABB. _____

b)

Combination in confusion   X

Singing loud and slow   A

To the end it bears repeating   X

But giraffe and_____A

    What is the type of metrical line? How many feet in each line?_____

    What kind of stanza does it form? _____

    (bonus: what is this special stanza form?_____

    Now let's add the line "Win the hammer throw." What is the stanza's new form, and what is its rhyme scheme?_____

c)

Wait for a simplified good opportunity   A

sabotage pineapple certainly _____B

Come my identical purchase disunity,   A

Think of a reason to reach for a greater prize.   B

Helplessly wanting a better _____A

Tropical flowers astonish my northern eyes.   B

    What is the type of metrical line?_____

    What kind of stanza does it form?_____

    Were you able to match your rhyme choices to the meter?_____

    Is your A rhyme choice a single, double, or triple rhyme with the other As?

    _____

    What would the rhyme scheme be if the last lines were "Helplessly seeking to buffer their sabotage, / Ostriches dressed up in tropical camouflage."

    _____

2. Poetry in the 1600s tended to present short lines with frequent rhymes. Although most poems used conventional rhymes of AABB or ABAB, some poems branched out into more creative patterns. Name the rhyme scheme for each stanza; the last one is a full poem of two stanzas, because the pattern is only visible when you have both.

    a) How happy the lover,
    How easy his chain,
    How pleasing his pain;
    How sweet to discover
      He sighs not in vain.
    For love, every creature

Is formed by his nature;
  No joys are above
  The pleasures of Love.

b) Love thee! good sooth, not I!
  I've somewhat else to do;
Alas, you must go learn to talk,
  Before you learn to woo.
  Nay, fie! stand off, go to!

c) Mine's a flame beyond expiring,
Still possessing, still desiring,
  Fit for Love's imperial crown;
    Ever shining
    And refining
  Still the more 'tis melted down.

d) Then talk not of inconstancy,
  False hearts, and broken vows;
If I by miracle can be
This live-long minute true to thee,
  'Tis all that Heaven allows.

e) Phillis is my only joy,
  Faithless as the winds or seas,
Sometimes coming, sometimes coy,
  Yet she never fails to please;
    If with a frown
    I am cast down,
    Phillis smiling
    And beguiling
Makes me happier than before.

Though alas! too late I find
  Nothing can her fancy fix,
Yet the moment she is kind
  I forgive her all her tricks;
    Which though I see,
    I can't get free.
    She deceiving,
    I believing,
What need lovers wish for more?

3. Ben Jonson was writing during a time of rapid expansion of English verse forms. Some of his short lyrical poems use rhymes informally, irregularly, or even playfully. In "Slow, Slow, Fresh Fount," he paints a picture of the nymph Echo weeping for handsome Narcissus having been turned into a flower. On the other hand, these words might express a natural emotion felt in the early spring, when snow and flowers appear together and beauty lasts for only a few days.

    Label the rhyming pattern with letters. How do you feel about the penultimate line; is it an X end-rhyme, or does it self-rhyme internally? Does the irregularity of the rhyme scheme detract from the artistry? If not, how does it contribute?

Slow, Slow, Fresh Fount

Slow, slow, fresh fount, keep time with my salt tears;
Yet slower, yet, O faintly, gentle springs!
List to the heavy part the music bears,
Woe weeps out her division, when she sings.
        Droop herbs and flowers;
            Fall grief in showers;
Our beauties are not ours. O, I could still,
Like melting snow upon some craggy hill,
        Drop, drop, drop, drop,
Since nature's pride is now a withered daffodil.

Ben Jonson, 1572-1637

4. In this exercise, I've grouped three poems that use stanzas with regular rhyme schemes. In Dickinson's "If you were coming," Van Diemen's Land was an early name for the Island of Tasmania, probably to connote a very far-off place. The "goblin bee" does not seem to refer to any particular insect; she may mean an imaginary bee.

    a) For each poem, name the stanzas and their rhyme scheme. Circle or underline examples of slant rhymes and double rhymes.

    b) Choose one of the poems to write about. Write a paragraph about the sound elements: the meter and line lengths, and the rhyme scheme, and how they create an overall sound. Write a second paragraph about what you feel the poet is saying. What kind of feeling is he/she commemorating? How does the choice of sound artistry support the content? Imagine this poem written in the style of one of the others, for example, Dickinson's words in Housman's stanzas, or Housman's ideas in Yeats' quatrains. How does this alter the poem's tone and message?

"If You Were Coming in the Fall"

If you were coming in the fall,
I'd brush the summer by
With half a smile and half a spurn,
As housewives do a fly.

If I could see you in a year,
I'd wind the months in balls,
And put them each in separate drawers,
Until their time befalls.

If only centuries delayed,
I'd count them on my hand,
Subtracting till my fingers dropped
Into Van Diemen's land.

If certain, when this life was out,
That yours and mine should be,
I'd toss it yonder like a rind,
And taste eternity.

But now, all ignorant of the length
Of time's uncertain wing,
It goads me, like the goblin bee,
That will not state its sting.

Emily Dickinson, 1830-1886

When you are Old

When you are old and grey and full of sleep,
And nodding by the fire, take down this book,
And slowly read, and dream of the soft look
Your eyes had once, and of their shadows deep;

How many loved your moments of glad grace,
And loved your beauty with love false or true,
But one man loved the pilgrim soul in you,
And loved the sorrows of your changing face;

And bending down beside the glowing bars,
Murmur, a little sadly, how Love fled
And paced upon the mountains overhead
And hid his face amid a crowd of stars.

William Butler Yeats, 1865-1939

"I to my perils..."
I to my perils
Of cheat and charmer
Came clad in armour
By stars benign.

> Hope lies to mortals
> And most believe her,
> But man's deceiver
> Was never mine.
>
> The thoughts of others
> Were light and fleeting,
> Of lover's meeting
> Or luck or fame.
> Mine were of trouble
> And mine were steady;
> So I was ready
> When trouble came.
>
> *A. E. Housman*, 1859-1936

5. George Herbert's "The Collar" takes us back to the time of Ben Jonson and Shakespeare. Some of the words are difficult, since their meanings have changed. As a rule, when you see a sight rhyme, assume that when Herbert said the words, they actually did rhyme. The poem is a study in the effective use of irregular rhymes.

    a) Read the poem. Word notes: "Collar" meant a decorative gold chain, but Herbert's theme suggests also its modern meaning of a neck band that can attach to a rope. In his poem, he rages against the problems that make him feel unfree, and especially the ethical and moral rules that constrain him to behave patiently. The "board" that he strikes is a table. His word "suit" does not mean clothing; its meaning is connected to "pursuit" and "lawsuit," in which it suggests moving toward a goal. "Cordial fruit" means a heart-stimulating drink made from fruit, like berry wine. A "death's head" is a skull; it was an artistic and moral reminder not to live carelessly, since life is short. The skull image was also called *memento mori*, a reminder of death, and appears in many still life paintings.

    b) Make a study of the poem's use of rhymes, starting by labeling the rhyming sounds with letters. Most of the letters will be used only twice, but four of them are used three and four times. I used letters A ("more") through O ("Lord"). There are no X lines.

    b) What is the meter? Look also at the poem's use of irregular lines that may be end-stopped, enjambed, or broken by a caesura. Usually, phrases run past the line ending because the lines must be a certain number of feet, and the thought is longer; but here, the poet could choose freely how long to make each line. What do you make of his utter carelessness of line lengths, endings, and punctuation?

    c) How does the speaker's tone and attitude shift throughout the poem? Imagine that the same (or very similar) words were written in iambic pentameter or ballad/hymn form. How does the poetic form that Herbert chose support the feeling he wanted to commemorate through art?

The Collar

    I struck the board and cried, "No more;
        I will abroad!
    What? shall I ever sigh and pine?
My lines and life are free, free as the road,
      Loose as the wind, as large as store.
        Shall I be still in suit?
    Have I no harvest but a thorn
    To let me blood, and not restore
What I have lost with cordial fruit?
      Sure there was wine
    Before my sighs did dry it; there was corn
      Before my tears did drown it.
  Is the year only lost to me?
      Have I no bays to crown it,
No flowers, no garlands gay? All blasted?
      All wasted?
Not so, my heart; but there is fruit,
      And thou hast hands.
    Recover all thy sigh-blown age
On double pleasures: leave thy cold dispute
Of what is fit and not. Forsake thy cage,
      Thy rope of sands,
Which petty thoughts have made, and made to thee
    Good cable, to enforce and draw,
      And be thy law,
    While thou didst wink and wouldst not see.
      Away! take heed;
    I will abroad.
Call in thy death's-head there; tie up thy fears.
      He that forbears
    To suit and serve his need,
      Deserves his load."
But as I raved and grew more fierce and wild
      At every word,
Methought I heard one calling, *Child*!
    And I replied, *My Lord*.

George Herbert, 1593-1633

6. For further reading, here are three poems cited in the text, but not assigned for study. Further, if you enjoy studying irregular rhyme schemes, look for 20th century poet John Berryman's long narrative poem, "Homage to Mistress Bradstreet."

Neutral Tones

We stood by a pond that winter day,
And the sun was white, as though chidden of God,
And a few leaves lay on the starving sod;
– They had fallen from an ash, and were gray.

Your eyes on me were as eyes that rove
Over tedious riddles of years ago;
And some words played between us to and fro
On which lost the more by our love.

The smile on your mouth was the deadest thing
Alive enough to have strength to die;
And a grin of bitterness swept thereby
Like an ominous bird a-wing….

Since then, keen lessons that love deceives,
And wrings with wrong, have shaped to me
Your face, and the God curst sun, and a tree,
And a pond edged with grayish leaves.

Thomas Hardy, 1840-1928

"They Flee From Me"

They flee from me that sometime did me seek
With naked foot, stalking in my chamber.
I have seen them gentle, tame, and meek,
That now are wild and do not remember
That sometime they put themself in danger
To take bread at my hand; and now they range,
Busily seeking with a continual change.

Thanked be fortune it hath been otherwise
Twenty times better; but once in special,
In thin array after a pleasant guise,
When her loose gown from her shoulders did fall,
And she me caught in her arms long and small;
Therewithall sweetly did me kiss
And softly said, "Dear heart, how like you this?"

It was no dream: I lay broad waking.
But all is turned thorough my gentleness
Into a strange fashion of forsaking;
And I have leave to go of her goodness,
And she also, to use newfangleness.
But since that I so kindly am served
I would fain know what she hath deserved.

              Thomas Wyatt, 1503-1542

How Clear, How Lovely Bright

    How clear, how lovely bright,
    How beautiful to sight
        Those beams of morning play;
    How heaven laughs out with glee
    Where, like a bird set free,
    Up from the eastern sea
        Soars the delightful day.

    To-day I shall be strong,
    No more shall yield to wrong,
        Shall squander life no more;
    Days lost, I know not how,
    I shall retrieve them now;
    Now I shall keep the vow
        I never kept before.

    Ensanguining the skies
    How heavily it dies
        Into the west away;
    Past touch and sight and sound
    Not further to be found,
    How hopeless under ground
        Falls the remorseful day.

            A. E. Housman, 1859-1936

Eight:

Sonnets

The single most important verse form in English literature is the sonnet. We have sonnets from six centuries, and most famous poets have written at least a few sonnets. Some have left behind whole books of them, and in some cases, their sonnets are now better known than anything else they wrote.

1. The Sonnet's history

During the mid-1300s, Francesco Petrarch wrote a book of love poems to Laura, a beautiful married woman in his town. He had fallen deeply in love with her, although he did not know her and may have only spoken to her a few times. Petrarch was one of the important early scholars of Latin literature, but he wrote these poems in medieval Italian as it was spoken on the street (and was only beginning to be written down). The poetic form he developed became inseparably linked to the Renaissance period when each country's spoken language grew its own literature.

In the 16th century England, Italian clothing styles, music, and language were very fashionable. Italy was consciously leading the Western world into a new era of art, science and literature. When English scholars had learned their Latin, Greek and French, they turned next to Italian, the language of music and art. The English tradition of traveling in Italy as a finishing touch to the best education seems to have begun at this time; we see this fascination with Italy in many of Shakespeare's plays.

The English-speaking world first saw Petrarch's form in 1557, in a book called *Songs and Sonnets*. The publisher probably borrowed the term "sonnet" from the late Sir Thomas Wyatt, whose work he included. Wyatt had been King Henry VIII's ambassador to Italy. His private hobby had been translating and imitating Petrarch's forms in English. The form was quickly picked up by other noblemen at court, and Queen Elizabeth I herself wrote sonnets.

What was so exciting about Petrarch's form of verse? First, he chose an interesting number of lines: fourteen. Fourteen can be seen as 8 + 6, an octave plus a sestet. It can also be organized as 4 + 4 + 4 + 2, three quatrains and a couplet. Within each of the quatrains, sestets and octaves of the sonnet, more than one rhyme scheme is possible. Rhymes can link the parts or divide them, at the poet's choice.

Second, Petrarch's sonnets were all highly personal, emotional, artistic, and philosophical. Poetry had mostly been used to tell stories up to this time, but the Renaissance revived an older Greek form of short, personal, lyrical poems. Petrarch blended medieval troubadour love songs with Classical scholarship, creating a song that could be set to music but didn't need to be sung. It was a modern verse idea for a new time.

English sonnets were often love poems, like Petrarch's, but they were also philosophical or introspective. In the 17th century, they could be theological; in the 19th century, sonnets were often filled with romantic ideas about nature. In the 20th century, they could be experimental, merely hinting at meaning.

2. The English Sonnet form

The first type of sonnet to learn is Shakespeare's. His style was not the first, since he received the form from Petrarch and Wyatt. But because Shakespeare left us over 150 sonnets of very high quality, his preferred pattern set a model for other English writers to copy. It is usually called the *English sonnet*.

Shakespeare viewed the fourteen lines of iambic pentameter as three quatrains and a couplet.. Each quatrain was united by a rhyme scheme and usually held a complete thought. It was divided from the other quatrains by their using different rhyming sounds, but united to them by keeping to the same pattern, ABAB. When we name the rhyme scheme of an English sonnet, we use letters A through G.

Shakespeare's sonnets are named with Roman numerals, in the order that they were originally printed in 1609. Let's look at Sonnet XVIII:

Shall I compare thee to a summer's day?	A
Thou art more lovely and more temperate:	B
Rough winds do shake the darling buds of May,	A
And summer's lease hath all too short a date:	B
Sometime too hot the eye of heaven shines,	C
And often is his gold complexion dimm'd;	D
And every fair from fair sometime declines,	C
By chance or nature's changing course untrimmed;	D
But thy eternal summer shall not fade	E
Nor lose possession of that fair thou owest:	F
Nor shall Death brag thou wander'st in his shade,	E
When in eternal lines to time thou growest:	F
So long as men can breathe or eyes can see,	G
So long lives this and this gives life to thee.	G

You can see how the couplet gives the poem a sense of completion. The G rhyme is new, but we hear its match immediately in the next line. In the quatrains, by contrast, each rhyme has to wait while another one begins. The rhymes tie together the quatrain lines, but the short couplet is already tightly tied.

Sonnet XVIII is a self-conscious poem, and this too was typical of 16th century sonnets that posed the problem of mortality. It is usually addressed to a beautiful beloved, and it often asks what will happen when the beloved, or the poet, has died. The poet may ask to be forgotten, but he wants the beloved to be remembered forever. The solution is the sonnet itself, which preserves her beauty for future readers: "this gives life to thee."

Edmund Spenser was born around the time that Wyatt's sonnets were published; he was approximately a contemporary of Shakespeare. He was already famous for his long poems, especially *The Faerie Queene*, when he remarried in middle age. He commemorated his loving hopes and fears in a cycle of 89 sonnets dedicated to his young bride. Spenser developed his own twist on the English sonnet by linking the rhymes of each quatrain to the next. The first quatrain is like Shakespeare's, but watch the B and C rhymes:

One day I wrote her name upon the strand,	A
But came the waves and washed it away;	B
Again I wrote it with a second hand,	A
But came the tide and made my pains his prey.	B

"Vain man," said she, "that dost in vain assay	B
A mortal thing so to immortalize,	C
For I myself shall like to this decay,	B
And eke my name be wiped out likewise."	C
"Not so" quod I, "let baser things devise	C
To die in dust, but you shall live by fame;	D
My verse your virtues rare shall eternize	C
And in the heavens write your glorious name,	D
Where, whenas death shall all the world subdue,	E
Our love shall live, and later life renew."	E

Like Spenser's, many of the Elizabethan sonnets were individual stanzas of what the poet considered a complete larger work. They were connected by a single theme, and they built on each other to flesh out all the poet's thoughts on the theme. We call these collections *sonnet sequences* or *sonnet cycles*. Each sonnet can stand alone, but its meaning is fully developed in context.

It's worth noting a particular sonnet sequence called a *crown of sonnets*. In this sequence, the sonnets build on each other thematically, but each also uses the last line of the previous sonnet as its first line. Linking the crown, the last sonnet closes with the original first line. Look up John Donne's "La Corona," which depicts the life of Jesus in seven linked sonnets, beginning and ending, "Deign at my hands this crown of prayer and praise."

3. The Italian Sonnet form

The key difference between the English and Italian sonnets is that the fourteen lines are divided into 8 + 6: one octave and one sestet. The Italian sonnet does usually not close with a couplet.

The octave and sestet are each unified with a rhyme scheme. Whereas Shakespeare could choose a new set of rhyming sounds for the second quatrain, in the Petrarchan sonnet, the same rhyming sounds are used for the first eight lines. Even if a poet chooses to include a blank line between the eight, it will still be counted as an octave, not quatrains, as long as the lines are still unified by rhyme. It's the same with the sestet, and with the whole sonnet for that matter (many poets break up the 14 lines with blank space, but we overlook it).

The octave is rhymed ABBA, then again ABBA. If you're not looking for the pattern, ABBAABBA can look like it's rhymed in pairs, BB, AA, BB. The A rhymes, though, are intended to draw the ear and eye back to the previous lines, unifying the set. The sestet is usually rhymed CDE, CDE. If you aren't prepared for this pattern, it can seem like the lines have stopped rhyming.

John Donne, a near contemporary of Shakespeare, wrote many poems that meditated on ideals of human and divine love. He included some sonnets, and in this famous one, "Death be not proud," he mostly follows the Italian form, but apparently he wanted to close it with a couplet, like Shakespeare. This required him to innovate in the sestet:

Death, be not proud, though some have called thee	A
Mighty and dreadful, for thou art not so;	B
For those whom thou think'st thou dost overthrow	B
Die not, poor Death, nor yet canst thou kill me.	A
From rest and sleep, which but thy pictures be,	A
Much pleasure; then from thee much more must flow,	B

And soonest our best men with thee do go,	B
Rest of their bones, and soul's delivery.	A
Thou art slave to fate, chance, kings, and desperate men,	C
And dost with poison, waste, and sickness dwell,	D
And poppy or charms can make us sleep as well	D
And better than thy stroke; why swell'st thou then?	C
One short sleep past, we wake eternally	E/A
And death shall be no more; Death, thou shalt die.	E/A

In Donne's time, "die" was almost certainly pronounced "dee," so the couplet had a true rhyme, not a sight one. It's not clear if Donne wanted us to remember that "ee" was also the A rhyme. I think he structured the sonnet around the last line, liking the irony of "Death, thou shalt die," and only chose the A rhymes because "ee" is easy to work with. In that case, it was coincidence that E = A. But perhaps not; he may have liked the couplet's rhyme serving also to tie the whole poem together.

John Milton wrote some famous sonnets in addition to his epic poem, *Paradise Lost*. Milton was born (1608) around the time Shakespeare's Sonnets were published (1609), and the sonnet remained an important poetic form throughout his lifetime. Milton's century was a time of open civil war in England, Protestants against Catholics, and Parliament against the monarch. In 1655, there was a massacre of Protestants in northern Italy. Whereas in Elizabethan times, the sonnet had been mostly used as a sophisticated love poem, Milton chose the Italian sonnet form to commemorate England's national outpouring of grief and outrage.

Avenge, O Lord, thy slaughtered saints, whose bones	A
Lie scattered on the Alpine mountains cold,	B
Even them who kept thy truth so pure of old,	B
When all our fathers worshiped stocks and stones;	A
Forget not: in thy book record their groans	A
Who were thy sheep and in their ancient fold	B
Slain by the bloody Piedmontese that rolled	B
Mother with infant down the rocks. Their moans	A
The vales redoubled to the hills, and they	C
To Heaven. Their martyred blood and ashes sow	D
O'er all th' Italian fields where still doth sway	C
The triple tyrant; that from these may grow	D
A hundredfold, who having learnt thy way	C
Early may fly the Babylonian woe.	D

The rhyme scheme works with Milton's choice of rhymes to create a wailing, moaning poem. "Bones" and "cold," the A and B rhymes, share the long O that people say when they're in pain. In the sestet, Milton uses only two rhyme sounds, C and D, and again both are groaning pain sounds. The D rhyme is very close to both A and B; so much sound repetition supports the poem's grieving tone.

Over the years, the sonnet model of Petrarch seems to be generally more popular than that of Shakespeare. There's no clear reason why this should be true. Probably the fact that the Italian rhyme scheme is more interlocked makes it a more appealing artistic choice: it sounds *prettier*, to put it very simply. It's a little bit harder to write, because the poet must find four A and B rhymes, rather than just two, and that might have some appeal. However, Spenser's interlocking-rhyme variant on the English sonnet is certainly just as difficult. But for whatever reason, it is easier to find Italian sonnets among modern collections.

4. Modern variations on the sonnet

The Puritan era of Donne and Milton closed when King Charles II was restored to the throne in 1660. There was no reason why sonnets should fall out of fashion, but they did. We have no famous sonnets in the literary record until more than a century had passed. Around 1800, a group of young poets became friends and settled in a part of England called the Lake District. They are known as the Lake Poets, who set off the new Romantic fashion in poetry. William Wordsworth, one of the leading Lake Poets, revived the sonnet. He wrote in the Italian form, but he altered both the octave's and the sestet's rhyme schemes.

Surprised by joy—impatient as the wind	A
I turned to share the transport—Oh! with whom	B
But Thee, deep buried in the silent tomb,	B
That spot which no vicissitude can find?	A
Love, faithful love, recalled thee to my mind—	A
But how could I forget thee? Through what power,	C
Even for the least division of an hour,	C
Have I been so beguiled as to be blind	A
To my most grievous loss?—That thought's return	D
Was the worst pang that sorrow ever bore,	E
Save one, one only, when I stood forlorn,	D
Knowing my heart's best treasure was no more;	E
That neither present time, nor years unborn	D
Could to my sight that heavenly face restore.	E

If Wordsworth had been a student, his teacher would have marked the C rhymes as mistakes, because in an Italian sonnet, they should be B's. But as an artist, Wordsworth could choose to jostle the rhyme scheme in exchange for two very good lines. His sestet is unified, but his rhyming choices are not the CDECDE of Petrarch. Instead, he followed Milton's pattern CDCDCD; had he rhymed those middle lines to B, the rhyme scheme would be exactly Milton's.

Wordsworth's variation was only the beginning. As modern poets revived the sonnet form, they never stopped playing with it. Its form was so carefully structured that it became a temptation to see how far it could be stretched and still qualify. You have read "Ozymandias," written by Shelley, who was a generation younger than the Lake poets, but very much influenced by them. Can we call "Ozymandias" a sonnet?

I met a traveller from an antique land,	A
Who said—"Two vast and trunkless legs of stone	B
Stand in the desert…. Near them, on the sand,	A
Half sunk a shattered visage lies, whose frown,	B
And wrinkled lip, and sneer of cold command,	A
Tell that its sculptor well those passions read	C
Which yet survive, stamped on these lifeless things,	D
The hand that mocked them, and the heart that fed;	C

And on the pedestal, these words appear:	E
My name is Ozymandias, King of Kings,	D
Look on my Works, ye Mighty, and despair!	E
Nothing beside remains. Round the decay	F
Of that colossal Wreck, boundless and bare	E
The lone and level sands stretch far away."	F

Some of Shelley's rhyme are not even true ones; the B rhymes "stone" and "frown" are slant rhymes, as are the E rhymes "appear" and "despair." There's no question that his rhyme scheme misses both English and Italian sonnets by a mile, but this poem is often counted as a sonnet anyway. Its theme *feels* like a sonnet, it has fourteen lines, and its rhyming pattern feels sonnet-like even when it isn't.

In the years since "Ozymandias," poets have created even more variations on the sonnet, though many modern poets have also written pure sonnets. Sometimes there are poems of about fourteen lines, but rhymed AABBCC and so on. Are they meant to count as sonnets? One type runs too long, but we call it a *caudate sonnet*, that is, a sonnet with a coda (Italian for tail, and also used in music). Poems with as many as 24 lines have been considered caudate sonnets.

Gerard Manley Hopkins, a reclusive Catholic priest, wrote true sonnets, but he also wrote some in which each part grew shorter, so that the result was only ten and a half lines. It is so different that I don't recognize it as a sonnet, but it is counted as a variation, called by Hopkins a *curtal sonnet* (curtal = curtailed, cut short). The most famous is "Pied Beauty," a celebration of unusual, spotted, striped, and odd things. This curtal sonnet is itself "counter, original, spare, strange."

Glory be to God for dappled things—	A
For skies of couple-colour as a brinded cow;	B
For rose-moles all in stripple upon trout that swim;	C
Fresh-firecoal chestnut-falls; finches' wings;	A
Landscape plotted and pierced — fold, fallow and plough;	B
And áll trádes, their gear, tackle and trim.	C
All things counter, original, spare, strange;	D
Whatever is fickle, freckled (who knows how?)	B
With swift, slow; sweet, sour; adazzle, dim;	C
He fathers-forth whose beauty knows no change:	D
Praise Him.	C

Hopkins was an enthusiast for obsolete and variant words, so his poems can be difficult to understand. He was also trying to adapt and loosen meter, sometimes indicating with added stress marks that he wanted extra weight to fall in places where poetry traditionalists would not expect (here, "áll trádes").

Hopkins was writing during the late 1800s; he died about 25 years before the First World War. From the 1920s on, the structure of meter and rhyme was unpopular. Sonnets were still written, often still true to either English or Italian model, but they were increasingly experimental. While their themes might still be of love, these sonnets only sometimes expressed conventional attitudes to love and society. Edna St. Vincent Millay wrote about the impermanence of love; Claude McKay, a Jamaican-American poet, depicted his harsh experience of segregated America.

These new sonnets not only enjambed lines, allowing the sentence to "step over" the line ending, they might break words across a line ending. They might invent words, ignore punctuation, and not even bother to complete sentences. Whenever they used the true sonnet form, perhaps they felt even freer to ignore other structure. If they were going to the trouble of following a rhyme scheme or counting lines, *surely* nobody would mind if they broke some syntax or spelling rules.

E. E. Cummings wrote highly experimental poetry (he is most famous simply for using no punctuation or capital letters). He wrote some sonnets that ran more or less true to form (although he wrote at least one 13-line "sonnet"). He seems to have preferred the English sonnet's structure. Notice his casual attention to rhyme, using slant rhymes or just ignoring the requirement, as in this ABAB quatrain:

life is more true than reason will deceive	A
(more secret or than madness did reveal)	B
deeper is life than lose: higher than have	A (slant)
—but beauty is more each than living's	no B rhyme

In the next generation, John Berryman wrote not just one sonnet, but an old-fashioned sonnet sequence. During the 1950s and 60s, any kind of meter, rhyme, or format rule was out of fashion. Berryman's sonnets followed the Italian rhyme scheme, but he combined very modern thought and language with strict observation of the sonnet's form. The most famous, Sonnet 73, recycled a theme used by Shakespeare: comparing the grief of an absence to the seasons.

> You should be gone in winter, that Nature mourn
> With me your anarch separation, call-
> ing warmth all with you: as more poetical
> Than to be left biting the dog-days, lorn
> Alone when all else burgeons, brides are born...

The closing couplet adds the very non-Shakespearean sentiment, "Than gin & limes you are cooler, darling." Berryman's work is recent enough that it is still under copyright protection, so I cannot give you the full poem. Please find it in a collection, in a book or on the internet; it's worth the trouble.

And so the sonnet has come all the way from the 1300s to the 2000s. The variations make it more important to know the original form, just as you can't recognize a face in disguise unless you know its usual appearance. There are also hundreds of poems that were clearly influenced by the sonnet, even if they don't follow the exact form. Since the time of the sonnet's introduction to English, it has shaped poems by forcing them to follow its model, modify its rules, copy its tendencies, or avoid it altogether.

SUMMARY AND DEFINITIONS

The *sonnet* is the most important English verse form. It has fourteen lines of iambic pentameter and can be divided into quatrains and a couplet, or into an octave and a sestet. Rhyme schemes vary.

The *English sonnet* (also called *Shakespearean*) is made of three quatrains with a closing couplet; its rhyme scheme is ABABCDCDEFEFGG. Shakespeare's sonnets follow this model, so it has become the most famous.

The *Italian sonnet* (also called *Petrarchan*) is made of one octave with a sestet; its rhyme scheme varies, but the standard pattern is ABBAABBACDECDE.

Sonnets can be written as parts of a thematic collection, called a sonnet sequence or cycle. There are variants of the sonnet that stretch longer or fall short. Modern variations may use just enough of the rhyme scheme to let the reader know that they're intended to be sonnets.

EXERCISES 8

Review:

a) What is a rhyme scheme?

b) Below is the second stanza of John Berryman's "Homage to Mistress Bradstreet." What kind of stanza is it? _____ Some of the lines (for example the first and last) are metrical, some are not; what is the meter for those that are? _____

c) If "sea" is one C rhyme, what is the other? _____

If "stands" is the B rhyme, what kind of rhyme does it form with "stunned"? _____

Find an internal rhyme for "rigor." _____

How does the A rhyme tie the stanza together? _____

> Outside the New World winters in grand dark
> white air lashing high thro' the virgin stands
> foxes down foxholes sigh,
> surely the English heart quails, stunned.
> I doubt if Simon than this blast, that sea,
> spares from his rigor for your poetry
> more. We are on each other's hands
> who care. Both of our worlds unhanded us. Lie stark…

1. Follow the rhyme scheme to assemble a modern Petrarchan/Italian sonnet, using its missing lines, shown below. This poem was written by Robert Crutchfield (2009), used with permission.

Line	Rhyme
Circe turned Odysseus' men to swine;	A
and something in the story as it's told	B
*	B
*	A
un-humans us; and everything that's fine	A
*	B
*	B
our hoped-for vintage dying on the vine.	A
The hero lives forever in the song—	C
*	D
*	C
as mortal beings, so our pride must be	D
in things of transient beauty said or done,	E
*	E

<u>missing lines:</u>
proves our resemblance to the men of old.
or noble in our nature slips our hold,
like water-droplets, blazing in the sun.
leaving a chattel to be bought and sold—
We, anyway, will never live so long,
Our daily business, like the poisoned wine
or lives as long as human eyes can see.

2-7: For the following sonnet pairs and groups, the study directions are similar in each case.

    a) Always read through the lines, attentive to the meter (count out the 5 iambs with your fingers), and mark the rhyme scheme with letters. Is it Shakespeare's three quatrains and a couplet? Or is it some variation on the Italian octave and sestet? If so, how is the sestet rhymed? Are you looking at true rhymes or slant rhymes?

    b) When you think about how the poets laid out their ideas in the sonnet form, observe whether the ideas match the form: does each quatrain have a separate idea? Or do the ideas run over from one quatrain to the next? Is the octave unified in its idea, not just its interlocked rhymes? How does the sestet or couplet relate to the first part? Is it a separate idea, or does the same sentence jump from octave to sestet, or from one quatrain to the couplet?

    c) The sonnets are paired for thematic contrast, as you will see. Compare their word use, emotional tone, and message. Choose one set to write about, following the questions above as an outline to write three or four paragraphs.

2. Petrarch's sonnets were written in praise of Laura's beauty, and many of the earliest sonnets in English followed his lead. In his Sonnet IX, Sir Philip Sidney compares Stella's face to a queen's court where everything is beautiful and elegant. Shakespeare's sonnet CXXX turns the convention around: his love is nothing like a beautiful goddess, but he loves her anyway.

Astrophel and Stella, IX

Queen Virtue's court, which some call Stella's face,
Prepar'd by Nature's choicest furniture,
Hath his front built of alabaster pure;
Gold in the covering of that stately place.
The door by which sometimes comes forth her Grace
Red porphyr is, which lock of pearl makes sure,
Whose porches rich (which name of cheeks endure)
Marble mix'd red and white do interlace.
The windows now through which this heav'nly guest
Looks o'er the world, and can find nothing such,
Which dare claim from those lights the name of best,
Of touch they are that without touch doth touch,
Which Cupid's self from Beauty's mine did draw:
Of touch they are, and poor I am their straw.

Sir Philip Sidney, 1554-1586

Sonnet CXXX

My mistress' eyes are nothing like the sun;
Coral is far more red than her lips' red;
If snow be white, why then her breasts are dun;
If hairs be wires, black wires grow on her head.
I have seen roses damask'd red and white,
But no such roses see I in her cheeks;
And in some perfumes is there more delight
Than in the breath that from my mistress reeks.
I love to hear her speak, yet well I know
That music hath a far more pleasing sound;
I grant I never saw a goddess go;
My mistress, when she walks, treads on the ground:
And yet, by heaven, I think my love as rare
As any she belied with false compare.

William Shakespeare, 1564-1616

3. Growing old is another major theme of traditional sonnets. Shakespeare's Sonnet LXIII compares old age to autumn, twilight, and a fire going out. John Milton mourns lost time when he is still only 23, because he does not feel as capable and mature as he thinks he should be. John Keats, who worked in medicine until he was 21, had high ambitions in poetry but saw early deaths from tuberculosis all around him. It turned out that he had only about five years left, himself, so although he wrote the sonnet when he was still well and young, it takes on a sharper pain since we know that his worries were well-founded.

Sonnet LXIII

That time of year thou mayst in me behold
When yellow leaves, or none, or few, do hang
Upon those boughs which shake against the cold,
Bare ruin'd choirs, where late the sweet birds sang.
In me thou see'st the twilight of such day
As after sunset fadeth in the west,
Which by and by black night doth take away,
Death's second self, that seals up all in rest.
In me thou see'st the glowing of such fire
That on the ashes of his youth doth lie,
As the death-bed whereon it must expire
Consumed with that which it was nourish'd by.
This thou perceivest, which makes thy love more strong,
To love that well which thou must leave ere long.

William Shakespeare, 1564-1616

"How Soon Hath Time"

How soon hath Time, the subtle thief of youth,
Stol'n on his wing my three and twentieth year!
My hasting days fly on with full career,
But my late spring no bud or blossom shewth.
Perhaps my semblance might deceive the truth,
That I to manhood am arrived so near,
And inward ripeness doth much less appear,
That some more timely-happy spirits endu'th.
Yet be it less or more, or soon or slow,
It shall be still in strictest measure even
To that same lot, however mean or high,
Toward which Time leads me, and the will of Heaven;
All is, if I have grace to use it so,
As ever in my great Taskmaster's eye.

John Milton, 1608-1674

When I Have Fears That I May Cease To Be

When I have fears that I may cease to be
    Before my pen has gleaned my teeming brain,
Before high-piled books, in charactery,
    Hold like rich garners the full-ripened grain;
When I behold, upon the night's starred face,
    Huge cloudy symbols of a high romance,
And think that I may never live to trace
    Their shadows, with the magic hand of chance;
And when I feel, fair creature of an hour!
    That I shall never look upon thee more,
Never have relish in the faery power
    Of unreflecting love; then on the shore
Of the wide world I stand alone, and think
    Till love and fame to nothingness do sink.

John Keats, 1795-1821

4. Sonnets have also been used for philosophical musing, such as about the nature of Time. Shakespeare's sonnet looks at how Time destroys all things; the conclusion, that time "will come and take my love away," is anti-climactic compared to the large, profound images he has been sketching. This sonnet is particularly rich in choosing words for parallel and contrasting sounds. The sonnet by Wilfrid Blunt is simpler: he considers the awareness of Time as a necessary evil.

Sonnet LXIV

When I have seen by Time's fell hand defaced
The rich proud cost of outworn buried age;
When sometime lofty towers I see down-razed
And brass eternal slave to mortal rage;
When I have seen the hungry ocean gain
Advantage on the kingdom of the shore,
And the firm soil win of the watery main,
Increasing store with loss and loss with store;
When I have seen such interchange of state,
Or state itself confounded to decay;
Ruin hath taught me thus to ruminate,
That Time will come and take my love away.
   This thought is as a death, which cannot choose
   But weep to have that which it fears to lose.

William Shakespeare, 1564-1616

If I Could Live

If I could live without the thought of death,
Forgetful of Time's waste, the soul's decay,
I would not ask for other joy than breath,
With light and sound of birds and the sun's ray.
I could sit on untroubled day by day
Watching the grass grow, and the wild flowers range
From blue to yellow and from red to grey
In natural sequence as the seasons change.
I could afford to wait, but for the hurt
Of this dull tick of time which chides my ear.
But now I dare not sit with loins ungirt
And staff unlifted, for death stands too near.
I must be up and doing—ay, each minute.
The grave gives time for rest when we are in it.

Wilfrid Scawen Blunt, 1840-1922

5. Traditionally, sonnets promise eternal love that will endure after death. Here, three poets consider the relationship between love and remembrance. Shakespeare suggests that it's better for his beloved to forget him, while Elizabeth Barrett Browning hopes to love after death. Edna St. Vincent Millay vows to love someone only as long as her cigarette lasts.

Because E. B. Browning's sonnet has become a sort of cliché, it's good to realize that there is an unusual story behind it. She was a middle-aged invalid who believed she was dying, when Robert Browning (some years younger) fell in love with her at sight. A year and a half of courtship had to be masked as poetry conferences due to her father's unreasonable rules. Finally they secretly married, although she could barely walk. She wrote a sequence of sonnets during that period; they reflect her difficulty in adjusting to the idea that Browning could actually love her. "How Do I Love Thee? Let Me Count the Ways" was the last of the sequence.

Sonnet LXXI

No longer mourn for me when I am dead
Than you shall hear the surly sullen bell
Give warning to the world that I am fled
From this vile world, with vilest worms to dwell:
Nay, if you read this line, remember not
The hand that writ it; for I love you so
That I in your sweet thoughts would be forgot
If thinking on me then should make you woe.
O, if, I say, you look upon this verse
When I perhaps compounded am with clay,
Do not so much as my poor name rehearse,
But let your love even with my life decay,
Lest the wise world should look into your moan
And mock you with me after I am gone.

William Shakespeare, 1564-1616

Sonnet XLIII

How do I love thee? Let me count the ways.
I love thee to the depth and breadth and height
My soul can reach, when feeling out of sight
For the ends of Being and ideal Grace.
I love thee to the level of everyday's
Most quiet need, by sun and candlelight.
I love thee freely, as men strive for Right;
I love thee purely, as they turn from Praise.
I love thee with the passion put to use
In my old griefs, and with my childhood's faith.
I love thee with a love I seemed to lose
With my lost saints,—I love thee with the breath,
Smiles, tears, of all my life!—and, if God choose,
I shall but love thee better after death.

Elizabeth Barrett Browning, 1806-1861

Sonnets

"Only Until This Cigarette"

Only until this cigarette is ended,
A little moment at the end of all,
While on the floor the quiet ashes fall,
And in the firelight to a lance extended,
Bizarrely with the jazzing music blended,
The broken shadow dances on the wall,
I will permit my memory to recall
The vision of you, by all my dreams attended.
And then adieu,—farewell!—the dream is done.
Yours is a face of which I can forget
The colour and the features, every one,
The words not ever, and the smiles not yet;
But in your day this moment is the sun
Upon a hill, after the sun has set.

Edna St. Vincent Millay, 1892-1950

6. Battles have always been foremost among the experiences that poets want to commemorate. In ancient times, victories were celebrated as days of glory, while the dead were eternal heroes. Modern times have prompted us to look more at the individual's role in the battle. Does he know why he's dying; does he believe in the cause; does he have a fair chance?

Wilfrid Owen died in battle one week before the Armistice that closed the First World War. His sonnet expresses anger at war. (Compare Owen's sonnet, too, with "The Lads in their Hundreds;" how is his attitude similar to Housman's, how different?) Claude McKay, an immigrant to America from Jamaica, described his struggles against racial segregation in terms of a battle. His death in battle would be glorious if only he could fight back and not be passive.

Anthem for Doomed Youth

What passing-bells for these who die as cattle?
Only the monstrous anger of the guns.
Only the stuttering rifles' rapid rattle
Can patter out their hasty orisons.
No mockeries now for them; no prayers nor bells,
Nor any voice of mourning save the choirs,—
The shrill, demented choirs of wailing shells;
And bugles calling for them from sad shires.
What candles may be held to speed them all?
Not in the hands of boys, but in their eyes
Shall shine the holy glimmers of good-byes.
The pallor of girls' brows shall be their pall;
Their flowers the tenderness of patient minds,
And each slow dusk a drawing-down of blinds.

Wilfrid Owen, 1893-1918

"If We Must Die"

If we must die, let it not be like hogs
Hunted and penned in an inglorious spot,
While round us bark the mad and hungry dogs,
Making the mock at our accursed lot.
If we must die, O let us nobly die,
So that our precious blood may not be shed
In vain; then even the monsters we defy
Shall be constrained to honor us though dead!
O kinsmen! we must meet the common foe!
Though far outnumbered let us show us brave,
And for their thousand blows deal one deathblow!
What though before us lies the open grave?
Like men we'll face the murderous, cowardly pack,
Pressed to the wall, dying, but fighting back!

Claude McKay, 1889-1948

7. Dawn in the city looks very different depending where you are standing. Wordsworth's sonnet sees London stripped of its laboring, bustling crowds and looks only at the artistry of river and buildings in the sun. McKay's sonnet sees New York with the eyes of a poor man or woman who works very hard in the ugliest streets and dreads dawn.

Composed upon Westminster Bridge

Earth has not anything to show more fair:
Dull would he be of soul who could pass by
A sight so touching in its majesty:
This City now doth, like a garment, wear
The beauty of the morning; silent, bare,
Ships, towers, domes, theatres, and temples lie

Open unto the fields, and to the sky;
All bright and glittering in the smokeless air.
Never did sun more beautifully steep
In his first splendour, valley, rock, or hill;
Ne'er saw I, never felt, a calm so deep!
The river glideth at his own sweet will:
Dear God! the very houses seem asleep;
And all that mighty heart is lying still!

William Wordsworth, 1770-1850

THE TIRED WORKER

O whisper, O my soul! The afternoon
Is waning into evening, whisper soft!
Peace, O my rebel heart! for soon the moon
From out its misty veil will swing aloft!
Be patient, weary body, soon the night
Will wrap thee gently in her sable sheet,
And with a leaden sigh thou wilt invite
To rest thy tired hands and aching feet.
The wretched day was theirs, the night is mine;
Come tender sleep, and fold me to thy breast.
But what steals out the gray clouds red like wine?
O dawn! O dreaded dawn! O let me rest
Weary my veins, my brain, my life! Have pity!
No! Once again the harsh, the ugly city.

Claude McKay, 1889-1948

8. Challenge question: How far can you stretch a sonnet's rules before it stops being a sonnet? E. E. Cummings knew the rules perfectly, and he wrote some traditional sonnets. He also wrote some that...well. In this poem, look at the rhyme scheme and the meter, and more. What do you think of his making "wink" into a word that rhymes with "in"? Overall, what's your opinion: is this a sonnet?

MY SONNET IS

my sonnet is A light goes on in
the toiletwindow, that's straightacross from
my window,night air bothered with a rustling din

sort of sublimated tom-tom
which quite outdoes the mandolin-
man's tiny racket. The horses sleep upstairs.
And you can see their ears. Ears win-

> k,funny stable. In the morning they go out in pairs:
> amazingly one pair is white
> (but you know that) they look at each other. Nudge.
>
> (If they love each other, who cares?)
> They pull the morning out of the night.
>
> I am living with a mouse who shares
> my meals with him,which is fair as i judge.
>
> E. E. Cummings, 1894-1962

9. For further reading, there are great sonnet collections. Foremost is Shakespeare's *Sonnets*; you could also search for:

Petrarch's *Canzoniere*, in translation

Dante's *La Vita Nuova*, 25 sonnets to Beatrice, in translation

Sir Philip Sidney's *Astrophel and Stella*

Edmund Spenser's *Amoretti*

Elizabeth Barrett Browning's *Sonnets from the Portuguese* (it's in English)

Dante Gabriel Rossetti's *The House of Life*

George Meredith's *Modern Love* (his sonnets have 16 lines)

John Berryman's *Sonnets for Chris*

For something completely different, look for fiction/horror writer H. P. Lovecraft's sonnet sequence *Fungi from Yuggoth*; the style is reminiscent of "The Raven" but appears to tell a fantasy/horror story with the sonnets.

Review 2

This review is based on a poem by the Scottish poet Robert Burns. He uses some words that may be difficult: *stone*, a measure of weight; *bumper*, glass filled to the brim; *lucubration*, a scholarly, detailed study.

> Fourteen, a sonneteer thy praises sings; (a)
> What magic myst'ries in that number lie!
> Your hen hath fourteen eggs beneath her wings (b)
> That fourteen chickens to the roost may fly.
> Fourteen full pounds the jockey's stone must be;
> His age fourteen –(c)– a horse's prime is past.
> Fourteen long hours too oft the Bard must fast;
> Fourteen bright bumpers — bliss he ne'er must see!
> Before fourteen, a dozen yields the strife;
> Before fourteen—e'en thirteen's strength is vain.
> Fourteen good years — a woman gives us life;
> Fourteen good men — we lose that life again.
> What lucubrations can be more upon it?
> Fourteen good measur'd verses make a ___(d)____.
>
> *Robert Burns* (1759-1796)

1. the punctuation at point (a) is _____.

    [enjambed; caesura; end-stopped; slant]

2. The sentence at point (b), regarding its punctuation, is _____.

    [enjambed; caesura; end-stopped; slant]

3. At point (c), the punctuation forms a _____.

    [enjambed; caesura; end-stopped; slant]

4. The metrical foot used here is the _____.

    [trochee; iamb; dactyl; accentual]

5. Because each line has _____ metrical feet, it is _____.

    [trimeter; tetrameter; pentameter; Alexandrine]

6. The missing word at (d) is _____.
   [blank verse; sonnet; pawn it; stanza]

7. Burns' poem is rhymed: _____.
   [ABABCDCDEFEFGG; ABBACDDCEFFEGG; ABABCDDCEFEFGG]

8. The poem's rhyme scheme is irregular. To correct it, which lines would you switch? _____
   (Note: there are two correct solutions.)
   [4 and 5; 5 and 6; 7 and 8; 13 and 14]

9. The first four lines of this poem are called a _____.
   [couplet; sonnet; tercet; quatrain]

10. The last two lines of this poem are called a _____.
    [couplet; sonnet; stanza; quatrain]

11. There are two types of this poem's form. Which one is this? _____
    [Italian; English; Greek; Accentual]

12. What famous poet used the same form? _____
    [Wordsworth; Browning; Shakespeare; Petrarch]

13. If we filled in (d) with the word "tonic," what kind of rhyme would that be? _____
    [sight; double; slant; internal]

14. If we filled in (d) with the word "curses," what kind of rhyme would that be? _____
    [sight; double; slant; internal]

15. When (d) has the correct word, what kind of rhyme does it form? _____
    [sight; double; slant; internal]

16. What poem form is the verse below? _____

    [couplet; Italian; sonnet; ballad; hymn]
    Your setting hen hath fourteen eggs
    Your horse just fourteen years;
    Drain fourteen bumpers to the dregs
    And cry out fourteen cheers.

17. In the stanza below, the meter is_____

    [iambic; trimeter; accentual; blank]
    My hen hath a hundred eggs
    And that I know is true.
    Whenever I count them in one breath,
    I turn completely blue.

18. The poem below is what kind of verse? _____

    [ballad; blank; accentual; couplet]
    Your hen hath fourteen eggs beneath her wings
    That fourteen chickens to the roost may fly.
    Your coop hath fourteen broken, splintered boards
    That weasels may at will their meals enjoy.
    O sluggard, if you never fix the holes
    Your fourteen eggs and hen will soon be gone!

19. The poem below is a _____.

    [couplet; tercet; quatrain; limerick]
    If you would brave and humble be,
    ignore the lessons of the wasp
    and imitate the bumblebee.

20. What kind of rhyme is shown in the lines in 19? _____

    [slant; double; sight; triple]

Nine:

Repetition and Variation of Sound

Repetition has always been one of the artist's most useful tools. Music uses repeated patterns of rhythm and melody to please the ear; visual art uses repeated color themes. In the same way, poetry can use repeated patterns of sound, word or phrase.

Rhyming words use repetition of end-sounds. The identical or similar ending of the words chime like bells at the end of each line. We find that the repeated sound is pleasing; it's comforting to hear what we expect. At the same time, rhyme involves the opposite partner of repetition: variation. The same *sound* comes, but not the same word. While you *can* use the same word to rhyme with itself, it's considered bad form in English verse. The best rhymes are the ones that repeat the key sounds, while not only differing but even surprising the ear with other sounds.

Too much exact repetition is boring. As a rule of thumb, after some element appears three times, we get bored unless there is some variation. Popular songs have a formula for managing repetition so that it won't be too boring. The first verse of the song goes by, and it's all new; the second verse is the same tune as the first, and this is familiar. The third verse can be the same again, but now it's very familiar. Too familiar? The song has a fourth verse awaiting, but instead, it presents a different tune, sometimes in a different key. This is called the bridge; it breaks up the familiarity. When the fourth verse comes back, it's *pleasantly* familiar, not boring.

Longer musical works take a melody, rhythm, or chord sequence and after repeating it a few times, they repeat parts of it with differences. The chord sequence might be the same, but with a new melody. Part of the melody might be repeated, but in a different rhythm, or with a different melody branching from it. When the piece comes back to the original motif, the listener's ear is usually eager for it, so that the symphony ends with a feeling of completeness.

Repetition and variation work together. They can alternate or combine in surprising ways. In both music and poetry, there are more ways to do this than we can easily list. Poetry has even more room for repetition and variation because it's supposed to be carrying forward a coherent thought, which requires words to be chosen for meaning, not sound. Language's natural default, then, is variation: a new word for each part of the idea. Introducing repetition of sound is usually a process of artistic choice; it stands out.

1. Alliteration

Rhymes repeat the ending sound of a word. *Alliteration* repeats the initial sound. We usually think of this as a consonant: Frank's Fried Fish. But it can also be a vowel, when the vowel is in the initial position: Auntie Allen's Ambergris. Tongue-twister rhymes use a lot of them: "Peter Piper picked a peck of pickled peppers…"

Old English poetry leaned exclusively on alliteration for its repetitive effects, not using rhyme at all. Look back at the brief samples of Old English verse in Lesson 2, as well as Tolkien's modern English imitations.

Not only were four strong accentual beats struck, as pointed out in that lesson; also, three of the stressed words had to begin with the same sound. It was usually the first three, with the fourth stressed word using a different first letter, but this was an artistic choice and different patterns can be seen. Anglo-Saxon bards treated all vowels as the same sound, so that words like "earth," "Edward," and "old" could be considered to alliterate. In modern English, we ask for exact matches.

When it's used in modern English poetry, alliteration is neither as rigidly placed as it was in Old English, nor as obviously forced as it is in tongue twisters and advertising jingles. Repeated sounds may not be next to each other. As long as they are in the same line or two lines, so that our ears are still remembering the previous sound, it counts as alliteration. Herbert's "The Collar" gives us a beautiful example with four L words in two lines:

> My lines and life are free, free as the road,
> Loose as the wind, as large as store.

If the line read "My lines live loose and large," it would also feel overdone and jingle-ly, like Frieda's Fried Fish. Too much alliteration is distracting, which is why shop names and advertising slogans like to use it. They want you to stop and look again at the phrase so that you will remember it. In poetry, this would be too much, because alliteration is only one of the sound elements. Even in Old English poetry, where it was the main sound element, part of the artistry was in varying the patterns with non-alliterating words.

Alliteration is not usually the main sound feature of a poem; instead, it is a decoration. In Herbert's lines of L's, the repeated sounds unify the phrases. They also just please the ear; it's hard to say why. The answer may just be the simplest one: we like to hear familiar sounds. Alliteration used in this light way doesn't shape the poetry, but it feels like a touch of decoration, like carved wood on a chair or extra serifs on letters.

Alliteration can also imitate a physical sound. Words that directly imitate a sound, like "meow," are called *onomatopoeia*, which just means the noun (Greek *onoma*, name) is made (Greek *poeia*, as in poem) of its sound. But alliteration isn't exactly like that, although we could create an onomatopoeic effect by having a talking cat use only words beginning with M. Alliteration imitates physical sounds by being aware of what actual sounds might be in the environment of what the poem is talking about. It's more likely to be used in a dramatic, story-telling, or description poem. Sounds like the wind in leaves or people whispering could be conveyed by a line of S alliteration; gunshots could be suggested with alliterated B's.

Using alliteration to convey physical sounds should be done with care. It's very easy to overdo, and the result might strike readers as comic. In a comic poem, that's wonderful. If it wasn't intended to be funny, the poet will be disappointed. Alliteration is better used lightly as artistic embellishment; all repetition works best when mixed with variation.

2. Assonance and Consonance

The middle sounds of a word can repeat as well. When they are vowels, we call the repetition *assonance*. If we repeat middle consonant sounds, it's called *consonance*. Of these two, assonance is more often noted.

We don't tend to notice assonance and consonance the way we notice alliteration. It takes some work to notice the assonance in Herbert's opening lines. The long I's are most noticeable in "My lines and life," and again in "there was wine /Before my sighs did dry it." Once I noticed the assonance in those lines, I began looking for other long I's. Of course, there's the pronoun "I," which is prominent all through the poem. By itself, the pronoun doesn't seem like enough to create assonance (and after all, we could equally call it alliteration, since it's just one letter). But in this context, it does become part of a strong pattern of sound repetition. I'm also going to include the word "wind," which in modern English is a short I; it may have been the same long I in Herbert's time. Here are the I's in boldface:

>I struck the board and cried, "No more;
>>I will abroad!
>What? shall I ever sigh and pine?
>My lines and life are free, free as the road,
>>Loose as the wind, as large as store.
>>Shall I be still in suit?
>Have I no harvest but a thorn
>>To let me blood, and not restore
>What I have lost with cordial fruit?
>>Sure there was wine
>Before my sighs did dry it; there was corn
>>Before my tears did drown it.
>Is the year only lost to me?

After I've singled out the long I's, I see some clusters of repeated sounds, in both cases centered around the word "sigh." The long I's seem to evoke the plaintive sighing. But alternating with the clusters of I's, there are groups with O and U assonance (and these sounds are somewhat similar, often using the same letters). Here, I'll underline the I's already pointed out, using bold for the new O and U sounds:

>I struck the board and cried, "No more;
>>I will abroad!
>What? shall I ever sigh and pine?
>My lines and life are free, free as the road,
>>Loose as the wind, as large as store.
>>Shall I be still in suit?
>Have I no harvest but a thorn
>>To let me blood, and not restore
>What I have lost with cordial fruit?
>>Sure there was wine
>Before my sighs did dry it; there was corn
>>Before my tears did drown it.
>Is the year only lost to me?

When I read these lines, my feeling is that the open O's are part of the life he's missing out on: the O's are whatever is open, long, strong, loose, round, and full. The I's are the thin, puny leavings that he has: tight, windy, dry, crying, sighing. I don't know if Herbert had an idea like this, but it's fair to recognize the way the poet's use of sound influences a reader's feeling about the work.

Let's look at one more example, from Shelley's "Mutability." Here, the poet had to choose from among one-syllable verbs to describe the appearance of clouds at night around the moon. None of them are needed for rhyming, so he could presumably have chosen from hundreds.

> We are as clouds that veil the midnight moon;
> How restless**ly** they sp**ee**d, and gl**ea**m, and quiver,
> Str**ea**king the darkness radiant**ly**! — yet soon
> Night closes round and they are lost forever.

In the lines that describe the clouds, three of the four verbs have the long E sound in the middle. Two adverbs reinforce the E sound's repetition. What is the effect of this assonance? First, it is just pretty, because we like repetition. Each line has three E's, and in the middle, so that it doesn't get boring, we have a different but related sound, the short I of "quiver." Second, the E sound may evoke some sense of movement, like shooting stars. It's a high, thin sound that holds on for a split second longer than short I. The clouds speeeeed, gleeeeeam, and streeeeeak.

Assonance and consonance may beautify a line of poetry without having any literal interpretation. But I think assonance may lend itself to giving a sense of feeling because vowels are like emotional sounds of crying, groaning, or laughing. If O sounds remind a reader of grief expressions, using them for deliberate repetition in a passage about sorrow will create a connection between sound and feeling. Assonance should be used carefully, like alliteration, but it's less likely to turn comic if overplayed.

3. Repetition of words and phrase structure

Repetition of words and grammatical constructions is also decorative, and this repetition also partners with variation. Look at Herbert's lines one more time, and now I have italicized some phrases while putting the question marks in boldface.

> I struck the board and cried, "No more;
>   I will abroad!
>   What**?** shall I ever sigh and pine**?**
> *My lines and life are free, free as the road,*
>   *Loose as the wind, as large as store.*
>   Shall I be still in suit**?**
>   Have I no harvest but a thorn
>   To let me blood, and not restore
> What I have lost with cordial fruit**?**
>   *Sure there was wine*
> *Before my sighs did dry it; there was corn*
>   *Before my tears did drown it.*
> Is the year only lost to me**?**

Looking first at the boldface question marks, we see that the passage gives us the repeated motif of questions, varying in length from one word to three lines. We get a pattern like this: statement; question, question; statement; question, question; statement; question. If we read the lines out loud, we must turn our sentence intonation upward at the end to indicate questions. So each question creates a kind of intonation repetition that carefully skirts the line where too many questions would be boring, but doesn't cross that line. You can observe this pattern in the rest of the poem, too.

In the italicized portions, we see some parallel phrasing. The second one is simpler, so let's start there.

> Sure there was wine /Before my sighs did dry it;
> there was corn /Before my tears did drown it.

If we added "sure" to the second phrase, they would be identical except for specific nouns and verbs. The first phrase is repeated, but with the slight variation of not including "sure" the second time. Of course, just varying corn for wine, and drowning for drying, also counts as variation to partner with the repetition.

Looking back at the first passage I pointed out, we see a more complicated repetition and variation of phrasing. It begins with the subject of the sentence, "my lines and life." To the side, I've swapped letters for the specific words so that it's easier to see the structure.

My lines and life are free,	My subject is A,
free as the road,	A as the B,
Loose as the wind,	C as the D,
as large as store.	as E as F.

The first repetition is the word "free." It appears in the first phrase, then it's immediately repeated as an idea to expand on. We get two comparisons with identical phrasing: free *as the* road, loose *as the* wind. "X *as the* Y" is the formula, and Herbert could easily have used it a third time. But he didn't. Instead, he used something almost the same, but with a variation: *as* large *as* store. ("Store" probably means a storage warehouse or cellar.) It's close to a repetition, but it's different. As a reader (and as a poet), I love this kind of phrasing repetition and variation.

We see the same techniques of phrasing repetition and variation in "Mutability" as well.

> We rest.—A dream has power to poison sleep;
> We rise.—One wandering thought pollutes the day;
> We feel, conceive or reason, laugh or weep;
> Embrace fond woe, or cast our cares away:

The first two lines repeat an almost identical phrasing. "We R-verb. — A thing does something." The third line could have said, "We reason — a feeling rises to change our logic." Then it would have been identical to the other lines, including alliteration in the verb (rest, rise, reason!). But instead, Shelley varied the structure by giving us a series of verbs, only one of which alliterates with R: We feel, conceive, *reason*, laugh, weep, embrace, or cast.

In the series of verbs, he also varies the phrasing. The first three verbs are in a simple list: We feel, conceive or reason. Laugh and weep are tied together with a second "or," while the last line expands the "or" alternatives to include phrases: Embrace fond woe, *or* cast our cares away.

So the list of options grows in length and complexity. I've also marked here, with boldface, the letters that form clusters of alliteration. As mutable humans:

> We rest;
> We rise;
> We {feel, conceive *or* reason},
> {laugh *or* weep};
> {embrace fond woe
> *or* cast our cares away}.

We saw effective musical use of word and phrase repetition in Tennyson's songs, too. In "The Splendour Falls," each stanza closed with a call for the bugle to blow. Here are those three sets of closing lines, which could be called couplets, but taken as a group, they are more than couplets:

(1) Blow, bugle, blow, set the wild echoes flying,
Blow, bugle; answer, echoes, dying, dying, dying.

(2) Blow, let us hear the purple glens replying,
Blow, bugle; answer, echoes, dying, dying, dying.

(3) Blow, bugle, blow, set the wild echoes flying,
And answer, echoes, answer, dying, dying, dying.

We see here alliteration of B sounds, which not only alliterate but call to mind the start of a trumpet sound. (If so, it may be less the poet's choice than just the way the language developed to have some onomatopoeia in words like boom, bang, blast, blow and bugle.) There's assonance of O sounds, especially in "blow" and "echoes." We also see the literal repetition, within a line, of the words "blow" and "dying."

But there are important variations that make it musical, not boring. When the first line is repeated in stanza 2, it doesn't repeat "blow, bugle, blow," but instead just "Blow, let us hear." Stanza 3 returns to the original identical form in its first line. The second line of each set is identical in the first two times we see it, so there is perfect repetition. However, when the poem closes with the third repeat, we see an identical line 1 "Blow, bugle, blow, set the wild echoes flying," but not an identical line 2. Now, it skips "Blow bugle" entirely, going straight to the echoes.

Word repetition is a powerful tool in poetry, but also one that must be used carefully. When words are repeated, we pay so much attention that if this attention wasn't wanted, the poet may be sorry (as with alliteration, the effect may seem comic). The best way to handle intentional word repetition is to keep varying the context of the word. Every word may have a basic meaning, but the context gives it a specific meaning in that sentence, and sometimes context can shift its specific meaning a lot. Context can reverse its meaning, or it can give the repeated word an ironic sense. A repeated word can become an idea that is developed throughout the poem, with new light, facts or viewpoints exposed each time we see it again.

Summary and Definitions

Repetition is a tool for artistic embellishment because we like hearing a familiar sound, but it should be used carefully and only in combination with *variation*. As a rule of thumb, after three repetitions it may become boring. Even a little variation can bring the repeated sound to life again.

Alliteration is the repetition of initial sound.

Assonance is the repetition of a middle vowel sound. Repetition of a middle consonantal sound is called consonance, but we usually pay less attention to this sound effect.

Onomatopoeia is the sound effect of a word that imitates a sound, like bang or meow. It can be part of alliteration and assonance, but only in specific contexts.

Repetition and variation can also apply to words, phrases, and grammatical structures, such as questions or comparisons.

Exercises 9

Review

> Avenge, O Lord, thy slaughtered saints, whose bones
> Lie scattered on the Alpine mountains cold...

a) In this Italian/Petrarchan sonnet, what will the next two rhymes be? (-oans, -old; -old, -oans; -old, -ine)

b) What rhyming sounds will be used in the second set of four lines? (same as first four; half the same, half new rhymes; entirely new rhymes)

c) How will the last six lines be rhymed? (ABABBA; CDCDEE; CDECDE)

> Shall I compare thee to a summer's day?
> Thou art more lovely and more temperate...

d) In this English/Shakespearean sonnet, what will the next two rhymes be? (-ate, -ay; -ee, -ay; -ay, -ate)

e) Will the next set of four lines need to rhyme with the first four?

f) How are the last six lines organized in this form? (two sets of three lines; three sets of two lines; four lines plus a couplet)

1. A monkey with a smart tablet has attempted to reproduce the first two stanzas of "The Raven." That darn autocorrect! Every underlined word is close but not right; it is related to the correct word through either alliteration or assonance. In two cases, there is *no* similar sound at all. Your task is to sort the wrong word and its correction into the proper column. The first one is done for you, as an example. ("Padding" and "church" appear twice but need only be corrected once.)

"The Rambler" (or was it "The Maven"?)

> Once upon a midnight <u>steamy</u>, while I pondered, <u>wan</u> and weary,
> Over many a <u>quiet</u> and curious <u>vanguard</u> of forgotten <u>hoard</u>—
> While I <u>blogged</u>, nearly <u>laughing</u>, suddenly there <u>called</u> a tapping,
> As of some one <u>gingerly</u> <u>padding</u>, padding at my <u>church</u> door.
> "'Tis some <u>vagabond</u>," I <u>said</u>, "tapping at my church door—
> Only this and nothing <u>serious</u>."

> Ah, <u>daily</u> I <u>robot</u> it was in the <u>sweet</u> December;
> And each <u>sooty</u> <u>mile</u> ember <u>popped</u> its <u>gamble</u> upon the floor.
> Eagerly I <u>kissed</u> the <u>matron</u>;—<u>never</u> I had sought to borrow
> From my <u>banks</u> surcease of sorrow—sorrow for the <u>soft</u> Lenore—
> For the <u>vain</u> and <u>random</u> <u>lady</u> whom the <u>attendants</u> name Lenore—
> Nameless <u>steel</u> for evermore.

Alliteration	Assonance	No sound repetition
	Steamy/dreary	

2. In 1711, Alexander Pope published a long poem, *Essay on Criticism*. It was in verse, but really was more of an essay about what's wrong with literary critics. Pope wrote in iambic pentameter, rhymed AABBCCDD, etc. This format was known as *heroic couplets*; it competed with blank verse in 18th century popularity. Pope's poem gave us the famous line, "A little learning is a dangerous thing," so first you'll read that line and its context. Notice the line number at the right margin; we skip about 100 lines between the two passages.

   But the second passage is our focus. Pope criticizes the simplistic way people of his time were reading poetry; he says they mostly judge "by numbers," that is, whether the meter is correct. If the meter is right and the words seem sweet, they consider the poetry good or great. However, Pope is seeking a higher standard: "the sound must seem an echo to the sense." (365)

   In this passage, Pope's lines provide examples of what he is talking about. Try to observe in what ways the "sound echoes the sense." In which examples do you see the use of repeated sounds? In what other ways, unique to each topic, do the lines self-illustrate his meaning?

   At each marked place (line number and asterisk to help locate it), observe how Pope is choosing sounds to be "an echo to the sense." If it's really not clear, check the answer key and then look back.

   a) 345
   b) 347
   c) 348 and 349
   d) 356 and 357
   e) 360
   f) 362 and 363
   g) 366 and 367
   h) 368 and 369
   i) 371
   j) 373

A little learning is a dangerous thing;   215
Drink deep, or taste not the Pierian spring.
There shallow draughts intoxicate the brain,
And drinking largely sobers us again.
Fired at first sight with what the Muse imparts,
In fearless youth we tempt the heights of arts,
While from the bounded level of our mind
Short views we take, nor see the lengths behind;
But more advanced, behold with strange surprise
New distant scenes of endless science rise!

But most by numbers judge a poet's song,   337
And smooth or rough with them is right or wrong.
In the bright Muse though thousand charms conspire,
Her voice is all these tuneful fools admire,   340
Who hount Parnassus but to please their ear,
Not mend their minds; as some to church repair,
Not for the doctrine, but the music there.
These equal syllables alone require,
*Though oft the ear the open vowels tire,   345
While expletives their feeble aid do join,
*And ten low words oft creep in one dull line:
*While they ring round the same unvaried chimes,
*With sure returns of still expected rhymes;
Where'er you find "the cooling western breeze,"   350
In the next line, it "whispers through the trees";
If crystal streams "with pleasing murmurs creep,"
The reader's threatened (not in vain) with "sleep";
Then, at the last and only couplet fraught
With some unmeaning thing they call a thought,   355
*A needless Alexandrine ends the song
*That, like a wounded snake, drags its slow length along.
Leave such to tune their own dull rhymes, and know
What's roundly smooth or languishingly slow;
*And praise the easy vigor of a line   360
Where Denham's strength and Waller's sweetness join.
*True ease in writing comes from art, not chance,
*As those move easiest who have learned to dance.
'Tis not enough no harshness gives offense,
The sound must seem an echo to the sense.   365
*Soft is the strain when Zephyr gently blows,
*And the smooth stream in smoother numbers flows;
*But when the loud surges lash the sounding shore,
*The hoarse, rough verse should like the torrent roar.

> When Ajax strives some rock's vast weight to throw,   370
> *The line too labors, and the words move slow;
> Not so when swift Camilla scours the plain,
> *Flies o'er the unbending corn, and skims along the main.

Alexander Pope, 1688-1744

3. In the short poems presented here, Wallace Stevens uses word repetition and variation to create much of the artistic effect.

   a) In "The Wind Shifts," there are many parallel phrases, on the patterns of "the wind shifts..." "like..." and "who..." Look at each set of similar lines. How does Stevens use variation amid the repetition? If you're interested, try rewriting the poem to make the repetitions more identical. How would it change the poem if "this is how the wind shifts" was exactly the same all four times? What about the "like" and "who" phrases? Notice, too, the careful neutrality of gender in the poem, except in one central line. How does this choice strike you?

   b) The second Stevens poem is one section, numbered III, of a longer group of short poems, all titled "Carnet de Voyage." In this poem, he uses more traditional poetic effects. What is the kind of meter? Notice the rhymes he chooses; they could be very trite and expected in such short couplets, but he provides some unexpected descriptions. When you see the opening lines repeated at the end, do they seem different after the middle lines have expanded the idea?

THE WIND SHIFTS

> This is how the wind shifts:
> Like the thoughts of an old human,
> Who still thinks eagerly
> And despairingly.
> The wind shifts like this:
> Like a human without illusions,
> Who still feels irrational things within her.
> The wind shifts like this:
> Like humans approaching proudly,
> Like humans approaching angrily.
> This is how the wind shifts:
> Like a human, heavy and heavy,
> Who does not care.

Speak Like Rain

Carnet de Voyage
III.

Here the grass grows,
And the wind blows.
And in the stream,
Small fishes gleam,
Blood-red and hue
Of shadowy blue,
And amber sheen,
And water-green,
And yellow flash
And diamond ash.
And the grass grows,
And the wind blows.

Wallace Stevens, 1879-1955

4. Gerard Manley Hopkins was keenly aware of the sound effects of language. He often wrote with such attention to showcasing the sounds that his sentences can be hard to understand. In these two sonnets, he uses alliteration almost in the Old English way (three alliterative repetitions per line).

   a) Study both poems for sound and word repetition. You may want to use different colors of pens or pencils, to circle or underline alliteration, internal rhyme, and word repetition. Look especially for sequences where alliterative patterns get repeated in groups of words (as Pope did in line 368).

   b) In "God's Grandeur," which was written while he was in seminary, he expresses strongly a sense of nature fighting back against mankind's pollution. "Reck his rod" means "recognize his sovereignty." Try to imagine the same message in a less musical style; how does Hopkins' rich use of sound elements support his message? How does the repetition in line 5 serve his purpose? Look closely at the last line, and notice the alliterative pattern: W B, W B, B W.

   c) "No Worst" came from a later time in Hopkins' life when he was clinically depressed. In this sonnet, he tries to capture the extremes of dark emotion not only in his statements, but in the sounds. What is the effect of the F alliteration when Fury shrieks? How do other repetitions support his message? ("Let me be fell: force I must be brief" means that if the depression is more severe or deadly, then it must be briefer; it's a beautiful sentence but is not true of clinical depression.)

God's Grandeur

The world is charged with the grandeur of God.
It will flame out, like shining from shook foil;
It gathers to a greatness, like the ooze of oil
Crushed. Why do men then now not reck his rod?
Generations have trod, have trod, have trod;
And all is seared with trade; bleared, smeared with toil;
And wears man's smudge and shares man's smell: the soil

Is bare now, nor can foot feel, being shod.

And for all this, nature is never spent;
There lives the dearest freshness deep down things;
And though the last lights off the black West went
Oh, morning, at the brown brink eastward, springs—
Because the Holy Ghost over the bent
World broods with warm breast and with ah! bright wings.

No Worst, There Is None

No worst, there is none. Pitched past pitch of grief,
More pangs will, schooled at forepangs, wilder wring.
Comforter, where, where is your comforting?
Mary, mother of us, where is your relief?
My cries heave, herds-long; huddle in a main, a chief
Woe, wórld-sorrow; on an áge-old anvil wince and sing—
Then lull, then leave off. Fury had shrieked "No lingering! Let me be fell: force I must be brief."

O the mind, mind has mountains; cliffs of fall
Frightful, sheer, no-man-fathomed. Hold them cheap
May who ne'er hung there. Nor does long our small
Durance deal with that steep or deep. Here! creep,
Wretch, under a comfort serves in a whirlwind: all
Life death does end and each day dies with sleep.

G. M. Hopkins, 1844-1889

5. This last poem is very famous, and its sound elements are more subtle than in the selections above. "Dover Beach" is remarkable for the overall beauty of its words, both sounds and ideas. Read it through a few times, including at least once out loud so you can hear the sounds. What type of meter is Arnold using, and how does he use rhyme? Study the poem for repetitions of initial and middle sounds (it's not as loaded as Hopkins' sonnets!). How do they contribute to its beauty? I think the line "Its melancholy, long, withdrawing roar" meets Pope's standard of the sound echoing the sense. Do you agree, and if so, what sounds achieve this effect? If you are working with this book for school credit, use "Dover Beach" to practice writing at least five paragraphs about the sound elements and how they support the message.

Dover Beach

The sea is calm tonight.
The tide is full, the moon lies fair
Upon the straits—on the French coast the light
Gleams and is gone; the cliffs of England stand,
Glimmering and vast, out in the tranquil bay.
Come to the window, sweet is the night air!
Only, from the long line of spray
Where the sea meets the moon-blanched land,
Listen! you hear the grating roar
Of pebbles which the waves draw back, and fling,
At their return, up the high strand,
Begin, and cease, and then again begin,
With tremulous cadence slow, and bring
The eternal note of sadness in.

Sophocles long ago
Heard it in the Aegean, and it brought
Into his mind the turbid ebb and flow
Of human misery; we
Find also in the sound a thought,
Hearing it by this distant northern sea.

The Sea of Faith
Was once, too, at the full, and round earth's shore
Lay like the folds of a bright girdle furled.
But now I only hear
Its melancholy, long, withdrawing roar,
Retreating, to the breath
Of the night wind, down the vast edges drear
And naked shingles of the world.

Ah, love, let us be true
To one another! for the world, which seems
To lie before us like a land of dreams,
So various, so beautiful, so new,
Hath really neither joy, nor love, nor light,
Nor certitude, nor peace, nor help for pain;
And we are here as on a darkling plain
Swept with confused alarms of struggle and flight,
Where ignorant armies clash by night.

Matthew Arnold, 1822-1888

6. Challenge Question. Here is a little poem by Wallace Stevens that includes a rare example of *consonance*, the deliberate repetition of middle consonant sounds. Stevens' repetition of the sound combination FT (or FK and ZK) is unusual in every way. He echoes this opening consonant combination in line 5, "Fat!" He is probably using it for onomatopoeia, imitating the birds. ("FT" could be their feet scratching among pine needles as they search for insects?)

The poem depicts a bantam rooster strutting around, threatening Stevens (the "ten-foot poet" from the rooster's point of view) and perhaps crowing. Lines 3 and 4 suggest that the rooster is so bright he makes the sun look dark. The "inchlings" are probably pine seedlings, which the chickens cannot eat. But the poem is best read for the sound effects, rather than trying to puzzle out a concrete meaning. Could you pick this rooster out of a line-up of chicken photos, based on the way he's depicted?

Bantams in Pine-Woods

Chieftain Iffucan of Azcan in caftan
Of tan with henna hackles, halt!

Damned universal cock, as if the sun
Was blackamoor to bear your blazing tail.

Fat! Fat! Fat! Fat! I am the personal.
Your world is you. I am my world.

You ten-foot poet among the inchlings. Fat!
Begone! An inchling bristles in these pines,

Bristles, and points their Appalachian tangs,
And fears not portly Azcan nor his hoos.

Wallace Stevens, 1879-1955

TEN:

REPETITION OF LINES

In this chapter and the next, we will look at two opposite ways of using the sound elements of language in poetry. They form the endpoints of a wide spectrum of word art, with most poems falling somewhere in the middle. At one extreme, the format prescribes so much of what the poet must write that there is very little room to innovate. At the other extreme, nothing is prescribed at all, so that the poet has freedom to innovate, even to innovate so much that the result isn't immediately recognizable as a poem.

Both extremes were initiated and encouraged by translations of poems from other languages. The poems from medieval French and Italian lent us ways to use the sound element of repetition to create highly complex, structured forms. Poems from Chinese and Japanese, on the other hand, lost their sound elements in translation. Imitating their style led to changes in how we present images and ideas in English, but with little or no focus on the sound elements.

You've already seen the sonnet form, which comes to us from Petrarch's medieval Italian poetry. In the sonnet, the rhyme scheme restricts the poet's innovation to only what can fit into quatrains and couplet or octave and sestet. Poets can adapt the sonnet form or break its rules, but the rules remain the definition of the form.

Some of the song forms that came to us from the Middle Ages are even more restrictive because they require whole lines to be repeated, not just words or sounds. They may have begun with carol songs, in which a simple repeated chorus alternates with verses. For example, "Deck the halls with boughs of holly / Fa la la la la, la la la la / 'Tis the season to be jolly / Fa la la la la, la la la la." The Fa la la's form a very simple chorus so that a group of people singing as they dance won't need their part written down. That's a very basic European song model.

Popular ballads sung by minstrels could also have repeated choruses, especially a repeated last line (which might have been echoed back by an audience). In modern times, we differentiate between ballad form (Emily Dickinson's quatrains), "ballads" that tell a story, and a form called *ballade* (bal-AHD). In the ballade, the last line is repeated in each stanza. It's the simplest of the patterns developed by troubadours.

The troubadours of 12th century southern France lived at the intersection of three major cultures. To the north was France, which was culturally connected to England and Germany; it was mostly dominated by village folk dances, carols and story-ballads. To the south was Andalusia, the Arabic region of central and southern Spain. Andalusia was culturally connected to Baghdad, Alexandria, and the far-off cities of Persia. The troubadours themselves were part of the shared Mediterranean culture of northern Spain, southern France, and much of Italy.

Out of this mix, borrowing from Arabic as well as Latin sources, the troubadours created a sophisticated set of song forms. Most were sung with music, but some may have only been spoken, so that it was truly poetry. They sang at the courts of the many castles in the region; their listeners were often musicians and poets themselves, so their standards were very high. "Fa la la" would never do; they wanted to hear something that was at once beautiful, philosophical, and very clever.

The troubadours' song forms spread to northern Europe, but they lost popularity when the sonnet became the dominant form. In the late 19th century, new translations of the troubadours brought the old song forms into English. Every generation is looking for something new, so the old forms were suddenly popular again. It was a new challenge to take such a stiff, difficult form and express modern ideas with it.

Of course, the following generation rebelled against these prescribed forms, veering to the opposite extreme. But just as sonnets continued to be written during the whole 20th century, so too did these forms. In the 21st century, some contemporary poets have been reviving the prescribed forms, again seeking to take the old form and fit it to new ideas and expressions.

1. Triolet, Rondeau, and Villanelle

Three of the troubadour song forms are similar enough that the troubadours may have thought of them as pretty much the same, just as we would not make up a new name for a hymn with a different number of lines, or for a pop song that repeated its bridge. However, when later poets took them up in modern French and English, the forms became fixed so that they are distinct from each other: triolet, rondeau, and villanelle.

All of these forms have exact rhyming patterns and, additionally, they all require that certain lines must be repeated in certain places. I need a new kind of notation for repeated lines, so when the A *line*, not just the A rhyme, must be repeated, it will be "A1"

The *triolet* is one stanza of eight lines, which can also be written as two quatrains. Its rhyme scheme is: ABAA, ABAB. But of those A's and B's, some must be repeated. It's almost a typical ABAB quatrain set, but instead, the repeated A line throws a curve, and then comes back like a boomerang.

To illustrate how this works with minimal confusion, I'm going to turn part of "The Raven" into a triolet (and then into the other forms). I need only two lines, A and B:

| Once upon a midnight dreary | A |
| Quoth the Raven, "Nevermore." | B |

To create a triolet, I start by making blank lines where I need new material, and repeating lines where they must be repeated:

Once upon a midnight dreary	A
Quoth the Raven, "Nevermore."	B
*	A
Once upon a midnight dreary	A1
*	A
*	B
Once upon a midnight dreary	A1
Quoth the Raven, "Nevermore."	B1

Now, since I am not serious in my effort here, I don't need to try very hard on the new material. It only has to rhyme in the right places. Notice that I need two A-rhyming lines, but only one fresh B-rhyme.

Once upon a midnight dreary	A
Quoth the Raven, "Nevermore."	B
At first I didn't find it eerie:	A
Once. Upon a midnight dreary,	A1
Such repeated quotes are weary	A
When you've heard them twice before.	B
Once upon a midnight dreary	A1
Quoth the Raven, "Nevermore."	B1

In a serious triolet, the repeated line develops its meaning as the poem goes on. In fact, that is why a modern poet would choose to write a triolet or any of the fixed forms with repeated lines: because some ideas gain strength from being repeated in a slightly different setting. Writing a poem this way is hard, but if you like words, it's also fascinating because it's a puzzle at the same time that it's art.

I wrote a triolet as a memorial for a cat who had been very timid and attached to me. When he died, I thought with some guilt, "He loved me more than I loved him." But on reflection, I knew that by loving me so much, he had created a bond that I hadn't chosen. My thought that "he loved me more than I loved him" suddenly seemed to have more layers of meaning, and I jotted down this "Triolet for Tishe."

He loved me more than I loved him.	A
He knew love when he felt my touch.	B
To me, to them, love was a whim;	A
He loved me more. Then I loved him	A1
Because he knew love was a limb,	A
An ear, a nose: he knew Love much,	B
He loved me *more*. Then I loved him.	A1
He knew love, when he felt my touch.	B1

Let's look at how the idea developed, and also at the way I altered the punctuation and word use when the line repeated. I have to admit that I cheated in one key place to make it possible, by swapping "then" for "than." But in both of the A1 lines, I split up the phrase with different punctuation. That's not only fair, it's the part that fascinates poets. Some lines can be cut in different places and made into parts of other sentences. When poets write in a fixed form like this, they try to devise a repeated line that has flexible phrasing.

Take a phrase like, "I've had enough of all my friends!" If I had to repeat it, I could do this: "...apple and cherry, pumpkin too, the pies / *I've had! Enough! Of all my friends* / you alone could eat as much." The meaning is very different when I split it up like that.

In my cat poem, the second A-rhyme line sets up a comparison of lesser love, mere whims, so that I can use A1 "He loved me more" to mean that the cat loved more intensely than we humans do. The third A1 uses "He loved me more" to compare the cat's practice of love with the cat's knowledge of love. These comparisons cast the cat's love into greater sizes.

The other half of the A1 line, too, shifts in use; granted here's where I cheated by swapping in a similar but different word. But the first time "Then I loved him" appears, it signals a point in time at which I began to love the cat, while in the second repeat, it signals a logical conclusion: Then I loved him.

The B1 line in the cat poem benefits especially from development. When it first appears, saying that the cat knew love when he felt my touch, it sounds like the cat might be mistaken since I didn't love him that much. When it appears at the end, the idea has grown around it, and now we see that it's true. That's what is so fascinating about the forms with repeated lines: how the same thing can appear, in identical words, and yet mean something different. This is why some modern poets love triolets!

The *rondeau* may have originally been much like the triolet, but even during the Middle Ages, some writers began to abbreviate that repeated line. It was too much effort to write out the whole thing, or perhaps it used up too much paper. From this, we've developed the modern rondeau that uses a repeated *half* line. The use of an abbreviated line sounded too interesting, to modern ears, to go back to using a whole line.

The rondeau is made of a quintet, then a tercet, then a quintet. But the half line that repeats is in addition to these. So really the rondeau has five lines, then three and a half lines, then five and a half. The phrase that opens the first quintet has to repeat; it will close the tercet and the second quintet. The first two feet become the repeated half-line. In addition, of course, there is a rhyming scheme that must be followed. The thirteen lines use only two rhymes, A and B: AABBA, AAB(half-line), AABBA(half-line).

Let's build a rondeau using "The Raven." I'm ignoring meter and line length, which I'd think about if I were writing a serious poem. But I do have to consider the half-line. I don't want to start with "Once upon a midnight dreary," because "once upon a" makes a lousy half-line. But I think "While I pondered" will be okay. So here are my basic A and B lines/rhymes:

While I pondered, weak and weary,	A
Quoth the Raven, "Nevermore."	B

First I lay out my rhyme scheme with As and Bs, noting where I need to repeat the half-line. That line isn't rhymed, which is part of its charm (too many rhymes can get monotonous). Now I will think of A and B rhyming words to fill in some kind of content that will lead to my half-lines:

While I pondered, weak and weary,	A
once upon a midnight dreary,	A
over some quaint, curious lore,	B
I heard a tapping at my door.	B
Tapping at that hour is eerie.	A
To use a slant rhyme: it's too *scary*	A
sitting high up in an eyrie	A
All alone with ghosts galore,	B
While I pondered.	1/2
Although I dreaded and was leery,	A
I did my best to form a theory:	A
Perhaps my aunt? or sophomore-	B
Year boyfriend, whom I still abhor?	B
I tried to make myself look cheery	A
While I pondered.	1/2

Of course, that's a goofy rondeau. Some years ago I wrote a serious rondeau, as well. Just as when I wrote a triolet, I had an idea that could be developed through repetition: what is love? I could say what it isn't, and then what it is; and each time, the required half-line would be in a new setting. When the phrase was seen in three different contexts, its meaning would open up.

I had to choose my repeating phrase carefully so that its grammar could be flexible. I decided to use "So much is love." The lines are iambic tetrameter, and I chose to add a 3rd B rhyme in the last stanza.

So much is love a notion shared	A
in common speech, not often bared	A
to microscope, nor well explained	B
that Love's trademark may be maintained	B
by saints and sinners lightly paired.	A
By those who cursed and those who cared,	A
who sulked, laughed, bitched, pretended, glared	A
or walked alone: by all is feigned,	B
"So much is love."	1/2
Let us walk true where these ill fared,	A
that Love's good name may be repaired.	A
Allow my darling's sun, where rained	B
my own soul's clouds—my joy sustained	B
by your eyes' touch—nor be disdained	B
your triumphs and sweet comforts shared:	A
So much is love.	1/2

My serious rondeau is a much better example of the form than the silly one, of course. You can see how the phrase "so much is love" means something different each time it appears. At first it means "so much" as in "this much," then it is a quotation summing up false ideas of love. In its last appearance, it sums up the poem's definition of love. In plain words, the poem says that when another person's happiness makes you happy also, that is love.

As an example of how meter can affect a line, swap "laughed" and "bitched," so that "bitched" no longer gets a stress accent. It sounds all wrong that way. When people use this harsh word to describe complaining behavior, they always put a heavy stress on it. That's why it only works at this exact point in the line.

The *villanelle* is made of tercets with interlocking repeated lines. Like the triolet and rondeau, it uses only two rhymes, A and B. This is because each tercet has to rhyme ABA, and both A rhyming lines must be used *three more times*. In each tercet, the B line can be fresh, and the first A line is also new; but the third line has to be one of the lines we've already seen. The last tercet repeats both of them, so it's really a quatrain.

This means that the villanelle sets a different kind of puzzle. In addition to expressing a meaningful idea, one that the poet wanted to commemorate with art, it needs lines that make sense both together and apart. The form is best for an idea that has, perhaps, two pieces. Each time one of them comes back, the new lines can develop it. At the end, with a parting thought, we see them together as a final statement.

I'm not going to fill in an entire villanelle with "The Raven," but a few stanzas give the idea:

While I pondered, weak and weary,	A1
a bird was tapping on my door,	B
once upon a midnight dreary;	A2
its coloration was not cheery.	A
I munched some tuna (albacore)	B
while I pondered. Weak and weary,	A1
I searched for a solid theory	A
to explain the football score.	B
Once upon a midnight dreary,	A2
In a campground by Lake Erie,	A
heavy rain began to pour	B
While I pondered weak and weary.	A1

When done in a serious way, the villanelle sounds meditative and calm. Most serious ones also use iambic pentameter, which is much calmer than the trochaic tetrameter used in my goofy example. The repeated lines aren't as close together as in the triolet, so they leave room for new ideas to come in. Someone could read a villanelle and not immediately notice that the lines are repeating. By the second time we hear each of them, they do sound familiar, and then they close the poem together.

As an amateur poet, I have loved all of these forms, so I can share a non-goofy villanelle. It expresses its idea less directly than the rondeau did, because it is harder to develop a direct idea in a villanelle. The lines repeat so many times; they keep having to be reused, and they can't be altered. So the fresh lines in each tercet can create a new setting, but the villanelle's form suggests sameness and even weariness. Of course, it doesn't need to be that way; but it is a challenge not to build the poem around the concept of repetition.

In my villanelle, the repeating lines reinforce a friend's unwillingness to accept grief, while the fresh lines set up new contexts to suggest how things could be different. Will anything change? The closing repetition suggests not.

Days and hours of drumming April rain:	A1
Surrender to the murmur, dear, and sleep.	B
You look for shining sun to dry my pain.	A2
Last autumn's leaves block up the gutter's drain,	
Then downpours spill and overflow the deep;	
Days and hours of drumming April rain.	A1
The spring is always late here, so explain	
Why you dislike to see me wisely weep;	
You look for shining sun to dry my pain.	A2
I see a happier wisdom through the pane:	
Umbrellas bright like blossoms, branches steep.	

Days and hours of drumming April rain	A1

Should cure my fever, wash away the stain	
Of tears. Drops sow what you may never reap;	
You look for shining sun to dry my pain.	A2

How will we live if always clouds remain:	
A paradox, a secret we must keep?	
Days and hours of drumming April rain,	A1
You look for shining sun to dry my pain.	A2

There are some beautiful villanelles that are still under copyright protection. The most famous is Dylan Thomas's "Do Not Go Gentle Into That Good Night." It is addressed to his elderly father, who seems to accept old age and death too passively. Thomas depicts four poetic, surreal scenes of how wise men, good men, wild men, and grave men face old age; for their various reasons, they all refuse to accept "the dying of the light."

Almost as famous and beautiful is Theodore Roethke's "The Waking." Its opening stanza lays out three mysterious statements:

> I wake to sleep and take my waking slow.
> I feel my fate in what I cannot fear.
> I learn by going where I have to go.

The villanelle continues, of course repeating the first and third lines, playing out a theme of surfing on chaos to maintain equilibrium. "This shaking keeps me steady," says the last stanza.

Elizabeth Bishop wrote "The Art of Losing." Compared to the villanelles of Thomas and Roethke, Bishop's message is straightforward: "The art of losing isn't hard to master." Of course, it isn't really as simple as that; accepting loss is never easy. Her villanelle is irregular because for the A2 repeated line, she chooses to repeat only its last word, "disaster." This allows the poet more flexibility in suggesting what sort of disaster various losses are. Bishop's rhymes for "master" are unusually clever, including the slant rhymes "fluster" and "gesture," and the phrase "my last, or."

In recent years, there has been some revival of these forms in contemporary poetry. In 1998, Chryss Yost published a terzanelle, a villanelle form with a twist on the rhyme scheme (taken from another medieval Italian form, Dante's *terza rima*). The poem, "Terzanelle in Blonde," meditates on the loss of love through dyeing her hair to become a different person — one who isn't in pain. Study the rhyme pattern as you read. The first stanza is ABA like a villanelle, but what happens next? What is the line repetition pattern?

TERZANELLE IN BLONDE

> Some things can be changed. Not yesterday
> And not your leaving me. I'll dye my hair.
> This blonde is too much yours for me today:
>
> Too long and sentimental, unaware.
> The insistent "if" of blonde, and "then,"
> And not "you're leaving me." I'll dye my hair,

> Until it's black as yours, and then again.
> I'll dye until it's red or grey, to drown
> The insistent "if" of blonde, and then
>
> Your words becoming tied to hers, the sound
> Of lovers' voices. Should be mine with yours.
> I'll dye until it's red or grey, to drown
>
> The echo of your whispers on my shoulders,
> Saturate the swish of my own heart,
> Of lovers' voices. Should be mine with yours
>
> Tangled up for days, not torn apart.
> Some things can be changed. Not yesterday,
> Not your leaving, not the hardest part.
> This blonde is too much yours for me today.
>
> *Chryss Yost*

The poem is a wonderful study in repetition and variation, as punctuation and spelling changes alter the meaning of repeated lines. When "Not your leaving me" is repeated for the last time, in the closing lines, it isn't identical to the first two. Instead, the line changes: "not the hardest part." Because we know what the line should say, the change is attention-getting. It focuses the poem on its central contradiction, its claim that a change in appearance can salve emotional pain, when actually it can't.

Mary Jo Salter's villanelle "Complaint for Absolute Divorce" appeared in *The New Yorker* in 2012. Salter's use of the repetitions is particularly sharp and witty, as she speaks drily of how grief gets processed with official forms.

> A little something to endorse:
> *Download attachment, print and sign*
> *Complaint for Absolute Divorce,*
>
> the lawyer wrote with casual force.
> Yet why complain? The suit was mine...

I've quoted only five lines, but the villanelle form tells you what the sixth will be. You can find Salter's poem at newyorker.com, and also in her book, *Nothing by Design* (Knopf, 2013).

2. Sestina

The *sestina* is quite different from the three previous forms, but it too comes directly from the medieval troubadours. It's different in that it doesn't use the sound elements of rhyme and repetition in the musical way that the others did. It doesn't rhyme at all, in fact, and words are repeated at such distance that they don't feel like repetitions until the whole poem is taken in. The sestina represents the more sophisticated tradition of the troubadours, who were often reciting or singing poetry for kings who were themselves poets. It is long, meditative, and complex.

In a sestina, there are six sestets (36 lines) closed by a special tercet. The six lines end with six words, and those words must be repeated, in a different order, in every stanza. The closing tercet has to use all six of them, two per line. It is called the *envoi*, which means the send-off. In medieval sestinas, the envoi was usually addressed to the lord who was hosting the artist.

To illustrate how it works, I'm choosing five words drawn from "The Raven," and for the sixth, I've chosen the generic word "word." Notice how for the sestina, I don't mark a rhyme scheme; instead, I am numbering the words so that you can see them falling into a different order.

Upon a Friday midnight dark and *dreary*	1
I tried to form a poem about a *raven*.	2
Perhaps sestina's form can be the *door*	3
That leads me, weak and weary, to *ponder*	4
The meaning of the bird as black as *midnight*	5
In myths and verse. And what of the sixth *word*	6
That has to end this line? Choose the wrong *word*,	6
And then the whole sestina turns out *dreary*!	1
It's not an easy task, even with *midnight*	5
Madness helping to sculpt a verbal *raven*.	2
Rhymes look hard, but sestinas make you *ponder*	4
The plight of endless rooms without a *door*.	3

The sestina would go on like this for another four stanzas. (There is a prescribed order for the words, but it is complex. A sestina reader doesn't need to know the rules.) A modern sestina may not observe the custom of the final-tercet envoi, which uses all six words to close the meditation. Troubadours' envois were a compliment to the hosting prince or duchess:

O prince! forgive this *raven* for the *dreary*
Use of Poe's dark *word*s, sung out at *midnight*.
Very soon, you *ponder* running out the *door*.

When sestinas are done well, they can be very fine. There are two famous sestinas, "Paysage Moralisé" by W. H. Auden, and "A Miracle for Breakfast," by Elizabeth Bishop. Both are under copyright, but you can find them in collections or on the internet.

Auden's six words in "Paysage Moralisé" are *valleys*, *mountains*, *water*, *islands*, *cities*, and *sorrow*. Just by themselves, the words set a scene in our minds, suggesting large land forms and distant horizons. Four of the words are natural objects, while people enter the poem through "cities" and "sorrow." The sestina uses the six words to meditate on our ambivalent relationship to the cities we build. In some stanzas, the cities are cast in a positive light, creating a home for people who came over mountains; in others, their people are sad, missing out on dreams of distant places.

Elizabeth Bishop's six words in "A Miracle for Breakfast" set a scene that's equally distinct and very different: *coffee*, *crumb*, *balcony*, *miracle*, *sun*, and *river*. Just by looking at the words, we can see there will be people and a house ("balcony") by a river. The title suggests that it's morning, and the coffee and crumb must refer to breakfast. But why is "miracle" in the list? As Bishop rotates through the words, she outlines a story of people expecting food that doesn't materialize. "Waiting for a miracle" and "like a miracle" give way to the sad comment, "not a miracle." The placement and use of "miracle" trace the human emotions through hope and disappointment to, in the last stanza, miraculous peace.

Summary and Definitions

Modern English poetry has borrowed some forms that originally came to us through Spanish and French medieval troubadours. They all feature some type of line or word repetition that restricts the poem's content.

The *ballade* is the simplest; it repeats the last line in each stanza. It may close with an *envoi*, a short stanza that troubadours used to end their songs.

The *triolet* has eight lines, but the first two are also the last two, and the first line is additionally repeated in the middle.

The *rondeau* repeats only half a line. The opening two feet for this half-line, which then closes the 2nd and 3rd stanzas. The rondeau also has a complex pattern of A and B rhymes, but the repeated half-line stands apart from them.

The *villanelle* is made up of tercets rhymed ABA. The first stanza's two A-rhyme lines must be repeated, alternating with each other, to close the next four stanzas. The last stanza is lengthened to four lines because it repeats both A-rhyme lines to close.

The *sestina* has six stanzas of six lines each, and they don't rhyme. Instead, there are six words ending the lines, and they are repeated as end-words in every stanza, in a different order. Like the ballade, the sestina often closes with an *envoi*, which must use all six words in three lines.

Exercises 10

Review

One stanza from *The Ballad of the White Horse*, Book I, G. K. Chesterton:

> A sea-folk blinder than the sea
> Broke all about his land;
> And Alfred up against them bare
> And gripped the ground and grasped the air,
> Staggered, and strove to stand.

Give an example of:
  a) alliteration
  b) assonance
  c) internal rhyme
  d) repeated word
  e) repeated phrase structure
  f) an X end-rhyme

1. There is another very rare verse form with repeated lines. This one comes from the poetry of Malaysia; its name, pantoum, comes from Malay *pantun*, poem. Victor Hugo was very excited about seeing it translated into French, and most of its few examples were written by his friends in the 1870s or so, in French or English.

Instead of just reading a description, for this exercise you will work out its rules like a detective. Here is a pantoum I wrote a long time ago. The poem speaks of Nova Scotia, where they typically paint their houses in bright colors, see also the bagpiper photo. Now work out the clues to the pantoum's rules:

a) What metrical line did I use?

b) What is the rhyme scheme?

c) What rule does the line repetition follow?

d) How does the poem close?

e) From Malay tradition, there is a convention about how the meaning must be developed. This is subtle, but can you spot it? Super bonus points if you can, just check answer key if you can't.

Cape Breton

Bright colors on a ground of green and gray
Announce the town flung open to the sea.
Pipes fill the silence with a breath and say,
With mourners' chant that floats across the lea:

Announce the town! Flung open to the sea
She suffers from its salt-spray laden gale.
With mourners' chant that floats across the lea
A nimble tune defies the numbing wail.

She suffers from its salt-spray laden gale;
Her bright paint chips with age and storm-sent shocks.
A nimble tune defies the numbing wail,
Picking a careful way on stubborn rocks.

Her bright paint chips. With age and storm-sent shocks
Proud foundations are tested; they prove strong.
Picking a careful way on stubborn rocks,
The piper's plaid seems woven from his song.

Proud foundations are tested. They prove strong
Who brave time's storms undaunted by the spray.
The piper's plaid seems woven from his song,
Bright colors on a ground of green and gray.

2. Here are two ballades with very different subjects and tones. For each one:

   a) what is the kind of metrical line used? What rhyme scheme does each one follow?

   b) What is the pattern of repeated lines in each?

   c) Looking at either poem, why do you think the writer chose the ballade, in which the last line will be repeated (never forget he could have written something else!)? What is the poet developing with each stanza that closes with the same line? If you asked him what new information we now have about the line, that we didn't have before, what might he say?

Ballade of Dead Actors

Where are the passions they essayed,
And where the tears they made to flow?
Where the wild humours they portrayed
For laughing worlds to see and know?
Othello's wrath and Juliet's woe?
Sir Peter's whims and Timon's gall?
And Millamant and Romeo?
Into the night go one and all.

Where are the braveries, fresh or frayed?
The plumes, the armours — friend and foe?
The cloth of gold, the rare brocade,
The mantles glittering to and fro?
The pomp, the pride, the royal show?
The cries of war and festival?
The youth, the grace, the charm, the glow?
Into the night go one and all.

The curtain falls, the play is played:
The Beggar packs beside the Beau;
The Monarch troops, and troops the Maid;
The Thunder huddles with the Snow.
Where are the revellers high and low?
The clashing swords? The lover's call?
The dancers gleaming row on row?
Into the night go one and all.

William Ernest Henley, 1849-1903

The Ballade of the Automobile

When our yacht sails seaward on steady keel
And the wind is moist with breath of brine
And our laughter tells of our perfect weal,
We may carol the praises of ruby wine;
But if, automobiling, my woes combine
And fuel gives out in my road-machine
And it's sixteen miles to that home of mine—
Then ho! For a gallon of gasoline!

When our coach rides smoothly on iron-shod wheel
With a deft touch guiding each taut drawn line
And the inn ahead holds a royal meal,
We may carol the praises of ruby wine;
But when, on some long and steep incline,
In a manner entirely unforeseen
The motor stops with a last sad whine—
Then ho! For a gallon of gasoline!

When the air is crisp and the brooks congeal
And our sleigh glides on with a speed divine
While the gay bells echo with peal on peal,
We may carol the praises of ruby wine;
But when, with perverseness most condign,
In the same harsh snowstorm, cold and keen,
My auto stops at the six-mile sign—
Then ho! For a gallon of gasoline!

ENVOY

When yacht or Coach Club fellows dine
We may carol the praises of ruby wine;
But when Automobile Clubmen convene
Then ho! For a gallon of gasoline!

Ellis Parker Butler, 1869-1937

3. Here are two triolets, also of very different tone and subject. One portrays a simple winter scene, while the other speaks in a sophisticated way about heartbreak. (Note: in Hardy's poem, the shrub "cotoneaster" rhymes with faster, not Easter.) For each one

   a) How are the repeated lines varied in phrasing and punctuation?

   b) How has the meaning in each changed and developed by the time the two opening lines appear again?

Around the House

Around the house the flakes fly faster,
And all the berries now are gone
From holly and cotoneaster
Around the house. The flakes fly!—faster
Shutting indoors that crumb-outcaster
We used to see upon the lawn
Around the house. The flakes fly faster,
And all the berries now are gone!

Thomas Hardy, 1840-1928

When First We Met

When first we met we did not guess
That Love would prove so hard a master;
Of more than common friendliness
When first we met we did not guess.
Who could foretell this sore distress
This irretrievable disaster
When first we met?—We did not guess
That love would prove so hard a master.

Robert Bridges, 1844-1930

4. For the rondeau, there are three beautiful examples to compare. Again, they are all very different in subject and tone, although they all fulfill the rules of the form. For each one, observe the type of meter the poet uses and any unusual rhyme choices. For each instance that the half-line phrase repeats, write a simple sentence showing its use, like this: "We do not know what is to come. We need not care what is to come. We may not share what is to come." Is there development of new meaning for the phrase, in each stanza?

Choose one poem, or a contrasting pair, to write five or six paragraphs about the use of the rondeau form to express and support the meaning.

   a) William Ernest Henley was a Victorian poet who battled a tuberculosis infection all his life, first resulting in an amputation and peg leg, and eventually ending his life in middle age. He was R. L. Steven's inspiration and model for Long John Silver; but more importantly, he was one of the leading poets who helped to revive the troubadour forms.

What Is To Come

What is to come we know not. But we know
That what has been was good—was good to show,
Better to hide, and best of all to bear.
We are the masters of the days that were;
We have lived, we have loved, we have suffered...even so.

Shall we not take the ebb who had the flow?
Life was our friend. Now, if it be our foe—
Dear, though it spoil and break us!—need we care
What is to come?

Let the great winds their worst and wildest blow,
Or the gold weather round us mellow slow;
We have fulfilled ourselves, and we can dare
And we can conquer, though we may not share
In the rich quiet of the afterglow
What is to come.

William Ernest Henley, 1849-1903

b) You may have seen "In Flanders Fields" before, since it is probably the most famous poem from World War I, often quoted for Veterans Day. Its author was a Canadian doctor serving in the trenches; he wrote this poem in a few minutes, sitting by a fresh grave after the Battle of Ypres, 1914.

In Flanders Fields

In Flanders Fields the poppies blow
Between the crosses row on row,
That mark our place; and in the sky
The larks, still bravely singing, fly
Scarce heard amid the guns below.

We are the Dead. Short days ago
We lived, felt dawn, saw sunset glow,
Loved and were loved, and now we lie
In Flanders fields.

Take up our quarrel with the foe:
To you from failing hands we throw
The torch; be yours to hold it high.
If ye break faith with us who die
We shall not sleep, though poppies grow
In Flanders fields.

John McCrae, 1872-1918

c) Paul Laurence Dunbar is one of the great poets of the Harlem Renaissance, a literary movement of black writers in the early 20th century. His rondeau clearly speaks of the difficulty he experienced living under racial segregation. As Dunbar develops the meaning of "wearing the mask," what does each stanza tell you about it?

We Wear the Mask

We wear the mask that grins and lies,
It hides our cheeks and shades our eyes —
This debt we pay to human guile;
With torn and bleeding hearts we smile
And mouth with myriad subtleties.

Why should the world be over-wise,
In counting all our tears and sighs?
Nay, let them only see us, while
We wear the mask.

We smile, but oh great Christ, our cries
To Thee from tortured souls arise.
We sing, but oh the clay is vile
Beneath our feet, and long the mile;
But let the world dream otherwise,
We wear the mask!

Paul Laurence Dunbar, 1872-1906

5. Edward Arlington Robinson was a shy boy who loved words, in a Maine town with an unusually strong literary tradition. (It was also the home of Julia Ward Howe, who wrote "The Battle Hymn of the Republic.") In this villanelle, Robinson describes children playing around an abandoned house.

   a) What is the meter? I think it works better if you read "they are" as "they're" and "there is" as "there's," as Robinson might have done when reading out loud.

   b) When "they are all gone away" or "there is nothing more to say" gets repeated, does it have added information from being in a new stanza setting?

   c) What is the emotional effect of those repeated lines closing the poem, as they opened it?

The House on the Hill

They are all gone away,
The House is shut and still,
There is nothing more to say.

Through broken walls and gray
The winds blow bleak and shrill;
They are all gone away.

Nor is there one to-day
To speak them good or ill:
There is nothing more to say.

Why is it then we stray
Around that sunken sill?
They are all gone away,

And our poor fancy-play
For them is wasted skill:
There is nothing more to say.

There is ruin and decay
In the House on the Hill:
They are all gone away,
There is nothing more to say.

d) Robinson and two of his brothers were all in love with the same pretty neighbor girl. She suddenly decided to marry the oldest brother, who had started a business in the far-off Midwest. The teenage poet refused to attend their wedding, and during the ceremony time, he wrote this poem below. "Cortège" means a funeral procession, but in the poem, the only real "procession" was the train that would take them west. When he says that they are going to their "grave," he is referring to their new home.

Observe the patterns of line and word repetition. Would you call this poem a villanelle? How it is like a villanelle, and how different?

Cortège

Four o'clock this afternoon,
Earth will hide them far away:
Best they go to go so soon,
Best for them the grave to-day.

Had she gone but half so soon,
Half the world had passed away.
Four o'clock this afternoon,
Best for them they go to-day.

Four o'clock this afternoon
Love will hide them deep, they say;
Love that made the grave so soon,
Fifteen hundred miles away.

Four o'clock this afternoon—
Ah, but they go slow to-day:
Slow to suit my crazy tune,
Past the need of all we say.

Best it came to come so soon,
But for them they go to-day:
Four o'clock this afternoon,
Fifteen hundred miles away.

E. A. Robinson, 1869-1935

6. For further reading, find the villanelles and sestinas mentioned in the text:

W. H. Auden, "Paysage Moralisé"

Elizabeth Bishop, "The Art of Losing" and "A Miracle for Breakfast"

Theodore Roethke, "The Waking"

Mary Jo Salter, "Complaint for Absolute Divorce"

Dylan Thomas, "Do Not Go Gentle"

If you like these forms, try the 1888 collection, *Ballades, Rondeaus, Chants Royal, Sestinas, Villanelles and etc.* edited by Gleeson White. White collected many of the troubadour-forms being written by his friends and contemporaries, when they were a very new, fresh idea. The book has been reprinted; you can also look at a scanned copy for free, at the Internet Archive:

https://archive.org/details/balladesrondeaus00whituoft

Eleven:
Free Verse

By the time of the First World War, English poetry had reached great heights of artistry in using the sound elements of the language. We could have seen several generations of amazing villanelles and sonnets, but instead the young generation was seeking something even newer.

In the late 19th century, a group of French poets experimented with extremes of artistic style. They were part of the revival of troubadour forms, but they also tried out writing verse with no form at all. *Vers libre*, they called it: free verse. Their experiments were influential among the young writers in London.

American poets also had the example of Walt Whitman's *Leaves of Grass*, which was published for the first time in 1855. Whitman's poems used no meter or rhyme; they were all unstructured. It's not clear that his work had any immediate visibility, which freed him to republish it over and over, with added poems, until his death in 1892. His work was only widely read after 1923, when a popular book series included his poems.

Around the time Whitman first published, both China and Japan had been forced into trade with Europe and America. Scholars began sending back translations and studies of Asian poetry. Both languages used sounds and styles that did not translate easily into English. Early translations imposed a Victorian style on Asian poems, but it felt wrong.

By about 1910, all of these influences came together in London, where a small group of young poets had gathered. They included the American Ezra Pound, who was working on translating the medieval troubadours. Translating from French and Provençal, and reading translation notes for Chinese and Japanese, they became convinced that a "new English" must be invented for the new century's literature. It had to be rid of ornate, antique words and structures. It had to be clean and efficient.

By the 1920s, when the First World War had left Europe in ruins, the principles of free verse had moved beyond experiments. Unstructured poetry seemed to capture the chaotic world order. Sonnets and other forms were *sometimes* used for ironic contrast with the ugly subject matter they talked about. You heard this ironic tone in "Only Until This Cigarette," "The Tired Worker," and "If We Must Die": beautiful form, ugly truths. But for the rest of the century, free verse was the dominant (and sometimes the only) form.

That's why most people see free verse before they ever read Shakespeare's sonnets. By the 1970s, schools stopped focusing on older, formal poems. When I was in school in the 70s, I learned only that a poem had irregular lines (with the option of rhyming), and each line should begin with a capital letter. Free verse appears to be the only kind from this point of view, but that's a distortion. We can't really see the artistic choices of free verse without going back to the early experimental years, when the poet's education consisted entirely of metered, rhymed poems. The free verse experimenters had been raised on Shakespeare, while most adults alive today were raised on free verse—-how different are our presuppositions!

One modern poet and critic wrote, "Poetry to be beautiful must separate itself from the ordinary — by extravagance, by purity, by precision, by original vision or imagination." (Hall, 168) When the musical, rhythmic elements of poetry are downplayed or avoided, then the words have to carry the burden of being beautiful in other ways. Free verse is typically extravagant or precise. It presents fanciful, imaginative images when it clusters words together, or it presents something very ordinary that is torn from its daily context so that it seems strange. Let's look at the three historical strands that resulted in the free verse we see today.

1. THE GRAND GESTURE OF LONG LINES

Walt Whitman's most successful poem in his lifetime was an 1865 elegy to Abraham Lincoln. Titled "O Captain! my Captain!" it followed conventions of meter and rhyme:

> O Captain! my Captain! our fearful trip is done,
> The ship has weather'd every rack, the prize we sought is won,
> The port is near, the bells I hear, the people all exulting,
> While follow eyes the steady keel, the vessel grim and daring;
> But O heart! heart! heart!
> O the bleeding drops of red,
> Where on the deck my Captain lies,
> Fallen cold and dead.

At the time he was writing "O Captain!" Whitman was privately experimenting with unstructured lines. His free verse experiments sometimes used grand, conventionally-poetic language much like "O Captain!" but without rhyming or rhythm, while other times, he tried to capture a conversational English tone. And without form: the longest poem in *Leaves of Grass*, "Song of Myself," ran to over a thousand lines. I'm presenting just the opening lines and a snip from its Part II:

> I CELEBRATE myself, and sing myself,
> And what I assume you shall assume,
> For every atom belonging to me as good belongs to you.
>
> I loafe and invite my soul,
> I lean and loafe at my ease observing a spear of summer grass...
>
> II
>
> ...Stop this day and night with me and you shall possess the origin
> of all poems,
> You shall possess the good of the earth and sun, (there are millions
> of suns left,)
> You shall no longer take things at second or third hand, nor look
> through the eyes of the dead, nor feed on the spectres in
> books,
> You shall not look through my eyes either, nor take things from me,
> You shall listen to all sides and filter them from your self...

As a poetry pioneer, Whitman seems to have written straight out of his own taste and invention, without following other models. His intention was to strip away the formalities of poetry and get to the core of experience, seeking authenticity. He wanted to take down the formal wall between his mind and the reader's mind. Authenticity and direct communication are still the goal of some modern free verse.

Whitman's use of words was extravagant and exuberant, even verbose. His greatest concern appears to have been that something important might get left out, so he added lines and words to capture it all.

Whitman followed no model, but his poetry became a model. We see lines like Whitman's in some famous 20th century poetry. In 1916, Carl Sandburg used similarly exuberant lines and wordy diction:

CHICAGO

Hog Butcher for the World,
Tool Maker, Stacker of Wheat,
Player with Railroads and the Nation's Freight Handler;
Stormy, husky, brawling,
City of the Big Shoulders:

They tell me you are wicked and I believe them, for I
have seen your painted women under the gas lamps
luring the farm boys.
And they tell me you are crooked and I answer: Yes, it
is true I have seen the gunman kill and go free to
kill again.
And they tell me you are brutal and my reply is: On the
faces of women and children I have seen the marks
of wanton hunger.
And having answered so I turn once more to those who
sneer at this my city, and I give them back the sneer
and say to them:
Come and show me another city with lifted head singing
so proud to be alive and coarse and strong and cunning.
Flinging magnetic curses amid the toil of piling job on
job, here is a tall bold slugger set vivid against the
little soft cities;

Fierce as a dog with tongue lapping for action, cunning
as a savage pitted against the wilderness,

Bareheaded,
Shoveling,
Wrecking,
Planning,
Building, breaking, rebuilding,

Under the smoke, dust all over his mouth, laughing with
white teeth,
Under the terrible burden of destiny laughing as a young
man laughs,
Laughing even as an ignorant fighter laughs who has
never lost a battle,
Bragging and laughing that under his wrist is the pulse,
and under his ribs the heart of the people,

Laughing!

Laughing the stormy, husky, brawling laughter of
Youth, half-naked, sweating, proud to be Hog
Butcher, Tool Maker, Stacker of Wheat, Player with
Railroads and Freight Handler to the Nation.

Carl Sandburg, 1878-1967

Whitman and Sandburg both became models for later poets. We see long lines and extravagant, word-spending phrases again in Allen Ginsberg's 1955 "Howl." It begins:

I saw the best minds of my generation destroyed by madness,
starving hysterical naked,
dragging themselves through the negro streets at dawn looking
for an angry fix,
angelheaded hipsters burning for the ancient heavenly
connection to the starry dynamo in the machinery of night...

The artistry in wordy free verse is in finding words that have a greater impact when they are grouped together; they add up to more together than separately. They may pile up their meanings, like "starving hysterical naked." They may clash in meaning, perhaps with irony like Ginsberg's tying "angelheaded" (a drug reference) to the literal *heaven* of stars and night. They build meaning, like Sandburg's "laughing" as it piles up details: "dust all over his mouth, laughing with white teeth," "as a young man laughs, "as an ignorant fighter laughs." They create colorful pictures, as Sandburg does with his phrases listing the painted women, gunmen, and starving children.

2. THE CUT GEMSTONE OF A HAIKU

Ezra Pound named the little London-based poetry movement "Imagism." He remained its most influential figure, in both writing and getting other poets published. Fairly early, they were deeply influenced by Chinese and Japanese poetry, because in 1913, a scholar's widow gave Ezra Pound boxes of her husband's notebooks on Asian art and poetry.

Pound had already been translating poetry from medieval Provençal and Anglo-Saxon. When he tried to create new poems from the translations, he found that they sounded silly when forced into 19th century language. The effect was even worse when Asian poems were forced to rhyme, or even to use conventional "poetic" words that Pound had previously admired. Calling those older styles a "dead crust" of English, he and his friends set out to reinvent poetic style.

We can learn a lot about Imagism by looking first at the haiku. When I was a child in school, we learned that the haiku is written in three lines: the first must have five syllables, the next seven, and last five again. It was a convenient way to teach light poetry while reinforcing syllables and spelling. Of course, it turns out that it's not so simple. There is a lot more to the haiku, and it is this "lot more" that mattered to the Imagists.

In early medieval Japan, the haiku was just a line or stanza in a long poem. In the phrasing of Japanese, it's natural to have a pause, breath, or change in intonation after five or seven syllables. Each 17-syllable line fell naturally into these divisions, although it was usually written in one line of Japanese characters. Japanese doesn't use rhyme in its poetry, because words already rhyme too much. Instead, it uses alliteration and clever word play.

Haiku artistry is also based in more subtle feelings about how the words sound together and how they present a picture. The haiku's aesthetic ideal is minimalist, precise, and concentrated. It uses hints and details to tell a human story. Each brief verbal picture drops a hint about when and where the image takes place, usually including a detail about the seasons. There is usually an implied human story, but we see only the corner of one small frame in someone's life.

Translating a Japanese haiku into English means completely disregarding our metrical stress and rhyme. When we write a haiku in English, we carefully count syllables, even if isn't natural to our language. But the key point of a haiku was not this 5-7-5 count, it was the brief expression of one concentrated image. Meaning had to be implied, not stated. To convey the essence of the Japanese line's meaning, English poets had to focus on using very few words, carefully chosen.

One of Ezra Pound's first haiku-influenced poems was published in *Poetry* magazine in 1913. In 1911, he had walked into the dark Paris subway station and glimpsed beautiful faces here and there in the crowd; it gave him a certain feeling and image he wanted to remember. He first wrote a poem of 30 lines, but after he started learning about Japanese poetry, he simply wrote:

IN A STATION OF THE METRO

The apparition of these faces in the crowd;
Petals on a wet, black bough.

Pound put a lot of thought into choosing these words. In "apparition," he focuses on his own *perception* of the faces, not on the real people in the real station. Japanese haikus try to connect the viewer (or speaker) and the image through hints like that. He didn't include a verb, so in a school paper, his lines might be marked "fragment." But no verb was needed to convey just his mental picture of petals against a dark background; in the Asian tradition, anything extra gets cut. In these lines, only the title tells us what it's actually about; without it, we would have to guess.

In addition to haikus with translations, the scholar's notebooks also discussed Chinese poetry. It is very difficult to translate Chinese poetry into English, partly because the Chinese language uses four musical tones that can be arranged in melodies, the way English word stress is arranged in rhythms. It's not clear that the young poets who tried to turn these notes into their own experimental poems even understood how much had been lost. Instead, they focused on how the poems presented scenes and emotion in Chinese court life.

Pound's first great work was to turn translation notes for Chinese poems into his 1915 book, *Cathay*. Although the poems were presented as translations (still credited to the Chinese or Japanese authors), Pound was really writing something new, and now we credit them just to him. He used the opportunity of this new material to create the "new language" they had been seeking. One prime directive was the rule that anything extra gets cut. Every word had to be there for a reason or it was suspected of being extra.

Let's look at one short example:

SEPARATION ON THE RIVER KIANG

Ko-jin goes west from Ko-kaku-ro,
The smoke-flowers are blurred over the river.
His lone sail blots the far sky.
And now I see only the river,
 The long Kiang, reaching heaven.

First, notice what is *not* in Pound's short poem: meter of any kind, rhyme of any kind, alliteration or assonance. There are also no "poetic" words such as English poets had learned to use; no "form'd," or "o'er," and no references to Greek mythology. There are only three adjectives, "lone," "far," and "long," and no adverbs except "only." The verbs are few and unpoetic in sound and meaning, especially "blots." There is no scene painted out in description: we don't know anything about the boat or river apart from the lone sail and the length of the river. We are given only one detail of "smoke-flowers" that become blurred as the poet watches. Does the boat have a steam engine in addition to its sail? Or did the smoke come from some other place? We aren't told.

"Separation on the River Kiang" is clearly art made with words, but it's art made in a new way. It used a few direct statements to suggest much more than was said, leaving us with questions and hinted answers. Who are these people, and why did one sail away? Why does the river seem to reach to heaven? What is the emotional effect of singling out, of all the boat's details, its "lone sail"?

We can really see Pound's re-invention of poetic language in a tiny poem that was based on a 19th century translation. In the Chinese poem, a former mistress of the Emperor speaks to her silk fan, saying that soon it, too, will be set on a shelf. The Victorian English version ran to ten lines and spoke without hints: "And yet I fear, ah me! that autumn chills, / Cooling the dying summer's torrid rage / Will see thee laid neglected on the shelf..."

I don't know how long the original Chinese poem was, but Pound turned the Victorian translation into a little haiku in which everything extra was cut:

FAN-PIECE, FOR HER IMPERIAL LORD

O fan of white silk,
clear as frost on the grass-blade,
You also are laid aside.

Like a good traditional haiku, the poem hints at a season, "*frost* on the grass-blade," and has just one hint of where it is set: the court, because of "Imperial." It only glances at the human scene. The speaker is here only in two words: "Her," in the title, and "also," in the last line. Even if we didn't know any story, we could still understand that a woman, speaking to a fan, says "you also" to mean that the same thing happened to her.

Ezra Pound's influence reached past his London circle of friends, to friends of theirs in America, and to complete strangers who read his work and were, in turn, discovered by Pound. His circle of influence includes famous names like T. S. Eliot, an American who moved to London, and William Carlos Williams, Pound's college roommate who became a doctor in New Jersey. Wallace Stevens, whose poems have already appeared, was another contemporary pulled into Pound's orbit. Their Asian-influenced, minimalist style of Imagism was directly opposite to the expansive style of Walt Whitman.

In 1923, Pound's friend Williams published a famous short poem that might as well be a haiku. It is precise, with tiny stanzas of three words, then one word. Like a haiku, it barely hints at the viewer's or speaker's connection to the picture it forms. But unlike the *Cathay* poems, its subject matter is not dependent on the foreign scenery of medieval China. It is drawn from a small yard in a poor neighborhood in New Jersey, so it is completely American:

THE RED WHEELBARROW

so much depends
upon

a red wheel
barrow

glazed with rain
water

beside the white
chickens.

3. PICTURES ON THE PAGE: USING WHITE SPACE

Most poems form a straight line at the left margin, whether they are traditional or free verse. But even within traditional poetry, some poets used the placement of words on the page in a creative way.

In 1633, George Herbert published a book of poems that included "Easter Wings." Not only were the lines laid out to form angelic wings, the block of type was even turned 90 degrees so that the reader had to tilt his head, or turn the book, to read it.

```
Then shall the fall further the flight in me.
    And sing this day thy victories,
      As larks, harmoniously,
        O let me rise
          With thee
        Most poore:
      Till he became
   Decaying more and more,
 Though foolishly he lost the same,
Lord, who createdst man in wealth and store,
```

This kind of poem is called a *calligram*. It uses the words as image, to illustrate its theme. It may have been borrowed into English from Arabic, whose letters lend themselves well to being stretched and curved into a picture. Islamic custom forbade making direct images of living things, so one way for artists to work around the rule was to use passages from the Quran as calligrams. The Shi'ite branch of Islam uses a lion calligram as a symbol of Ali, Mohammed's son-in-law; the words are a prayer instructing believers about Ali. Here is one very famous version of this image; the tiger is vividly alive!

Calligrams have never been a major vehicle of poetry in English, although Herbert's angel-wings created a short-lived fad in the 17th century. In the 20th century, as free verse pushed the boundaries of poetry wider, there were more experiments. One of the best-known images was in French, of course using the same Latin letters that English uses. It was published in a collection of inventive calligrams by Guillaume Apollinaire, at the close of the First World War. It means something like, "Hello, world, of which I am the eloquent language that thy mouth, O Paris, fires and will fire forever at the Germans." We all recognize the Eiffel Tower!

```
            S
            A
           LUT
            M
           O   N
           D    E
           DONT
          JE SUIS
          LA LAN
          GUE  É
          LOQUEN
         TE QUESA
         BOUCHE
         O  PARIS
         TIRE ET TIRERA
         TOU      JOURS
        AUX       A  L
       LEM            ANDS
```

The other way to use creative line and word placement is to use the spacing to control the reader's flow of thought. By breaking up lines, phrases, and even words, the poet speeds up and slows down our perception. Stéphane Mallarmé, who published a long poem of this type in 1897, found it difficult to get the printer to cooperate with the crazy way he wanted the words laid out. He admitted that only about one-third of the paper was used by words, while the rest was white space. "The paper intervenes," he explained. It "disperses" the words that might otherwise march along in measured order; it breaks the ideas into "prismatic subdivisions."

Mallarmé tried out using type of different sizes; his poem's title was spread out through the poem itself, in the largest type. Experimental poems have even used the little images that appear in a Wingdings font (such as the skull and crossbones for poison). It's hard to use Wingdings in a serious, non-gimmicky way. There has to be a compelling reason for why this kind of unusual element makes the poem better *as art*.

Mallarmé's use of white space, on the other hand, has been well accepted. Many 20th century poets writing in English enhance meaning with line placement. Creative use of space and line permits the reader to follow more than one line of thought at the same time. It points out parallels and juxtapositions by literally positioning them in parallel, or at angles, or at a distance. Sometimes it's not clear why a poet placed words as he did, but other times, we can learn directly from the way white space sets some words apart.

For example, contemporary Canadian-Ukrainian poet Lidia Wolanskyj uses a lot of white space placement in this 1986 poem to commemorate her mother's death at age 38. The poem provides both a formal, photographic memory and a skeptical, realistic commentary, and literal position on the page often juxtaposes them directly. "Pure & pretty" is immediately undercut with the murmur: "not so pure, not always pretty."

Additionally, Wolanskyj uses white space and word placement to align words that flow not from logic or grammar, but from word association. Some words sound alike, others are close synonyms, and these associations allow the poet to imitate the drift of memory: "posterity / prosperity / paternity / patterns." Similarly, she nearly puns with "MAZES / & mazes / amazingly lonely and cold." Mazes suggest walking, which suggests following behind — something. The vertical alignment gives us two equivalent possibilities: a man, or all ways. "All ways," of course, suggests "always." As you'll see, this free verse is not "free" of the artistic sound elements of language.

As you read, use a pencil to connect words that are linked by their placement. Look for uses of white space and alignment to suggest contrasting attitudes, as well as equivalencies.

Elegy for a Woman Unknown

```
salmon spawning young on the steps of THE TEMPLE OF LIFE
killing themselves for posterity
                    prosperity
                    paternity
patterns of living & checkerboard brains cooking
                                        stewing
                                        steaming up clams in a
CHOWDER OF LOVE
of stewy, creamy, tasty love                what nonsense what's stewy about love?
cauldron of the cosmic
babbling on, bubbling on
rising, falling                             fouling up
a pristine image of self                    not self
mother standing in the corner
pure & pretty                               not so pure, not always pretty
my mother                                   woman unknown
standing there
```

dropped into her grave   so bony & cold
dropped by our father   dropped by us all
dropped by life in general & cancer in particular &
        MAZES
     & mazes
      amazingly lonely & cold
mazes to walk through
  to walk behind
      a man
      all ways
crowded out by life in general & cancer in particular

left behind
under a cold stone,
   cold bones
below a cross of crucifixion
   cross of unholy communion
      the union of blood & ashes
        meat & dust
killed by the presence of a random tumour

THAT'S LIFE   what life that's no life at all
  up at six
  curls uncurled
  beds unfurled
  breakfast made
  husband fed
  kids fed too, off to school & did she really do it
  baby to take into arms to play & cuddle with
  beds to make
  shoes to bake
  all taken care of
  garden spaded
  grey hair faded
  mind stayed
  with
the pressure of lonely years
& unshed tears climbing higher every day
BAROMETER RISING i
      think i'm gonna rain today
        rain this way
        rain that way
     let the floodgates open wide
open open
    cry baby cry

Free Verse

```
                                revolution number thirty-nine
    every year a turning of the old worm
            a turn of the screw
                    & screwed in the turning
                                                    RETURNING
    to the empty womb
        the empty room, no place for me
                    no mother standing in the corner
        she's
                                            gone

    out of this world
    dropped through the bottom of life
        into the belly of nothingness–


                will i find her eyes
                behind someone else's hair
                one day peek
                into an ancient heart of love

                in another's innocently foreign face?
```

Lidia Wolanskyj

    We can see how the word placement is not random; in each case, the proximity or distance of a word speeds or slows the reader's thought. Words placed directly under each other make the word-play more obvious, showing the reader how the associations flow. In the middle section, short phrases in a line demonstrate the repetitive tasks of life (sometimes emphasized by rhyme). Words placed far away are distanced from each other: "she's.../gone" uses so much white space that at first, the reader may miss the phrase's completion. Finally, the closing lines form a cluster in the middle of the page, although by themselves they are left-aligned in conventional poetic style. They play the role of a couplet, bringing the poem to a sense of rest.

    Many free verse poems are less accessible than Wolanskyj's, such that we can't determine why this word or phrase is in the place that it is. Some poems try hard to communicate, while other contemporary poems seem indifferent to clarity of message.

    Free verse was born in the minds and pens of writers who were deeply part of the old traditions. They could not hear any speech without noticing its English sound elements; they had memorized many poems in childhood. By avoiding the deliberate use of rhyme and meter, they were playing with them, like a painter using the unpainted spaces of his canvas as part of the picture.

    They chose words for how they sounded together, and they played with *nearly* rhyming or falling into meter. They listened to the sounds formed when words bumped against each other, as the end of one word slid into the beginning of the next. They heard the flow of natural word stress as it fell into and out of patterns, and sometimes they planned little pauses into lines, not marked by commas, but created by the way we speak.

    When you can hear these things as a reader, you are equipped to appreciate the artistry in their words. Then you really understand the sound elements of English poetry.

Summary and Definitions

Free verse is poetry that is not directly structured around the sound elements of meter, rhyme and repetition. It can still use any of these elements.

English free verse has three roots: Walt Whitman, Chinese and Japanese translations, and the late 19th century French Symbolists. These roots give us three basic line styles: long and wordy; short and precise; loose and creative.

The best-known Asian poetry form in English is the Japanese *haiku*. It organizes 17 syllables as a pattern of 5, 7, and 5, with no meter or rhyme.

A *calligram* uses writing to form a picture; some free verse poems have been shaped as calligrams. Others use white space to communicate at a nonverbal level, using reading pace and association of ideas by placement.

Exercises 11

Review:

> When our yacht sails seaward on steady keel
> And the wind is moist with breath of brine
> And our laughter tells of our perfect weal,
> We may carol the praises of ruby wine;
> But if, automobiling, my woes combine
> And fuel gives out in my road-machine
> And it's sixteen miles to that home of mine—
> Then ho! For a gallon of gasoline!

a) Most of these lines have ten syllables, while others have nine or eleven. Why is that all right in this poem?

b) What kinds of sound repetition do you see in lines 1, 2, and 3?

c) The last five lines end in "-ine." Are "combine" and "machine" examples of sight rhymes?

d) Cite an example for each: end-stopped line; enjambed line; caesura.

1. Like the early Imagists, try to write in the Japanese style. You may choose which of three ways to do this—-or do them all if you like!

    a) The University of Virginia's library has a Japanese Text Initiative where you can read original haikus and translation notes, perhaps much like the notebooks Ezra Pound received: http://jti.lib.virginia.edu/japanese/shiki/beichman/BeiShik.utf8.html (or search "Japanese Text Initiative" if the link has changed). Using these notes, choose a few to make into art. You can keep yourself to the pattern of 5-7-5 syllables in English, or you can write a different version that you feel is art.

b) Here is a haiku-like poem written by F. S. Flint, another of Pound's London friends. None of the stanzas follow the 5-7-5 pattern. Edit them so that they follow the syllable rule, without losing artistry.

CONES

The blue mist of after-rain
fills all the trees;

the sunlight gilds the tops
of the poplar spires, far off,
behind the houses.

Here a branch sways
and there
a sparrow twitters.

The curtain's hem, rose-embroidered,
flutters, and half reveals
a burnt-red chimney pot.

The quiet in the room
bears patiently
a footfall on the street.

F. S. Flint, 1885-1960

c) Yone Noguchi, an immigrant from Japan, was also experimenting with the haiku form in English at this time. His "Hokku" was published in 1919. It's a bit different in tone, perhaps because he does not feel bound by imitating a "Japanese style," since he was writing in English directly from the Japanese tradition. His stanzas are strictly in the 5-7-5 pattern, but they don't provide concrete sensory details or clues about setting. Instead, they develop an idea, perhaps more like a poem in the English tradition. Follow Noguchi's lead by writing a series of haiku phrases that develop an idea you have been thinking about.

HOKKU

I
Bits of song—-what else?
I, a rider of the stream,
Lone between the clouds.

II
Full of faults, you say.
What beauty in repentance!
Tears, songs—-thus life flows.

III

But the march to life—
Break song to sing the new song!
Clouds leap, flowers bloom.

IV

Song of sea in rain,
Voice of the sky, earth and men!
List, song of my heart.

Yone Noguchi, 1875-1947

2. *Poetry magazine* published Carl Sandburg's Chicago poems in its March, 1914 issue, including "The Harbor."

   a) Find at least one example each of alliteration, assonance, and internal rhyme. "Walls" and "gulls" form a slant rhyme: do you think we're supposed to hear it, to remember "walls" when we read/hear "gulls"? Or is it a coincidental resemblance?

   b) What is the impact of the series of descriptive words beginning with H? Which phrase is repeated?

   c) How do the words change after the view opens up "at the city's edge"? What kinds of descriptors are used, and what kinds of sounds prevail in the second half?

   d) Find two phrases that are parallel to "blue burst of lake" (that is, "adjective noun of noun"). How many phrases follow the pattern of "two adjectives followed by a noun"? Do you see any other patterns in the phrasing?

   e) How did Sandburg determine where to end a line, in general?

   f) Contrast the tone and image of the first five lines with the tone and image of the second half. Which tone are humans associated with?

The Harbor

Passing through huddled and ugly walls,
By doorways where women haggard
Looked from their hunger-deep eyes,
Haunted with shadows of hunger-hands,
Out from the huddled and ugly walls,
I came sudden, at the city's edge,
On a blue burst of lake,
Long lake waves breaking under the sun
On a spray-flung curve of shore;
And a fluttering storm of gulls,
Masses of great gray wings
And flying white bellies
Veering and wheeling free in the open.

Carl Sandburg, 1878-1967

Free Verse

3. In "The River Merchant's Wife," Ezra Pound created something that feels foreign in tone and theme, but uses easy, natural English. He depicts the feelings of the teenage wife, who does not know how to tell her equally young husband that she loves him. Her love for him, and how much she misses him, are suggested by some details.

    a) Do you see any role here for sound elements like alliteration?

    b) The poem moves through five time periods, including the present time at the end. How are the time transitions marked?

    c) Generally, how did Pound handle line breaks? Compare with Sandburg, above.

    d) The speaker has one direct statement of emotion, "They hurt me. I grow older." What details does she use to convey her feelings indirectly? Outside of this context, would those details convey sadness to you?

    e) One word is repeated in this poem; what is the effect of its repeated use?

The River Merchant's Wife: A Letter

While my hair was still cut straight across my forehead
I played about the front gate, pulling flowers.
You came by on bamboo stilts, playing horse,
You walked about my seat, playing with blue plums.
And we went on living in the village of Chokan:
Two small people, without dislike or suspicion.

At fourteen I married My Lord you.
I never laughed, being bashful.
Lowering my head, I looked at the wall.
Called to, a thousand times, I never looked back.

At fifteen I stopped scowling,
I desired my dust to be mingled with yours
Forever and forever and forever.
Why should I climb the look out?

At sixteen you departed,
You went into far Ku-to-en, by the river of swirling eddies,
And you have been gone five months.
The monkeys make sorrowful noise overhead.

You dragged your feet when you went out.
By the gate now, the moss is grown, the different mosses,
Too deep to clear them away!
The leaves fall early this autumn, in wind.
The paired butterflies are already yellow with August
Over the grass in the West garden;
They hurt me. I grow older.
If you are coming down through the narrows of the river Kiang,

> Please let me know beforehand,
> And I will come out to meet you
> As far as Cho-fu-Sa.
>
> *Ezra Pound*, 1885-1972

4. E. E. Cummings wrote many free verse poems with loose, creative line placement. He broke conventions of capitalization, punctuation, and spelling, in addition to using white space. One of his most famous works is "in Just-," where he tries to capture the feeling of children playing.

   a) How does the poet handle line breaks? What can you observe about his choices?

   b) Which phrase is repeated three times, and how does it change in each repetition?

   c) "spring" is also repeated three times, but it always appears alone and at the left. Can you observe any other similarities or differences in how the poet places the word? Does it open or close "stanzas"?

   d) The words "whistles far and wee" appear in a different arrangement each time we see them. Do the variations convey a different whistle-hearing experience to you? Similarly, what about the way "balloonman" changes to "balloonMan"?

   e) When you read this, out loud or in your mind, do you pause at each long space, and at the end of each line, even if it breaks up words or phrases? How does the speeding and slowing alter your impression of the words, compared to how it would be as prose?

>   in Just-
>
> springwhen the world is mud-
> luscious the little
> lame balloonman
>
> whistlesfarand wee
>
> and eddieandbill come
> running from marbles and
> piracies and it's
> spring
>
> when the world is puddle-wonderful
>
> the queer
> old balloonman whistles
> farand wee
> and bettyandisbel come dancing
>
> from hop-scotch and jump-rope and
>
> it's
> spring
> and
>
>   the
>
> goat-footed

> balloonManwhistles
> far
> and
> wee
>
> *E. E. Cummings, 1894-1962*

5. In "Rain," William Carlos Williams freely uses white space to shape and pace our mental experience of his words.

    The poem begins with an epigraph, a quotation that is only indirectly part of the poem. It means, "What is this place, what region, what area of the world?" The text continues the pattern of asking questions.

    a) What place contrasts with the rain, as worldly to its unworldliness?

    b) how are rain and love alike, in the poet's telling?

    c) who does "you" seem to address?

    d) Suppose the poem rhymed like this:

    As the rain falls so does your love
    Bathe every open object of the world—
    In dry houses, priceless chairs are symbols of
    Hiding from love, useless and neatly curled.

    Or imagine that his lines were all aligned at the left, in a long string, without the creative use of white space. How does the free verse format, as he actually used it, shape or support the message he seems to be conveying about love?

Rain

As the rain falls
so does
    your love

bathe every
    open
object of the world—

In houses
the priceless dry
    rooms

of illicit love
where we live
hear the wash of the
    rain—

There
    paintings
and fine

    metalware
woven stuffs—
all the whorishness
of our
    delight
sees
from its window

the spring wash
of your love
    the falling
rain—

The trees
are become
beasts fresh-risen
from the sea—
water

trickles
from the crevices of
their hides—

So my life is spent
    to keep out love
with which
she rains upon

    the world

of spring

    drips

so spreads

    the words

far apart to let in

    her love

And running in between

the drops

    the rain

is a kind physician

    the rain

of her thoughts over

the ocean
    every

where

    walking with
invisible swift feet
over

    the helpless
        waves—

Unworldly love
that has no hope
    of the world

    and that
cannot change the world
to its delight—

    The rain
falls upon the earth
and grass and flowers

come
    perfectly

into form from its
    liquid

clearness

    But love is
unworldly

    and nothing
comes of it but love

following
and falling endlessly
from
    her thoughts

    William Carlos Williams, 1883-1963

6. Challenge Question. As a relatively unknown American, in 1914 Wallace Stevens started submitting radically experimental poems to literary journals. "Thirteen Ways of Looking at a Blackbird" was among these early poems. For a reading public whose idea of a blackbird poem was Poe's "The Raven," Stevens' work was shocking. Even now, a century later, it's hard to understand. It helps to view each stanza as a little haiku, presenting a glimpse of some human connection to nature, which is represented by the blackbird.

   a) Do you see any role for the sound elements of verse (meter, rhyme, repeated sounds and words)?

   b) Japanese haikus must provide some indirect hint of where and when the image exists. From how many of Stevens' sketches could you deduce a place or time (seasonal or time of day)?

   c) In some of the stanzas, the blackbird is actually present. When you add up these glimpses of the blackbird, what parts of him do we see?

   d) In other vignettes, the blackbird is present only by *not* being present. When the blackbird is not visible or present, what is perceived instead, and how is it connected to the blackbird? Sometimes the blackbird is just an idea, either a comparison in an analogy, or standing in as a symbol for something else. Do these add up to anything? If you removed the blackbird from these statements and instead put in a word that would make sense to you, what kinds of words would you substitute for the bird?

   e) How does the poet handle line breaks, as compared to the previous poems in this section?

Thirteen Ways of Looking at a Blackbird

I
Among twenty snowy mountains,
The only moving thing
Was the eye of the blackbird.

II
I was of three minds,
Like a tree
In which there are three blackbirds.

III
The blackbird whirled in the autumn winds.
It was a small part of the pantomime.

IV
A man and a woman
Are one.
A man and a woman and a blackbird
Are one.

V
I do not know which to prefer,
The beauty of inflections
Or the beauty of innuendoes,
The blackbird whistling
Or just after.

VI
Icicles filled the long window
With barbaric glass.
The shadow of the blackbird
Crossed it, to and fro.
The mood
Traced in the shadow
An indecipherable cause.

VII
O thin men of Haddam,
Why do you imagine golden birds?
Do you not see how the blackbird
Walks around the feet
Of the women about you?

VIII
I know noble accents
And lucid, inescapable rhythms;
But I know, too,
That the blackbird is involved
In what I know.

IX
When the blackbird flew out of sight,
It marked the edge
Of one of many circles.

X
At the sight of blackbirds
Flying in a green light,
Even the bawds of euphony
Would cry out sharply.

XI
He rode over Connecticut
In a glass coach.
Once, a fear pierced him,
In that he mistook
The shadow of his equipage
For blackbirds.

XII
The river is moving.
The blackbird must be flying.

XIII
It was evening all afternoon.
It was snowing
And it was going to snow.
The blackbird sat
In the cedar-limbs.

Wallace Stevens, 1879-1955

7. There is more to the art of haiku, for although Japanese does not use meter and rhyme, it does use sound elements. Faubion Bowers provides this 17th century haiku transliterated into Latin letters: *kokoro koko ni / naki ka nakanu na / hototogisu.* The "hototogisu" is a cuckoo frequently mentioned in Japanese poetry, and in this line, the poet wonders why he had not been hearing the cuckoo. Read out loud even by a non-Japanese speaker, the sounds clearly imitate the cuckoo. You can find many more informative notes and classic poems in Bowers' *The Classic Tradition of Haiku: An Anthology* (Dover Publications, 1996). It's available as an inexpensive digital book at Dover's website.

If you are interested in seeing some Chinese poetry, there are many poems and English translations at www.poetry-chinese.com. The first thing an English-language reader notices is that the Chinese originals all form perfect rectangle blocks. The page "What is Jintishi?" explains how the musical tones of the Chinese language are used as sound elements. In Chinese poetry, you don't choose a meter, you choose a tune.

To learn more about early free verse, look for Ezra Pound's 1918 editorial essay, "A Retrospect," from *Poetry* magazine. https://www.poetryfoundation.org/articles/69409/a-retrospect-and-a-few-donts

Additionally, *Poetry* has archives online, including some whole issues: https://www.poetryfoundation.org/poetrymagazine/issue/70335/march-1914

For a very different look at early experimental poets, try to find *The Mechanic Muse* by Hugh Kenner. In this book, Kenner suggests that some of the key inventions of the 20th century shaped the writers' work. He identifies the alarm clock with T. S. Eliot and the typewriter (and other printing machines) with Ezra Pound, who wrote, "The good forms are in the parts of the machine where the energy is concentrated." It's not an easy book to find.

REVIEW 3

Review questions 1-10 are based on G. M. Hopkins' poem "Binsey Poplars."

BINSEY POPLARS
felled, 1879

My aspens dear, whose airy cages quelled,
Quelled or quenched in leaves the leaping sun,
All felled, felled, are all felled;
Of a fresh and following folded rank
Not spared, not one   5
That dandled a sandalled
Shadow that swam or sank
On meadow and river and wind-wandering weed-winding bank.

O if we but knew what we do
When we delve or hew—   10
Hack and rack the growing green!
Since country is so tender
To touch, her being só slender,
That, like this sleek and seeing ball
But a prick will make no eye at all,   15
Where we, even where we mean
To mend her we end her,
When we hew or delve:
After-comers cannot guess the beauty been.
Ten or twelve, only ten or twelve   20
Strokes of havoc únselve
The sweet especial scene,
Rural scene, a rural scene,
Sweet especial rural scene.

1. In lines 1 and 2, there are three examples of _____

    [assonance; alliteration; consonance; word repetition]

2. Line 5 has an example of _____

    [assonance; alliteration; consonance; word repetition]

3. In line 7, all of the words except for "or" form an example of _____.

   [assonance; alliteration; consonance; word repetition]

4. In line 8, "winding" and "wandering" show us alliteration, rhyme, and also the much less common sound element of _____.

   [assonance; alliteration; consonance; word repetition]

5. Lines 10 and 18, together, use _____

   [assonance; alliteration; consonance; word repetition]

6. Lines 12 and 13 together form a _____

   [alliteration; internal rhyme; couplet; word repetition]

7. In line 14, the adjectives describing the eye use both _____ and _____

   [alliteration; internal rhyme; couplet; word repetition]

8. Line 15's only repetitive sound element, in "prick" and "make," forms _____ (and there is another one in line 14, do you see it?)

   [alliteration; assonance; consonance; slant rhyme]

9. Line 17 shows us _____

   [alliteration; internal rhyme; couplet; word repetition]

10. Lines 6 and 17 also show us _____

    [double rhyme; slant rhyme; sight rhyme; alliteration]

Review questions 11-20 are about formal and free verse forms.

11. The simplest Provençal troubadour form repeats the same last line in each stanza.
    It is the _____.

    [triolet; ballade; villanelle; rondeau]

12. In this troubadour form, only a half-line needs to be repeated; we see this half-line come back twice in the _____.

    [triolet; ballade; villanelle; rondeau]

13. In this short eight-line poem, two full lines must be repeated; one of them is repeated three times. It is the _____.

    [triolet; ballade; villanelle; rondeau]

14. This troubadour song form requires the poet to repeat two of the lines more than once. Each tercet, rhymed ABA, includes one of the repeated lines. It is the _____.

    [triolet; villanelle; sestina; envoi]

15. The troubadours' longest song form required 36 lines for the main poem. Instead of repeating lines or using a rhyme scheme, it required lines to end with the same words. It is the _____.

    [triolet; villanelle; sestina; envoi]

16. Troubadour songs sometimes closed with a special stanza that re-used the repeated lines or words in a closing thought. It is called the _____

    [triolet; villanelle; sestina; envoi]

17. The Japanese haiku is usually composed in English by following this pattern of syllables: _____

    [7-9-7; 10-10-8; 5-7-5; 7-3-7]

18. In English poetry history, the haiku formed part of the history of modern _____.

    [free verse; French verse; Provençal troubadour poetry; Arabic poetry]

19. The calligram, in which the words of a poem are shaped into a picture, is *not* part of this tradition: _____

    [free verse; French verse; Provençal troubadour poetry; Arabic poetry]

20. The poetic form that uses blank space to speed and slow the words is called _____

    [free verse; French verse; Provençal troubadour poetry; Arabic poetry]

21. (Bonus point) The Malay poetic form that uses many repeated lines is called a _____

    [tanka; pantoum; kanshi; cinquain]

Twelve:
Image in Description

Poetry is art made with words. It uses the sound elements of language as artistic tools to shape a beautiful way to present some kind of image. Now that we've surveyed all of the sound elements used to create poetry, we turn to the ways it can present images.

An image is something we can see, whether with our eyes or in our mind's eye. In its simplest form, poetry can describe what the poet sees. A witness to the writing of "Flanders Fields" averred that its image was a perfect photographic capture of what he saw from where he sat on the ground:

> In Flanders Fields the poppies blow
> Between the crosses row on row,
> That mark our place; and in the sky
> The larks, still bravely singing, fly
> Scarce heard amid the guns below.

Other images may have an abstract purpose, providing ideas instead of exact pictures. The image may not even be possible to see, as it may be imaginary:

> O the mind, mind has mountains; cliffs of fall
> Frightful, sheer, no-man-fathomed.

The next chapters will look at the ways images can be used. We'll start with the simplest: images used in descriptions, and images that are made of descriptions.

1. Traditional descriptive poetry

Poetry has usually been used to tell stories, and with a story there must be at least some description in the narrative. In the 17th, 18th, and 19th centuries, description was central to poetry; it was a feature that made readers pick up new volumes with pleasure. Perhaps this was because there were far fewer pictures available at the time. Books that described foreign travel were equally popular, and they rarely had illustrations. Readers expected to hear careful descriptions of unfamiliar things, but they also appreciated the words chosen to make these verbal pictures. It was natural that poetry would excel in "painting" verbal art.

When I was about sixteen, I felt the power of one of these old descriptive passages when I picked up a book at random in my father's library and read:

> Deep in the shady sadness of a vale
> Far sunken from the healthy breath of morn,
> Far from the fiery noon, and eve's one star,
> Sat gray-hair'd Saturn, quiet as a stone,
> Still as the silence round about his lair;
> Forest on forest hung about his head
> Like cloud on cloud. No stir of air was there,
> Not so much life as on a summer's day
> Robs not one light seed from the feather'd grass,
> But where the dead leaf fell, there did it rest.
> A stream went voiceless by, still deadened more
> By reason of his fallen divinity
> Spreading a shade: the Naiad 'mid her reeds
> Press'd her cold finger closer to her lips.

Before this, I had only seen poetry in school, and I had not been impressed with any of it. I felt that the poems we saw had been chosen to try to make us think a certain way. They seemed at best like a vase of cut flowers, or often like an array of silk flowers at a dime store. (My assessment was probably quite unfair to the poems.)

By contrast, this descriptive passage by John Keats shocked me. It seemed untamed, like something that perhaps my teachers didn't even *know* about. The lines drew me immediately into an unknown world ("forest on forest"?), although I did not know what world it was. It was heavy, sad, and completely still. It wasn't like the real world, but it felt vivid and palpable. I memorized these lines so that I could remind myself of them during very boring moments at school. I can't say that the rest of *Hyperion*, Keats' story poem about the Greek Titans, drew me in though I wanted it to. But its opening descriptive passage still leaves me with the impression that I *saw* the stream, the dead leaf, the deep and shady vale, the forest upon forest like cloud on cloud.

Descriptive passages could show the reader familiar or unfamiliar scenes, using many or few words. The poet's skill lay in selecting the details that would pique a reader's interest, using the right words to make it vivid or dramatic. If the reader was drawn into feeling and seeing with the narrative voice, it was good verse. If the poet only gave routine details, using words that had been used before, and not assembling them into a whole that felt real, it was poor work. Length was not an issue, except that if the poetry was good, then more was better.

Descriptions in the 17th and early 18th centuries tended to be ornate and formal, though much loved by readers at the time. Here is an early passage from best-seller *The Seasons*, published in 1726. James Thomson is describing birds in spring:

> When first the Soul of Love is sent abroad,
> Warm thro the vital Air, and on the Heart
> Harmonious seizes, the gay Troops begin,
> In gallant Thought, to plume the painted Wing;
> And try again the long-forgotten Strain,
> At first faint-warbled. But no sooner grows
> The soft Infusion prevalent, and wide,

> Than, all alive, at once their Joy o'erflows
> In Musick unconfin'd. Up-springs the Lark,
> Shrill-voic'd, and loud, the Messenger of Morn…

But in 1785, William Cowper published *The Task*, a six-part blank verse ramble through various views and ideas that came to his mind while walking in the country. Although his tone seems formal to our age, it was revolutionary in its informality; he was a model for the Lake Poets who came just after, including Wordsworth, Coleridge, and Keats about 30 years later. They all had read this poem; Robert Burns said that he carried a copy in his pocket on walks. Jane Austen read and quoted from it, too.

It's hard for readers of our time to imagine re-reading this long poem with never-ending delight, since the fashion for such verse has ended. But let's look at a typical (and good) descriptive passage about greenhouses, which every wealthy estate had in plenty.

> Who loves a garden, loves a greenhouse too.
> Unconscious of a less propitious clime
> There blooms exotic beauty, warm and snug,
> While the winds whistle and the snows descend.
> The spiry myrtle with unwithering leaf
> Shines there and flourishes. The golden boast
> Of Portugal and Western India there,
> The ruddier orange and the paler lime,
> Peep through their polished foliage at the storm,
> And seem to smile at what they need not fear.
> The amomum there with intermingling flowers
> And cherries hangs her twigs. Geranium boasts
> Her crimson honours, and the spangled beau,
> Ficoides, glitters bright the winter long,
> All plants, of every leaf, that can endure
> The winter's frown if screened from his shrewd bite,
> Live there and prosper. Those Ausonia claims,
> Levantine regions these; the Azores send
> Their jessamine; her jessamine remote
> Caffraria: foreigners from many lands,
> They form one social shade, as if convened
> By magic summons of the Orphean lyre.
> Yet such arrangement, rarely brought to pass
> But by a master's hand, disposing well
> The gay diversities of leaf and flower,
> Must lend its aid to illustrate all their charms,
> And dress the regular yet various scene.
> Plant behind plant aspiring, in the van
> The dwarfish, in the rear retired, but still
> Sublime above the rest, the statelier stand.
> So once were ranged the sons of ancient Rome,

A noble show, while Roscius trod the stage;
And so, while Garrick, as renowned as he,
The sons of Albion, fearing each to lose
Some note of Nature's music from his lips,
And covetous of Shakespeare's beauty, seen
In every flash of his far-beaming eye.
Nor taste alone and well-contrived display
Suffice to give the marshalled ranks the grace
Of their complete effect. Much yet remains
Unsung, and many cares are yet behind
And more laborious; cares on which depends
Their vigour, injured soon, not soon restored.
The soil must be renewed, which often washed
Loses its treasure of salubrious salts,
And disappoints the roots; the slender roots,
Close interwoven where they meet the vase,
Must smooth be shorn away; the sapless branch
Must fly before the knife; the withered leaf
Must be detached, and where it strews the floor
Swept with a woman's neatness, breeding else
Contagion, and disseminating death.
Discharge but these kind offices (and who
Would spare, that loves them, offices like these?)
Well they reward the toil. The sight is pleased,
The scent regaled, each odoriferous leaf,
Each opening blossom, freely breathes abroad
Its gratitude, and thanks him with its sweets.

Cowper gives us sight (golden peeping through foliage, flowers glittering through the winter), smell (jessamine/jasmine, oranges), texture (smooth, spiny, withered), temperature (warm and snug, wind howls outside), and even some implied sounds of the gardener at work clipping and sweeping. He describes the stages of plant care: care for soil, root, branch and leaf. He decorates the passage with interesting names of plants, like ficoides and jessamine, and places, like Portugal and India, the Azores and "Caffraria," an outdated name for South Africa. Proper names have an essential charm: geranium, orange, lime, myrtle...

He brings in other images, too: the plants are typically ranged in height, shortest to tallest, like an audience at a Shakespeare play (David Garrick was a famous actor). There's some light-hearted personification: the oranges and limes "seem to smile at what they need not fear." And the human reader/viewer is connected to the scene directly, since he is describing what may have been many ladies' favorite outing in winter, a trip to the conservatory (greenhouse) to see how the gardener's work was getting along and perhaps help trim leaves.

Descriptive passages like this often paired with didactic verse, usually theological and philosophical reflections about life. They described people and social situations as well as natural beauty or buildings. As the 19th century began, the Romantic view of nature created more interest in both natural descriptions and philosophical reflections about how the heart is elevated by nature. You've read some sonnets by Wordsworth, but his main poetic works were long descriptive poems such as "Lines composed a few miles above Tintern Abbey" (a famous ruin by the Wye River). Here's how he opens, with a rich description of English countryside:

> Five years have past; five summers, with the length
> Of five long winters! and again I hear
> These waters, rolling from their mountain-springs
> With a soft inland murmur. Once again
> Do I behold these steep and lofty cliffs,
> That on a wild secluded scene impress
> Thoughts of more deep seclusion; and connect
> The landscape with the quiet of the sky.
> The day is come when I again repose
> Here, under this dark sycamore, and view
> These plots of cottage ground, these orchard tufts,
> Which at this season, with their unripe fruits,
> Are clad in one green hue, and lose themselves
> 'Mid groves and copses. Once again I see
> These hedgerows, hardly hedgerows, little lines
> Of sportive wood run wild; these pastoral farms,
> Green to the very door; and wreaths of smoke
> Sent up, in silence, from among the trees!
> With some uncertain notice, as might seem
> Of vagrant dwellers in the houseless woods,
> Or of some Hermit's cave, where by his fire
> The Hermit sits alone.

Wordsworth gives us creeks, cliffs, cottage plots, orchards, groves of trees, hedges, and farms; he hints at three different shades of green (dark sycamore, orchard, farm weeds). He describes the motion of the eye going from one shape to another, following lines of hedges or smoke. He hints at his own human connection to the landscape and sketches other people who might be part of it, gypsies or hermits. The varied nouns create contrast, though here they are all homely English features, not exotic words like "Azores" or "jessamine." "Tintern Abbey" goes on for a mere 159 lines, which was very short by their standards. His masterpiece, the never-finished memoir titled *The Prelude*, was divided into fourteen books averaging 500 or 600 lines.

John Keats (then 22 years old) was one eager reader of Cowper's and Wordsworth's poetry. He set out to write a long descriptive story poem as his first work, but as he toiled at *Endymion*, friends sometimes asked him why he was not content with the sonnets and other short verse he had already mastered. Keats replied, "Do not the Lovers of Poetry like to have a little Region to wander in, in which the images are so numerous that many are forgotten and found in a second Reading, which may be food for a Week's stroll in the Summer? Do they not like this better than what they can read before Mrs. Williams comes down stairs? a Morning work at most. Besides, a long poem is a test of invention, which I take to be the Polar star of poetry, as Fancy is the Sails——and Imagination the rudder. Did our great Poets ever write short pieces?"[Oct. 18, 1817, letter to B. Bailey] *Endymion* was not a success, but ironically, only its first line (a short piece!) is still well known: "A thing of beauty is a joy for ever."

2. EKPHRASIS: WORD ART DESCRIBING VISUAL ART

There's a subset of descriptive verse that dates to before 500 BC. *Ekphrasis* means a verbal description of visual art. The classic example is Homer's long passage describing the miraculous artwork on the shield of Achilles in Book XVIII of the *Iliad*. Here's one short passage, translated and versified by Alexander Pope:

> Two cities radiant on the shield appear,
> The image one of peace, and one of war.
> Here sacred pomp and genial feast delight,
> And solemn dance, and hymeneal rite;
> Along the street the new-made brides are led,
> With torches flaming, to the nuptial bed:
> The youthful dancers in a circle bound
> To the soft flute, and cithern's silver sound:
> Through the fair streets the matrons in a row
> Stand in their porches, and enjoy the show.

Ekphrasis doesn't require the description to be word art itself, and often it isn't. But some famous poems are best seen as ways to present a visual image in words. Keats' "Ode on a Grecian Urn" is one such, and you will see it in the homework section. In the later 1800s, one standard theme for painting was a girl looking in a mirror, her face showing only in the mirror, her back to the viewer. Swinburne, an English poet, wrote a poem inspired by his friend Whistler's mirror painting, now called "Symphony in White, No. 2." Swinburne copied the poem onto gold paper and attached it to the painting's gold frame when it was exhibited in London, 1865.

In "Before the Mirror," Swinburne chose to describe the mood of the painting, with references to details but no direct description. Although there is no direct description, you could probably pick the correct painting out of a line-up of other mirror paintings, because it so well captures the mood and general impression. The poem has nine stanzas, in three parts; each part has a repeated rhyme common to its three stanzas, as you see here in the last part.

> Glad, but not flush'd with gladness,
> Since joys go by;
> Sad, but not bent with sadness,
> Since sorrows die;
> Deep in the gleaming glass
> She sees all past things pass,
> And all sweet life that was lie down and lie.
>
> There glowing ghosts of flowers
> Draw down, draw nigh;
> And wings of swift spent hours
> Take flight and fly;
> She sees by formless gleams,
> She hears across cold streams,
> Dead mouths of many dreams that sing and sigh.

Face fallen and white throat lifted,
With sleepless eye
She sees old loves that drifted,
She knew not why,
Old loves and faded fears
Float down a stream that hears
The flowing of all men's tears beneath the sky.

In the 20th century, both William Carlos Williams and W. H. Auden created ekphrastic poems for famous paintings. Williams' last published collection, *Pictures from Breughel*, came out in 1962, so it's still under copyright protection. The most famous is his description of Breughel's "The Kermess," also the poem's title. Williams decided to focus on implied sounds and motion:

...the
tweedle of bagpipes, a bugle and fiddles
tipping their bellies (round as the thick-
sided glasses whose wash they impound)
their hips and their bellies off balance
to turn them...

Auden wrote some ekphrastic poems during the World War, using the allusion to famous art to set up a philosophical point. In "The Shield of Achilles," he depicts the same scene that Homer did, in which Achilles' goddess mother sees the shield, but the smith has changed the images to dismal ones from the 1930s. Stanzas in trimeter remind us of the original Homeric scene,

She looked over his shoulder
    For vines and olive trees,
Marble well-governed cities
    And ships upon untamed seas...

But then stanzas of pentameter spell out the grimness of the new picture:

Barbed wire enclosed an arbitrary spot
Where bored officials lounged (one cracked a joke)
And sentries sweated for the day was hot...

Auden also wrote a poem to go with Breughel's "Landscape with the Fall of Icarus." In Greek mythology, Icarus and his father were escaping from the island of Crete by flying with wings made of feathers and wax. Icarus carelessly flew too close to the sun, the wax melted, and he fell into the sea. In the painting, the foreground is dominated by a medieval peasant plowing a field, while the background shows a green-tinted sea with ships and a more distant harbor town. Icarus appears only as a pair of legs splashing into the water.

The poem picks up the inherent message in the painting and makes it explicit: Icarus' death was barely noticed at the time, because we are all the center of our own worlds and we pay little attention to others. In "Musée des Beaux Arts," Auden notes that,

the ploughman may
Have heard the splash, the forsaken cry,
But for him it was not an important failure.

But he places the painting's message in a larger picture, saying:

About suffering they were never wrong,
The old Masters...
...how it takes place
While someone else is eating or opening a window
or just walking dully along...

Auden uses the painting's image and story, but he also ties it philosophically into this larger scene. An ekphrastic poem can dwell on the painting in a literal sense, or it can incorporate what the poet feels the art is suggesting into a larger idea or emotional impression he wants to convey.

3. Imagist description

The influence of Asian poetry radically altered the way English poems can present description. Imagism's goal was to present "things" in a way that either removed or exposed the narrator, with minimal or no storytelling. Ideally, the words would capture the essence of the things described, portrayed *just as they are*, close to a photograph. But as soon as you describe a thing in words, you have inserted yourself into the process, so the Imagists also wanted us to be conscious of how we, the human viewers (both describer and reader), connect to the images.

Here's how Ezra Pound summarized the goals (quoted in "A Retrospect," *Poetry* magazine, 1918) that he and his friends Hilda Doolittle and Richard Aldington set for their new method:

I. Direct treatment of the "thing," whether subjective or objective.
II. To use absolutely no word that does not contribute to the presentation.
III. As regarding rhythm: to compose in sequence of the musical phrase, not in sequence of the metronome.

The first rule, "direct treatment of the 'thing,'" would not permit Cowper's extended analogy between greenhouse plants arranged in order of height and a theater audience. There are too many lines taken up with name-dropping actors and making grand phrases about Shakespeare's "far-seeing eye." These lines really add little to the greenhouse description, though the simple analogy to a theater with raised seats in back might help. What about Swinburne's girl at the mirror? The first rule allows for description of something subjective, like the mood of a scene. But Swinburne, one of the poets the young Imagists most abhorred, piled up phrases like "wings of swift spent hours," which do not treat directly of the "thing."

The second rule might be applied to Pope's "shield of Achilles" passage to object to phrases like "the fair streets" or the "sacred pomp" and "solemn dance." What do the words "fair," "sacred," and "solemn" add to the description? The matrons standing in their porches contribute directly to the picture, and in the line where "the youthful dancers in a circle bound," each word contributes a new meaning. But what about "new-made brides"? Pound his friends would probably argue that "new-made" is redundant with "bride." Words like these should be struck out of the description.

To an Imagist, a poem formed a connection, a bridge, between human minds and "things." The human viewpoint could be explicit (a subjective "thing") or it might exist only in the fact that "things" don't write out their descriptions themselves. They were keenly interested in the way the "things" and the human connected. The connection might be implied in a direct, photographic treatment of an object, or it might be the subject of the poem: how objects make us feel.

William Carlos Williams left two poems (with the same title) that show how he experimented with making the word bridge as narrow as possible by cutting, cutting, and cutting more. By 1935, when this set of lines was published, the Imagists had been experimenting for twenty years and kept pushing the limits of the possible. We can imagine a group such as Pound and his friends looking at the first poem and questioning every word: is "the leaves" really necessary for a more direct treatment? And what does "wrist-thick" add to the presentation? Is it valuable enough to account for taking up space? The end result is the poem on the right, even more minimal than the first.

The Locust Tree in Flower	The Locust Tree in Flower
Among	Among
the leaves	of
bright	green
green	stiff
of wrist-thick	old
tree	bright
and old	broken
stiff broken	branch
branch	come
ferncool	white
swaying	sweet
loosely strung——	May
come May	again
again	
white blossoms	
clusters	
hide	
to spill	
their sweets	
almost	
unnoticed	
down	
and fall	
quickly	

How do you feel about the two "Locust" poems? At what point is an Imagist description too minimal to be an effective bridge between the locust tree in flower and your mind?

Some Imagist descriptions depict little glimpses of a story, while others give very specific details, a bit like traditional poetry. Williams wrote "Good Night" in 1916:

> In the brilliant gas light
> I turn on the kitchen spigot
> and watch the water plash
>
> into the clean white sink.
> On the grooved drain-board
> to one side is
> a glass filled with parsley—-
> crisped green...

Here, Williams' description would be enough for Wordsworth and Keats; but would they consider it "poetic"? How much distance is there between the diction in "Good Night" and in Cowper's greenhouse passage?

We can contrast the Imagist style with W. H. Auden's poem about Icarus, because Williams too wrote a series of poems about Breughel's paintings in the last years of his life. Where Auden connects this painting to general ideas about human life and the Old Masters, Williams keeps his description to the "thing" itself in "Landscape with the Fall of Icarus:"

> ...it was spring
>
> a farmer was ploughing
> his field
> the whole pageantry
>
> of the year was
> awake tingling
> near
>
> the edge of the sea...

His sense of message and attitude comes through in just a few subjective words, especially when he calls Icarus' death "a splash quite unnoticed." The two poems are different kinds of beauty, worth looking up to compare side by side while studying the painting by Breughel.

Summary and Definitions

Poetry is word art that uses the sound elements of language while providing an *image*.

Traditional descriptive poetry uses vivid details in a story-like way to please readers, drawing them into "a little Region to wander in." It uses color and shape, proper nouns, and implied sound and motion to recreate the visual scene.

One subset of description is ekphrastic poetry, which uses word art to describe visual art.

In the 20th century, the Imagist poets focused on description in a minimal, stripped-down manner, trying for "direct treatment of the 'thing.'"

Exercises 12

Review questions are about this shaped poem by George Herbert:

              A broken ALTAR, Lord, thy servant rears,
              Made of a heart and cemented with tears;
              Whose parts are as thy hand did frame;
              No workman's tool hath touch'd the same.
                    A HEART alone
                    Is such a stone,
                    As nothing but
                  Thy pow'r doth cut.
                Wherefore each part
                  Of my hard heart
                Meets in this frame
                  To praise thy name.
            That if I chance to hold my peace,
            These stones to praise thee may not cease.
            Oh, let thy blessed SACRIFICE be mine,
            And sanctify this ALTAR to be thine.

a) What is the rhyme scheme?

b) What kind of meter, and how many feet are in the lines of the central "pillar" of the altar? How many feet in the "top" and "base" of the altar?

c) The meter forces one of the words to be read in an unnatural way; what is that word?

d) What is another name for a shaped poem?

1. Select any photograph that means something to you; it can be a personal picture or one from the internet. (You may also choose a painting, of course.) If you were going to write a poem that describes it, what descriptive details would you choose? Use the outline below to think about descriptive detail; if something doesn't apply to the picture you have in hand, you can skip it.

    a) something brightly colored

    b) an implied sound

    c) the names of three plants or animals in the picture

    d) something in process (object falling, person moving, water running)

    e) a detail that shows the season of the year

    f) a detail that might identify the place and/or time of day

    g) a way that human beings can relate to the things in the picture

    h) two different things that have a similar shape or color

    i) something that isn't easy to spot

    j) two more details of your choice

2. William Wordsworth was born in the town of Cockermouth, Cumbria, in England. The Rivers Cocker and Derwent flow together at this town, and apparently Wordsworth's childhood home had the Derwent River at the back edge of its garden. Mount Skiddaw was one of the nearby peaks of the Northern Fells mountains. In his memoir, Wordsworth evoked his early childhood by describing the river and a child's experience of playing in it, in this passage in Book I of *The Prelude*.

   a) Counting: how many colors do you find here? How many different land features? How many proper nouns? What kinds of implied sounds and motion?

   b) Wordsworth makes an explicit connection here between Nature and the viewer. What does Nature do for mankind, as shown in this passage? What is the message of the analogy that closes this passage?

   c) How well does the passage evoke a clear description for you, such that you can imagine being there, seeing or feeling these things?

"Childhood and School-time"

...Was it for this
That one, the fairest of all rivers, loved   270
To blend his murmurs with my nurse's song,
And, from his alder shades and rocky falls,
And from his fords and shallows, sent a voice
That flowed along my dreams? For this, didst thou,
O Derwent! winding among grassy holms
Where I was looking on, a babe in arms,
Make ceaseless music that composed my thoughts
To more than infant softness, giving me
Amid the fretful dwellings of mankind
A foretaste, a dim earnest, of the calm   280
That Nature breathes among the hills and groves.

When he had left the mountains and received
On his smooth breast the shadow of those towers
That yet survive, a shattered monument
Of feudal sway, the bright blue river passed
Along the margin of our terrace walk;
A tempting playmate whom we dearly loved.
Oh, many a time have I, a five years' child,
In a small mill-race severed from his stream,
Made one long bathing of a summer's day;   290
Basked in the sun, and plunged and basked again
Alternate, all a summer's day, or scoured
The sandy fields, leaping through flowery groves
Of yellow ragwort; or, when rock and hill,
The woods, and distant Skiddaw's lofty height,

> Were bronzed with deepest radiance, stood alone
> Beneath the sky, as if I had been born
> On Indian plains, and from my mother's hut
> Had run abroad in wantonness, to sport
> A naked savage, in the thunder shower. 300

3. In these poems, four early Imagist poets trace the seasons: early spring, middle and late summer, autumn, winter. Their styles are a little bit different.

   a) In each poem, look for haiku-like clues about the setting: not just what season, but what time of day and in what sort of place? Note, too, the colors mentioned in each poem ("sepia" is a red-brown tone we see in antique photographs).

   b) In which poems do you find sound elements of verse, and what are they?

   c) In which poems do you find human emotional attributes given to non-human objects? How does this attribution form a connection between humans and things? In which poems do you find the purest description of things without any human attributes?

   d) How do the four poets handle line breaks? Are they looking for complete thoughts, dramatic presentation, or something more arbitrary? Choose one to try re-organizing; how does it alter the poem, and which version do you like better?

   e) Which poems give you the clearest mental picture? Which ones connect with your emotions best? Choose two and write five or six paragraphs about what you see and feel.

Spring Storm

> The sky has given over
> its bitterness.
> Out of the dark change
> all day long
> rain falls and falls
> as if it would never end.
> Still the snow keeps
> its hold on the ground.
> But water, water is seething
> from a thousand runnels.
> It collects swiftly,
> dappled with black
> cuts a way for itself
> through green ice in the gutters.
> Drop after drop it falls
> from the withered grass stems

William Carlos Williams, 1883-1963

IMAGE IN DESCRIPTION

SUMMER

A butterfly,
Black and scarlet,
Spotted with white
Fans its wings
Over a privet flower.

A thousand crimson foxgloves,
Tall bloody pikes,
Stand motionless in the gravel quarry;
The wind runs over them.

A rose film over a pale sky
Fantastically cut by dark chimneys
Candles winking in the windows
Across an old city-garden.

Richard Aldington, 1892-1962

NEW ENGLAND LANDSCAPE

On a sepia ground
Shot with orange light
The pines
In blue-black lines;
And birches, slender,
Diagonal, and white,
Stencil compact designs.
The inevitable wall,
As it leaves the woods,
Breaks to a sprawl
Of separate stones,
Echoing the tones
Of sepia and orange
With high-lights
Of chrome and red,
Until they find a bed
In the splotched lilac
Of the meadow,
Or chill to blue in shadow.
In the valley's cupped palm
Lies a handful of ripening grain.
And, riding the high blue calm,
Over Monadnock

A decorous cloud
Is slowly unwinding its skein.

DuBose Heyward, 1885-1940

Autumn

A touch of cold in the Autumn night—-
I walked abroad,
And saw the ruddy moon lean over a hedge
Like a red-faced farmer.
I did not stop to speak, but nodded
And round about were the wistful stars
With white faces like town children.

T. E. Hulme, 1883-1917

Blizzard

Snow:
years of anger following
hours that float idly down—-
the blizzard
drifts its weight
deeper and deeper for three days
or sixty years, eh? Then
the sun! a clutter of
yellow and blue flakes—-
Hairy looking trees stand out
in long alleys
over a wild solitude.
The man turns and there—-
his solitary track stretched out
upon the world.

William Carlos Williams, 1883-1963

4. Samuel Taylor Coleridge wrote one of his most famous poems to capture a dream he had after reading about Emperor Kubla Khan's summer palace: "In Xandu did Cublai Can build a stately Pallace, encompassing sixteen miles of plaine ground with a wall, wherein are fertile Meddowes, pleasant Springs, delightfull streames, and all sorts of beasts of chase and game, and in the middest thereof a sumptuous house of pleasure, which may be moved from place to place." — Samuel Purchas (1614) paraphrasing Marco Polo (1299). "Xanadu" was later called Shangdu, the summer palace; it was closer to Kubla Khan's homeland of Mongolia than his official capital (modern Beijing). The "house of pleasure" that could be "moved from place to place" was probably a tent with bamboo poles, engineered to fold up for travel, but Marco Polo reported that it was of enormous size.

Coleridge wrote these lines in 1797, although he did not publish them until 1816, after Lord Byron begged him to do so. Coleridge intended the poem to be much longer, so he always called it a fragment.

a) What is the course of the Alph River; is its geography realistic? What descriptive details does the poet offer?

b) In the second part, Coleridge devotes descriptive energy to a dream-like place and figure, the "pleasure dome" and the Abyssinian maid. Is his description more objective or subjective? What is he mainly describing?

c) Observe the irregular way Coleridge uses meter and rhyme; try to mark the rhyme scheme. What patterns can you observe? Where he changes his use of meter, how does it alter the feeling of the verse? Which feels more like song, and why?

d) These lines are often considered among the most beautiful in English verse. What sound elements do you see at work in this art?

Kubla Khan

Or a Vision in a Dream. A Fragment.

In Xanadu did Kubla Khan
A stately pleasure dome decree:
Where Alph, the sacred river, ran
Through caverns measureless to man
    Down to a sunless sea.
So twice five miles of fertile ground
With walls and towers were girdled round:
And there were gardens bright with sinuous rills,
Where blossomed many an incense-bearing tree;
And here were forests ancient as the hills,
Enfolding sunny spots of greenery.

But oh! that deep romantic chasm which slanted
Down the green hill athwart a cedarn cover!
A savage place! as holy and enchanted
As e'er beneath a waning moon was haunted
By woman wailing for her demon lover!

And from this chasm, with ceaseless turmoil seething,
As if this earth in fast thick pants were breathing,
A mighty fountain momently was forced:
Amid whose swift half-intermitted burst
Huge fragments vaulted like rebounding hail,
Or chaffy grain beneath the thresher's flail:
And 'mid these dancing rocks at once and ever
It flung up momently the sacred river.
Five miles meandering with a mazy motion
Through wood and dale the sacred river ran,
Then reached the caverns measureless to man,
And sank in tumult to a lifeless ocean:
And 'mid this tumult Kubla heard from far
Ancestral voices prophesying war!

    The shadow of the dome of pleasure
    Floated midway on the waves;
    Where was heard the mingled measure
    From the fountain and the caves.
It was a miracle of rare device,
A sunny pleasure dome with caves of ice!

    A damsel with a dulcimer
    In a vision once I saw:
    It was an Abyssinian maid,
    And on her dulcimer she played,
    Singing of Mount Abora.
    Could I revive within me
    Her symphony and song,
    To such a deep delight 'twould win me,
That with music loud and long,
I would build that dome in air,
That sunny dome! those caves of ice!
And all who heard should see them there,
And all should cry, Beware! Beware!
His flashing eyes, his floating hair!
Weave a circle round him thrice,
And close your eyes with holy dread,
For he on honey-dew hath fed,
And drunk the milk of Paradise.

    Samuel Taylor Coleridge, 1772- 1834

5. John Keats' famous "Ode to a Grecian Urn" was published in 1820; an *ode* is a lyrical poem that addresses a person or thing, as here he is speaking to the urn. During the preceding years, the Earl of Elgin had been importing large amounts of Greek antiquities to the British Museum. Before that time, Englishmen had to travel to Greece to see its marble and pottery ruins, so relatively poor men like Keats would have seen only travelers' sketches. Keats viewed the exhibit in London, sketched some of the artifacts, and wrote this richly-descriptive poem.

   If you are a student, this poem would be a good theme to practice writing an essay, perhaps using the questions below as prompts or ideas.

   a) What are the Ode's metrical plan and rhyme scheme? What other sound elements do you see Keats using? How would you describe Keats' tone?

   b) What scenes were on the urn, based on Keats' descriptions?

   c) In this poem, why is art immortal?

   d) What do you think of his last lines? We usually see them quoted out of context, but the poem's context suggests Keats imagines they are what the urn is saying. Does Keats agree with the urn? Do you?

ODE ON A GRECIAN URN

Thou still unravished bride of quietness,
    Thou foster-child of silence and slow time,
Sylvan historian, who canst thus express
    A flowery tale more sweetly than our rhyme:
What leaf-fringed legend haunts about thy shape
    Of deities or mortals, or of both,
        In Tempe or the dales of Arcady?
    What men or gods are these? What maidens loth?
What mad pursuit? What struggle to escape?
    What pipes and timbrels? What wild ecstasy?

Heard melodies are sweet, but those unheard
    Are sweeter; therefore, ye soft pipes, play on;
Not to the sensual ear, but, more endeared,
    Pipe to the spirit ditties of no tone:
Fair youth, beneath the trees, thou canst not leave
    Thy song, nor ever can those trees be bare;
        Bold Lover, never, never canst thou kiss,
Though winning near the goal—yet, do not grieve;
She cannot fade, though thou hast not thy bliss,
    For ever wilt thou love, and she be fair!

Ah, happy, happy boughs! that cannot shed
    Your leaves, nor ever bid the Spring adieu;
And, happy melodist, unwearièd,
    For ever piping songs for ever new;

By John Keats.

More happy love! more happy, happy love!
    For ever warm and still to be enjoyed,
        For ever panting, and for ever young;
All breathing human passion far above,
    That leaves a heart high-sorrowful and cloyed,
        A burning forehead, and a parching tongue.
Who are these coming to the sacrifice?
    To what green altar, O mysterious priest,
Lead'st thou that heifer lowing at the skies,
    And all her silken flanks with garlands drest?
What little town by river or sea shore,
    Or mountain-built with peaceful citadel,
        Is emptied of this folk, this pious morn?
And, little town, thy streets for evermore
    Will silent be; and not a soul to tell
        Why thou art desolate, can e'er return.

O Attic shape! Fair attitude! with brede
    Of marble men and maidens overwrought,
With forest branches and the trodden weed;
    Thou, silent form, dost tease us out of thought
As doth eternity: Cold Pastoral!
    When old age shall this generation waste,
        Thou shalt remain, in midst of other woe
Than ours, a friend to man, to whom thou say'st,
    "Beauty is truth, truth beauty,"—that is all
        Ye know on earth, and all ye need to know.

John Keats, 1795-1821

6. For further reading, try any of the long poems cited in this lesson:

   The Iliad, translation and versification by Alexander Pope

   The Task, by William Cowper

   The Prelude, by William Wordsworth

   Hyperion, by John Keats (because Keats abandoned his epic, it's relatively short)

   Look also for the ekphrastic poems of W. H. Auden and William Carlos Williams; if you are interested in the intersection of art and poetry, try to find some of the "double works" by Dante Gabriel Rossetti, in which he paired a sketch or a painting with a poem. You can also find some very interesting contemporary ekphrastic poems at www.poetryfoundation.org.

Thirteen:
Image as Analogy

One of the key differences between poems and essays is that poems are free to use analogies in an artistic way. A poem and an editorial could present the same idea about society, but in an essay or editorial, we expect an attempt to persuade us with logic and facts. In a poem, we expect to see images described so that we can *see* the similarities in the mind's eye.

Analogies are usually very persuasive even when they are factually quite wrong. We may know a lot about one thing and less about the other, so as soon as someone tells us to use what we know about A to understand B, we're on it. When the analogy seems to have *many* parallels, it can be so persuasive that we don't even realize we've been persuaded. But what if A and B are only alike in trivial details, and the analogy is misleading about other points? When in doubt, we usually believe the analogy because the *image* is compelling.

In an editorial, this can be a very dishonest way of persuading readers, but in poetry, it's fair because poetry is art. It may present ideas, like "this is what love means" or "this is how you should feel about death," but its main purpose is to be artistic. If a poem seems to be saying something you don't agree with, it's still art, just as a portrait of a person you dislike is still a painting. If you don't even understand what the analogy is saying but it's still beautiful, it's definitely art. We don't need to agree that "Beauty is truth" or understand why "a man and a woman and a blackbird are one" to appreciate the artistry of the images.

So poetic analogies don't need to be entirely factual or even *helpful*, but the poet must have some artistic purpose in mind. It might be to explain his idea; poets are usually trying to be helpful even if it doesn't seem like it. But especially in modern poetry, the analogy may be intended just to give you a feeling, or even to force you to think of two dissimilar images at the same time. A poet's analogy may be deliberately *unhelpful*, misleading you with a comparison you can't figure out. Maybe the poet felt it was the best way to commemorate this particular moment, feeling, or insight.

When poets show us a likeness to bring in new meaning, it's in the form of a simile, a metaphor, or a symbol. The differences between these forms are not as clear as it might seem; I'll draw clear distinctions, but in application they may not be simple, and there may be readers who don't think my definitions are the best. Usually, books explain that similes use "like" or "as," while metaphors say "is." I'm going to approach them differently, and then I'll tackle symbols in the next lesson. If you disagree with my approach, try to form your own thoughts into clear words: how do you see them?

1. Simile: Keeping the images separate

By using the comparison words "like" and "as," the *simile* makes it very clear to us which object is the main one we're talking about, and which one is the comparison image. In terms of basic grammar, the thing that comes after the comparison word cannot be the main object. This doesn't sound like a big deal, but when analogies are used in poetry, sometimes it is difficult to know which object or image the poem is "about." Poets adore ambiguity, and metaphor and symbol allow them more room for confusion and blurring lines. Similes, however, force them to be at least somewhat clear.

When we read "Like a thunderbolt, he falls," it's clear that the eagle (not the thunderbolt) is the main subject; the thunderbolt is just the comparison image. We see also that the comparison is limited to the way that lightning and the eagle both drop downward very rapidly. There's no need to explain, because understanding analogies appears to be a built-in function of the brain, so most people understand what the two things have in common. When a simile is unclear or unhelpful, it's probably because the comparison image isn't familiar enough to make the similarity spring to mind.

Any explicit comparison counts as a simile, even if it does not say "like" or "as." Shakespeare's sonnet begins, "Shall I compare thee to a summer's day?" He continues to compare these two things, the traits of a summer day and the traits of the beloved. Summer weather can be extreme, and the season ends; the poet denies that these traits are true of the beloved. It's a very direct comparison that keeps the two compared objects clear and separate, using terms like "more than" rather than the classic like/as.

Similes can be simple or extended. In the simple, direct sort, we use our knowledge of the comparison image to fill in the details. "Impatient as the wind" makes us quickly call up the aspects of wind that can be like impatience; the wind doesn't wait, and it knocks things over. Emily Dickinson told us that the butterfly steps out of its cocoon "as a lady from her door." This may not be scientifically accurate, but it shows us the attitude she wants us to have toward the butterfly. In Dickinson's time, ladies learned posture and style for simple things like stepping out of a door, immediately accessible to readers of her time (though now we must lean on historical dramas to recreate that image).

George Herbert invoked three similes in a row to demonstrate how his life should be: free, loose, and large. Free as the road, which may go on for miles without end or wall. Loose as the wind, which also has no walls and may blow anywhere. Large as a storehouse that might keep a year's wine, flour and salt. With each ideal of freedom, the poet borrows images that he wishes could apply to his life.

Similes in love poems are often used to compare beauty or goodness to idealized images like the sun or pearls. Shakespeare turned this expectation on its head in Sonnet CXXX by listing many negative similes: not like a goddess, not like the snow, not like the sun.

Poets sometimes extend the simile to elaborate on the aspect of the comparison they want you to focus on. Shelley's "Mutability" makes several similes that carefully explain what he wants us to think about human nature:

> We are as clouds that veil the midnight moon;
> How restlessly they speed, and gleam, and quiver,
> Streaking the darkness radiantly!—yet soon
> Night closes round, and they are lost for ever:
>
> Or like forgotten lyres, whose dissonant strings
> Give various response to each varying blast,
> To whose frail frame no second motion brings
> One mood or modulation like the last.

In each case, the poet tells us enough that we can imagine the sight or sound the way he wants us to. This is helpful if we don't happen to be as familiar with midnight clouds or forgotten lyres as he is, or perhaps if our idea of them is different. The extended simile also carries the weight of the poem, taking a simple idea (that we are changeable) and making something beautiful by describing these other images. An extended simile like this could become the whole poem.

We saw an extended simile also in the Imagist poem about autumn:

> A touch of cold in the Autumn night—-
> I walked abroad,
> And saw the ruddy moon lean over a hedge
> Like a red-faced farmer.
> I did not stop to speak, but nodded
> And round about were the wistful stars
> With white faces like town children.

The poet is walking in the country outside London, and he sees the full moon rising. Because it is near the horizon, it appears larger than usual and its color is reddish. He envisions the moon as a sunburnt countryman, and this suggests another image for the stars: children in town who don't get sunburnt because they have to go to school. It's a complete picture, and the "wistful" stars suggest an emotion borrowed from the children. They're looking on, not allowed to become ruddy like the moon. The extended simile fills in the poet's attitudes and feelings.

When the purpose of speech is clear communication, the best simile is familiar and direct: "like a lightning bolt." Poets, of course, may have other things in mind than simplicity and clear communication. Some similes are simple in grammar but do not give us easy or expected images to compare. Emily Dickinson's "If You Were Coming in the Fall" has several similes that are emotionally suggestive but not quite clarifying. The last particularly stands out:

> It goads me, like the goblin bee,
> That will not state its sting.

If you search for "goblin bee," it does not turn out to be some species like fire ant or carpenter wasp. It seems to be just the poet's evocative way of naming a bee that flies where you can't see it, so that you never know if you're about to be hurt. The point of the simile is not some property of a real bee, but the unreal property of an imaginary one.

In Eliot's poem "La Figlia Chè Piange," he says that he wants to pose the weeping girl in a gesture that is "simple and faithless as a smile or a shake of the hand." I pause when I read this, because "faithless" isn't the trait of a smile (or handshake) that I think of first. In daily speech, a smile is associated with happiness, sunshine, welcome, and things like that. But Eliot is directing our attention to a particular kind of smile, the faithless one. This smile or handshake can distract us from picking up clues that we're being deceived. His analogy redirects my attention to the falseness of the girl's emotion: she is posing, like a faithless smile. The simile does tell me something, but I have to pay attention to detail and be open to less obvious ideas.

In the same poem, Eliot says that some man left this weeping girl behind,

> As the soul leaves the body torn and bruised,
> As the mind leaves the body it has used.

Again, the simile startles me. First, the girl is compared to a dead body; and second, the simile suggests that the mind or soul should be held responsible for bodily damage, like a careless driver. Really? Instead of being familiar and clear, the comparisons raise more questions about how men and women, and souls and bodies, relate. Why would a poet deliberately muddy his images? (Simple answer: because it supports his artistic purpose, which gives us even more to ponder, this time about art.)

Wallace Stevens makes an extended comparison in "The Wind Shifts," but none of his five similes is very helpful. Taken by themselves, the comparisons tell us little about how the wind shifts, because each one is more complicated than the wind. The wind shifts:

1. Like the thoughts of an old human,
   Who still thinks eagerly
   And despairingly.

2. Like a human without illusions,
   Who still feels irrational things within her.

3. Like humans approaching proudly,

4. Like humans approaching angrily.

5. Like a human, heavy and heavy,
   Who does not care.

The first two similes are especially complicated. Both of them describe people with contradictory impulses: "eagerly and despairingly," and "without illusions" but still "irrational." I don't picture either of these clearly. The last three images are clearer, but they are contradictory among themselves: approaching or sitting still ("heavy and heavy")? How can these similes tell me anything about the wind?

The simile ("the wind shifts like a human") clearly states that we're primarily talking about the wind and only using humans for comparison, to illustrate the wind. However, the poem makes more sense if we turn the words around and see the *wind* as the comparison image for all of these types of people. They are hard to understand; their motives and feelings clash and change direction, like the wind. Sometimes their emotions blow steadily in an angry or proud direction, and other times, humans knock things down, the way the wind does, when they fail to care.

When I understand it that way and then go back to the poem, I like the way Stevens presented it. I picture the poet walking to work in Connecticut, perhaps caught by wind coming in off the Atlantic Ocean as it clashes with wind moving east across the continent. It reminds him of contradictions in human nature, and he decides to write similes that turn the comparisons around. This is how the wind shifts: like a poet using a simile backwards.

2. Metaphor: blurring the boundaries

Metaphors are also a kind of analogical comparison. They can be clear and simple, but they avoid using plain-spoken comparison language. They don't say "this is *like* that;" instead, they confuse the two things in some way. It may be as direct as saying "this is that," or it may be indirect, talking about one with language that implies the other. Metaphors are all about blurring the boundaries between the things they compare.

Shakespeare could have written, "My old age is like the autumn," but instead, he wrote, "That time of year thou mayst in me behold, /when yellow leaves, or none, or few, do hang /upon the trees..." The comparison idea is simple and clear: the end of life is like the end of a year. But it's phrased as though "time of year" is something that can be observed directly in a human being, the way seasons are observed. Similarly, he goes on to say that we see in him "the twilight of such day," and "the glowing of such fire" as both are about to end. All three are clear, direct comparisons but framed as metaphors, not similes.

Metaphor means something like "what has been transferred." The traits and truths of one thing are transferred to another thing: yellow leaves of autumn are transferred to human old age. It's a way of saying that they are alike, while taking a bit more risk: "I don't have to tell you they are alike, I'll just act like they're identical and you'll figure it out."

We can usually translate metaphors into similes, with a little thought. Matthew Arnold spoke in metaphor when he said, in "Dover Beach," that the "Sea of Faith" is retreating. "Sea of Faith" is, in a sense, shorthand for "the church is *like* the ocean because it was all over the world." The metaphorical name "Sea of Faith" allows him to speak about Christianity by borrowing the ocean's trait of rising and falling tides. G. M. Hopkins' sonnet about depression, "No Worst, There is None," spoke metaphorically about the mind: it has "mountains" and "cliffs." In literal terms, this is a comparison: traits of the mind are *like* cliffs, in that they produce severely painful feelings that are hard to recover from, like injuries from falling off a cliff. The kind of fear he's talking about is as scary as hanging over the edge of a cliff, or as hard to climb as a mountain. But he doesn't tell us so directly.

Emily Dickinson made an extended metaphor in "Hope is the Thing with Feathers." Put simply, hope is like a bird. But by using the phrase "a thing with feathers" for "bird," she could transfer it to hope: hope is a *thing*, but instead of literal "feathers," the thing of hope has emotional "feathers" that allow it to rise up unintentionally. The poem talks about hope entirely with words appropriate for birds: it sings, eats, and travels to distant places. At the same time, the poem makes it clear that none of this is meant literally, since the "thing with feathers" perches "in the soul." It's up to the reader to understand which truths about hope are parallel to the image of giving crumbs to a bird.

How is metaphor different from simile? That is, how does it change the effect when we disregard comparison language and just blur the separate identities of the things? By insisting on confusing the identities of the two things, a metaphor opens up the possibility that they are alike in many other ways. Context doesn't restrain it as much as in a simile, where it's usually clear that just one aspect of the comparison is relevant (the eagle falls like a thunderbolt, but it does not start fires).

Metaphor is also more dramatic, more insistent. It makes the same point as a simile, but it's emotionally stronger. The overt comparing language of a simile admits that the things are merely *alike*, while the metaphor refuses to make that admission. Along with opening up the comparison, this forces the reader to consider emotional associations that may accompany the image in the metaphor.

Metaphor also opens up a new range of words. Poets are often searching for an unusual or dramatic verb, or perhaps for a word that fits a metrical or rhyme scheme. By employing her extended metaphor, Emily Dickinson could use bird-related words, instead of just the usual set we use about emotion or ideas. The entire vocabulary gets transferred to the new object, as needed. The poet can mix the two vocabularies, even switching images, because he has blurred them into one combination image.

George Herbert used metaphor briefly in his lines, "Forsake thy cage, thy rope of sands, which petty thoughts have made…" When he says that "petty thoughts" have made the "cage" and "rope," it's clear that the cage and rope are just ideas. But although he calls the rules that restrict his life "cage" and "rope" just in passing, he can go on using the vocabulary of ropes by calling them "good cable" that can drag him around. However, since he is blurring the separation of life restrictions and ropes via metaphor, he can switch right back to words more appropriate to restrictions. He doesn't have to be consistent.

Metaphor also engages the imagination by confusing the two images. I wrote a poem using an extended metaphor that could be expressed as a simile: "words are like rain." Words are like rain because there are many of them, and they may come in bursts or drizzles. They may be overwhelming; people may feel that as listeners, they are being showered with words too heavily. However, words are not like rain in many ways: they are not made of H_2O, they are not wet. When we talk, nothing gets muddy. But it's much more fun to imagine that words might really fall down into puddles or drip off the roof.

In my poem, I wanted to convey an emotion about words, so I borrowed how we feel about rain. I talked about reading old emails by using the vocabulary of rain and clouds, transferring their literal meanings to the new subject. In the third stanza, I introduced the rain with a simile, but even there, the simile was already just part of a metaphor. Instead of saying, "I piled words on words *like* cumulus clouds," I called them "cumulus speeches," and off goes the metaphor of words = rain. The clouds grow thicker and darker, then it begins to rain, first a patter, then a drenching shower:

Gratitude

I open an old file to search a word
Lost, like the farmer's needle, in a stack
Of conversations, to be read not heard,
To play back.

Our notes are like ourselves: yours are terse,
Informative, and bright. Scheherazade,
I filled the nights, but played back, mine seem worse
And sometimes odd.

I piled the words on words like cumulus
Speeches, cottony heaps of metaphor:
True histories, fantastic tales of us,
More and more.

The past grows wet as syllables like rain
Fall on the grass, an alphabetic patter
Of fears and feelings, notions, sighs and plain
Daily chatter.

I wander in the downpour that I wrote.
The flood and fog of talk obscure the view
Of when and why my weather rained each note
On you.

But dear, you read with drier eyes and used
My rain in season. Where I only see
A hopeless mud, failed, sopping and confused,
You saw me.

By confusing the objects I'm comparing, blurring the boundaries until it's hard to tell which one I'm talking about, I can convey the sincerity of emotion better. In literal terms, as I read back over past emails, I felt ashamed of how many words I had used. But if I wrote it with a simile, "I was ashamed of my words, as if they were mud," it would only convey the idea. With metaphor, I draw the reader's mind into the experience of word-rain, borrowing human feelings about downpour, flood, fog, and mud. While applying rain words to ideas, I apply idea words to the rain. Mud can't really be "failed" or "confused," but words and feelings can. Words can't really be muddy or "sopping," but when they're depicted that way, you can feel my sense of defeat.

Metaphor provides opportunities to be dramatic or make strong statements without displays of overt emotion that might embarrass both writer and reader. Here's another personal example. One of my children experienced a lot of illness at a young age; it was very frightening to realize that these years were supposed to be his springtime, his time of strength and joy, but instead the years were largely spent on survival and sorrow. If I wrote about how I felt then, I would have to reach for strong emotional words, adding "very, very" and "really, really" to them all. Talking out loud, I might start to wave my hands in the air or raise my voice and walk around. All this may be acceptable in a conversation with a close friend, but it's uncomfortable and disturbing in writing; it sounds hysterical and the reader wants to back away.

Instead, I could write by creating a metaphor of seasons, as Shakespeare did. In my metaphor, the year was scaled to childhood: spring is like the baby and preschool years; summer is like the elementary school years; fall is adolescence; here, winter is just adulthood, the end of childhood, rather than the end of life. I can tell you how scary and difficult the illness was by describing seasons that have the wrong weather, and I can describe both the seasons and the weather in strong, colorful ways — without sounding hysterical.

I titled the poem "Amicus Curiae," which means "a friend of the court." It's the name of a legal document filed as an addition to a case that isn't your own. It was a way to express my sense of helplessness as the mother who stood outside the illness; it was really between my child and God, but perhaps I, a friend and stakeholder, could register this complaint. Each stanza of complaint should be read as almost a haiku that hints at the season (therefore at the child's age) by mentioning colorful details.

Amicus Curiae
(on behalf of a sick child)

In the days of pale yellow green
at dawn's first rays
I saw fingers of lightning.

In a time of robin's grass and
white violets under bees
I heard a low sick moan of thunder.

In the night of a dragonfly moon
and singing in the wetlands
I felt the gale force rise and howl.

As all heaven rushed by in streams
of white on blue
I felt dark clouds press heavily.

> In apple days, in times when all
> grew red and green
> I saw hail bend trees into bones.
>
> In days that honked and flew
> beyond any shadowed hills
> I heard a lowering vacant silence.
>
> O God, such unseasonable weather!
> What will I see when days are white and cold?

In each seasonal stanza, the last line states how the weather was wrong: violent storms when spring should be gently nurturing the bees and frogs, hail when the trees should be loaded with apples, and ominous silence when the sky should be filled with migrating geese (days that "honked and flew"). The last line makes the complaint direct, addressing God, and it closes with one line of deliberate iambic pentameter. To me, iambic pentameter is the sound of rational thought; it means that somehow the world will make sense. The last line asks: so will things be okay, and will all this someday make sense? It felt right to ask the question in a metered line.

There's simply no way I could write about such an intense experience without using metaphor. I've tried; but I notice that I'm repeating myself, over-acting, and using imprecise words. When I cast it into a metaphor that allowed me to write about "robin grass" and the "dragonfly moon," and only indirectly about the emotion, it became the only way I could express feelings without censoring myself. It created *art* to commemorate an important feeling with truth, but without hysteria.

Successful metaphor may reach beyond observable likeness and tap into spiritual images we seem to carry in our hearts and minds. That's important for both the poet and the reader. Reaching for something well outside himself allows the poet to be both inside and outside of the experience he's trying to capture. For the reader, the poem may only touch his feelings as it resonates with these deeper images. We'll talk about this more when considering image as symbol and myth.

For all these reasons, metaphor is the universal language of poetry. There are great poems without metaphor, and there are other ways to use images. But over and over, you find metaphor stepping in to carry the burden of indirect expression of emotion.

Summary and Definitions

Images can be used in analogies, showing how much alike two things are. In *simile*, two objects or images are compared directly, often with "like" and "as." In *metaphor*, the traits and truths of one object or image are transferred to the other without using comparison terms. Simile keeps the two compared objects apart, while metaphor blurs their boundaries.

Both simile and metaphor can be simple or *extended*, in which the poet sketches more of the image to spell out aspects of the comparison.

IMAGE AS ANALOGY

Exercises 13

Review:
Compare these two sestets; the first is from Coleridge's "Kubla Khan", the second is from Eliot's "The Love Song of J. Alfred Prufrock."

> The shadow of the dome of pleasure
> Floated midway on the waves;
> Where was heard the mingled measure
> From the fountain and the caves.
> It was a miracle of rare device,
> A sunny pleasure dome with caves of ice!

> For I have known them all already, known them all:
> Have known the evenings, mornings, afternoons,
> I have measured out my life with coffee spoons;
> I know the voices dying with a dying fall
> Beneath the music from a farther room.
> So how should I presume?

a) From each poem, choose a set of lines that forms a couplet of iambic pentameter.

b) It's possible for a longer metrical line (more feet) to use fewer letters than a shorter metrical line. In each poem, find a set of lines for which this is true.

c) Which rhyme scheme does neither sestet use? ABBACC, ABCABC, ABABCC

1. Translating between simile and metaphor: Turn metaphors into similes by separating the compared things, and similes into metaphors by blurring the boundaries. In each of four metaphors and four similes, the first one is done for you as an example.

    a) "...I'd wind the months in balls, /and put them each in separate drawers..."

    The language of *yarn balls in drawers* is applied to *the passage of a year*.

    A simile would compare *how I store yarn* and *how I perceive the year*.

    Simile in my words: *I put the months in order in my mind, as if they were balls of yarn put away in little drawers.*

    b) "the Sea of Faith was once, too, at its full /and round earth's shore /Lay like the folds of a bright girdle furled. /But now I only hear /Its melancholy, long, withdrawing roar..."

    The language of _____ is applied to _____.

    A simile would compare _____ and _____.

    Simile in my words: _____.

c) "Hope is the thing with feathers /That perches in the soul… /Yet, never, in extremity /it asked a crumb of me."

   The language of _____ is applied to _____.

   A simile would compare _____ and _____.

   Simile in my words: _____.

d) "I was angry with my foe: /I told it not, my wrath did grow. /And I watered it in fears, /Night and morning with my tears… /And it grew both day and night, /Till it bore an apple bright…"

   The language of _____ is applied to _____.

   A simile would compare _____ and _____.

   Simile in my words: _____.

e) "I'd brush the summer by… /as housewives do a fly."

   The simile compares *brushing away a fly* and *perceiving time passing in a summer* .

   A metaphor would apply the language of *waving at flies* to *perceiving summer*.

   Metaphor in my words: *the summer buzzed around my head but I shooed it away.*

f) "If we must die, let it not be like hogs /Hunted and penned in an inglorious spot…"

   The simile compares _____ and _____.

   A metaphor would apply the language of _____ to _____.

   Metaphor in my words: _____.

g) "How like a winter hath thine absence been!"

   The simile compares _____ and _____.

   A metaphor would apply the language of _____ to _____.

   Metaphor in my words: _____.

h) "This City now doth, like a garment, wear /the beauty of the morning…"

   The simile compares _____ and _____.

   A metaphor would apply the language of _____ to _____.

   Metaphor in my words: _____.

i) Bonus: "Forsake thy cage, thy rope of sands which petty thoughts have made…"

   Can you recast this as either simile or metaphor in your own words?

2. John Keats was apprenticed to a doctor at a young age, so he missed out on the classical education wealthier boys received. At 21, he stopped working as a medic and began making up for lost time in literature, but he was not able to read Greek. When Keats began reading the Shakespeare-era translation of *The Iliad* by George Chapman, he was delighted enough to commemorate how he felt with a poem.

    a) In this sonnet, Keats uses both metaphor and simile. Notice where he turns from one to the other; it is right where the octave ends and the sestet begins. In the metaphor, what two things does he compare? What are "realms," "states," and "islands"? How are they ruled? Does this metaphor communicate its meaning to you clearly?

    b) There are two similes. To what two other kinds of people does Keats compare himself?

    c) It's worth noting that his facts about the discovery of the Pacific Ocean were off; it was Balboa, not Cortez, who glimpsed the other ocean while in the new Spanish province of "Darien," that is, modern Panama. Keats extends this simile into a little dramatic story: what is their wild surmise? Why are they silent? What does this tell us about Keats' feeling?

    d) Notice that the last line's first foot is a trochee, not an iamb. How does this change the feeling of the line?

On First Looking Into Chapman's Homer

Much have I travelled in the realms of gold,
    And many goodly states and kingdoms seen;
    Round many western islands have I been
Which bards in fealty to Apollo hold.
Oft of one wide expanse had I been told
    That deep-browed Homer ruled as his demesne;
    Yet did I never breathe its pure serene
Till I heard Chapman speak out loud and bold:
Then felt I like some watcher of the skies
    When a new planet swims into his ken;
Or like stout Cortez when with eagle eyes
    He stared at the Pacific—and all his men
Looked at each other with a wild surmise—
    Silent, upon a peak in Darien.

John Keats, 1795-1821

3. "Fire and Ice" appears to be about the end of the world, but Frost is using the idea metaphorically to talk about human emotions. He has completely blurred the boundaries of these ideas, so that he speaks of emotions in terms of apocalyptic disasters, and those disasters in terms of emotion.

    a) What are fire and ice? What might "the end of the world" mean in emotional terms?

    b) Note the rhyme scheme and meter. Frost's use of these sound elements combines with the compelling metaphor to make this poem one of the easiest to memorize. He varied the four-foot lines with three short lines of dimeter. How do these change the feeling of the poem?

Fire and Ice

Some say the world will end in fire,
Some say in ice.
From what I've tasted of desire
I hold with those who favor fire.
But if it had to perish twice,
I think I know enough of hate
To say that for destruction ice
Is also great
And would suffice.

Robert Frost, 1874-1963

4. John Donne's poetry was noted for inventive and even disturbing metaphors. His poetry falls roughly into three categories: early poems that plead with various unnamed girls to like him, midlife poems about his passionately happy marriage to Anne More, and late-life poems to or about God. "Valediction" means saying good-bye; Donne wrote more than one poem on the theme of parting. In this one, he must go on a journey away from Anne, and we should remember that journeys were always dangerous in early centuries, without any way to call home. Leaving England meant getting onto a ship, which was doubly dangerous. Ships often sank just in the short passage to France.

Donne presents three pictures of what tears are like, based first on the fact that tears are round, as are all of these things.

a) Tears are coins because:

Tears are globes because:

His loved one is (more than) a moon because:

in this 3rd image, tears are:

and sighs are:

b) Each metaphor creates a kind of logic for why it's dangerous to weep. The logic isn't factual or very logical, but can you state in your own words what he concludes from each metaphor? If tears are like _____, then why are they dangerous?

c) Note Donne's use of rhyme and meter. Some of the rhymes don't rhyme for us, such as "tear" and "wear." They may have rhymed in Donne's time, or in his regional speech, or he may have accepted them as sight rhymes (as they would be now). There also some archaic words, for example, "divers," which means separate or different. What does the meter tell you about how Donne pronounced "Asia"?

A Valediction: Of Weeping

Let me pour forth
My tears before thy face, whilst I stay here,
For thy face coins them, and thy stamp they bear,
And by this mintage they are something worth.
For thus they be
Pregnant of thee;
Fruits of much grief they are, emblems of more;
When a tear falls, that thou fall'st which it bore;
So thou and I are nothing then, when on a divers shore.

On a round ball
A workman, that hath copies by, can lay
An Europe, Afric, and an Asia,
And quickly make that, which was nothing, all.
So doth each tear,
Which thee doth wear,
A globe, yea world, by that impression grow,
Till thy tears mix'd with mine do overflow
This world, by waters sent from thee, my heaven dissolvèd so.

O! more than moon,
Draw not up seas to drown me in thy sphere;
Weep me not dead, in thine arms, but forbear
To teach the sea, what it may do too soon;
Let not the wind
Example find
To do me more harm than it purposeth:
Since thou and I sigh one another's breath,
Whoe'er sighs most is cruellest, and hastes the other's death.

John Donne, 1572-1631

5. John Milton was an ambitious political writer during the years of English rule by Parliament, but he became completely blind a few years before that period ended. He must have felt that his life was effectively over (although he wrote his masterpiece *Paradise Lost* by dictation, while blind). This sonnet captures how he felt when he tried to make peace with losing his sight. As a deeply religious man, he expressed the loss in terms of his usefulness to God.

Milton's use of the word "talent" should be seen chiefly as referring to Jesus' story of a man who had a certain measure (a "talent") of silver and chose to bury it, rather than invest it. (Matthew 25: 14-30, Luke 19: 12-28; if you're not familiar with the story, look it up.) It's not clear if the word "talent" had acquired the modern meaning of aptitude or giftedness yet in the 1650s. There's another antique word use: "fondly" should be read not as a loving attitude toward the question he keeps asking, but that he habitually asks it. And a third: those who "stand and wait" are not waiting for an event, they are standing at the edge of a great lord's hall, prepared to get or do things at need. It's the same meaning as in "waiter" at a restaurant.

Milton uses four main metaphorical images to stand for his blindness. Explain your understanding of the comparison each metaphor is suggesting.

   a) light/lack of light:

   b) the talent:

   c) yoke:

   d) servant:

On His Blindness

When I consider how my light is spent
Ere half my days, in this dark world and wide,
And that one talent which is death to hide,
Lodged with me useless, though my soul more bent
To serve therewith my Maker, and present
My true account, lest he returning chide;
"Doth God exact day-labor, light denied?"
I fondly ask; but Patience to prevent
That murmur, soon replies, "God doth not need
Either man's work or his own gifts; who best
Bear his mild yoke, they serve him best. His state
Is kingly. Thousands at his bidding speed
And post o'er land and ocean without rest:
They also serve who only stand and wait."

John Milton, 1608-1674

6. Challenge Question. Elizabeth Barrett Browning's famous sonnet tries to describe very true, intense love. Before she loved Robert Browning, she was cynical about romantic love, considering its usual forms untrue and mostly self-deception. To demonstrate the nature of true love, she reached for some unusual imagery. While we think of similes as usually simpler and more obvious than metaphors, in a case like this, her two similes take some unpacking.

   a) "I love thee freely, as men strive for right." How do humans strive for right, and what would love be like if it were better compared to "as men neglect right" or "as men strive for wrong"? Why "freely"?

   b) "I love thee purely, as they turn from praise." How and why do humans turn from praise? What does this tell us about their motivation, and how does that apply to love? Why "purely"?

How do I love thee? Let me count the ways.
I love thee to the depth and breadth and height
My soul can reach, when feeling out of sight
For the ends of being and ideal grace.
I love thee to the level of every day's
Most quiet need, by sun and candle-light.
I love thee freely, as men strive for right.
I love thee purely, as they turn from praise.
I love thee with the passion put to use
In my old griefs, and with my childhood's faith.
I love thee with a love I seemed to lose
With my lost saints. I love thee with the breath,
Smiles, tears, of all my life; and, if God choose,
I shall but love thee better after death.

Elizabeth Barrett Browning, 1806-1861

7. For further reading, there are some modern poems still under copyright that have beautiful and intriguing metaphors. In "Elegy for Jane," Theodore Roethke commemorates his student, who has just died in a horse-riding accident, by speaking of Jane as if she is a bird. In "The Heavy Bear," Delmore Schwartz talks about his physical body as if it is a clumsy circus bear that insists on following him everywhere. The bear ruins everything: eating too much sugar, showing off, and even getting between his soul and the one he loves.

Also, a Challenge Question: here is an Imagist metaphor from William Carlos Williams. Do you think the image helps you understand more clearly? If not, what does it do?

TO WAKEN AN OLD LADY

Old age is
a flight of small
cheeping birds
skimming
bare trees
above a snow glaze.
Gaining and failing
they are buffeted
by a dark wind—-
But what?
On harsh weedstalks
the flock has rested,
the snow
is covered with broken
seedhusks
and the wind tempered
by a shrill
piping of plenty.

Fourteen:

Image as Symbol

In a broad sense, any image used to convey a meaning could be called a symbol. Any metaphor could be called symbolic language, and in trying to explain its meaning, we might say that the image "symbolizes" this or that. However, there are symbols that are not metaphors. This lesson will tackle two questions: what is a symbol and why does it have meaning? And, separately, how do we distinguish between a metaphor and a symbol in a poem?

I'm going to talk first about the key difference between metaphor and symbol in poetry, because defining symbols in a general way gets into deeper water. Unfortunately, although I can try to delineate cases when an image is definitely a symbol, not a metaphor, we really don't have a mathematically accurate definition of any of these words. They are all figurative speech, that is, words loaded with images and meaning. But I think it will be helpful to simplify and clarify at first, then later look at what's less clear.

1. Real objects with meaning

When an image is used as a symbol, it is different from a metaphor in that the object is "real" in the poem (as much as anything is real). It may be the main subject; it is a thing we are looking at and talking about. It is not there just as a comparison image or as language being borrowed.

By contrast, in my poem "Gratitude," presented in the last chapter, the rain was metaphorical, not real. The poem presented a human situation: I was sitting at a computer, opening an old file, reading through emails to find something. The words were "real" in that sense. My feelings were real. The rain? The poem doesn't present it as though I had taken my laptop outside and it began to rain. No, clearly the rain is present only in the metaphor to convey how I felt about my words. Similarly, Donne's coins and globe are not "real," but his grief at parting is. John Keats did not discover the Pacific Ocean, rather he used it as a comparison image, while his discovery of a book that excited him was the real thing. One could still say that Donne's coins and globes symbolize grief at parting, and I could say that my rain metaphor symbolized the confusion and embarrassment I felt when it looked like I had portrayed myself in an unflattering, undisciplined way by writing too much. It wouldn't be wrong to say those things, but neither would it be precise.

Let's look first at a poem in which the symbolic object is real and primary. William G. Salter, a contemporary poet, writes about inheriting his father's watch. In the years before digital time could be seen on every screen, fathers often wore large, sturdy wristwatches. Seeing the familiar old watch on the table, the poet thinks of everything it means to be the one everyone depends on. It is a larger inheritance than the watch itself; he must become the sentry, provider, and many other roles, too. It is sobering to realize that he will grow old too, while trying not to let his children down, but it is also a test, a challenge.

In the poem, the watch is definitely real, not just a comparison object, but it *means* these ideas. It's a symbol.

My Father's Watch

My inheritance lies before me here, unbidden,
and I am not so much surprised as numb -
it is both the loss outright,
and that it's augury of what's to come.
My instinct is to leave it where it lies,
it can carry on without me – self-sufficient –
yet there's another message etched within it,
not just my name it scrives with every tick,
but that there's neither rescue, nor respite, nor nick
of time to save us, only what we can gather
in both arms' endless flailing sweep
before we lose our hold and fall to sleep.
So. How shall I take up my duties
as sentry, generous provider, great heart and faithless tool,
conscientious amnesiac, brave loner and beloved fool?
How can this manacle aid my grasping extremity?
I look at his watch and know likewise I have been
a two-fisted drinker of my father's once full cup.
I pause. It doesn't. Then I take it up.

William G. Salter

If the poem described only the watch's appearance, we might not know if the watch was supposed to symbolize an idea. In "My Father's Watch," however, we're clearly shown that the watch means more, and the poem interprets its own symbol. The poet might have conveyed something similar by telling memories of the watch, connecting it with human history and feelings. It's the way the image is connected with human ideas and feelings that gives it the status of a symbol.

The poem uses two other images in passing. The manacle is a metaphor, since wristwatches and handcuffs are both things we put around our wrists, and the restrictive meaning of the handcuff can be transferred to the wristwatch by calling it a manacle. The last image is of a cup, another metaphor. Unlike the watch, which is very present in the poem as a real object on the table, the cup is an analogy for his father's providing ability and even his life force. Like the watch, the speaker has eaten away his father's essence tick by tick.

Frost's "Road Less Traveled" does the same thing. The road is clearly real, not merely an idea. He describes the "yellow wood" in which the road or trail forked, and he makes it plain that he had to make a literal, concrete decision about going left or right. However, his last lines make it clear to us that the road means an idea, too. Otherwise he would not be thinking about how he'll remember it for ages, or how it changed his whole life. The Y-branching road is a symbol for major life decisions.

Frost wrote a sonnet about a little warbler, the oven-bird. The bird's name appears only in the title, but its symbolic meaning derives from key traits of the species. Many birds only sing during the spring, while their chicks are imprinting the song. Once their chicks have left the nest, the territorial and communication reasons for singing drop off. However, the oven-bird continues to sing all through the summer. It also sings in the middle of the day, while other birds sing mainly in twilight of morning and evening. How does this shape the bird's symbolic meaning?

The Oven-bird

There is a singer everyone has heard,
Loud, a mid-summer and a mid-wood bird,
Who makes the solid tree trunks sound again.
He says that leaves are old and that for flowers
Mid-summer is to spring as one to ten.
He says the early petal-fall is past
When pear and cherry bloom went down in showers
On sunny days a moment overcast;
And comes that other fall we name the fall.
He says the highway dust is over all.
The bird would cease and be as other birds
But that he knows in singing not to sing.
The question that he frames in all but words
Is what to make of a diminished thing.

Robert Frost, 1874-1963

To Frost, the oven-bird is the poet of the late season, when things are no longer fresh and new. He suggests that the bird's song means that leaves are old, petals are gone, many flowers are past blooming, and roadside plants are dusty. Opportunities are past, and things will only shrink from now on. The season is "diminished," compared to spring.

"What do we make of a diminished thing?" is the universal question asked by most poetry. How should we feel about old age or failure? What about lost love? What about memories of a happier past? Frost's poetry puts words to the oven-bird's supposed question. The bird, in this poem, symbolizes the poet himself. By singing about memories and love when nobody else is trying to make beauty, he is like the bird who still sings in late summer. The bird is not a metaphor; he's really talking about a warbler who can be found on the forest floor. However, the bird means more than just a bird, it means the idea of speaking up about loss and fear, as poets do.

An object's being "real" in the poem is one strong indicator that it is acting as a symbol, but an object could also be a symbol while being just an idea. Sometimes the line between metaphor and symbol is not clear. In the poem below, for example, Christina Rossetti asks if she is a "stone" or a "sheep." The poem develops the idea of why she is concerned—-her lack of personal feeling about Jesus' death on the cross—-but it assumes that we know what the stone and sheep mean. A sheep is someone who is in the flock, who belongs to the Shepherd, like all of the people she mentions who wept; a stone is hard and cold, without feeling. The verses do not develop those images further, but instead they draw pictures around the central images:

Good Friday

Am I a stone, and not a sheep,
    That I can stand, O Christ, beneath Thy cross,
    To number drop by drop Thy Blood's slow loss,
And yet not weep?

> Not so those women loved
>> Who with exceeding grief lamented Thee;
>> Not so fallen Peter weeping bitterly;
> Not so the thief was moved;
>
> Not so the Sun and Moon
>> Which hid their faces in a starless sky.
>> A horror of great darkness at broad noon—
> I, only I.
>
> Yet give not o'er,
>> But seek Thy sheep, true Shepherd of the flock;
> Greater than Moses, turn and look once more
>> And smite a rock.

Christina Rossetti, 1830-1894

The poem references several Bible stories in just a few lines. The people in the second stanza can be found in Luke 22 and 23, as can the "darkness at broad noon." Jesus' statement "I am the true Shepherd" comes from John 10, while Moses smiting a rock (so that water gushed out) is told in Numbers 20.

We could argue that the "stone" and "sheep" are metaphors; the *language* of Moses striking the rock is *applied* to the speaker's emotional state. But I think it's a weak case for these images as metaphor, because the language of stones is not really applied to the speaker (stones don't count drops of blood), nor is sheep language applied to the speaker apart from invoking the Shepherd.

I'm classing the stone and sheep as symbols because Rossetti uses them a bit like chess pieces, moving them about and talking about them as though we already know what they stand for. There aren't real stones and sheep in the poem, but the poem depicts as "real" only (if anything) the speaker standing by a Crucifix and not feeling moved. Everything else is an idea or a person she's comparing herself to. However, "stone" and "sheep" are used as shorthand for fuller ideas about how we respond to faith and feeling. The stone and sheep are like pictures she can flash at us, counting on us to see through them to the larger meaning each carries with it. She expects us to know what she means, so she is drawing on a shared cultural sense.

2. Archetypes: universal symbols

Symbolism is embedded in our thought processes, perhaps at the root of all perception. There seems to be an alternation and partnership of directly sensing a shape or experience and forming an idea or memory of it. The direct experience is concrete and detailed, but the impression that's left may be more abstract. It is also tied to emotions we felt during the experience. Over time, these impressions form general meanings that are tied to the shapes and experiences. In this way, things can be linked strongly to memories and feelings, inheriting from memories the emotional polarity of our experiences.

The linkage of things to meaning can be highly personal, drawn only from one person's experiences. Poetry specializes in using this kind of personal symbol, creating a context with word art that recreates salient features of the experience that we want to commemorate and share. But symbols also have a group meaning that isn't as logically derived. Some of it can be explained by thousands of people sharing similar experiences that left similar impressions. For example, we all know the new hope that can dawn with morning, the sense that a tired, failed yesterday is gone with the night. That's an experience that millions have had thousands of times, and it does become part of a shared understanding of the symbolic meaning of "morning."

But there's a more mysterious layer to symbols, as though some of them are parts of instinctive knowledge that's built into the brain's neural structure. First, we can see that they are widely shared across many cultures and times. Second, a few linkages of thing and meaning appear to show up in studies of what human babies know at very young ages. While common experiences (like waking up in the morning) can account for some widely-shared symbols, it's harder to account for babies knowing some symbols. The implication of both points is that symbols could be built into the brain at some very simple but profound level.

Because infant knowledge is so difficult to pinpoint, there are only a few examples that overlap between babies and world cultures. One of these is the snake, a shape that strikes fear into most people's minds. Many animals are innately afraid of snakes, too; indoor cats with no relevant reptile experience jump out of their skin if they suddenly see a cucumber nearby. So let's compare snakes in infant knowledge, world symbols, and poetry.

Babies readily associate snakes with fear, even if they have no personal experiences with snakes. In one study, babies looked more closely at snake films if they overheard adults talking in frightened voices. In another, they readily associated snakes with "scary" emoticon faces, but appeared surprised if researchers prompted them to associate fear with flowers. The individual children didn't know much (or anything) about snakes or danger yet, but their brains made sense of associating snakes with danger. We can think of this as a template waiting to gather facts and experiences that will flesh it out into real knowledge. (For these studies and more discussion of infant knowledge, see my book *Re-Modeling the Mind: Personality in Balance*, pages 37-9.)

Around the world, snakes show up as common symbols. They may symbolize evil, especially evil knowledge as in the Bible story of Eve talking to the serpent. Even when they are used as symbols for something friendly, like fertility, there's a special zing to handling snakes in a ritual because they are so often dangerous. Handling deadly danger, but surviving, feels very *important* to a template that's highly alert to patterns of danger. In the same vein, serpents have sometimes been worshipped. Perhaps the most ironic use of a snake symbol was in the Bible, when Moses commanded metalworkers to make a serpent image out of bronze. People suffering from snake-bite sickness would be cured if they looked at the image: braving the inborn fear cured them. That's why a snake draped over a pole is a symbol for medicine.

Snakes show up in art and poetry, and their meaning is often ambivalent: wicked and dangerous, or just animals? In 1921, D. H. Lawrence wrote about encountering a snake and feeling constantly torn between the innate sense that he must defend himself from danger, and the plain observation that he is in danger.

Snake

A snake came to my water-trough
On a hot, hot day, and I in pyjamas for the heat,
To drink there.

In the deep, strange-scented shade of the great dark carob tree
I came down the steps with my pitcher
And must wait, must stand and wait, for there he was at the trough before me.

He reached down from a fissure in the earth-wall in the gloom
And trailed his yellow-brown slackness soft-bellied down, over the edge of the stone trough
And rested his throat upon the stone bottom,

And where the water had dripped from the tap, in a small clearness,
He sipped with his straight mouth,
Softly drank through his straight gums, into his slack long body,
Silently.

Someone was before me at my water-trough,
And I, like a second-comer, waiting.

He lifted his head from his drinking, as cattle do,
And looked at me vaguely, as drinking cattle do,
And flickered his two-forked tongue from his lips, and mused a moment,
And stooped and drank a little more,
Being earth-brown, earth-golden from the burning bowels of the earth
On the day of Sicilian July, with Etna smoking.

The voice of my education said to me
He must be killed,
For in Sicily the black, black snakes are innocent, the gold are venomous.

And voices in me said, If you were a man
You would take a stick and break him now, and finish him off.

But must I confess how I liked him,
How glad I was he had come like a guest in quiet, to drink at my water-trough
And depart peaceful, pacified, and thankless,
Into the burning bowels of this earth?

Was it cowardice, that I dared not kill him?
Was it perversity, that I longed to talk to him?
Was it humility, to feel so honoured?
I felt so honoured.

And yet those voices:
If you were not afraid, you would kill him!

And truly I was afraid, I was most afraid,
But even so, honoured still more
That he should seek my hospitality
From out the dark door of the secret earth.

He drank enough
And lifted his head, dreamily, as one who has drunken,
And flickered his tongue like a forked night on the air, so black,
Seeming to lick his lips,
And looked around like a god, unseeing, into the air,
And slowly turned his head,
And slowly, very slowly, as if thrice adream,
Proceeded to draw his slow length curving round
And climb again the broken bank of my wall-face.

And as he put his head into that dreadful hole,
And as he slowly drew up, snake-easing his shoulders, and entered farther,
A sort of horror, a sort of protest against his withdrawing into that horrid black hole,
Deliberately going into the blackness, and slowly drawing himself after,
Overcame me now his back was turned.

I looked round, I put down my pitcher,
I picked up a clumsy log
And threw it at the water-trough with a clatter.

I think it did not hit him,
But suddenly that part of him that was left behind convulsed in undignified haste,
Writhed like lightning, and was gone
Into the black hole, the earth-lipped fissure in the wall-front,
At which, in the intense still noon, I stared with fascination.

And immediately I regretted it.
I thought how paltry, how vulgar, what a mean act!
I despised myself and the voices of my accursed human education.

And I thought of the albatross,
And I wished he would come back, my snake.

For he seemed to me again like a king,
Like a king in exile, uncrowned in the underworld,
Now due to be crowned again.

And so, I missed my chance with one of the lords
Of life.
And I have something to expiate:
A pettiness.

D. H. Lawrence, 1885-1930

Lawrence attributes the inner voice to kill the snake to "education" coming from outside himself. Certainly, the knowledge that golden snakes are venomous in Sicily was something he had learned. But his whole inner struggle strikes me as going much deeper than just a decision whether to follow cautious advice or not. He's deeply afraid and deeply attracted, at once. During the time that the snake was nearby without harming him, it became "my" snake, a relationship the poet briefly had with not only an animal but a symbol. After the snake had gone, his impression of the snake linked to another image: a king. (He links the snake also to "the albatross," an image from *The Rime of the Ancient Mariner*, which is presented in Lesson 16.)

Profound, basic images that we all sort of understand are called archetypes (*ch* = *k*). We have basic archetypes of human roles like mothers, innocent babes, and kings, but these universal symbols also cover non-human roles and things. The color white, for example, has an archetypal meaning of purity, while our innate fear of the dark may have shaped the color black's archetypal negative meanings of evil and grief. Some cultures may have different conscious symbolic meanings for images, such as Japan's symbolic attribution of grief to the color white. But to a surprising degree, people do have the same basic impressions of things.

Poetry often deals in archetypes, as well as in symbolic meanings that we can draw out of the specific poem. We don't always know if the poet consciously thought about the archetype, but it's often likely since these are such strong impressions. Was Lawrence aware of the snake's archetypal significance? Almost certainly he was, since his education had also shown him many stories and poems with snake imagery. But in another sense, it doesn't matter. Creating art employs nonverbal, unconscious processes in the brain, and our brain processes may not be overtly aware of something that is, in fact, there. A reader may be able to sense and name what even the poet could not.

Art stands as a mediator between our senses and the deep archetypes and symbols of another person's mind. When I wrote the poem about my child's illness, I needed to avoid direct description lest both I and the reader become overwhelmed by the intensity, and that's how art functions as mediator. The poem can recreate some of the symbolic meanings in a reader's mind, but without needing to intrusively press them in or shout about them. The symbols link writer and reader, reaching down to this deep layer of the mind where we know without knowing why.

3. Interpreting symbols in poetry

We can interpret symbols in poems both by drawing a meaning out of the poem, and by reading a meaning into it. In the examples in Section 1 of this lesson, I drew the meaning out. Whereas clocks generally symbolize time, in Salter's poem the watch means paternal responsibility. If we took an external "clock = time" idea and forced it into the poem, we'd miss the real message. However, sometimes a poem doesn't really interpret its symbol much, and then it's fair to import a cultural symbolic meaning.

In Laurence Dunbar's "Sympathy," the cultural meaning is clearly intended. It's from this poem that poet Maya Angelou took her autobiography's title: *I Know Why the Caged Bird Sings*. The line alone resonates as a title *because* the poem uses conventional symbolism:

Sympathy

I know what the caged bird feels, alas!
When the sun is bright on the upland slopes;
When the wind stirs soft through the springing grass,
And the river flows like a stream of glass;
When the first bird sings and the first bud opes,
And the faint perfume from its chalice steals —
I know what the caged bird feels!

I know why the caged bird beats his wing
Till its blood is red on the cruel bars;
For he must fly back to his perch and cling
When he fain would be on the bough a-swing;
And a pain still throbs in the old, old scars
And they pulse again with a keener sting —
I know why he beats his wing!

I know why the caged bird sings, ah me,
When his wing is bruised and his bosom sore, —
When he beats his bars and he would be free;

> It is not a carol of joy or glee,
> But a prayer that he sends from his heart's deep core,
> But a plea, that upward to Heaven he flings —
> I know why the caged bird sings!

Paul Laurence Dunbar, 1872-1906

Dunbar develops facets of the bird's unhappiness and his sympathy, but he does not create a unique meaning for the bird or its cage. Birds have always readily symbolized the soul, able to range far and free through the "flight" of imagination or emotion. If we accept this conventional meaning for the bird, there are two possibilities for the cage. The soul may feel imprisoned in the body, especially if the body is sick or crippled. On the other hand, the cage may refer to circumstances of injustice: literal imprisonment in a cell, or figurative imprisonment with laws. We recall Herbert's reference to laws as a cage: "Forsake thy cage, /Thy rope of sands, /Which petty thoughts have made, and made to thee /Good cable, to enforce and draw, /And be thy law…"

Dunbar seems content to assume that we intuitively know the meaning of his caged bird symbolism. In his life's context, we can assume that the "cage" was the set of restrictions by race known as "Jim Crow laws." But the poem would still resonate if its context were something else. The cage could be a prison or a body, and he would still feel sympathy with why the "caged bird" is beating against the walls and crying out.

We've seen two other symbolic images that seem to carry the burden of traditional archetypal meaning. In Frost's "The Road Not Taken," the road is a real object, not a metaphor, but it symbolizes a decision process in how we "travel" through life. We can draw this meaning out of the poem, but we can also import to it the generalized, traditional symbolism of roads as symbols of our lives and actions. In this case, the meaning in context and the traditional meaning are identical.

In Poe's "The Raven," importing the traditional symbolic meaning may be more important, since the poet never explains why the visitor is (among all possible birds, animals, insects, and people) a raven. The poem is also loaded with other symbolic images: the dark night, the door, angels, and the goddess Athena. The poet is reading a book of "forgotten lore," perhaps one in which the Raven stands as a symbol of knowledge of death. Real ravens are battlefield scavengers who circle the scene of a fight, waiting for the dying to be still. In Norse mythology, Odin carries two ravens, each symbolizing a type of knowledge. If we import this meaning, "knowledge of death," into Poe's verses, does it help us? In this case, I think it does. The Raven's single word "Nevermore" seems to be telling the narrator that death is final and grief is everlasting: the Raven does, indeed, have special insight about death. So in this case again, the meaning we can draw out of the context is identical to the cultural archetypal meaning.

What about reading an archetypal meaning into Lawrence's "Snake" poem? Does it add to the poem's meaning if we give special consideration to cultural meanings for the snake? What about, for example, Eve's serpent in the garden, or Moses' serpent on a pole? The poet was certainly aware of these symbolic meanings of the snake, and even if he wasn't, we can be aware of them as readers. Going a step further, what does it add to "Snake" if we see the snake as a symbol of evil knowledge? Other worldwide symbolic meanings of snakes include eternity (because the snake biting its own tail forms a ring), creation, and fertility. Any of these meanings might, on careful reading, provide insight.

How much these additional layers of meaning illumine the poem has to be a reader's personal sense. When I read Lawrence's lines, I don't gain much from imposing those meanings. It's important to be aware that this isn't an ordinary animal he's talking about, nor even an animal we don't like to get close to (such as a skunk). He's talking about an animal that makes us deeply anxious, that seems purely *evil* to many people.

I need this basic archetypal meaning to understand the poem, but it's not clear to me that imposing Moses' bronze snake, or an eternal ring, helps me. I don't need to interpret his fascination as temptation to evil knowledge (which then slithered back into darkness) to understand why he felt "petty" after he threw a log at the animal's tail. However, it wouldn't take more than five minutes at a poetry seminar to find readers and writers of poetry who completely disagree with me, and that's fair.

Beyond the special case of the circular snake biting its tail, every circle carries a deeply symbolic meaning of both eternity and perfection. Our love for the visual perfection of a circle may be one of the things built into the brain's neural structure. We could even make the case that the circles formed on still water are signs that it contains nothing dangerous to us; perhaps there are so many situations in nature where circles are evidence of tranquility that it's really an important visual clue for staying safe. In any case, we like circles; we feel them as balanced, smooth, and perfect. Tracing around the circle, we never come to a plain ending, but instead we go around again. Circles have always had a major place in religious and traditional art; the circle may symbolize God himself, perfect and eternal. Can we import this into poems, reading these meanings into the lines?

Let's consider two poetic circles in which the meaning of "perfect and eternal" may or may not be inherent—or helpful. We saw the first in Stevens' "Thirteen Ways of Looking at a Blackbird." In the ninth stanza, he writes:

When the blackbird flew out of sight,
It marked the edge
Of one of many circles.

The poem already feels loaded with symbols and archetypes of simple, primary things, even if we're not sure what they mean: man, woman, tree, mountain, light, shadows, numbers 3 and 20, and even a fairy-tale glass coach. When I try to draw a unified meaning out of the poem's many contexts for the bird (see Lesson 11 Answer Key notes), I come up with something like "nature" or "life force." If I pencil this meaning into the stanza with circles, what do I get? First, the poem tells us that there are many circles. They are in the sky, serving as perfect boundaries for zones that we don't really understand. Right where we cease to see the blackbird, a circle's boundary runs. Are we inside the circle, or outside of it? Since there are many circles, it could be either. I think it's very likely that Stevens wants us to access the archetypal symbolic meaning of circles here, and also the archetypal senses of any other figures in the poem. But I have to admit that the verses remain as mysteriously opaque as ever, at least for now.

Here's a short, well-known epigram about circles, written by the Poet Laureate of the State of Oregon in the 1920s.

Outwitted

He drew a circle that shut me out—
Heretic, a rebel, a thing to flout.
But Love and I had the wit to win:
We drew a circle that took him in!

Edwin Markham, 1852-1940

We can draw a firm meaning out of the poem's context: the circles symbolize lines that we draw when we refuse to relate to someone in a normal way. While one circle shuts a man out, he can draw another to enclose his enemy, because there are as many circles as we can draw. Circles mean exclusion or inclusion and symbolize how we relate to others. But what if Markham had chosen a different word, for example, "he drew a boundary" or "We drew an oval"? Is the meaning more precise, or enhanced, by the lines forming perfect, eternal circles? If you see the circle as an archetypal symbol, what more can the poem tell you? I'll leave this an open question for you (and me) to think about.

Summary and Definitions

A *symbol* is an image that presents a real object imbued with extra meaning. Poems often provide a full interpretation of the symbol's meaning or clues so that we can figure it out. Some modern poems use symbols without much interpretation, but they at least give hints that make it clear that the object means more than itself.

Symbols also exist outside poetry as *archetypes*. They have widely-shared cultural and deeply-held emotional meanings. These meanings may be part of a poem consciously, used and instilled by the poet, or unconsciously, seen and felt by the reader.

Exercises 14

Review
(lines 49-61 from "The Love Song of J. Alfred Prufrock," T. S. Eliot)

> For I have known them all already, known them all:
> Have known the evenings, mornings, afternoons,
> I have measured out my life with coffee spoons;
> I know the voices dying with a dying fall
> Beneath the music from a farther room.
> So how should I presume?
> And I have known the eyes already, known them all-
> The eyes that fix you in a formulated phrase,
> And when I am formulated, sprawling on a pin,
> When I am pinned and wriggling on the wall,
> Then how should I begin
> To spit out all the butt-ends of my days and ways?
> And how should I presume?

a) The first stanza compares "my life" to coffee, measured out with spoons. The comparison is framed as a _____.

b) The second stanza gives us an extended analogy, comparing what two things? Why is it not a simile?

c) There are several sound elements done in nearly identical form in these stanzas. What do you see that's the same in both; and what variations appear in the second set?

1. "All things are symbols." Longfellow gives us this sonnet about symbols; in it, he suggests that we see symbols in many things (even *all* things) because of the way we process the world. A mental image inside the mind has some analogy to an external image in the world. (In the sonnet, italics are mine for emphasis.)

> It is the Harvest Moon! On gilded vanes
> And roofs of villages, on woodland crests
> And their aerial neighborhoods of nests
> Deserted, on the curtained window-panes
> Of rooms where children sleep, on country lanes
> And harvest-fields, its mystic splendor rests!
> Gone are the birds that were our summer guests,
> With the last sheaves return the laboring wains!
> *All things are symbols: the external shows*
> *Of Nature have their image in the mind,*
> As flowers and fruits and falling of the leaves;
> The song-birds leave us at the summer's close,
> Only the empty nests are left behind,
> And pipings of the quail among the sheaves.

"All things are symbols: the external shows /of Nature have their image in the mind."

Taking our task from Longfellow's sonnet, what images in the mind are mirrored in outside things? In each case, you can identify a general meaning that you've seen in literature or daily speech, and a private meaning that the thing symbolizes for you. For example, if you grew up in a family that moved every year, summer might symbolize the sadness of losing friends. If you have no private symbolic feeling about something, just identify the general one that society seems to feel (research if you're not sure). Also, you can choose a particular thing here, so that you can select ones that have personal meaning to you, if you like.

a) a season: _____

   general: _____

   personal: _____

b) a natural object (flower, tree, root, creek...): _____

   general: _____

   personal: _____

c) a time of the day (morning, twilight...) _____

   general: _____

   personal: _____

d) a color _____

   general: _____

   personal: _____

e) a building feature (stairs, door, window, roof...) _____
   general: _____
   personal: _____

f) an animal that preys on other animals or is the victim/prey itself (tiger, hawk, wolf...; rabbit, fawn, sheep...) _____
   general: _____
   personal: _____

If you are a student using this book for a credit course, choose one of the four following poems to write about at greater length. Don't forget to look at the sound elements, as well as the use of images.

2. Edmund Waller was a contemporary of George Herbert, John Donne and John Milton; he was a member of Parliament and a wealthy landowner. His poetry was later greatly admired for its "sweetness," which stood out in a time when many other poets were philosophical and intellectual.

   In this poem, he addresses a rose. He is sending the rose as a gift to a young woman, and he wants the rose to remind her of all that it symbolizes. (Note that Waller uses "deserts" in an archaic sense to mean a place deserted by humans. He doesn't mean a hot, dry, sandy desert where it would be very strange to find a rose. He just means a wilderness of meadow or forest.) How does each part of the cut flower's life cycle symbolize this young woman's life?

   a) still growing, perhaps in a "desert"
   b) now that's it is a cut-flower gift
   c) next week when its petals fall off

   What is the overall symbolic meaning of the Rose, as drawn out of the poem? How does this compare with its cultural symbolic meaning?

Go, Lovely Rose

Go, lovely Rose—
Tell her that wastes her time and me,
That now she knows,
When I resemble her to thee,
How sweet and fair she seems to be.

Tell her that's young,
And shuns to have her graces spied,
That hadst thou sprung
In deserts where no men abide,
Thou must have uncommended died.

Small is the worth
Of beauty from the light retired:

Bid her come forth,
Suffer herself to be desired,
And not blush so to be admired.

Then die—that she
The common fate of all things rare
May read in thee;
How small a part of time they share
That are so wondrous sweet and fair!

Edmund Waller, 1606-1687

As a further note on Waller's "Rose," compare it with William Blake's "The Sick Rose." He, too, addresses the Rose. Does it have the same symbolic meaning? Would you draw its meaning out of the poem, or read a cultural meaning into the poem?

THE SICK ROSE

O Rose thou art sick.
The invisible worm,
That flies in the night
In the howling storm:

Has found out thy bed
Of crimson joy:
And his dark secret love
Does thy life destroy.

William Blake, 1757-1827

3. Claude McKay's sonnet is about water, but he also suggests that he means more than water. What might water symbolize?

   a) What phrases suggest that "water" has a non-literal meaning?

   b) Drawing from the poem alone, what might "water" symbolize?

   c) Drawing from what you know of Claude McKay's life as a Jamaican immigrant who found racial segregation in the United States almost unbearable, what can you add to the symbolism of "water"? (Look back at "The Tired Worker" and "If We Must Die")

   d) Look up "symbolism of water" online to find archetypal meanings from psychology and literature. Do they add to your sense of the meaning of water in this poem?

THIRST

My spirit wails for water, water now!
My tongue is aching dry, my throat is hot
For water, fresh rain shaken from a bough,
Or dawn dews heavy in some leafy spot.
My hungry body's burning for a swim
In sunlit water where the air is cool,
As in Trout Valley where upon a limb
The golden finch sings sweetly to the pool.
Oh water, water, when the night is done,
When day steals gray-white through the window-pane,
Clear silver water when I wake, alone,
All impotent of parts, of fevered brain;
Pure water from a forest fountain first,
To wash me, cleanse me, and to quench my thirst!

Claude McKay, 1889-1948

4. G. M. Hopkins' "Spring and Fall" can be difficult to read because he used creative syntax and words ("unleaving" = un-leaf-ing). It seems to comment on a young girl who wept when she saw the autumn leaves falling. The word "Spring" in the title symbolizes the first part of life, where the girl still is. What does Hopkins predict about her thoughts when she is an adult, in the "fall" stage? How will she feel about the leaves then? Why does he think she is weeping now? Putting it together, what do the autumn leaves symbolize? Does the poet see Margaret as aware of the symbolism?

Notice, of course, Hopkins' beautiful sound elements! How does the meter of line 9 support the meaning?

SPRING AND FALL

Margaret, áre you gríeving
Over Goldengrove unleaving?
Leáves, líke the things of man, you
With your fresh thoughts care for, can you?
Áh! ás the heart grows older
It will come to such sights colder
By and by, nor spare a sigh
Though worlds of wanwood leafmeal lie;
And yet you wíll weep and know why.
Now no matter, child, the name:
Sórrow's spríngs áre the same.
Nor mouth had, no nor mind, expressed
What heart heard of, ghost guessed:
It ís the blight man was born for,
It is Margaret you mourn for.

G. M. Hopkins, 1844-1889

5. One of the most puzzling poems in the Modernist canon is Wallace Stevens' "Anecdote of the Jar." An anecdote is a little story, but this isn't much of a story, on the surface. Spoiler alert: he put a jar on a hill.

    a) As a step toward finding symbolic meaning in the jar, list the facts we know about the jar.

    b) How do the jar's traits contrast with "slovenly" Tennessee? Why was the wilderness no longer wild? What might the jar symbolize?

ANECDOTE OF THE JAR

I placed a jar in Tennessee,
And round it was, upon a hill.
It made the slovenly wilderness
Surround that hill.

The wilderness rose up to it,
And sprawled around, no longer wild.
The jar was round upon the ground
And tall and of a port in air.

It took dominion everywhere.
The jar was gray and bare.
It did not give of bird or bush,
Like nothing else in Tennessee.

Wallace Stevens, 1879-1955

6. Jean Toomer was part of the Harlem Renaissance, but he settled in Georgia to work as a school principal. In his poem about a cotton flower, he indicates that the flower means something more, but he only suggests what it might be. (Note: "drouth" is an alternative (Scots) spelling of "drought.") The flower may be the fluffy white cotton fruit that is frequently called a flower, but the cotton plant *Gossypium barbadense* also has a real flower that is yellow with a brown center. Either one could be the "brown eye."

    a) What is the literal situation that the poem describes?

    b) What phrases does Toomer use to suggest a meaning for the flower? How would you interpret it, in your words?

    c) Look closely at the poem's structure. Why and why not should this poem be considered a sonnet?

NOVEMBER COTTON FLOWER

Boll-weevil's coming, and the winter's cold,
Made cotton-stalks look rusty, seasons old,
And cotton, scarce as any southern snow,
Was vanishing; the branch, so pinched and slow,
Failed in its function as the autumn rake;

Drouth fighting soil had caused the soil to take
All water from the streams; dead birds were found
In wells a hundred feet below the ground—
Such was the season when the flower bloomed.
Old folks were startled, and it soon assumed
Significance. Superstition saw
Something it had never seen before:
Brown eyes that loved without a trace of fear,
Beauty so sudden for that time of year.

Jean Toomer, 1894-1967

7. Challenge question: In this 1920 poem by Jamaican intellectual Walter Adolphe Roberts, what does the tiger lily symbolize? How does it differ from the other flowers presented in this homework set?

Tiger Lily

Gray are the gardens of our Celtic lands,
Dreaming and gray,
Tended by the devotion of pale hands,
On barren crags, or by disastrous sands,
That night and day
Are drenched with bitter spray.
There rosemary and thyme are plentiful,
Larkspur that lovers cull,
Love-in-the-mist that is most sorrowful.
Flowers so wistful that our teardrops start….
Scarcely one understands that regal, rare,
Bravely the tiger lily blossoms there,
Bravely apart.

Our gardens are enamored of the spring,
Of silver rain,
The cloudy green of buds slow-burgeoning,
The sorrow of last apple blooms that cling
And are not fain
To yield their fruit again.
We do not long for tropic pageantry,
Yet surge with love to see
The tiger lily's muted ecstasy.
Watered by mist and lashed by wind-blown rime,
She is no alien thing; but vivid, free,
She has no heed for paler rosemary,
Larkspur or thyme.

It is in vain they worship her who knows
Pity nor pride.
Their petals whirl down every wind that goes
South to the palms or northward to the snows,
Mourning they died
So distant from her side.
But the brave tiger lily blossoms on,
Never to be undone
Till the last rosemary and thyme are gone.
Tattered by autumn storms, she will not fling
Herself to sullen foes. The winter rain
Alone can beat her down, to bloom again
Spring after spring.

Walter Adolphe Roberts, 1996-1962

8. For further reading, there are many works on symbols and archetypes. Try Joseph Campbell's *The Hero of a Thousand Faces* or *The Power of Mythology,* or Carl Jung's (as editor) *Man and His Symbols*. My own book *Re-Modeling the Mind*, referenced in the text, is a recasting of Jung's ideas on how human personality is organized; in one chapter, I go over instances of inborn knowledge and some basics of universal archetypes. For particular study of archetypal images in poetry, see the works of Northrop Frye, such as *Anatomy of Criticism* or *The Educated Imagination.*

Fifteen:

Image as Myth

The word "myth" means a simple story shared by a whole culture. It's usually very old, and its plot outline may have influenced other stories. There are two more meanings, one useful to the study of poetry, the other not relevant at all.

When people use "myth" in daily speech, they are usually suggesting that an idea is untrue, even if it's believed by many to be factual. That's how "Myth Busters" uses the term. We can't use this meaning in literature because factual truth is not important in either fiction or poetry. They are both kinds of word art, and there is no problem with art portraying something that is not factual.

The other meaning of "myth" is relevant because it means specifically the stories of gods from Greece. This use of "myth" is essentially a shortcut for "Greek myth." Greek myths are the most important outside reference source for English poetry because they were so much part of European education for many centuries. The Latin poet Ovid wrote out many of them in *Metamorphoses*, one of the most-read texts of Latin-based schooling. The *Metamorphoses* told over 250 stories, from the creation of the world through Rome's founding and the life of Julius Caesar. The characters' names were as familiar to any educated Englishman in medieval times as Batman and Robin are to you.

"Myth" also refers to stories about the creation of the world and its things, such as how the tiger got its stripes, or how trouble came into the world. Every ancient culture had its own stories of this kind, and in our time, more of them are being retold. But "myth" in poetry functions mainly as a way to refer to a well-known story; it's a story reference. And Greek myths have an outsized role in traditional English poetry.

The Bible is the other great source of story references. Its stories can be called myths only in the first sense of the word: a basic story shared by a whole culture. I don't mean to imply that the stories are not factual, and they are certainly not Greek. But we can count as "shared cultural stories" the near-sacrifice of Isaac, the selling of Joseph into slavery, and the epic of how the Israelites left Egypt. Many people know what you mean if you say, "the parting of the Red Sea," or mention "the plague of the frogs." Many of the Gospel stories of Jesus also count in that sense: the feeding of the 5000, walking on water, and of course the Christmas story of the birth of Jesus: Mary, Joseph, Bethlehem, shepherds, Magi. We saw in the last lesson a poem that centered around facts about the death of Jesus, too.

We should also count as "myths" historical facts that have been reduced to outline form and widely shared through society. For example: the fall of Rome, King Arthur, and the Crusades. They're historical, but their popular image has been reduced to a sort of myth. We've seen one of these myth-facts used in a poem already, when "stout Cortez" sighted the Pacific Ocean, "silent upon a peak in Darien." The discovery of the Americas by Europeans went into shared cultural history, although Columbus and the Pilgrims are better-known than Balboa.

Fairy tales are part of the body of "myth" for this purpose, too. Most European ones memorialize a generalized view of medieval life, an image that mixes things from many places and time periods into a mythical "once upon a time." Stories like "Goldilocks and the Three Bears" or "Cinderella" are firmly part of our myth-story heritage. All you must do is cite one line or detail from them, and everyone knows what you're talking about. Let's wrap up this introduction while it is not too short, not too long, but just right – and before you turn into a pumpkin.

1. Myth as allusion, reference or symbol

Greek myths could be narrative explanations of natural phenomena like the seasons, while others told about the creation of the world; still others were basically just stories using the gods as characters. The myths that refer to seasons or creation have a close connection to archetypal symbols, as discussed in the last lesson. In the Greek creation story, the Sky Father (Uranus) fathered the first gods, the Titans, with the Earth Mother (Gaia), but then he was castrated by his son Cronos—-a name very close in sound to the Greek word for "time." Everything was created from Uranus' spilled blood. The story doubles as a story about characters and a sort of eternal truth: that time slays even the greatest, and new life comes from wounds and death.

Because the Cronos story serves this dual purpose as tale and truth, it feels larger and more important than a mere story. That's the feeling of an archetypal myth. They often tell about births and deaths: children killing their parents (Cronos' son Zeus killed him in his turn), or mysterious birth circumstances (babies set adrift in boxes or born in odd ways). They may directly explain seasons, like the story of how Hades forced Persephone, daughter of the Hearth and Harvest goddess Demeter, to spend seven months in the Underworld. Only when her daughter returns can Demeter bring happiness and life to the ground. Archetypal myths may tell us about desperate quests to defeat amazing monsters like the many-headed hydra, and in the story's structure, we can sense the way we all feel about trying to defeat terrifying and chronic problems in our lives.

By invoking an archetypal myth, a poem may reference both the shared cultural story and the archetypal symbol. Some scholars of mythology see all traditional myths as archetypal, and they include not just the Greek/Latin set of stories, but also the Norse myths, and non-European myths of Asia, Africa, and the Americas. This may be so, but poetry does not always use mythological references for archetypal symbols. A poem may treat a myth as shared story for a dramatic situation or even for irony.

Myths are often used as name-dropping references that imply a story background or attitude that the poem wants us to use. This works fairly well in modern times for figures like "Cupid," who is still very well known. It's much tougher when the poem demands that we know names of all the gods, alternative nicknames they went by, and small details of their stories. Another challenge is that the Latin-speaking people adopted many of Greece's myths, but tied them to their own gods who had similar roles. So in order to understand mythology, you have to know a number of pairs:

Role	Greek name	Latin name
King	Zeus	Jupiter
Queen	Hera	Juno
Wisdom	Athena	Minerva
War	Ares	Mars
Love	Aphrodite	Venus
Ocean	Poseidon	Neptune
Death	Hades	Pluto

For poetry, perhaps the most important set is Aphrodite/Venus, the goddess of love, and her son Eros/Cupid. The names Venus and Cupid were used more often in English, since Latin was the foundation of European education. But the Latin and Greek stories become mixed; Greek Aphrodite was born as an adult woman out of the sea, then Latin Venus took on this story at some point. Botticelli's painting "The Birth of Venus" shows her standing in a seashell. Eros or Cupid was the son of Love and War, but to match Venus's new watery origin, Cupid began riding on dolphins in paintings. Cupid, as you know, also carried a bow and arrows to shoot humans with love; sometimes stories say he is blindfolded, which demonstrates why love often goes wrong. Cupid is a chubby preschooler in some depictions, a naked but athletic teenager in others.

John Donne mentioned both Venus and Cupid in his early love poems; their names are a clear signal that the poem is intended to be about love *problems*. His sonnet on Cupid is clearly ironic in tone; what is he saying about love?

Cupid, I Hate Thee

Cupid, I hate thee, which I'd have thee know;
A naked starveling ever may'st thou be.
Poor rogue, go pawn thy fascia and thy bow
For some few rags wherewith to cover thee.
Or, if thou'lt not thy archery forbear,
To some base rustic do thyself prefer,
And when corn's sown or grown into the ear,
Practise thy quiver and turn crow-keeper.
Or, being blind, as fittest for the trade,
Go hire thyself some bungling harper's boy;
They that are blind are often minstrels made;
So may'st thou live, to thy fair mother's joy,
That whilst with Mars she holdeth her old way,
Thou, her blind son, may'st sit by them and play.

Edgar Allen Poe was in love with Greek and Roman mythology. "The Raven" is sprinkled with allusions to the pagan gods. First, the poet claims to have a "bust of Pallas" in his room; Victorians loved the truncated statues called busts, which showed only the head and shoulders of someone, and his bust is of Athena, goddess of wisdom, whose other name was Pallas. In stanzas 8 and 17, he refers to night as "the Plutonian shore." Pluto was the Roman name for the god of death, so he is associating night and death.

Certain stories from *The Metamorphoses* were known so well that mere details would be enough to tip off readers. Many of the stories involved people being turned into animals and birds. Famously, a princess of Athens named Philomela was turned into a nightingale after she suffered trauma that left her unable to speak. Sir Philip Sidney, Queen Elizabeth I's courtier, wrote about Philomela in "The Nightingale," and much later, Matthew Arnold wrote a "Philomela." T. S. Eliot brought Philomela into "The Wasteland" by placing a painting of her story on someone's wall:

Above the antique mantel was displayed
As though a window gave upon the sylvan scene
The change of Philomel, by the barbarous king
So rudely forced; yet there the nightingale
Filled all the desert with inviolable voice
And still she cried, and still the world pursues,
"Jug Jug" to dirty ears...

In "Slow, Slow, Fresh Fount," Ben Jonson wrote of another famous transformation: Narcissus, who fell in love with his own reflection and was turned into a waterside flower. He never mentioned the name, he just described the situation and said that "Nature's pride" is now a daffodil. You can appreciate the poem without knowing the story, but it makes more sense if you do. In Jonson's time, anyone who could read knew about Narcissus.

The Iliad and *The Odyssey* are another rich source of mythical stories. "Helen of Troy" becomes a shorthand name for blinding beauty. Poe wrote an ode "To Helen" that also uses Psyche (from a different myth) as a reference for a woman's beauty. The poem was probably written for someone he knew, someone whose inner beauty felt like "home" to him.

To Helen

Helen, thy beauty is to me
Like those Nicaean barks of yore
That gently, o'er a perfumed sea,
The weary, way-worn wanderer bore
To his own native shore.

On desperate seas long wont to roam,
Thy hyacinth hair, thy classic face,
Thy Naiad airs have brought me home
To the glory that was Greece,
And the grandeur that was Rome.

Lo, in yon brilliant window-niche
How statue-like I see thee stand,
The agate lamp within thy hand,
Ah! Psyche, from the regions which
Are Holy Land!

Edgar Allen Poe, 1809-1849

Odysseus's wanderings produced more stories; you saw one reference in Robert Crutchfield's sonnet that appeared in the Exercises 8 set:

Circe turned Odysseus' men to swine;
and something in the story as it's told
proves our resemblance to the men of old...

The sonnet can be enjoyed without knowing the story, since it interprets the reference, but it helps to know who Circe and Odysseus are. Crutchfield's purpose in alluding to the Greek myth is to use the archetypal feeling of a story that's universal – and feels somehow larger than us – to frame his observation about human nature:

...Our daily business, like the poisoned wine
un-humans us; and everything that's fine

or noble in our nature slips our hold,
leaving a chattel to be bought and sold—
our hoped-for vintage dying on the vine.
The hero lives forever in the song—
or lives as long as human eyes can see.
We, anyway, will never live so long,
as mortal beings, so our pride must be
in things of transient beauty said or done,
like water-droplets, blazing in the sun.

The Bible is the other hugely important source of common cultural stories, perhaps especially in America where the Bible was the one book found in every house. Edgar Allen Poe could count on his reading public to know that "is there balm in Gilead?" (Raven, stanza 15) referred to a medicinal perfume mentioned in Jeremiah 8:22. Robert Frost knew that his readers would know this odd name "Abishag" in "Provide, Provide":

The witch that came (the withered hag)
To wash the steps with pail and rag,
Was once the beauty Abishag...

If you know Bible stories well, you recognize her as the young girl hired to be King David's nurse in old age, later sought in marriage by one of his sons. Frost could use her name to evoke Hollywood starlets who are only valued in their youth and then thrown away. His message is the complement of Waller's: knowing that someday you will be a wilted rose, plan ahead for the rejection: "provide."

Milton assumed you would know the story that Jesus told, in which a rich man went on a long journey and gave sums of money, in silver talents, to his employees to invest. The one who brought shame on himself was the servant who didn't want to earn any profit with his sum: since the profit would belong to his boss, he buried the silver in a hole. Milton compares his blindness to this man's action; when he mentions "that talent which is death to hide" he assumes that he can evoke the whole story with one reference.

There are countless poems that reference Adam, Eve, Eden (it appears as "Aidenn" in "The Raven"), Abraham, Moses, and Jesus. Christina Rossetti brought both Jesus and Moses into her image of herself as a rock:

Greater than Moses, turn and look once more
And smite a rock.

The only way to know all the stories that are referenced this way is to read widely and look up anything unfamiliar. Most Americans are still very familiar with the Bible, which may be taught as literature even when it isn't believed in faith. Anyone who wants to get every reference in classic English poetry would certainly be well-advised to read *The Odyssey* and *The Metamorphoses*, as well as the Bible.

2. Myth as dramatic situation

The Greek and Latin myths, stories from the Bible, tales of King Arthur, and fairy tales have provided many poets with dramatic situations for their own story development. Let's say you want to meditate on some difficult personal situation, but you don't want to write a confessional poem that lays it all bare, or you want to take some of the partisan sting out of your thoughts on a national situation. You can find a myth that sets up a dramatic situation you can talk about, and in doing so, you say what you wanted to say that's personal or controversial. The myth, being such a commonly-known story, doesn't need the same type of set-up and backstory that the real story would need. You can drop a few names or details and your readers will be on board.

Matthew Arnold's "Philomela" considers whether time heals grief and pain. Hearing a nightingale in England, he imagines that it is the same one Philomela became, and asks,

> O Wanderer from a Grecian shore,
> Still, after many years, in distant lands,
> Still nourishing in thy bewilder'd brain
> That wild, unquench'd, deep-sunken, old-world pain—
> Say, will it never heal?
> And can this fragrant lawn
> With its cool trees, and night,
> And the sweet, tranquil Thames,
> And moonshine, and the dew,
> To thy rack'd heart and brain
> Afford no balm?

It's not much of a stretch to see that Arnold is talking about the general case: can a tranquil environment heal emotional pain? We don't know any backstory on his writing this poem; he might have been struggling with grief, or he might have been close to someone who was. But the story isn't what he wants to share with us. By choosing the dramatic situation of Philomela, he touches on what's common to all who suffer from injustice and trauma, asking whether what's external to the soul can touch it inside.

Tennyson chose to develop the dramatic situation of Odysseus, the Greek lord who went to Troy and did not return home for many years. Using the Latin version of the name, Ulysses, he presents the man now home, ruling his people, sighing for his old freedom:

> It little profits that an idle king,
> By this still hearth, among these barren crags,
> Match'd with an aged wife, I mete and dole
> Unequal laws unto a savage race,
> That hoard, and sleep, and feed, and know not me.
> I cannot rest from travel: I will drink
> Life to the lees: All times I have enjoy'd
> Greatly, have suffer'd greatly, both with those
> That loved me, and alone, on shore, and when
> Thro' scudding drifts the rainy Hyades
> Vext the dim sea: I am become a name;
> For always roaming with a hungry heart...

We think of a homecoming as joyous, leading to an ideal resolution, and so the voyage of Ulysses/Odysseus is presented in the original epic poems. But what about later, Tennyson asks? What about when you've won your prizes against all odds, but the next morning the sun comes up and life's meaning has changed? Tennyson himself may have experienced some of this, becoming Poet Laureate, Britain's most honored writer, at the age of 41. There was no higher goal to reach, but it was only the midpoint of his life.

Myths may serve as allusions or straightforward dramatic situations, but they may also be a familiar point from which to veer into contrasting or unexpected themes. New ideas can be a sequel to the myth, a new twist on the myth's events, or some other layer of commentary.

In a poem about Hades and Persephone, I imagined that after Hades kidnapped Persephone and forced her into seven months of marriage each year, it turned out to be a huge mistake. I had been thinking about unhappy marriages, so I took the dramatic situation of Persephone, sitting in the underworld as queen, and imagined them bickering like a modern unhappy couple. As immortal gods, they were not able to separate or divorce, nor even to dodge each other's presence by, say, choosing to take a shower just when the other was having breakfast. It was comic to mix modern details into the Greek scene that still included Charon, the ferryman who helped souls cross the River Styx. The reference to spring only makes sense if you realize that the myth of Persephone explained the seasons: when Persephone returns to the topside of earth for a while, it will be spring and summer.

Persephone

Not for them the shower or newsprint screen;
no perky morning broadcast made a wall
between their thrones in Hell's enormous hall.

She took a folding mirror, checked her eyes,
redrew her red, red lips, then smiled and pursed.
He watched her, slammed his forehead hard, and cursed.

"O God!" he groaned, "up there they talk of spring!
It can't come soon enough: I'd see you pack
tomorrow if I could and send you back."

"He blames me *now*," she told her fingernails,
"but I was picking flowers in the hay,
had he not snatched me, there I'd be today."

"Then go," he cried. "Gladden the earth, goddess!
Bring summer everlasting, stay all year!
You bring nothing but cold and darkness here!"

"Those pomegranate seeds, all your idea!
You liked me *then*" (the mirror caught her pout)
"and anyway, I tried to spit them out!"

"Like hell you did," he growled, "as if you'd spit—-"
The clock chimed; Charon started taking tolls;
Their bailiff brought the morning's crop of souls.

Persephone and Hell left off their quarrel:
they lost expression, gripped their chairs and froze.
To rule the dead required this dual pose.

No, not for them the suitcase or the grave;
divinities are permanently mated.
Through centuries of seasons, still they hated.

For a very different meditation, I chose the story of Psyche, who is another favorite of literary references. Psyche's name means "soul," and she was secretly married to Eros, the god of love. She had been tied to a hillside, sacrificed to a monster, but Eros had rescued her without her seeing his face; he put her in a safe place but only visited her in the dark. In the myth, her sisters visit her new palace but in their jealousy, they tempt her to use a forbidden light to see her husband, to prove he isn't a monster. When Psyche does this, she spills a drop of hot oil from her lamp, and when it awakens Eros, he leaves her in his anger. Her myth goes on to tell how she earns back his favor with quests.

But I was interested in using Psyche's story in a symbolic way: Soul meets Love in the physical body. In my retelling, her husband actually does turn out to look like an animal, but in the darkness and lamplight, she sees that they are both covered with fur; if he is a monster, so is she. My poem is really about how difficult it can be for us to accept the body's limitations when our minds feel immortal, and how love often forces us to do just this. It opens with the dramatic situation of Psyche's sisters tempting and mocking her:

PSYCHE

They said her love was beastly, not divine.
She said she was prohibited from seeing.

They promised her that light would be benign.
She bit her lip in doubt, perhaps agreeing.

She dared: on fur and claw the lamp did shine,
but her hand, too, was fur. So truth was freeing,

For both were meat and ghost, pelt and divine.
She snuffed the lamp to keep her god from fleeing.

Their story is the same as yours and mine,
How Soul meets Flesh: the romance of our being.

I could have written the same idea without using Psyche's story, but the myth provided a basic framework that allowed me to sketch it briefly with a dramatic flair. Because Psyche's name means "soul," she is a ready-made symbol for the human spirit. In this case, I certainly wanted to invoke the archetypal images that come with her myth.

In 1940, W. H. Auden wanted to say something about the modern world. He saw reckless decadence, discontent, luxury, and poverty, and he feared that disunity and inequality would lead to the fall of civilization. The myth ready to his hand was the fall of Rome, which is real history; the phrase, though, has become a cliché to us, a simplified story from the past. Auden could take the idea of "The Fall of Rome" and portray it with modern details mixed in:

The piers are pummeled by the waves;
In a lonely field the rain
Lashes an abandoned train;
Outlaws fill the mountain caves.

This isn't much like historical Rome, starting with the anachronism of a train. But it portrays the dismaying mood of a place in free fall: the piers, where foreign merchants should be unloading their wares, are being smashed into splinters by bad weather, possibly by a rising sea level; the train, a symbol of progress and travel, has been abandoned; and the city is not the focus at all, rather its outlying caves where robbers prey on travelers.

The poem goes on to mix historical names, such as Caesar and Cato, with modern details: clerks, evening-gowns, Marines, and a flu epidemic. At the close, Auden shows nature going about its business while the city grows miserable and sick. Nature is "unendowed with wealth or pity." The poem's closing lines suggest that ultimately our cities are unimportant to the history of the natural world, which endures:

> Altogether elsewhere, vast
> Herds of reindeer move across
> Miles and miles of golden moss,
> Silently and very fast.

3. Poetry to create myths

Henry Wadsworth Longfellow, a professor of Romance Languages at Bowdoin and Harvard Colleges, was keenly aware of the role of myth in Europe's literature. His special calling as a poet was to create American myths by writing poetry about American events and people. We've all heard of Paul Revere, but it's likely that the silversmith of Boston was never famous until Longfellow wrote his story in a collection of narrative poems. We have all heard the opening lines:

> Listen, my children, and you shall hear
> Of the midnight ride of Paul Revere,
> On the eighteenth of April, in Seventy-five;
> Hardly a man is now alive
> Who remembers that famous day and year.
>
> He said to his friend, "If the British march
> By land or sea from the town to-night,
> Hang a lantern aloft in the belfry arch
> Of the North Church tower as a signal light,—
> One, if by land, and two, if by sea;
> And I on the opposite shore will be,
> Ready to ride and spread the alarm
> Through every Middlesex village and farm,
> For the country folk to be up and to arm."

Longfellow's poem appeared in *The Atlantic Monthly* in 1861, as the Union states gathered energy to fight the Confederacy. As the poem notes, the last men who had been children during the American Revolution had recently died. Longfellow wanted to provide the Union with a myth to encourage them to emulate their great-grandfathers. During the 19th century, school children memorized many poems, so "Paul Revere's Ride" quickly became part of their school recitation programs. Revere, a minor figure even in Boston, became a legend.

Native American legend told of an Iroquois leader who worked to unite the related tribes in New York and around the Great Lakes. We might not know the name "Hiawatha" if Longfellow had not chosen to celebrate his story in another myth-making poem. The story of how the "Six Nations" came to be united was told only among its member tribes (the Mohawk, Onondaga, Oneida, Cayuga, Seneca, and Tuscarora), and the historical Hiawatha may have lived as long ago as 1142 AD, one of the years when a solar eclipse occurred, matching a detail in the legend. It is likely that the legends would have faded into obscurity, but Longfellow chose to write them into a narrative poem that celebrated unity among American peoples.

In "The Song of Hiawatha," Longfellow blended Iroquois words with trochaic meter, seeking to imitate in English the effect of a Native American drummer's beat.

> On the shores of Gitche Gumee,
> Of the shining Big-Sea-Water,
> Stood Nokomis, the old woman,
> Pointing with her finger westward...

Nokomis was Hiawatha's grandmother; his deceased mother's name, Wenonah, has come into mainstream American culture as Winona. People who have never read "The Song of Hiawatha" have still heard the name of Minnehaha, Hiawatha's bride, because Longfellow used the name of a beautiful waterfall in Minneapolis for her name, in "Hiawatha's Wooing." Minnesota was part of the land of the Dakota Sioux:

> At the doorway of his wigwam
> Sat the ancient Arrow-maker,
> In the land of the Dacotahs,
> Making arrow-heads of jasper,
> Arrow-heads of chalcedony.
> At his side, in all her beauty,
> Sat the lovely Minnehaha,
> Sat his daughter, Laughing Water,
> Plaiting mats of flags and rushes
> Of the past the old man's thoughts were,
> And the maiden's of the future.

Poetry and myth feed back and forth into each other. The Greek myths came to us in poetry, as did the stories about Troy and Odysseus (in the *Iliad* and the *Odyssey*). Many of our tales of King Arthur came through medieval poems that took the bare facts, names and dramatic situations, developing them as new stories. So did the stories of Robin Hood.

How much of what we think we know about Santa Claus actually comes from Clement Clarke Moore's "A Visit from St. Nicholas," published in a New York newspaper in 1823?

> 'Twas the night before Christmas, when all thro' the house
> Not a creature was stirring, not even a mouse;
> The stockings were hung by the chimney with care,
> In hopes that St. Nicholas soon would be there...

Without this poem, we might not even care about Santa himself, let alone his individual reindeer:

> "Now! Dasher, now! Dancer, now! Prancer and Vixen,
> "On! Comet, on! Cupid, on! Donder and Blixen;
> "To the top of the porch! To the top of the wall!
> "Now dash away! Dash away! Dash away all!"

It's probably also the first time St. Nicholas (an early medieval saint) was called an elf, giving rise to the whole legend of his North Pole toy workshop and elves. Would we know the names of Santa's mythical reindeer without poetry? Would we even think he *had* a sleigh pulled by reindeer? How much of our American Christmas, and now the world's Christmas, was created by this one poem's myth-making effort?

Summary and Definitions

A *myth* is a simplified, traditional story that is common to all the people in some culture or nation. The term often refers to the stories about Greek and Roman gods and goddesses, but English poetry draws not only from these, but also from Bible stories, folk tales, and events of history. Names, events and details from some common story can be mentioned to bring in the attitudes or morals of the story. They can also introduce symbolic meaning.

Poetry often develops a myth or Bible story by shaping its meaning. Since most myths owe their original fame to poetry, it is hard to completely separate the two literary forms.

Exercises 15

Review: "The Coat," W. B. Yeats
a) Describe the meter.
b) What is the rhyme scheme?
c) How is the image of the coat used here? What does it tell us about his poetry?

The Coat

> I made my song a coat
> Covered with embroideries
> Out of old mythologies
> From heel to throat;
> But the fools caught it,
> Wore it in the world's eyes
> As though they'd wrought it.
> Song, let them take it
> For there's more enterprise
> In walking naked.

1. Greek heroes A to Z: how well do you know the superheroes of the Classical world? Here's a list of people and places; a few letters didn't get used, while a few of them had too many important names to give just one. A few of the names are double, showing you the Greek and Latin names. See how many you can get on the first try, then use reference materials to figure out the remaining names. If you can match all of them, good work! (they're scrambled within three sets of ten, to keep the matching simple)

Achilles	1 god of wine
Aeneas	2 god of the sun, prophecy, and poetry
Ajax	3 the "heaven" of the Greek underworld
Apollo	4 magical lady of an island, turned men into pigs
Athena	5 hero of Trojan War who had a weak heel
Bacchus/Dionysus	6 she was turned into a nightingale
Circe	7 the place where Apollo's priestess told futures
Delphi	8 hero of Trojan War, then founder of Rome
Elysian Fields	9 hero of Trojan War who was very strong
(F) Philomela	10 goddess of wisdom, also named Pallas
Gorgon	11 he flew too near the sun with wax wings
Helen	12 first woman, she opened a box of trouble
Icarus	13 best musician who sang for Hades/Pluto
Jason	14 beautiful queen who started the Trojan War
Lethe	15 the minor goddesses of the arts
Muses	16 Odysseus' wife who kept weaving for years
Narcissus	17 a monster, for example Medusa
Orpheus	18 he sailed in quest of the Golden Fleece
Pandora	19 he fell in love with his reflection
Penelope	20 the underworld's river of forgetfulness
Persephone	21 ancient city, site of long war
Pluto/Hades	22 the twin founders of Rome
(Q) Cupid/Eros	23 king of the gods
Romulus and Remus	24 hero of the Trojan war, wandered 10 years
Sisyphus	25 goddess of love, mother of Cupid/Eros
Troy	26 god of the underworld, married Persephone
Ulysses/Odysseus	27 boundary river of underworld
Venus/Aphrodite	28 god of love, carries a bow
(X) Styx	29 daughter of Demeter, kidnapped
Zeus/Jupiter	30 he pushes a rock uphill forever

2. John Keats' famous "Ode to a Nightingale" draws in several "myth" references at once. By writing about a nightingale, he tacitly draws on the story of Philomela, but Keats did not develop her story directly. His nightingale is pictured as real: he is sitting outdoors, and he hears the bird's song. The poem records his series of emotional responses. He wants to join the bird in complete happiness, and while his first thought is that wine could make him feel happy, he rejects this shortcut. Instead, he wants to use poetry-writing to achieve ecstasy. In the closing lines, the bird flies away.

   a) How does Keats' stanza here compare with the stanza he used in "Ode on a Grecian Urn"?

   b) The first two stanzas invoke four classical (either Greek or Roman) names. Hippocrene and Lethe are water sources (you just saw Lethe above). What do they stand for? Who is Flora, and what is a Dryad? Why is the nightingale a dryad?

   c) The third stanza has no mythological references, but it forms the emotional background of the poem. Keats' brother was dying of tuberculosis, which killed the poet shortly after. How many details of sadness in the world does Keats catalog as things the bird cannot know?

   d) In the fourth stanza, Keats rejects using wine for forgetfulness, with the line, "not charioted by Bacchus and his pards." Who is Bacchus? Notes: The stanza also cites the "Queen-Moon;" in Greek mythology, the sun-god Apollo's twin was Artemis, who ruled both the moon and hunting. "Pard" is a medieval shorthand for "leopard" (its Latin name is Panthera pardus). Keats was thinking of images like this Roman mosaic:

   e) In the next stanzas, Keats muses on the bird's immortality, to contrast with the death he feels all around him, so that to join the bird seems like a pleasant way to die. In stanza 7, he has one of the most memorable lines and images in all of his poetry. He invokes the Bible story of Ruth, great-grandmother of King David, who came to Israel as a stranger. (If you are not familiar with the Book of Ruth, please read it.) How does Keats develop the dramatic situation in just these few lines? What human story does he suggest, and what details does he add to the original story?

Ode to a Nightingale

My heart aches, and a drowsy numbness pains
    My sense, as though of hemlock I had drunk,
Or emptied some dull opiate to the drains
    One minute past, and Lethe-wards had sunk:
'Tis not through envy of thy happy lot,
    But being too happy in thine happiness—
        That thou, light-winged Dryad of the trees,
            In some melodious plot
    Of beechen green, and shadows numberless,
        Singest of summer in full-throated ease.

O, for a draught of vintage! that hath been
    Cooled a long age in the deep-delved earth,
Tasting of Flora and the country green,
    Dance, and Provençal song, and sunburnt mirth!
O for a beaker full of the warm South,
    Full of the true, the blushful Hippocrene,
        With beaded bubbles winking at the brim,
            And purple-stained mouth;
    That I might drink, and leave the world unseen,
        And with thee fade away into the forest dim:

Fade far away, dissolve, and quite forget
    What thou among the leaves hast never known,
The weariness, the fever, and the fret
    Here, where men sit and hear each other groan;
Where palsy shakes a few, sad, last gray hairs,
    Where youth grows pale, and specter-thin, and dies;
        Where but to think is to be full of sorrow
            And leaden-eyed despairs,
    Where Beauty cannot keep her lustrous eyes,
        Or new Love pine at them beyond tomorrow.

Away! away! for I will fly to thee,
    Not charioted by Bacchus and his pards,
But on the viewless wings of Poesy,
    Though the dull brain perplexes and retards:
Already with thee! tender is the night,
    And haply the Queen-Moon is on her throne,
        Clustered around by all her starry Fays;
            But here there is no light,
    Save what from heaven is with the breezes blown
        Through verdurous glooms and winding mossy ways.

I cannot see what flowers are at my feet,
    Nor what soft incense hangs upon the boughs,
But, in embalmed darkness, guess each sweet
    Wherewith the seasonable month endows
The grass, the thicket, and the fruit tree wild;
    White hawthorn, and the pastoral eglantine;
        Fast fading violets covered up in leaves;
        And mid-May's eldest child,
    The coming musk-rose, full of dewy wine,
        The murmurous haunt of flies on summer eves.

Darkling I listen; and for many a time
    I have been half in love with easeful Death,
Called him soft names in many a mused rhyme,
    To take into the air my quiet breath;
Now more than ever seems it rich to die,
    To cease upon the midnight with no pain,
        While thou art pouring forth thy soul abroad,
        In such an ecstasy!
    Still wouldst thou sing, and I have ears in vain—
        To thy high requiem become a sod.

Thou wast not born for death, immortal Bird!
    No hungry generations tread thee down;
The voice I hear this passing night was heard
    In ancient days by emperor and clown:
Perhaps the selfsame song that found a path
    Through the sad heart of Ruth when, sick for home,
        She stood in tears amid the alien corn;
        The same that ofttimes hath
    Charm'd magic casements, opening on the foam
        Of perilous seas, in faery lands forlorn.

Forlorn! the very word is like a bell
    To toll me back from thee to my sole self!
Adieu! the fancy cannot cheat so well
    As she is famed to do, deceiving elf.
Adieu! adieu! thy plaintive anthem fades
    Past the near meadows, over the still stream,
        Up the hill side; and now 'tis buried deep
        In the next valley-glades:
    Was it a vision, or a waking dream?
        Fled is that music:—Do I wake or sleep?

John Keats, 1795-1821

3. In the story of the birth of Jesus, there were two separate uninvited visiting parties. Shepherds from nearby hills came into the village to find the baby announced to them by angels (Luke 2: 8-20). Wise men from the East then arrived, led by their studies in astronomy to expect the birth of a great king (Matthew 2: 1-12). The stories are well known in Christian culture, so they formed a good setting for Sidney Godolphin to meditate on the sides of mankind that they demonstrate.

   a) The "highest Cause" in philosophy meant the purpose for which things are done. What other words and things does Godolphin associate with the "wise men"? What do they offer at the altar?

   b) By contrast, what words and ideas are associated with the shepherds? What do they offer at the altar?

   c) What parts of human nature do the wise men and shepherds seem to symbolize?

   d) Why do all ways lead to "wonder," according to the poet?

   e) What is the moral the poet draws from the story, for us?

> Lord, when the wise men came from far,
> Led to Thy cradle by a star,
> Then did the shepherds too rejoice,
> Instructed by Thy Angel's voice:
> Blest were the wise men in their skill
> And shepherds in their harmless will.
>
> Wise men in tracing Nature's laws
> Ascend unto the highest Cause;
> Shepherds with humble fearfulness
> Walk safely, though their Light be Life:
> Though wise men better know the way
> It seems no honest heart can stray.
>
> There is no merit in the wise
> But Love (the shepherds' sacrifice);
> Wise men, all ways of knowledge past,
> To the shepherds' wonder come at last:
> To know can only wonder breed,
> And not to know is wonder's seed.
>
> A wise man at the altar bows
> And offers up his studied vows,
> And is received,—may not the tears,
> Which springs too from a shepherd's fears,
> And sighs upon his frailty spent,
> Though not distinct, be eloquent?
>
> 'Tis true, the object sanctifies
> All passions which within us rise,

But since no creature comprehends
The Cause of causes, End of Ends,
He who himself vouchsafes to know
Best pleases his Creator so.

When, then, our sorrows we apply,
To our own wants and poverty,
When we look up in all distress
And our own misery confess,
Sending both thanks and prayers above—
Then, though we do not know, we love.

Sidney Godolphin (1610–1643)

Yeats, featured below, also wrote a poem about the Magi in 1916. If you find it hard to understand, you're not alone.

The Magi

Now as at all times I can see in the mind's eye,
In their stiff, painted clothes, the pale unsatisfied ones
Appear and disappear in the blue depth of the sky
With all their ancient faces like rain-beaten stones,
And all their helms of silver hovering side by side,
And all their eyes still fixed, hoping to find once more,
Being by Calvary's turbulence unsatisfied,
The uncontrollable mystery on the bestial floor.

W. B. Yeats, 1865-1939

4. Tennyson's 1832 poem "The Lotos-Eaters" takes a dramatic situation from *The Odyssey*, to rework with a new theme. In the original story, Odysseus and his sailors go on shore, where natives offer them lotos flowers to eat. The sailors who eat the lotos are lulled into a drugged state and refuse to go on. During Tennyson's lifetime, opium use had become a serious problem; it was used as legitimate medicine, but people also went to "opium dens" to smoke it. They became seriously addicted. Tennyson may not have intended to meditate on drug use per se, because in later sections of the poem, the lotos-eating sailors discuss other themes of society and morality, but opium's power clearly shapes his story.

Odysseus is probably the "he" who says "Courage!" The ship has been in distress, so they are glad to see land, with no premonition of the subtle danger.

   a) Each stanza has nine lines; its form is called the Spenserian stanza, invented by Edmund Spenser (1553-1599) for *The Faerie Queene*. What is the rhyme scheme? What is the meter? Notice the meter of the final line in each stanza. How does the irregular foot in the first line affect the feeling of the line's meaning?

   b) Much of the poem is descriptive, although the place is idealized and unrealistic. What are its geographical features? What plants grow there?

c) How does the poem depict time (as marked by sun and moon)?

The Lotos-Eaters

"Courage!" he said, and pointed toward the land,
"This mounting wave will roll us shoreward soon."
In the afternoon they came unto a land
In which it seemed always afternoon.
All round the coast the languid air did swoon,
Breathing like one that hath a weary dream.
Full-faced above the valley stood the moon;
And like a downward smoke, the slender stream
Along the cliff to fall and pause and fall did seem.

A land of streams! some, like a downward smoke,
Slow-dropping veils of thinnest lawn, did go;
And some thro' wavering lights and shadows broke,
Rolling a slumbrous sheet of foam below.
They saw the gleaming river seaward flow
From the inner land: far off, three mountain-tops,
Three silent pinnacles of aged snow,
Stood sunset-flush'd: and, dew'd with showery drops,
Up-clomb the shadowy pine above the woven copse.

The charmed sunset linger'd low adown
In the red West: thro' mountain clefts the dale
Was seen far inland, and the yellow down
Border'd with palm, and many a winding vale
And meadow, set with slender galingale;
A land where all things always seem'd the same!
And round about the keel with faces pale,
Dark faces pale against that rosy flame,
The mild-eyed melancholy Lotos-eaters came.

Branches they bore of that enchanted stem,
Laden with flower and fruit, whereof they gave
To each, but whoso did receive of them,
And taste, to him the gushing of the wave
Far far away did seem to mourn and rave
On alien shores; and if his fellow spake,
His voice was thin, as voices from the grave;
And deep-asleep he seem'd, yet all awake,
And music in his ears his beating heart did make.

They sat them down upon the yellow sand,

Between the sun and moon upon the shore;
And sweet it was to dream of Fatherland,
Of child, and wife, and slave; but evermore
Most weary seem'd the sea, weary the oar,
Weary the wandering fields of barren foam.
Then some one said, "We will return no more";
And all at once they sang, "Our island home
Is far beyond the wave; we will no longer roam."

Alfred Tennyson, 1809-1892

5. The lines that begin "On the shores of Gitche Gumee" open the ninth part of "The Song of Hiawatha," in which Nokomis urges her heroic grandson to attack Megissogwon, a magician. His name in English, Pearl Feather, is also used; and "Mama" does not mean mother; it is the Iroquois word for wood-pecker.

What heroic, unrealistic elements does Longfellow put into Hiawatha's tale? What fact of nature does the story explain?

...Westward thus fared Hiawatha,
Toward the realm of Megissogwon,
Toward the land of the Pearl-Feather,
Till the level moon stared at him,
In his face stared pale and haggard,
Till the sun was hot behind him,
Till it burned upon his shoulders,
And before him on the upland
He could see the Shining Wigwam
Of the Manito of Wampum,
Of the mightiest of Magicians.
Then once more Cheemaun he patted,
To his birch-canoe said, "Onward!"
And it stirred in all its fibres,
And with one great bound of triumph
Leaped across the water-lilies,
Leaped through tangled flags and rushes,
And upon the beach beyond them
Dry-shod landed Hiawatha.
Straight he took his bow of ash-tree,
On the sand one end he rested,
With his knee he pressed the middle,
Stretched the faithful bow-string tighter,
Took an arrow, jasper-headed,
Shot it at the Shining Wigwam,
Sent it singing as a herald,
As a bearer of his message,

Of his challenge loud and lofty:
"Come forth from your lodge, Pearl-Feather!
Hiawatha waits your coming!"
Straightway from the Shining Wigwam
Came the mighty Megissogwon,
Tall of stature, broad of shoulder,
Dark and terrible in aspect,
Clad from head to foot in wampum,
Armed with all his warlike weapons,
Painted like the sky of morning,
Streaked with crimson, blue, and yellow,
Crested with great eagle-feathers,
Streaming upward, streaming outward.
"Well I know you, Hiawatha!"
Cried he in a voice of thunder,
In a tone of loud derision.
"Hasten back, O Shaugodaya!
Hasten back among the women,
Back to old Nokomis, Faint-heart!
I will slay you as you stand there,
As of old I slew her father!"
But my Hiawatha answered,
Nothing daunted, fearing nothing:
"Big words do not smite like war-clubs,
Boastful breath is not a bow-string,
Taunts are not so sharp as arrows,
Deeds are better things than words are,
Actions mightier than boastings!"
Then began the greatest battle
That the sun had ever looked on,
That the war-birds ever witnessed.
All a Summer's day it lasted,
From the sunrise to the sunset;
For the shafts of Hiawatha
Harmless hit the shirt of wampum,
Harmless fell the blows he dealt it
With his mittens, Minjekahwun,
Harmless fell the heavy war-club;
It could dash the rocks asunder,
But it could not break the meshes
Of that magic shirt of wampum.
Till at sunset Hiawatha,
Leaning on his bow of ash-tree,
Wounded, weary, and desponding,
With his mighty war-club broken,

With his mittens torn and tattered,
And three useless arrows only,
Paused to rest beneath a pine-tree,
From whose branches trailed the mosses,
And whose trunk was coated over
With the Dead-man's Moccasin-leather,
With the fungus white and yellow.
Suddenly from the boughs above him
Sang the Mama, the woodpecker:
"Aim your arrows, Hiawatha,
At the head of Megissogwon,
Strike the tuft of hair upon it,
At their roots the long black tresses;
There alone can he be wounded!"
Winged with feathers, tipped with jasper,
Swift flew Hiawatha's arrow,
Just as Megissogwon, stooping,
Raised a heavy stone to throw it.
Full upon the crown it struck him,
At the roots of his long tresses,
And he reeled and staggered forward,
Plunging like a wounded bison,
Yes, like Pezhekee, the bison,
When the snow is on the prairie.
Swifter flew the second arrow,
In the pathway of the other,
Piercing deeper than the other,
Wounding sorer than the other;
And the knees of Megissogwon
Shook like windy reeds beneath him,
Bent and trembled like the rushes.
But the third and latest arrow
Swiftest flew, and wounded sorest,
And the mighty Megissogwon
Saw the fiery eyes of Pauguk,
Saw the eyes of Death glare at him,
Heard his voice call in the darkness;
At the feet of Hiawatha
Lifeless lay the great Pearl-Feather,
Lay the mightiest of Magicians.
Then the grateful Hiawatha
Called the Mama, the woodpecker,
From his perch among the branches
Of the melancholy pine-tree,
And, in honor of his service,

> Stained with blood the tuft of feathers
> On the little head of Mama;
> Even to this day he wears it,
> Wears the tuft of crimson feathers,
> As a symbol of his service...

Henry Wadsworth Longfellow, 1807-1882

6. In 1923 and 1924, two American women wrote poems that used myth-like stories as settings to criticize attitudes they saw developing in the modern world. Marjorie Allen Seiffert's "The New Eve" was part of three sonnets "Concerning the Knowledge of Good and Evil," published in *Poetry* magazine. Elizabeth J. Coatsworth's "Demeter" appeared in *Poetry* about six months later. In each poem, a single female figure is the central image, but they are used in different ways and to make different criticisms.

   a) How does Seiffert's poem want us to see the serpent? How does this view interact with the serpent's archetypal figure?

   b) How do the poems present their central female figures differently? How would it change the "Eve" poem if Eve spoke?

   c) The narrator of "The New Eve" makes a complaint against the younger generation. How would you put it in your words?

   d) In "Demeter," we must guess what the speaker is responding to. What has she been hearing? How would it change the poem if the same speech was given, but we had no tip that the speaker was Demeter? In your words, what is the poem's complaint about the modern world?

THE NEW EVE

> The wise and lovely serpent in the garden
> Where our first parents lived in innocence
> Offered them unknown fruit, and there commence
> The fever known as sin, the dream called pardon.
> Today a sturdier Eve confronts the warden
> Of the forbidden fruit. She circumvents
> Man's ancient thirst for sin with common sense,
> Fed on wild crab-apples their spirits harden.
>
> Cynical innocents, they cling together;
> It is a non-man's-land they wander in,
> A two-dimensional desert, flat and waste.
> The older generation wonder whether
> The fruit was really bitter to the taste
> Which opened to them the height and depth of sin.

Marjorie Allen Seiffert, 1885-1970

Demeter

And hearing the complaints of the reapers,
The Lady straightened her back among the sheaves,
Wiping the sweat from her eyes,
Towering like a golden pillar among them.
"Fools," she said,
"Are you not content with receiving the gift of grain
That you must grudge the flowers to Persephone?"

And then in their silence she spoke again:
"You are blind with greed," said she;
"Is the wheat enough? Is it enough to live?
Do you need nothing to fill your hearts?
You forget," said Demeter, "that it is the songs you sing
for joy of the flowers
That strengthen your arms for the swing of the heavy scythes."

Elizabeth J. Coatsworth, 1893-1986

7. For further reading, look up the poems cited in the text but not provided in full:

"The Nightingale," Sir Philip Sidney

"Philomela," Matthew Arnold

"Provide, Provide," Robert Frost

"Ulysses," Alfred Lord Tennyson

"The Fall of Rome," W. H. Auden

"Paul Revere's Ride" and *The Song of Hiawatha*, Henry Wadsworth Longfellow

"A Visit from St. Nicholas," Clement Clarke Moore

Of course, there are many further reading options concerning shared cultural stories and old mythology: The Bible, *The Arabian Nights*, collections of Greek and Norse myths, Ovid's *Metamorphoses*.

Last Review

1. What is poetry? _____
   _____

What are the basic sound elements of the English language that are used in poetry?

2. _____
3. _____
4. _____

Match the lines of poetry with the correct label:
[iambic pentameter; iambic tetrameter; iambic trimeter; trochaic tetrameter; accentual tetrameter; accentual dimeter; dactylic hexameter; no regular meter at all]

5. Leaped across the water-lilies,
   Leaped through tangled flags and rushes,
   And upon the beach beyond them
   Dry-shod landed Hiawatha. _____

6. They sat them down upon the yellow sand,
   Between the sun and moon upon the shore; _____

7. A cold coming we had of it,
   Just the worst time of the year
   For a journey, and such a long journey: _____

8. How clear, how lovely bright,
   How beautiful to sight
   Those beams of morning play; _____

9. Why should the world be over-wise,
   In counting all our tears and sighs? _____

10. Hang a lantern aloft in the belfry arch
    Of the North Church tower as a signal light,—
    One, if by land, and two, if by sea; _____

11. This is the forest primeval;
    but where are the hearts that beneath it

    Leaped like the roe, when he hears in the
    woodland the voice of the huntsman?_____

12. Gaily bedight,

    A gallant knight,_____

Some poems by Emily Dickinson shows us images used in various ways. Look carefully at each italicized image, and decide whether it is best described as simile, metaphor, symbol, or myth. (When two answers are required, count one of them as a bonus point.)

13. _____

    He ate and drank the precious words,
    His spirit grew robust;
    He knew no more that he was poor,
    Nor that his frame was dust.
    He danced along the dingy days,
    And this bequest of wings
    Was but a book. What liberty
    A loosened spirit brings!

14. Belshazzar _____ and the conscience reading on a wall _____

    Belshazzar had a letter,—
    He never had but one;
    Belshazzar's correspondent
    Concluded and begun
    In that immortal copy
    The conscience of us all
    Can read without its glasses
    On revelation's wall.

15. _____

    Portraits are to daily faces
    As an evening west
    To a fine, pedantic sunshine
    In a satin vest.

16. (the frigate) _____ and (the chariot) _____

> *There is no frigate like a book*
> *To take us lands away,*
> *Nor any coursers like a page*
> *Of prancing poetry.*
>
> *This traverse may the poorest take*
> *Without oppress of toll;*
> *How frugal is the chariot*
> *That bears a human soul!*

17. _____

> *Remembrance has a rear and front,—*
> *'T is something like a house;*
> *It has a garret also*
> *For refuse and the mouse,*
>
> *Besides, the deepest cellar*
> *That ever mason hewed;*
> *Look to it, by its fathoms*
> *Ourselves be not pursued.*

18. The slant of light on winter afternoons and the weight of cathedral tunes _____

> *There's a certain slant of light,*
> *On winter afternoons,*
> *That oppresses, like the weight*
> *Of cathedral tunes.*
>
> *Heavenly hurt it gives us;*
> *We can find no scar,*
> *But internal difference*
> *Where the meanings are.*
>
> *None may teach it anything,*
> *'T is the seal, despair,—*
> *An imperial affliction*
> *Sent us of the air.*
>
> *When it comes, the landscape listens,*
> *Shadows hold their breath;*
> *When it goes, 't is like the distance*
> *On the look of death.*

19. Jacob wrestling _____

> A little over Jordan,
> As Genesis record,
> *An Angel and a Wrestler*
> *Did wrestle long and hard.*
>
> Till, morning touching mountain,
> And Jacob waxing strong,
> The Angel begged permission
> To breakfast and return.
>
> "Not so," quoth wily Jacob,
> And girt his loins anew,
> "Until thou bless me, stranger!"
> The which acceded to:
>
> Light swung the silver fleeces
> Peniel hills among,
> And the astonished Wrestler
> Found he had worsted God!

20. Robert Frost wrote a very unusual _____. How is it unusual?

    Bonus: The image of the night is used as a _____.

> ### I HAVE BEEN ONE ACQUAINTED WITH THE NIGHT
>
> I have been one acquainted with the night.
> I have walked out in rain—and back in rain.
> I have outwalked the furthest city light.
>
> I have looked down the saddest city lane.
> I have passed by the watchman on his beat
> And dropped my eyes, unwilling to explain.
>
> I have stood still and stopped the sound of feet
> When far away an interrupted cry
> Came over houses from another street,
>
> But not to call me back or say good-bye;
> And further still at an unearthly height,
> One luminary clock against the sky
>
> Proclaimed the time was neither wrong nor right.
> I have been one acquainted with the night.

Sixteen:

Image as Story

Narrative verse uses some type of poetic style to tell a story. Perhaps because poetic style can help with memorization, many traditional stories were told in verse. When the whole story was not in verse, it often included sections that were, perhaps to introduce or close it. Stories told entirely in prose without *any* poetic elements seem to appear only in relatively modern times. Famous stories of the Middle Ages were told in verse: *The Song of Roland* in Old French, and in Middle English the Robin Hood cycle, Arthurian stories like *Gawain and the Green Knight*, and most famously, Chaucer's *Canterbury Tales*.

By the time of Geoffrey Chaucer (around 1400), stories in verse had developed the same characteristics we see in the Victorians: iambic pentameter and rhymed lines (heroic couplets). Both were new to English, having developed as a hybrid of Latin, French, and English poetic traditions. Chaucer set up a frame story, in which his narrator joined a company of assorted people on a pilgrimage to Canterbury. The narrator became the thirtieth member of the company, as lines 19-34 tell:

> Bifil that in that seson on a day,
> In Southwerk at the Tabard as I lay
> Redy to wenden on my pilgrymage
> To Caunterbury with ful devout corage,
> At nyght was come into that hostelrye
> Wel nyne and twenty in a compaignye,
> Of sondry folk, by aventure yfalle
> In felaweshipe, and pilgrimes were they alle,
> That toward Caunterbury wolden ryde.
> The chambres and the stables weren wyde,
> And wel we weren esed atte beste.
> And shortly, whan the sonne was to reste,
> So hadde I spoken with hem everichon
> That I was of hir felaweshipe anon,
> And made forward erly for to ryse,
> To take oure wey ther as I yow devyse.

The pilgrims take turns telling stories as their horses walk the roughly sixty miles along the road. The stories were probably based largely on Boccaccio's *Decameron*, a collection of stories told in Medieval Italian (in his frame story, people have fled the plague and are holed up in a country house, bored).

This pattern of metered, rhymed verse was how all stories were told until Daniel Defoe published the prose novels *Robinson Crusoe* and *Moll Flanders* in 1719 and 1722. After that, writers had a choice: which format would best convey the story they wanted to tell? What kind of art did they aim to create? When they chose to tell a story in verse, it was a deliberate choice.

The storytelling poet has to decide how to use the medium of poetry to convey what seems important in the story. Is the story more about an idea, or does it involve a lot of descriptions? Does it focus on a person's character and development? Is it presenting something from history, trying to make it come alive? Or is the story aiming at some other tone, like fear or mystery? And what's the purpose for choosing poetry, when prose might do as well?

In the excerpts from "Paul Revere's Ride" and "The Song of Hiawatha," you saw some famous narrative verse. Although written by the same poet, their tones were quite different. "Paul Revere's Ride" focused on story details and the urgency of time. Longfellow used a moment of pause effectively to create suspense. The Bostonian who is supposed to hang lanterns that Revere can see across the water takes a moment to look out on the peaceful pre-war countryside:

> Beneath, in the churchyard, lay the dead,
> In their night encampment on the hill,
> Wrapped in silence so deep and still
> That he could hear, like a sentinel's tread,
> The watchful night-wind, as it went
> Creeping along from tent to tent,
> And seeming to whisper, "All is well!"
> A moment only he feels the spell
> Of the place and the hour, and the secret dread
> Of the lonely belfry and the dead;
> For suddenly all his thoughts are bent
> On a shadowy something far away,
> Where the river widens to meet the bay,—
> A line of black that bends and floats
> On the rising tide like a bridge of boats.
>
> Meanwhile, impatient to mount and ride,
> Booted and spurred, with a heavy stride
> On the opposite shore walked Paul Revere.
> Now he patted his horse's side,
> Now he gazed at the landscape far and near,
> Then, impetuous, stamped the earth,
> And turned and tightened his saddle girth;
> But mostly he watched with eager search
> The belfry tower of the Old North Church...

Longfellow chose to use accentual tetrameter, really a perfect match for his purpose: four-foot lines keep the pace from dragging, and the accentual meter walks and runs along, not slowing down for unnatural word stress to even up iambs. Because he used rhyme (mostly AABB but irregularly), we hear the line endings chime; if he had chosen blank verse, we could not hear the line length as well. Sometimes a line rhymes with one that came earlier; in the stanza about Revere's impatient wait next to his horse, we get AABAB. The variation seems to say "I don't have time to make this work out perfectly because the errand is urgent."

In *The Song of Hiawatha*, Longfellow's purpose was entirely different, so he made other poetic choices. His trochees imitate the beat of a storytelling drum, and once he made that choice, he really had to stick to four feet in a line because drum-beats most naturally fall into twos and fours. Trochaic pentameter would sound a bit odd, and it certainly would not bring to mind the drums of an Iroquois campfire. Longfellow's tone in *Hiawatha* is not urgent; rather, it is magical without impatience. In fairy tales and myths, things often happen more than once (usually by threes), and the narrative does not take short cuts. So too, in his Iroquois tales, Longfellow allows the magical fish, birds and animals to play out their interactions with the hero.

Longfellow's poetic choices were different again in *Evangeline*, his long narrative poem about the eviction of French-speakers from the maritime provinces of Canada. *Evangeline* opens with the famous lines:

> This is the forest primeval. The murmuring pines and the hemlocks,
> Bearded with moss, and in garments green, indistinct in the twilight,
> Stand like Druids of eld, with voices sad and prophetic,
> Stand like harpers hoar, with beards that rest on their bosoms.
> Loud from its rocky caverns, the deep-voiced neighboring ocean
> Speaks, and in accents disconsolate answers the wail of the forest.
>
> This is the forest primeval; but where are the hearts that beneath it
> Leaped like the roe, when he hears in the woodland the voice of the huntsman?
> Where is the thatch-roofed village, the home of Acadian farmers,—
> Men whose lives glided on like rivers that water the woodlands,
> Darkened by shadows of earth, but reflecting an image of heaven?
> Waste are those pleasant farms, and the farmers forever departed!
> Scattered like dust and leaves, when the mighty blasts of October
> Seize them, and whirl them aloft, and sprinkle them far o'er the ocean.
> Naught but tradition remains of the beautiful village of Grand-Pré.
>
> Ye who believe in affection that hopes, and endures, and is patient,
> Ye who believe in the beauty and strength of woman's devotion,
> List to the mournful tradition, still sung by the pines of the forest;
> List to a Tale of Love in Acadie, home of the happy.

While the dactyls were not sustainable throughout the entire poem-story, Longfellow set up a very different feel by opening with them. His language is grandly descriptive, even stately. He wants to take the story of poor, evicted farmers and tell it with immense dignity and beauty. The lines of hexameter seem patient, not urgent; they add romantic phrases and words instead of hurrying as Paul Revere's lines did. The poem's point is to use the wanderings of Evangeline, seeking her lost fiancé, to tour the places where the French-Canadians resettled, giving the character and culture of each place.

Probably the most famous narrative English poem of the 19th century was Tennyson's cycle of 12 poem-stories, *The Idylls of the King*. The legends of King Arthur were built through poetry, each poet across many centuries adding details, characters and themes. Tennyson's work was the last poetic installment, summarizing and building on all the others. Much of what we think we know about Arthur comes from Tennyson, since *The Idylls* were a best-seller in his time.

Tennyson used blank verse for an effect quite different from Longfellow's. Since he did not impose rhyme on himself, he indulged mainly in poetic language. His tone is the most important feature: it is elegiac, lamenting the loss of something great. We see this in Arthur's last battle:

> Nor ever yet had Arthur fought a fight
> Like this last, dim, weird battle of the west.
> A deathwhite mist slept over sand and sea:
> Whereof the chill, to him who breathed it, drew
> Down with his blood, till all his heart was cold
> With formless fear; and ev'n on Arthur fell
> Confusion, since he saw not whom he fought.
>
> For friend and foe were shadows in the mist,
> And friend slew friend not knowing whom he slew;
> And some had visions out of golden youth,
> And some beheld the faces of old ghosts
> Look in upon the battle; and in the mist
> Was many a noble deed, many a base,
> And chance and craft and strength in single fights,
> And ever and anon with host to host
> Shocks, and the splintering spear, the hard mail hewn,
> Shield-breakings, and the clash of brands, the crash
> Of battleaxes on shatter'd helms, and shrieks
> After the Christ, of those who falling down
> Look'd up for heaven, and only saw the mist...

After Arthur's sword Excalibur has been given back to the Lady of the Lake, and Arthur himself laid in a mystical boat, the last knight closes the poem cycle. Tennyson was probably using the knight's words to speak about his own time, when the world was rapidly changing: trains and telegraphs replaced the slower (but more chivalrous!) carriages and riders. Men of business became the new aristocracy, perhaps more deserving but less romantically elegant than the old landed aristocracy, many of whom were titular knights. With Sir Bedivere, Tennyson bids farewell to the age of knights:

> Then loudly cried the bold Sir Bedivere:
> "Ah! my Lord Arthur, whither shall I go?
> Where shall I hide my forehead and my eyes?
> For now I see the true old times are dead,
> When every morning brought a noble chance,
> And every chance brought out a noble knight.
> Such times have been not since the light that led
> The holy Elders with the gift of myrrh.
> But now the whole Round Table is dissolved

> Which was an image of the mighty world,
> And I, the last, go forth companionless,
> And the days darken round me, and the years,
> Among new men, strange faces, other minds."

Today we remember Robert Browning for his dramatic monologues and lyric verse, but in his time, his early popularity sank into obscurity until, in old age, he published a verse-novel called *The Ring and the Book*. It retold a 1698 murder mystery from Italy, presenting different points of view as testimony. It was very popular, and a younger generation rediscovered (and valued) Browning's style, as their fathers had not. Browning closed the story (Book XII, lines 855-70) by asking why he wrote in verse: what can Art do, that plain truth cannot?

> ...Art may tell a truth
> Obliquely, do the thing shall breed the thought,
> Nor wrong the thought, missing the mediate word.
> So may you paint your picture, twice show truth,
> Beyond mere imagery on the wall, —
> So, note by note, bring music from your mind,
> Deeper than ever the Andante dived, —
> So write a book shall mean, beyond the facts,
> Suffice the eye and save the soul beside.
> And save the soul ! If this intent save mine, —
> If the rough ore be rounded to a ring,
> Render all duty which good ring should do.
> And, failing grace, succeed in guardianship, —
> Might mine but lie outside thine. Lyric Love,
> Thy rare gold ring of verse (the poet praised)
> Linking our England to his Italy !

There is a last narrative poem from the late Victorian period, *The Ballad of the White Horse*, worth looking at because it's quite different and people still read and quote from it. It's ironic that *The Idylls* and *Hiawatha* have fallen out of fashion, when their composers were artists of the first rank, while the amateur work of a journalist still has fans. Gilbert Keith Chesterton wrote a weekly op-ed column in a London paper between 1902 and 1935; he also wrote a series of detective stories about a priest, Father Brown. He was a cartoonist and satirist more than a poet.

During his time, the concept of the British Empire became controversial. Chesterton, among others, believed it would be better to let the colonies go and become simply England again. Their position was called "Little Englanders." To express and build romantic support for the idea of "Little England," Chesterton wrote a narrative poem about the events of the year 878, when the West Saxon King Alfred was temporarily defeated by invading Danes (Vikings). Alfred apparently led a resistance movement from hiding, then mustered an army to fight back and reconquer his land.

To tell this story, Chesterton chose accentual meter to connect with the roots of English folk verse. He generally followed ballad meter, in which a line of four feet is followed by a line of three feet (to allow a pause for breath). Also following ballad tradition, he rhymed it only on the 2nd and 4th lines. However, he freely used a variation in which the 3rd line suddenly started spawning extra rhyming lines, so that when the last rhyme comes back, which should be the 4th line but is now the 6th or 7th, its delayed return makes it as welcome as rain.

> Up across windy wastes and up
> Went Alfred over the shaws,
> Shaken of the joy of giants,
> The joy without a cause.
>
> In the slopes away to the western bays,
> Where blows not ever a tree,
> He washed his soul in the west wind
> And his body in the sea.
>
> And he set to rhyme his ale-measures,
> And he sang aloud his laws,
> Because of the joy of the giants,
> The joy without a cause.
>
> The King went gathering Wessex men,
> As grain out of the chaff
> The few that were alive to die,
> Laughing, as littered skulls that lie
> After lost battles turn to the sky
> An everlasting laugh.
>
> The King went gathering Christian men,
> As wheat out of the husk;
> Eldred, the Franklin by the sea,
> And Mark, the man from Italy,
> And Colan of the Sacred Tree,
> From the old tribe on Usk.

In *The Ballad of the White Horse*, everything feels larger than life, both archetypal and symbolic. Chesterton liked word play and magic, and he had no intention of being restricted to plain facts, any more than to one rhyme scheme. His real interest was in portraying the forging of an English identity out of Roman, Celtic, and Anglo-Saxon peoples. As the story of King Alfred acted as a symbol for this theme, so pretty much everything acts as a symbol for some idea. Personalities, emotions and even colors are unrealistic, since they are all symbolic. The sky can be green if Chesterton thinks the world has gone wrong, just as King Alfred can sing about measuring ale to show "joy without a cause."

Narrative verse has mostly fallen out of favor. After the First World War, few narrative poems were even attempted. Robert Frost was writing narrative poems that created short stories, during the first two decades of the century. And poem and prose have at times crossed boundaries: John Berryman wrote a long poem, *Homage to Mistress Bradstreet*, that almost tells a story, while James Joyce's *Finnegans Wake* might be better read as poetry in the French Symbolist tradition. But otherwise, for at least 100 years there has been a consensus that stories are best told in the direct language of prose.

Summary and Definitions

Narrative poetry uses all of the elements of poetry for the purpose of telling a story. The poet chooses meter, rhyme, and general tone and sound of words in order to support the theme and attitude he wants the story to have. He uses images as description, analogy and symbol in order to turn the bare facts of the story into artistry of ideas.

Exercises 16

1. Write a short narrative poem about a dramatic incident in your life. You can choose to write blank verse, heroic couplets, free verse, or any of the other forms you've seen modeled in this lesson. Choose an incident that has an exciting turning-point: danger, suspense, surprise, true love, or hope dashed.

   For example, when I was a baby, I began to slide toward a cliff's edge when my mother had set me down for a moment in a national park. (They caught me in time, and I remember nothing about it.) If I dramatized this incident in a narrative poem, I'd have to choose how much of the setting to describe. I could choose to tell it with a lot of dialogue between my parents, showing mainly the human setting of two 20-somethings trying to manage two babies in a park. Or I could play up the grandeur of the setting; it may have been only a ravine with a creek in it, but I could turn it into the Grand Canyon with a gaping hole in the safety fence. I could tell it from the baby's point of view, the parent's, or a hawk's. With these decisions made, I could decide which form would best convey my dramatic purpose: free verse that uses blank paper for dramatic effect, heroic couplets that might force some rhymes but would turn it into a stately adventure, or iambic tetrameter with here-and-there rhyming (like "Paul Revere's Ride").

   Whatever your choices, they should support the basic purpose you have chosen for your story.

2. In 1798, Samuel Taylor Coleridge first published his ghost story/sea shanty, "The Rime of the Ancient Mariner." (We generally use the 1817 text, with the side notes that help keep the reader oriented with a running summary.) From the start, it was controversial; Coleridge was the James Joyce of his time, writing in such an experimental way that many readers were put off. He deliberately used "archaic" spellings (sometimes spellings that he just made up); in 1800, nobody would write "rhyme" as "rime." Archaic spelling was acceptable when it was part of the usual poetic vocabulary, like *rhym'd* or *e'en*, but not like this. Coleridge's audience had been used to the smooth lines of Alexander Pope's contemporaries, mostly iambic pentameter and heroic couplets.

   Coleridge wanted his story to be magical and supernatural like the *One Thousand and One Nights*, translated from Persian (via French) in the 18th century. Persian genies don't operate by logic; good and bad luck comes upon characters without their having done much to deserve either one. He chose to tell the story of an English Sinbad-like sailor who ran into supernaturally bad luck on a voyage to the Antarctic.

   It opens with a frame story: the old sailor feels compelled to force random strangers to listen to his story. He is so focused on recounting his fearful tale that he ignores whatever is going on at the moment, in this case, a wedding at which the "Wedding-Guest" was supposed to be best man (but never makes it to the ceremony). We hear the story through the ears of the Wedding-Guest, as he is gradually drawn into the tale's horrors.

There is a key event at the close of Part I: the narrator admits that he killed an innocent animal for no reason. After it, his guilt haunts him as bad luck until the victim, an albatross, becomes a symbol of guilty bad luck. D. H. Lawrence referenced it when he regretted throwing a log at the golden snake:

> And I thought of the albatross,
> And I wished he would come back, my snake.

Read through the poem (using the side notes) to understand the basic plot. How would you summarize what happens here? What were Coleridge's choices of meter and rhyme? Describe some of the variations. Remembering how experimental these choices were, how do they support the tone and purpose of the story?

Study the many images presented in the story. Try writing about them: what do they say, what do they mean, how do they fit in and contribute to the whole? What does this story gain by being set in poetry, rather than told as a Stephen King-style horror novel? (Equally, what does it lose?) How does the language create the poem's atmosphere? How does Coleridge use repetition of sound, word and idea to build his story?

If you are a student, use this opportunity to develop a full-length paper that discusses all of these aspects of the poem. If you aren't, enjoy a good ghost story!

The Rime of the Ancient Mariner
ARGUMENT

How a Ship having passed the Line was driven by storms to the cold Country towards the South Pole; and how from thence she made her course to the tropical Latitude of the Great Pacific Ocean; and of the strange things that befell; and in what manner the Ancyent Marinere came back to his own Country.

PART I

It is an ancient Mariner,
And he stoppeth one of three.
'By thy long grey beard and glittering eye,
Now wherefore stopp'st thou me?

The Bridegroom's doors are opened wide,
And I am next of kin;
The guests are met, the feast is set:
May'st hear the merry din.'

The Wedding-Guest is spell-bound by the eye of the old sea-faring man, and constrained to hear his tale.

He holds him with his skinny hand,
'There was a ship,' quoth he.
Hold off! unhand me, grey-beard loon!'
Eftsoons his hand dropt he.

He holds him with his glittering eye—
The Wedding-Guest stood still,
And listens like a three years' child:
The Mariner hath his will.

The Wedding-Guest sat on a stone:
He cannot choose but hear;
And thus spake on that ancient man,
The bright-eyed Mariner.

'The ship was cheered, the harbour cleared,
Merrily did we drop
Below the kirk, below the hill,
Below the lighthouse top.

The Mariner tells how the ship sailed southward with a good wind and fair weather, till it reached the line.

The Sun came up upon the left,
Out of the sea came he!
And he shone bright, and on the right
Went down into the sea.

Higher and higher every day,
Till over the mast at noon—'
The Wedding-Guest here beat his breast,
For he heard the loud bassoon.

The Wedding-Guest heareth the bridal music; but the Mariner continueth his tale.

The bride hath paced into the hall,
Red as a rose is she;
Nodding their heads before her goes
The merry minstrelsy.

The Wedding-Guest he beat his breast,
Yet he cannot choose but hear;
And thus spake on that ancient man,
The bright-eyed Mariner.

The ship driven by a storm toward the south pole.

'And now the storm-blast came, and he
Was tyrannous and strong:
He struck with his o'ertaking wings,
And chased us south along.

With sloping masts and dipping prow,
As who pursued with yell and blow
Still treads the shadow of his foe,
And forward bends his head,
The ship drove fast, loud roared the blast,
And southward aye we fled.

And now there came both mist and snow,
And it grew wondrous cold:
And ice, mast-high, came floating by,
As green as emerald.

The land of ice, and of fearful sounds where no living thing was to be seen.

And through the drifts the snowy clifts
Did send a dismal sheen:
Nor shapes of men nor beasts we ken—
The ice was all between.

The ice was here, the ice was there,
The ice was all around:
It cracked and growled, and roared and howled,
Like noises in a swound!

Till a great sea-bird, called the Albatross, came through the snow-fog, and was received with great joy and hospitality.

At length did cross an Albatross,
Thorough the fog it came;
As if it had been a Christian soul,
We hailed it in God's name.

It ate the food it ne'er had eat,
And round and round it flew.
The ice did split with a thunder-fit;
The helmsman steered us through!

And lo! the Albatross proveth a bird of good omen, and followeth the ship as it returned northward through fog and floating ice.

And a good south wind sprung up behind;
The Albatross did follow,
And every day, for food or play,
Came to the mariners' hollo!

In mist or cloud, on mast or shroud,
It perched for vespers nine;
Whiles all the night, through fog-smoke white,
Glimmered the white Moon-shine.'

The ancient Mariner inhospitably killeth the pious bird of good omen.

'God save thee, ancient Mariner!
From the fiends, that plague thee thus!—
Why look'st thou so?' —With my crossbow
I shot the albatross.

PART II

The Sun now rose upon the right:
Out of the sea came he,
Still hid in mist, and on the left
Went down into the sea.

And the good south wind still blew behind,
But no sweet bird did follow,
Nor any day for food or play
Came to the mariners' hollo!

His shipmates cry out against the ancient Mariner, for killing the bird of good luck.

And I had done a hellish thing,
And it would work 'em woe:
For all averred, I had killed the bird
That made the breeze to blow.
Ah wretch! said they, the bird to slay,
That made the breeze to blow!

But when the fog cleared off, they justify the same, and thus make themselves accomplices in the crime.

Nor dim nor red, like God's own head,
The glorious Sun uprist:
Then all averred, I had killed the bird
That brought the fog and mist.
'Twas right, said they, such birds to slay,
That bring the fog and mist.

The fair breeze continues; the ship enters the Pacific Ocean, and sails northward, even till it reaches the Line.

The fair breeze blew, the white foam flew,
The furrow followed free;
We were the first that ever burst
Into that silent sea.

The ship hath been suddenly becalmed.

Down dropt the breeze, the sails dropt down,
'Twas sad as sad could be:
And we did speak only to break
The silence of the sea!

All in a hot and copper sky,
The bloody Sun, at noon,
Right up above the mast did stand,
No bigger than the Moon.

Day after day, day after day,
We stuck, nor breath, nor motion;
As idle as a painted ship
Upon a painted ocean.

And the Albatross begins to be avenged.

Water, water, every where,
And all the boards did shrink;
Water, water, every where,
Nor any drop to drink.

The very deep did rot: O Christ!
That ever this should be!
Yea, slimy things did crawl with legs
Upon the slimy sea.

About, about, in reel and rout
The death-fires danced at night;
The water, like a witch's oils,
Burnt green, and blue and white.

A Spirit had followed them; one of the invisible inhabitants of this planet, neither departed souls nor angels; concerning whom the learned Jew, Josephus, and the Platonic Constantinopolitan, Michael Psellus, may be consulted. They are very numerous, and there is no climate or element without one or more.

And some in dreams assurèd were
Of the Spirit that plagued us so;
Nine fathoms deep he had followed us
From the land of mist and snow.

And every tongue, through utter drought,
Was withered at the root;
We could not speak, no more than if
We had been choked with soot.

The shipmates, in their sore distress, would fain throw the whole guilt on the ancient Mariner, in sign whereof they hang the dead sea-bird round his neck.

Ah! well-a-day! what evil looks
Had I from old and young!
Instead of the cross, the Albatross
About my neck was hung.

PART III

There passed a weary time. Each throat
Was parched, and glazed each eye.
A weary time! a weary time!
How glazed each weary eye,
When looking westward, I beheld
A something in the sky.

The ancient Mariner beholdeth a sign in the element afar off.

At first it seemed a little speck,
And then it seemed a mist;
It moved and moved, and took at last
A certain shape, I wist.

A speck, a mist, a shape, I wist!
And still it neared and neared:
As if it dodged a water-sprite,
It plunged and tacked and veered.

At its nearer approach, it seemeth him to be a ship; and at a dear ransom he freeth his speech from the bonds of thirst.	With throats unslaked, with black lips baked, We could nor laugh nor wail; Through utter drought all dumb we stood! I bit my arm, I sucked the blood, And cried, A sail! a sail!
A flash of joy;	With throats unslaked, with black lips baked, Agape they heard me call: Gramercy! they for joy did grin, And all at once their breath drew in, As they were drinking all.
And horror follows. For can it be a ship that comes onward without wind or tide?	See! see! (I cried) she tacks no more! Hither to work us weal; Without a breeze, without a tide, She steadies with upright keel!
	The western wave was all a-flame. The day was well nigh done! Almost upon the western wave Rested the broad bright Sun; When that strange shape drove suddenly Betwixt us and the Sun.
It seemeth him but the skeleton of a ship.	And straight the Sun was flecked with bars, (Heaven's Mother send us grace!) As if through a dungeon-grate he peered With broad and burning face.
	Alas! (thought I, and my heart beat loud) How fast she nears and nears! Are those *her* sails that glance in the Sun, Like restless gossameres?
And its ribs are seen as bars on the face of the setting Sun. The Spectre-Woman and her Death-mate, and no other on board the skeleton ship.	Are those *her* ribs through which the Sun Did peer, as through a grate? And is that Woman all her crew? Is that a death? and are there two? Is death that woman's mate?
Like vessel, like crew!	*Her* lips were red, *her* looks were free, Her locks were yellow as gold: Her skin was as white as leprosy, The Night-mare life-in-death was she, Who thicks man's blood with cold.

Death and Life-in-Death have diced for the ship's crew, and she (the latter) winneth the ancient Mariner.	The naked hulk alongside came, And the twain were casting dice; 'The game is done! I've won! I've won!' Quoth she, and whistles thrice.
No twilight within the courts of the Sun.	The Sun's rim dips; the stars rush out: At one stride comes the dark; With far-heard whisper, o'er the sea, Off shot the spectre-bark.
At the rising of the Moon,	We listened and looked sideways up! Fear at my heart, as at a cup, My life-blood seemed to sip! The stars were dim, and thick the night, The steersman's face by his lamp gleamed white; From the sails the dew did drip— Till clomb above the eastern bar The hornéd Moon, with one bright star Within the nether tip.
One after another,	One after one, by the star-dogged Moon, Too quick for groan or sigh, Each turned his face with a ghastly pang, And cursed me with his eye.
His shipmates drop down dead.	Four times fifty living men, (And I heard nor sigh nor groan) With heavy thump, a lifeless lump, They dropped down one by one.
But Life-in-Death begins her work on the ancient Mariner.	The souls did from their bodies fly,— They fled to bliss or woe! And every soul, it passed me by, Like the whizz of my cross-bow!

PART IV

The Wedding-Guest feareth that a Spirit is talking to him;	'I fear thee, ancient Mariner! I fear thy skinny hand! And thou art long, and lank, and brown, As is the ribbed sea sand. I fear thee and thy glittering eye, And thy skinny hand, so brown.'—
But the ancient Mariner assureth him of his bodily life, and proceedeth to relate his horrible penance.	Fear not, fear not, thou Wedding-Guest! This body dropt not down.

Alone, alone, all, all alone,
Alone on a wide wide sea!
And never a saint took pity on
My soul in agony.

He despiseth the creatures of the calm,

The many men, so beautiful!
And they all dead did lie:
And a thousand thousand slimy things
Lived on; and so did I.

And envieth that they should live, and so many lie dead.

I looked upon the rotting sea,
And drew my eyes away;
I looked upon the rotting deck,
And there the dead men lay.

I looked to heaven, and tried to pray;
But or ever a prayer had gusht,
A wicked whisper came, and made
My heart as dry as dust.

I closed my lids, and kept them close,
And the balls like pulses beat;
For the sky and the sea, and the sea and the sky
Lay like a load on my weary eye,
And the dead were at my feet.

But the curse liveth for him in the eye of the dead men.

The cold sweat melted from their limbs,
Nor rot nor reek did they:
The look with which they looked on me
Had never passed away.

An orphan's curse would drag to hell
A spirit from on high;
But oh! more horrible than that
Is the curse in a dead man's eye!
Seven days, seven nights, I saw that curse,
And yet I could not die.

In his loneliness and fixedness he yearneth towards the journeying Moon, and the stars that still sojourn, yet still move onward; and every where the blue sky belongs to them, and is their appointed rest, and their native country and their own natural homes, which they enter unannounced, as lords that are certainly expected and yet there is a silent joy at their arrival.

The moving Moon went up the sky,
And no where did abide:
Softly she was going up,
And a star or two beside—

Her beams bemocked the sultry main,
Like April hoar-frost spread;
But where the ship's huge shadow lay,
The charmèd water burnt alway
A still and awful red.

Beyond the shadow of the ship,
I watched the water-snakes:
They moved in tracks of shining white,
And when they reared, the elfish light
Fell off in hoary flakes.

By the light of the Moon he beholdeth God's creatures of the great calm.

Within the shadow of the ship
I watched their rich attire:
Blue, glossy green, and velvet black,
They coiled and swam; and every track
Was a flash of golden fire.

Their beauty and their happiness.

O happy living things! no tongue
Their beauty might declare:
A spring of love gushed from my heart,
And I blessed them unaware:
Sure my kind saint took pity on me,
And I blessed them unaware.

He blesseth them in his heart.

The spell begins to break.

The self-same moment I could pray;
And from my neck so free
The Albatross fell off, and sank
Like lead into the sea.

PART V

Oh sleep! it is a gentle thing,
Beloved from pole to pole!
To Mary Queen the praise be given!
She sent the gentle sleep from Heaven,
That slid into my soul.

The silly buckets on the deck,
That had so long remained,
I dreamt that they were filled with dew,
And when I awoke, it rained.

By grace of the holy Mother, the ancient Mariner is refreshed with rain.

My lips were wet, my throat was cold,
My garments all were dank;
Sure I had drunken in my dreams,
And still my body drank.

I moved, and could not feel my limbs:
I was so light—almost
I thought that I had died in sleep,
And was a blessèd ghost.

And soon I heard a roaring wind:

It did not come anear;
But with its sound it shook the sails,
That were so thin and sere.

He heareth sounds and seeth strange sights and commotions in the sky and the element.

The upper air burst into life!
And a hundred fire-flags sheen,
To and fro they were hurried about!
And to and fro, and in and out,
The wan stars danced between.

And the coming wind did roar more loud,
And the sails did sigh like sedge;
And the rain poured down from one black cloud;
The Moon was at its edge.

The thick black cloud was cleft, and still
The Moon was at its side:
Like waters shot from some high crag,
The lightning fell with never a jag,
A river steep and wide.

The bodies of the ship's crew are inspired and the ship moves on;

The loud wind never reached the ship,
Yet now the ship moved on!
Beneath the lightning and the Moon
The dead men gave a groan.

They groaned, they stirred, they all uprose,
Nor spake, nor moved their eyes;
It had been strange, even in a dream,
To have seen those dead men rise.

The helmsman steered, the ship moved on;
Yet never a breeze up-blew;
The mariners all 'gan work the ropes,
Where they were wont to do;
They raised their limbs like lifeless tools—
We were a ghastly crew.

The body of my brother's son
Stood by me, knee to knee:
The body and I pulled at one rope,
But he said nought to me.

But not by the souls of the men, nor by daemons of earth or middle air, but by a blessed troop of angelic spirits, sent down by the invocation of the guardian saint.

'I fear thee, ancient Mariner!'
Be calm, thou Wedding-Guest!
'Twas not those souls that fled in pain,
Which to their corses came again,
But a troop of spirits blest:

For when it dawned—they dropped their arms,
And clustered round the mast;
Sweet sounds rose slowly through their mouths,
And from their bodies passed.

Around, around, flew each sweet sound,
Then darted to the Sun;
Slowly the sounds came back again,
Now mixed, now one by one.

Sometimes a-dropping from the sky
I heard the sky-lark sing;
Sometimes all little birds that are,
How they seemed to fill the sea and air
With their sweet jargoning!

And now 'twas like all instruments,
Now like a lonely flute;
And now it is an angel's song,
That makes the heavens be mute.

It ceased; yet still the sails made on
A pleasant noise till noon,
A noise like of a hidden brook
In the leafy month of June,
That to the sleeping woods all night
Singeth a quiet tune.

Till noon we quietly sailed on,
Yet never a breeze did breathe:
Slowly and smoothly went the ship,
Moved onward from beneath.

The lonesome Spirit from the south-pole carries on the ship as far as the Line, in obedience to the angelic troop, but still requireth vengeance.

Under the keel nine fathom deep,
From the land of mist and snow,
The spirit slid: and it was he
That made the ship to go.
The sails at noon left off their tune,
And the ship stood still also.

The Sun, right up above the mast,
Had fixed her to the ocean:
But in a minute she 'gan stir,
With a short uneasy motion—
Backwards and forwards half her length
With a short uneasy motion.

Then like a pawing horse let go,
She made a sudden bound:
It flung the blood into my head,
And I fell down in a swound.

The Polar Spirit's fellow-daemons, the invisible inhabitants of the element, take part in his wrong; and two of them relate, one to the other, that penance long and heavy for the ancient Mariner hath been accorded to the Polar Spirit, who returneth southward.

How long in that same fit I lay,
I have not to declare;
But ere my living life returned,
I heard and in my soul discerned
Two voices in the air.

'Is it he?' quoth one, 'Is this the man?
By him who died on cross,
With his cruel bow he laid full low
The harmless Albatross.

The spirit who bideth by himself
In the land of mist and snow,
He loved the bird that loved the man
Who shot him with his bow.'

The other was a softer voice,
As soft as honey-dew:
Quoth he, 'The man hath penance done,
And penance more will do.'

PART VI

First Voice

'But tell me, tell me! speak again,
Thy soft response renewing—
What makes that ship drive on so fast?
What is the ocean doing?'

Second Voice

'Still as a slave before his lord,
The ocean hath no blast;
His great bright eye most silently
Up to the Moon is cast—

If he may know which way to go;
For she guides him smooth or grim.
See, brother, see! how graciously
She looketh down on him.'

First Voice

'But why drive on that ship so fast,
Without or wave or wind?'

Second Voice

'The air is cut away before,
And closes from behind.

Fly, brother, fly! more high, more high!
Or we shall be belated:
For slow and slow that ship will go,
When the Mariner's trance is abated.'

I woke, and we were sailing on
As in a gentle weather:
'Twas night, calm night, the moon was high;
The dead men stood together.

All stood together on the deck,
For a charnel-dungeon fitter:
All fixed on me their stony eyes,
That in the Moon did glitter.

The pang, the curse, with which they died,
Had never passed away:
I could not draw my eyes from theirs,
Nor turn them up to pray.

And now this spell was snapt: once more
I viewed the ocean green,
And looked far forth, yet little saw
Of what had else been seen—

Like one, that on a lonesome road
Doth walk in fear and dread,
And having once turned round walks on,
And turns no more his head;
Because he knows, a frightful fiend
Doth close behind him tread.

The Mariner hath been cast into a trance; for the angelic power causeth the vessel to drive northward faster than human life could endure.

The supernatural motion is retarded; the Mariner awakes, and his penance begins anew.

The curse is finally expiated.

But soon there breathed a wind on me,
Nor sound nor motion made:
Its path was not upon the sea,
In ripple or in shade.

It raised my hair, it fanned my cheek
Like a meadow-gale of spring—
It mingled strangely with my fears,
Yet it felt like a welcoming.

Swiftly, swiftly flew the ship,
Yet she sailed softly too:
Sweetly, sweetly blew the breeze—
On me alone it blew.

And the ancient Mariner beholdeth his native country.

Oh! dream of joy! is this indeed
The light-house top I see?
Is this the hill? is this the kirk?
Is this mine own countree?

We drifted o'er the harbour-bar,
And I with sobs did pray—
O let me be awake, my God!
Or let me sleep alway.

The harbour-bay was clear as glass,
So smoothly it was strewn!
And on the bay the moonlight lay,
And the shadow of the Moon.

The rock shone bright, the kirk no less,
That stands above the rock:
The moonlight steeped in silentness
The steady weathercock.

The angelic spirits leave the dead bodies,

And the bay was white with silent light,
Till rising from the same,
Full many shapes, that shadows were,
In crimson colours came.

And appear in their own forms of light.

A little distance from the prow
Those crimson shadows were:
I turned my eyes upon the deck—
Oh, Christ! what I saw there!

Each corse lay flat, lifeless and flat,
And, by the holy rood!
A man all light, a seraph-man,
On every corse there stood.

This seraph-band, each waved his hand:
It was a heavenly sight!
They stood as signals to the land,
Each one a lovely light;

This seraph-band, each waved his hand,
No voice did they impart—
No voice; but oh! the silence sank
Like music on my heart.

But soon I heard the dash of oars,
I heard the Pilot's cheer;
My head was turned perforce away
And I saw a boat appear.

The Pilot and the Pilot's boy,
I heard them coming fast:
Dear Lord in Heaven! it was a joy
The dead men could not blast.

I saw a third—I heard his voice:
It is the Hermit good!
He singeth loud his godly hymns
That he makes in the wood.
He'll shrieve my soul, he'll wash away
The Albatross's blood.

PART VII

The Hermit of the Wood,

This Hermit good lives in that wood
Which slopes down to the sea.
How loudly his sweet voice he rears!
He loves to talk with marineres
That come from a far countree.

He kneels at morn, and noon, and eve—
He hath a cushion plump:
It is the moss that wholly hides
The rotted old oak-stump.

The skiff-boat neared: I heard them talk,
'Why this is strange, I trow!

Where are those lights so many and fair,
That signal made but now?'

Approacheth the ship with wonder.

'Strange, by my faith!' the Hermit said—
'And they answered not our cheer!
The planks looked warped! and see those sails,
How thin they are and sere!
I never saw aught like to them,
Unless perchance it were

Brown skeletons of leaves that lag
My forest-brook along;
When the ivy-tod is heavy with snow,
And the owlet whoops to the wolf below,
That eats the she-wolf's young.'

'Dear Lord! it hath a fiendish look—
(The Pilot made reply)
I am a-feared'— 'Push on, push on!'
Said the Hermit cheerily.

The boat came closer to the ship,
But I nor spake nor stirred;
The boat came close beneath the ship,
And straight a sound was heard.

Under the water it rumbled on,
Still louder and more dread:
It reached the ship, it split the bay;
The ship went down like lead.

The ship suddenly sinketh.

The ancient Mariner is saved in the Pilot's boat.

Stunned by that loud and dreadful sound,
Which sky and ocean smote,
Like one that hath been seven days drowned
My body lay afloat;
But swift as dreams, myself I found
Within the Pilot's boat.

Upon the whirl, where sank the ship,
The boat spun round and round;
And all was still, save that the hill
Was telling of the sound.

I moved my lips—the Pilot shrieked
And fell down in a fit;
The holy Hermit raised his eyes,
And prayed where he did sit.

I took the oars: the Pilot's boy,
Who now doth crazy go,
Laughed loud and long, and all the while
His eyes went to and fro.
'Ha! ha! quoth he, 'full plain I see,
The Devil knows how to row.'

And now, all in my own countree,
I stood on the firm land!
The Hermit stepped forth from the boat,
And scarcely he could stand.

The ancient Mariner earnestly entreated the Hermit to shrieve him; and the penance of life falls on him.

'O shrieve me, shrieve me, holy man!'
The Hermit crossed his brow.
'Say quick,' quoth he, 'I bid thee say—
What manner of man art thou?'

Forthwith this frame of mine was wrenched
With a woful agony,
Which forced me to begin my tale;
And then it left me free.

And ever and anon throughout his future life an agony constraineth him to travel from land to land;

Since then, at an uncertain hour,
That agony returns:
And till my ghastly tale is told,
This heart within me burns.

I pass, like night, from land to land;
I have strange power of speech;
That moment that his face I see,
I know the man that must hear me:
To him my tale I teach.

What loud uproar bursts from that door!
The wedding-guests are there:
But in the garden-bower the bride
And bride-maids singing are:
And hark the little vesper bell,
Which biddeth me to prayer!

O Wedding-Guest! this soul hath been
Alone on a wide wide sea:
So lonely 'twas, that God himself
Scarce seemèd there to be.

O sweeter than the marriage-feast,
'Tis sweeter far to me,
To walk together to the kirk
With a goodly company!—

To walk together to the kirk,
And all together pray,
While each to his great Father bends,
Old men, and babes, and loving friends
And youths and maidens gay!

Farewell, farewell! but this I tell
To thee, thou Wedding-Guest!
He prayeth well, who loveth well
Both man and bird and beast.

And to teach, by his own example, love and reverence to all things that God made and loveth.

He prayeth best, who loveth best
All things both great and small;
For the dear God who loveth us,
He made and loveth all.

The Mariner, whose eye is bright,
Whose beard with age is hoar,
Is gone: and now the Wedding-Guest
Turned from the bride-groom's door.

He went like one that hath been stunned,
And is of sense forlorn:
A sadder and a wiser man,
He rose the morrow morn.

Seventeen:

Voice as Image

The human voice is always part of making art with words, and in some poetry, individual voices are the main point. Meter and rhyme may be part of how those voices express themselves, but the key artistic feature is in capturing the voice. It must be both realistic and artistic, at the same time.

One way to present the human voice is to try to imitate speech through writing. Poems like this present not so much visual images as audible voices. The other way to use the voice for poetry is to maintain that the artistry lies not just in how it's written but also in how it is performed when spoken out loud.

1. Voice presented as the image

> Now that lilacs are in bloom
> She has a bowl of lilacs in her room
> And twists one in her fingers while she talks.
> "Ah, my friend, you do not know, you do not know
> What life is, you who hold it in your hands";
> (Slowly twisting the lilac stalks)
> "You let it flow from you, you let it flow,
> And youth is cruel, and has no remorse
> And smiles at situations which it cannot see."
> I smile of course,
> And go on drinking tea...
>
> ...The voice returns like the insistent out-of-tune
> Of a broken violin on an August afternoon:
> "I am always sure that you understand
> My feelings, always sure that you feel,
> Sure that across the gulf you reach your hand."

T. S. Eliot's "Portrait of a Lady" is very much about her voice, not just her visual portrait. In this short passage, his only simile is about sound, not appearance. We've been talking about images, but here we must make room for "images" that we cannot see. Her voice is like a violin, but of a certain type: it is insistent when the listener would rather hear silence, and it is both broken and out of tune in its strings. If you try to imagine the sound, you will flinch at its unpleasantness. The simile gives us context for how her voice paints her portrait.

Voice as Image

"Voice" first came into poetry because for a long time, stage plays were written in verse. Any speech could be taken out of context and quoted as a poem, and many of the speeches included elements of poetry. Robert Browning, now known as a poet, first wanted to be a famous dramatist for the stage. He wrote some plays that did very badly, partly because he wasn't really interested in providing entertainment. He wanted to portray stories and voices that might be unpopular because they appealed to his personal interests and sense of drama. After his plays flopped, he wrote dramatic monologues as poems. These weren't immediately successful either, but the next generation loved them.

By modern standards, Browning's character voices aren't that distinct, because they all had to speak in blank verse. I find the most distinctive one in the Renaissance painter Fra Lippo Lippi, whose poem opens with the night watch arresting him near a brothel:

> I am poor brother Lippo, by your leave!
> You need not clap your torches to my face.
> Zooks, what's to blame? you think you see a monk!
> What, 'tis past midnight, and you go the rounds,
> And here you catch me at an alley's end
> Where sportive ladies leave their doors ajar?
> The Carmine's my cloister: hunt it up,
> Do,—harry out, if you must show your zeal,
> Whatever rat, there, haps on his wrong hole,
> And nip each softling of a wee white mouse,
> Weke, weke, that's crept to keep him company!
> Aha, you know your betters! Then, you'll take
> Your hand away that's fiddling on my throat,
> And please to know me likewise. Who am I?
> Why, one, sir, who is lodging with a friend
> Three streets off—he's a certain . . . how d'ye call?
> Master—a ...Cosimo of the Medici,
> I' the house that caps the corner.

After revealing that his host is actually the ruler of the city, the painter sits down with the leader of the watch, telling his life story. His voice is always colorful and slangy; he belongs to the city rabble, but at the same time is separated from them by his art.

The best-known Browning monologue has a more formal voice: the Duke of Ferrara. He is showing a guest around his house; a portrait prompts him to stop and talk rather coldly about his late wife. He describes the portrait, so that the poem is almost ekphrastic, but it is mainly a character study. The Duke's speech uses both iambic pentameter and rhyme:

> That's my last Duchess painted on the wall,
> Looking as if she were alive. I call
> That piece a wonder, now; Fra Pandolf's hands
> Worked busily a day, and there she stands.
> Will't please you sit and look at her?

In "Caliban Upon Setebos," Browning presents the uncivilized beast-man Caliban from Shakespeare's *The Tempest*. Caliban is trying to understand why God might have made his island and the world, based on reasoning why he himself might have done such things. His voice is unrhymed but uses antique words like "thinketh," and his sentences are often strange. He leaves out the pronoun "I" and at times seems to speak of himself as if of another. At the same time, his reasoning and examples are concrete and simple. The formula, "Thinketh..." followed by the conclusion, "as do I, so He," is repeated as the voice ponders the nature of self and God.

> 'Thinketh, such shows nor right nor wrong in Him,
> Nor kind, nor cruel: He is strong and Lord.
> 'Am strong myself compared to yonder crabs
> That march now from the mountain to the sea;
> 'Let twenty pass, and stone the twenty-first,
> Loving not, hating not, just choosing so.
> 'Say, the first straggler that boasts purple spots
> Shall join the file, one pincer twisted off;
> 'Say, this bruised fellow shall receive a worm,
> And two worms he whose nippers end in red;
> As it likes me each time, I do: so He.

Other Victorians used dramatic monologues, but they did not try so hard to imitate individual humans. Technically, both "The Lotus-Eaters" and "Dover Beach" are also voices. It's hard to claim that each speaker's patterns of intonation and word use are the central feature of those works, as they are in Browning's monologues.

On the other hand, when the dramatic monologue came into the 20th century, it could be even more distinctive. William Carlos Williams, as a New Jersey doctor, sometimes captured his patients' voices in little snips. Some are just titled "Detail," with lines like this:

> She's always hungry but...
> She seems to gain all right, I don't know.
>
> Doc, I bin lookin' for you.
> I owe you two bucks.
> How you doin'?

Modern poetry could focus just on the voice, so that portraying its individuality became the chief artistic feature. Neither of Williams' patients in these "Details" is saying anything poetic, nor are their voices distinct from those of their neighbors. Williams seems to be claiming that these country folks' voices were distinctive or important in the context of the world. By capturing them out of context, he claims that *the human voice itself* is art.

The most famous modernist poem, T. S. Eliot's "The Waste Land," has many voices. Its first line, "April is the cruellest month," may be one of these voices. In the opening lines, we become aware that we are listening to an old woman (Countess Marie Larisch von Moennich) reminiscing about her childhood at the Austrian court. It closes with the voice really coming into focus as a person, not a poetic narrator, when she slips into irrelevant detail about her daily life:

And when we were children, staying at the archduke's,
My cousin's, he took me out on a sled,
And I was frightened. He said, Marie,
Marie, hold on tight. And down we went.
In the mountains, there you feel free.
I read, much of the night, and go south in the winter.

The voices carry on through this section, "The Burial of the Dead." Next we hear the "Hyacinth Girl," who speaks German (it could be Marie again), then a fortune-teller whose passage ends with asking the listener to take a message for one of her other clients, since "One must be so careful these days." The section closes with the narrator's voice calling out to the spirit of an old friend he has just recognized on the London street: literally, a voice calling out loud.

In the section called "A Game of Chess," most of the poem portrays voices. The first one is a nervous woman, probably taken straight from Eliot's first wife, Vivien. The quiet replies to the nervous, rapid voice may be the poet's silent reactions of frustration to his wife's unhappiness. At one point, she starts singing along with jazz on a gramophone record, then goes back to hounding the silent listener about what to do.

"My nerves are bad tonight. Yes, bad. Stay with me.
"Speak to me. Why do you never speak. Speak.
"What are you thinking of? What thinking? What?
"I never know what you are thinking. Think."

I think we are in rats' alley
Where the dead men lost their bones.

"What is that noise?"
    The wind under the door.
"What is that noise now? What is the wind doing?"
    Nothing again nothing.
        "Do
"You know nothing? Do you see nothing? Do you remember
"Nothing?"
I remember
Those pearls that were his eyes.
"Are you alive, or not? Is there nothing in your head?"
        But

O O O O that Shakespeherian Rag—-
It's so elegant
So intelligent
"What shall I do now? What shall I do?"
"I shall rush out as I am, and walk the street
"With my hair down, so. What shall we do tomorrow?
"What shall we ever do?"

> The hot water at ten.
> And if it rains, a closed car at four.
> And we shall play a game of chess,
> Pressing lidless eyes and waiting for a knock upon the door.

The poem then takes a surprising turn, steering away from Eliot's nervous, hysterical woman to a very different voice. We hear two working-class women in London chatting about the end of the First World War and how hard it will be to please the "demobbed" men (de-mobilized, that is, released into civilian life). At unexpected intervals, another voice interrupts them in an impersonal tone, like a loudspeaker:

> When Lil's husband got demobbed, I said——
> I didn't mince my words, I said to her myself
> HURRY UP PLEASE IT'S TIME
> Now Albert's coming back, make yourself a bit smart.
> He'll want to know what you done with that money he gave you
> To get yourself some teeth. He did, I was there.
> You have them all out, Lil, and get a nice set,
> He said, I swear, I can't bear to look at you.
> And no more can't I, I said, and think of poor Albert,
> He's been in the army four years, he wants a good time,
> And if you don't give it him, there's others will, I said.
> Oh is there, she said. Something o' that, I said.
> Then I'll know who to thank, she said, and give me a straight look.
> HURRY UP PLEASE ITS TIME
> If you don't like it you can get on with it, I said,
> Others can pick and choose if you can't.
> But if Albert makes off, it won't be for lack of telling.
> You ought to be ashamed, I said, to look so antique.
> (And her only thirty-one.)

The women chatter on, interrupted by the "loudspeaker," and the section closes with a chorus of people calling "Goodnight" to each other.

The voices of Marie, the hysterical woman, and the London gossips are all very distinct and could not be confused with each other. We could match the poetry passages to video clips of the speakers, if such clips existed. Eliot uses meter and rhyme, but only when he wants to. By ignoring their structure most of the time, he is free to depict the voices as idiosyncratically as possible.

These lines could be considered poetry of the city experience, where you might sit near strangers and overhear their intimate conversations. There is a lot of ugliness portrayed in "The Waste Land." Are the human voices part of the ugliness, or are their voices beautiful because they are so human? That seems to be one of the questions the poem poses.

2. Spoken word art

The oldest poetry was spoken, not written; it was chanted or sung, sometimes with musical accompaniment. We only know it through its written form, so we just don't know how it sounded. Was it shouted and whispered? Chanted to a steady beat? Did people take turns reciting the verses, making it into a play?

We owe the 20th century revival of spoken, performance poetry to W. B. Yeats in Ireland and Vachel Lindsay in America. Yeats writes that he naturally disliked pen and paper, but he also disliked singing. He wanted to hear poetry recited in a way that would blend voice and words, to be more musical than speech, and with an accompanying harp. At least once he heard a woman recite to the harp and said that if only the art could be taught to others, he would never open a book of verse again, preferring to hear it this way (*Ideas of Good and Evil*, 1902). He and his friends tried out systems of half-musical notation that could capture the half and quarter tones of speech, and a craftsman made a special lyre with chromatic intervals. Yeats was sure that his new art would catch on and develop. He was right, but not in the way he expected. Before his new art could grow, the idea had to move across the ocean to America.

Vachel Lindsay grew up in Springfield, Illinois during the 1880s. He dabbled in college and art studies, but to his parents' frustration, he seemed determined not to take up a profession that could make a real living. In 1905, in New York, Lindsay decided to try becoming a poetry-writing tramp. It had worked for medieval troubadours, so why wouldn't it work for him, now? Human nature hadn't changed; people still liked entertainment, and in small towns of that time, there wasn't much entertainment. Lindsay printed a pamphlet called "Rhymes to be Traded for Bread," then sailed to Florida. He walked across Florida, about 600 miles, into Kentucky. For room and board, he recited his verses and gave printed copies away.

By the time Lindsay had made three long circuits by foot—the last one all the way to New Mexico—he felt he had learned what people wanted to hear. They wanted to hear stories and ear-catching, foot-tapping rhythms. He shouted and sang, chanted and whispered, and sometimes he beat time on a drum or hired musicians to play along. By his third walking tour, he had struck upon methods that kept the money pouring in, more than he could carry. He became known as the "Prairie Troubadour."

When Lindsay returned to Chicago in 1912, the new *Poetry* magazine published his poem "General William Booth Enters Into Heaven," in commemoration of the death of the Salvation Army's founder. Lindsay cared most about the moral message of caring for the poor, but he wrote in the style that kept his audience's attention. He used accentual meter and rhyme, but his lines are also laced with alliteration, assonance, and consonance. But that's not all: the sections are marked for bass drum, banjo, flute and tambourine accompaniment or introductions. He chanted it to a hymn tune used often by the Salvation Army, "Are You Washed in the Blood of the Lamb?" Here's the first stanza:

> Booth led boldly with his big bass drum—
> (Are you washed in the blood of the Lamb?)
> The Saints smiled gravely and they said: "He's come."
> (Are you washed in the blood of the Lamb?)
> Walking lepers followed, rank on rank,
> Lurching bravoes from the ditches dank,
> Drabs from the alleyways and drug fiends pale—
> Minds still passion-ridden, soul-powers frail:—
> Vermin-eaten saints with mouldy breath,
> Unwashed legions with the ways of Death—
> (Are you washed in the blood of the Lamb?)

Yeats admired this poem, saying he recognized in it true craftsmanship, and that it was "stripped bare of ornament" with an "earnest simplicity" and "strange beauty" (recalled by Harriet Monroe in her introduction to Lindsay's *The Congo and Other Poems*). When he came to Chicago in 1914, Yeats asked Lindsay, "What are we going to do to restore the primitive singing of poetry?" They wrote to each other after Yeats went home, sharing ideas. Lindsay's tramping poetry readings were one answer; he referred to his style as a sort of "vaudeville," the live shows that traveled to cities with a variety of acts. But Lindsay also began experimenting with interactive verse performance.

Lindsay called his new idea "Poem Games." He envisioned an informal performance with several speakers and an audience acting as chorus. He wanted some dancing: less like ballet and more like a children's circle game. Repeated lines were for echoing back to a leader, questions were to be called out and answered by the chorus, and some actions were scripted into the poem. For example, in "John Brown," there is a scripted call-and-response in which the reciter will begin, "I've been to Palestine." The audience would act as chorus to ask him what he saw. The answers major in repetition and variation of sounds and words:

> I've been to Palestine.
> WHAT DID YOU SEE IN PALESTINE?
> I saw the ark of Noah—
> It was made of pitch and pine.
> I saw old Father Noah
> Asleep beneath his vine.
> I saw Shem, Ham and Japhet
> Standing in a line.
> I saw the tower of Babel
> In the gorgeous sunrise shine—
> By a weeping willow tree
> Beside the Dead Sea.
>
> I've been to Palestine.
> WHAT DID YOU SEE IN PALESTINE?
> I saw abominations
> And Gadarene swine.
> I saw the sinful Canaanites
> Upon the shewbread dine
> And drink the temple wine.
> I saw Lot's wife, a pillar of salt
> Standing in the brine—
> By a weeping willow tree
> Beside the Dead Sea…
>
> …I've been to Palestine.
> WHAT DID YOU SEE IN PALESTINE?
> I saw the harp and psalt'ry
> Played for old John Brown.

> I heard the ram's horn blow,
> Blow for Old John Brown.
> I saw the Bulls of Bashan—
> They cheered for Old John Brown...

While Yeats and Lindsay were trying to revive classical Greek verse and medieval minstrelsy, a separate stream of spoken verse was pouring into New York City. In earlier chapters, we've seen some poets of the "Harlem Renaissance," such as Paul Laurence Dunbar and Claude McKay. Vachel Lindsay mentored some of them, so there was a direct connection between Yeats and Harlem. But the primary tradition at work in jazz-soaked Harlem came from Africa.

Harlem had a lot of Jamaican immigrants (like Claude McKay) and a constant flow of cultural influence from the islands. In the Caribbean Islands, some African customs had been kept alive even more than in the American South. Among them was the West African custom of oral-history recitation by trained, specialized poets called *griots* (gree-ohs) or *djeli*. They had reams of history committed to memory, but they were also expected to improvise verses on current events. In Jamaica the griot tradition lingered, although African languages were soon lost. Storytelling was the main way of passing on family history and wisdom when few were able to read.

In the Jazz Age, the griot style developed into *toasting*, the art of rapid, rhyming improvisation in a monotone delivery. Toasters told stories or commented on current events and political complaints. Record companies sometimes released a jazz song with an instrumental-only version on the B-side. Jamaican toasters could play the instrumental song and make up chanted words to go with it. When they used records this way, they became known as deejays, short for "disk jockey," but in Jamaican use, it meant they were part of the music, not just playing the record. Toasters and deejays were spoken-word performers in their own right.

Jamaica influenced Harlem's style, which spread to other parts of New York and influenced white musicians and poets. In the 1950s, the cool poets of the Beat Generation imitated Harlem's blend of musical and verbal improvisation. In the chapter on free verse, you saw a sample of Allen Ginsberg's "Beat" poetry. This kind of poetry was often declaimed out loud, but it was not rhythmic like Vachel Lindsay's work. It tended to be emotional, unstructured, and rich in jarring images.

The contemporary descendants of Lindsay's and Harlem's art dwell on the border between poetry and something else. They are both art made with words, but both of them stipulate that without the *voice* (live or recorded), the art is not complete. We'll look separately at rap and spoken-word poetry. It's an open question: are these art forms still "art made with words," or are they "art made with words *and voice*," the way songs are "art made with words and music"?

At discos in the late 1970s, the men who kept music going on two turntables started filling in the quiet times and instrumental sections with rhymed chants like Jamaican toasters. They became known as MCs, short for "Master of Ceremonies." Within a few years, some MCs recorded songs that consisted of their chants over a beat, and the hiphop genre was born. ("Hiphop" seems to be a broader term for the style and culture, while "rap" seems to indicate just the verbal art, so I will refer to it as rap.) Its intense popularity in inner cities spread to suburbs, then worldwide, and then into other kinds of song. Now it's hard to go anywhere without hearing rap's half-sung, half-chanted, rapidly-delivered strings of rhymes.

Most commercial hiphop songs take an aggressive tone against the world, majoring in vulgarity and shunning beauty. However, there's a minority tradition that is philosophical, trying to explore the meaning of life. Rappers (MCs) in these songs use poetic imagery that, in some cases, meets the same artistic standard that written poetry hews to.

Rap is built around the three sound elements of language: rhythm, rhyme, and repetition. Its use of repetition is pretty much identical to the way classical poetry uses it: repeating phrases, words, and sounds, with repetition varied with partial changes.

Rhyme, though, is used in a much broader way. In rap, rhyme seems to mean any similar interior or ending sound. Slant rhyme and assonance count as rhyme, sometimes all called stretch rhymes. Spoken emphasis on the common sound, with de-emphasis on the differences, works with rapid delivery to make the audience hear only the "rhyme." In this way, *vibe*, *wise*, *slides*, *disguise* and *five* form a good set of rap rhymes. Rappers get extra appreciation for using words that match in two syllables, like *blacktop* and *jackpot*.

The rhythm of rap started with accentual verse, like nursery rhymes. The first rappers stayed with simple rhythms whose stressed words landed on a drum beat. Within a few years, they were looking for more complex rhythms. Chanting to a steady beat poses a question: how do you want your words to relate to that beat? Each performer's solution is called his *flow*. Adam Bradley, an English professor writing about the poetics of hiphop, explains: "Rappers' flows, their distinctive vocal cadences, establish reciprocal relationships with the beat. MCs can rap a little behind, or a little ahead, they can use their voices as counterpoint, or they can simply ride the beat where it wants to take them." (Bradley, 207-8)

Syllables aren't counted as they are in accentual-syllabic meters. Nor are natural strong stresses strictly counted, as in pure accentual meter. Rather, as Bradley describes, "Syllables can be light or heavy, long or short. An effective rap verse balances its linguistic weight in such a way that it can be performed without awkward pauses, gasps for breath, or other infelicities." (Bradley, 29)

Rap's use of rhythm may be exactly the opposite of classic poetry's use of it, since written poetry is built on the natural stresses of the language. Rap may work against these stresses, creating unnatural patterns that distort normal intonation. In fact, exposure to rap music might make it more difficult to learn to hear the patterns of classic poetic meter.

Rap may be a kind of poetry, but it's not the traditional kind, because it does not live separately from the live performance or recording. "As an oral idiom, rap's rhythm only partly exists on the page; it requires the beat and the distinctive rhythmic sensibility of the lyricist to make it whole. A lyrical transcription rarely provides all the information needed to reconstruct a rapper's flow." (Bradley, 35) As art, it does not consist only of words, but of words *and voice*. If the voice providing flow is not present, the art is gone.

The tradition of Vachel Lindsay and the Beat Generation led also to the rise of performance poetry in the 1980s. It may not be coincidental that academic poets turned to microphones at the same time that rappers were rising in popularity. Like Vachel Lindsay in his tramping days, people wanted to find out what audiences would pay to hear.

Since the Victorian years, there has been a place for poets to read their own works to an audience. In 1890, Tennyson recorded a reading of "The Charge of the Light Brigade," while in 1956, Robert Frost read "The Road Not Taken" in a recording session at his house. Frost and others did public readings, usually at universities, that contributed to their popularity.

But the new "performance poetry" was not just a way of reading written poetry to a listening audience. As in rap, the spoken interpretation was felt to be the primary art, and a written transcript nothing but a partial record of the art that had taken place. This view did not need to change the nature of the poetry, as we see from Lindsay's use of sound elements of language. However, since the form developed in a time when free verse was dominant, "spoken word" poetry came to be mostly dependent on the vocal performance alone. Metrical rhythm didn't play as well as other ways of organizing the words.

Spoken word poetry focuses on emotional and rhetorical rhythms, which are usually larger than metrical ones. Meter focuses on how a few syllables relate to each other, but a rhetorical or emotional structure takes in phrases or even whole sentences; it also brings in pacing, as the performance poet chooses how to speed or slow words. These vocal tools create types of rhythm, but only infrequently does it include metrical rhythm.

Spoken word poetry can use sound repetition; both alliteration and rhyme are used at will. However, since its emphasis is on the totality of the spoken voice, sound elements like rhyme may be seen as distractions from other features. Many spoken-word texts (written down, of course) don't appear to have any rhyme or alliteration.

Spoken-word poetry is best known for developing a competitive scoring system for events called *slams*. Originally, slams organized poets into regional teams, but they now give individual prizes too. Following the model of Olympic Games artistic scoring, poetry slams have a panel of judges who award a point number; the highest and lowest numbers are discarded, while the middle ones are averaged. However, it's only sometimes competitive. Probably most spoken-word poetry takes place during open-microphone evenings at coffee shops. These may also be called poetry jams, to rhyme with slams. People just gather to share and influence each other.

You can find spoken-word poetry easily on the internet, and you can also search for recordings of poetry slam events. Some sites also have the transcripts so that you can study them at your leisure, but they'd be the first to point out that you're not experiencing the true poem unless you're listening to it.

This kind of poetry is art made with words, but like rap, it needs the element of vocal interpretation. When it is reduced to words on a page, much spoken-word poetry is indistinguishable from prose, although it also may be identical to free verse in its irregular line organization.

Spoken-word poets feel that they are within the tradition of English poetry, while rap artists do not. Their goals in performing with words may be the same as those of written poets. Rap, on the other hand, may have more in common with written poetry in its attention to formal sound elements. Most of the sound elements of language receive more attention in rap than in spoken-word poetry, but the imagery and sheer range of subjects covered by traditional poetry are better covered by spoken-word poets.

I have a personal bias in favor of classic written poetry, but I have to admit that both of these newer kinds of word art are more popular in the 21st century. In his tramping days, Vachel Lindsay had to answer the question: for *what* will people pay scarce money or food? At a popular level, people want comedy, drama, surprise, and an open show of emotion. They don't want the sophisticated micro-arts favored at royal courts (in the past) and universities (now). Hiphop and poetry jam fans far outnumber subscribers to university poetry journals.

We end up back on the African farm with the Kikuyu boys who wanted to hear speech "like rain." Human minds love art made with words, and when one kind becomes remote from their daily experience, another form rises up.

For further reading and listening:

1. Listen to old recordings of W. B. Yeats and Vachel Lindsay reciting verse. The University of Pennsylvania has an online sound archive of authors, and both Yeats and Lindsay can be found there, reading (chanting) their best-known works:

   http://writing.upenn.edu/pennsound/x/Yeats.php

   http://writing.upenn.edu/pennsound/x/Lindsay.php

2. Watch two TED talks. One is by Sarah Kay, a young spoken-word poet; its title is, "If I Should Have a Daughter." Kay recites two poems, and she also tells how she got interested in this kind of poetry. The other is by British hiphop artist Akala, who is associated with the Hip-hop Shakespeare Company. In his "Hip-Hop and Shakespeare?" talk at TEDx Aldeburgh, he tests the audience to see if they can recognize Shakespeare's lines when they are mixed into selected rap lines.

After this book:

Speak Like Rain has focused on poetry published before 1925, with limited attention to interesting and important developments in more recent years. Of course, the traditional poets featured here have many more works you can enjoy, from the Elizabethans to the 1950s. You can find many of their works online, and Dover Publications has very inexpensive collections and anthologies (usually under $5) of anything published before 1925. If you read only poems published before 1900, it would probably take you some years to work through them all.

But perhaps you want to see what's being written recently or even currently. In *The New Formalism: A Critical Introduction* (Cincinnati: Textos Books, 2005), Robert McPhillips surveys the "New Formalists," the poets who revived metrical forms after 1970. If you want to know who's been writing what, this is a good place to start. Chryss Yost and Mary Jo Salter, mentioned in the text, are both discussed and there is a chapter on attempted revivals of narrative verse.

Subscribing to a poetry journal is a very good way to keep up with current writing. The Poetry Society of America (poetrysociety.org) keeps a complete list of current journals you can read online or subscribe to.

If you study or read a foreign language, learn about its poetry. For anyone who wants to write good poetry, this matters especially. Look at how many great poets started out as translators! It's a way to know the essence of word art because you see what's at the core as art crosses the boundaries of languages.

Do you wish to continue formal study? In 1938, American poets Robert Penn Warren and Cleanth Brooks published an influential college textbook, *Understanding Poetry*. It has gone through a number of editions that have kept it up to date with more contemporary poetry. Perhaps because it was originally written to develop a critical point of view, it doesn't have a strict textbook feeling. Its organization is based in categories of content and approach, rather than following the basic-elements approach I've taken in *Speak Like Rain*, so it would make a perfect sequel (so to speak). Its major publishing budget allows it to reprint many poets that I regret to have passed by.

There are many books about poetry written by poets, starting with Sir Philip Sidney's *Defense of Poesy*. I appreciated W. H. Auden's essay "Making, Knowing and Judging," in *The Dyer's Hand*. But you can find more recent, perhaps more approachable books with a simple internet search.

My parting advice: never neglect your own intuition, once it has received basic training. If a poem or poet bores you, skim the work if you need to know about it, but otherwise let it go. Revisit the poem or poet in 10 or 20 years, and it may strike you differently: Robert Frost has doubled in stature every decade that my eyes have aged. But don't do your taste the basic harm of telling yourself you like something that you don't, just because others say they do. Since word art has such a wide range of style and content, respect a poet's art but let yourself be pleased and displeased, excited and bored. To like everything is to love nothing.

Contemporary Works Cited

Akala. "Hip-hop or Shakespeare?" TEDx Talks, Aldenburgh. Posted on YouTube by TEDx Talks: https://www.youtube.com/watch?v=DSbtkLA3GrY

Auden, W. H. *The Dyer's Hand*. New York: Random House, 1962.

Bradley, Adam. *Book of Rhymes: the Poetics of Hip-Hop.* New York: BasicCivitas, 2009.

Bone, Paul and Rob Griffith, eds. *Measure: A Review of Formal Poetry*. Evansville, IN: Measure Press.

Bowers, Faubion. *The Classic Tradition of Haiku: An Anthology.* Mineola, NY: Dover, 1996.

Brooks, Cleanth and Robert Penn Warren. *Understanding Poetry*. New York: Holt, Rinehart and Winston, 1976.

Campbell, Joseph. *The Hero with a Thousand Faces*, 3rd ed. San Francisco, CA: New World Library, 2008.

Chang, Edward C. "What Is Jintishi?" *Bilingual Chinese Poetry and Prose.* www.chinese-poetry.com

Eliot, T. S. Old Possum's *Book of Practical Cats.* London: Faber, 1939.

Frye, Northrop. *Anatomy of Criticism: Four Essays*. Princeton, NJ: Princeton University Press, 1957.

Frye, Northrop. *Fables of Identity: Studies in Poetic Mythology.* San Diego, CA: Harcourt Brace 1963.

Hall, Donald. *Their Ancient Glittering Eyes.* New York: Ticknor and Fields, 1992.

Hollander, John. *Rhyme's Reason.* New Haven: Yale University Press, 1981.

Johnston, Ruth A. *Excavating English*. 2003.

Johnston, Ruth A. *Re-Modeling the Mind: Personality in Balance.* Gibsonia, PA: Pannebaker Press, 2015.

Jung, Carl, ed. *Man and His Symbols.* New York: Dell, 1968.

Kay, Sarah. "If I Should Have a Daughter." https://www.ted.com/talks/sarah_kay_if_i_should_have_a_daughter

Kenner, Hugh. *The Mechanic Muse.* New York: Oxford University Press, 1987.

McPhillips, Robert. *The New Formalism: A Critical Introduction*. Cincinnati, OH: Textos Books, 2005.

Poetry Foundation. *Poetry magazine*. www.poetryfoundation.org

Salter, Mary Jo. *Nothing by Design*. New York: Knopf, 2013.

Tolkien, J. R. R. *The Fellowship of the Ring* (audiobook narrated by Rob Inglis). Recorded Books, 1990.

Williams, William Carlos. *Pictures from Breughel and Other Poems.* New York: New Directions, 1962.

Yost, Chryss. "Terzanelle in Blonde." *Mouth & Fruit*. Santa Barbara, CA: Gunpowder Press, 2014.

SPEAK LIKE RAIN:
ANSWER KEY

LESSON ONE

1. Personal answer. Example: Once I was getting ready to move to another place, and I thought about the particular sort of sadness involved in leaving everyone behind; I wrote a poem to remember my thoughts.

2. Answers will vary. Example, for "A Poison Tree": a. the writer was thinking about how we harbor and feed negative feelings until they have grown into something really harmful; b. word rhythm; rhyme; repetition of some words and phrases like "I," "my wrath did," "And I"; unusual mark for accent on "sunned" to add to the rhythm; c. images of tree, shining apple, dead enemy; d. When I read it a second time after studying it, the artistic points are more obvious.

LESSON TWO

Review: a. Poetry is art made with words. b. We study arts that we can't do so that we know their terms and techniques; so we can understand them.

1. correct word matches in each group:

   tiger, hurry
   giraffe, believe
   banana, impressive

   fortunate, balcony
   oppose, garage
   cathedral, Italian

   record, project
   license, football
   approach, balloon

   majorette, personnel
   object, address
   thankless, saddle

   fantastic, appalling
   simple, menu
   triangle, elephant

   simplify, exercise
   approval, ballistic
   musketeer, lingerie

2.
FORtunate	garBANzo	refeREE	SOMber	deLIGHted	reFER
DeLIGHT	apPREciate	in the DARK	THEater	balLOON	SepTEMber
a BIRD	the HOUSE	THIS and THAT	THIS one	you SEE?	who's THERE?

3. fortunate, exercise, triangle
   Somber, this one, lion
   Garbanzo, approval, Norwegian

   giraffe, my car, the tree
   Who's there? It's me, a dog.
   referee, in the rain, balconette

4. but SOFT what LIGHT through YONder WINdow BREAKS?

    a LITtle LEARNing IS a DANgerous THING.

    the SEA is CALM toNIGHT the MOON shines FULL

    can YOU come Over HERE to EAT toNIGHT?

    shall I comPARE thee TO a SUMmer's DAY?

5. The words that don't fit in each set are: appreciate; alphabetize; arbitrary; community; sentimental; determination

6. give me ONE, like "referee"

    give ME one, like "banana"

    i'm right HERE, like "balconette"

    I'M right here, like "exercise"

    i DO, like "giraffe"

    I do, like "lion"

    this is my DOG, like "my guarantee"

    this is MY dog, like "California"

    THIS is my dog, like "hullabaloo"

Lesson Three

Review:

a) We make art to remember a significant feeling or experience.

b) in SUNshine COLD grey STONES a GALLant KNIGHT

    had JOURneyed from the DYing MOON in ENGland

    SHAven and SHORN of the SHAdow aCROSS the LAKES

c) You came back, in the dark… (personnel)

    Simplify, algebra… (pineapple)

    The last one, I can't wait… (a big deal)

    Abracadabra… (why did you say that)

    Circumvent, tell me now!... (smorgasbord)

1. Answers vary; my example:

    This is Jack with an app for sale
    Who met the girl with a phone so frail
    Who leashed the dog, a big Airedale,
    That bit the postman delivering mail
    That stopped the robber out on bail
    That mugged the boss (a Mr. Whale)
    That fired the tech all hooded and pale
    That made the patch
    That fixed the bug

That ruined the app
That Jack wrote.

2.
- a) 2; 2; 3; 2; 2; 3. this pattern continues in other stanzas, with one exception: "Down the Valley of the Shadow" has 4 beats. In "Fell AS he FOUND," "OF the MOON," normally unstressed words receive a strong stress.
- b) answers vary.

3. Sweet and Low: a) 4, 3, 4, 3, 4, 4, 3, 5; the stanzas are the same. b) answers vary. c) the repeated lines are the same

   Break, Break, Break: a) in the first 2 stanzas, each line has 3 beats; in the second two, it's 3, 3, 4, 3.. b) answers vary. c) repeated lines are a bit different the second time.

   The Splendour Falls: a) 4, 4, 4, 4, 6, 6; he stanzas are the same. b) answers vary. c) The 6-beat lines each repeat once identically, and once differently.

4. Pippa's Song has two beats per line. "Home Thoughts from Abroad" with stresses marked as I hear them:

   OH, to BE in ENGland (3)
   NOW that April's THERE, (3)
   And whoEVer WAKES in ENGland (3)
   SEES, some MORning, UNaware, (3)
   That the LOWest BOUGHS and the BRUSHwood SHEAF (4)
   Round the ELM-tree BOLE are in TIny LEAF, (4)
   While the CHAFfinch SINGS on the ORchard BOUGH (4)
   In ENGland—NOW! (2)

   And AFter APril, when MAY FOLlows, (4)
   And the WHITEthroat BUILDS, and ALL the SWAllows! (4)
   Hark, WHERE my BLOSsomed PEAR-tree in the HEDGE (4)
   LEANS to the FIELD and SCATters ON the CLOver (5)
   BLOSsoms and DEWdrops—AT the BENT spray's EDGE— (5)
   THAT'S the wise THRUSH; he SINGS each SONG twice Over, (5)
   Lest YOU should THINK he NEVer COULD reCAPture (5)
   The FIRST fine CAREless RAPture! (3)
   And THOUGH the FIELDS look ROUGH with HOAry DEW, (5)
   ALL will be GAY when NOONtide WAKE aNEW (5)
   The BUTterCUPS, the LITtle CHILdren's DOWer (5)
   —Far BRIGHTer THAN this GAUdy MELon-FLOWer! (5)

5.
- a) Two ROADS diVERged in a YELlow WOOD,
    And SORry I COULD not TRAvel BOTH
    And BE one TRAveler, LONG I STOOD
    And LOOKED down ONE as FAR as I COULD
    To WHERE it BENT in the UNderGROWTH;

b) Answers may vary. "Yet knowing how way leads on to way" seems to me a point where he's no longer being literal, since it's possible to circle back on literal roads and take the same one again.

c) The last stanza may be read with variations. I usually read it:

i SHALL be TELling this WITH a SIGH (or: I shall be TELLing THIS with a SIGH)

SOMEwhere AGes and AGes HENCE:

Two ROADS diVERged in a WOOD, and I—

I took the ONE less TRAveled BY, (or: i TOOK the ONE…)

And THAT has MADE all the DIFferENCE.

Lesson Four

Review:

a) Lollapalooza… (abracadabra); Opportunity… (Deuteronomy); Counterfactual… (sanctimonious); Determination… (extravaganza)

b) Possible answers: Old English or Anglo-Saxon verse; nursery rhymes; Romantic verse; early hiphop.

c) Break, break, break… (Oh, to be in England);

Then took the other as just as fair… (O, sweet and far from cliff and scar)

He met a pilgrim shadow… (Wind of the western sea)

All's right with the world!… (In England—now!)

1. Answers vary; here are examples.

    a) about a cat between garage

    Come here my friend refrigerate

    b) hurry saddle simple expert

    Combination in confusion

    c) beautiful sabotage certainly pineapple

    Come my identical such opportunity

    d) guarantee referee balconette do you see?

    In the dark an impossibly messy balloon

2.

   a) for questions about the meter, check the first two sample lines given in the lesson text.

   b) examples of words that would disrupt the meter, for lines 2-4:

   There's men from the barn and the forge and the mill and the *sheepfold*,

   The lads for the *women* and the lads for the *alcohol* are there,

   And there with the *others* are *many* lads that will never be old.

   c) answers vary; the poem looks ahead to how World War One will end these country boys' lives before they get old. Housman ironically casts the future dead as the "fortunate" because they will carry their looks and sense of truth to the grave, without feeling dirtied by the betrayal he feels about war's outcome.

3.
- a) Stanza 1: "Could frame thy fearful symmetry;" Stanza 3: "Could twist the sinews of thy heart," "And when thy heart began to beat;" Stanza 5: "And watered heaven with their tears," "Did he who made the Lamb make thee?" Stanza 6: "Dare frame thy fearful symmetry." Together, they are iambs; but they can be hard to spot because they don't interrupt the music of the poem.
- b) I see the stressed words as emphasizing the impossibility of getting any real answer to the questions. A normal question would be, "What hammer did you use?" Blake asks, "WHAT the HAMmer," which seems to say rather "it's an amazing hammer that I'll never know about" than actually asking, "which hammer in the catalog?"
- c) When "did he?" is a trochee, it's a more ordinary question, like "did he smile or not?" But when "did he?" becomes an iamb, it's asking if it's really the same "he" who smiled at the Tiger's sinews and heart, and then turned around and made the gentle lamb. The meter also emphasizes contrast between the lamb and the tiger.
- d) your personal answer. I feel that after asking so many unanswerable questions, Blake's poem would feel open, uncertain, and unfinished. He can't answer his questions, but he can complete the poem by restating the thought that we've now seen fleshed out.

4.
- a) trochees
- b) 4, 2, 4, 4, 2, 4.
- c) Ocean is the poet's soul; storms are emotion; the reef or coast is a page or book; the seaweed is poetry, art made with words to commemorate the poet's storm.

4.
- a) iambs, with five feet in each line. I don't think smoothing out the irregularity of "Something" improves the poem, because the first foot being a trochee makes the poem feel like the person walking along the wall stumbled, and I like that image. I find that same first-foot troche in these other lines:

    No one has seen them made or heard them made (NO one)

    One on a side. ("ONE on a SIDE" is the typical speech pattern)

    He is all pine and I am apple orchard. (to contrast He and I)

    Spring is the mischief in me (to emphasize the season that makes the mischief)

    "*Why* do they make good neighbours? (because he emphasizes "why")

    Bringing a stone grasped firmly by the top ("bringING" is just no good)
- b) Expanding ice moves the stones. Personal answers.

5. Limerick: 3, 3, 2, 3.

Lesson Five

Review:
- a) qualitative
- b) Two roads diverged in a yellow wood... (But the tender grace of a day that is dead)

Slight, to be crushed with a tap… (And whoever wakes in England)

Sleep, my little one, sleep, my pretty one, sleep… (That's the wise thrush; he sings each song twice over)

c) spondees; iambs; dactyls; trochees; anapests.

1. line; trespass; scale; look upon; stretch; real; looker; for; shoulder; obsidian; forward; remove.

2. The poem's meter is iambic, and the line lengths vary between one foot and five feet, but it does not settle into pentameter or tetrameter. The poet varies line lengths to bring forward certain words, such as "she" in the 3rd line. Because the lines are all end-rhymed, short lines place rhyming words very close together ("be," "she," "me"). (Note: the answer key will not usually try to discuss the meaning of a poem.)

3. The poem's meter is iambic; lengths are 4, 3, 4, 3. This form was popular for hymns because the 3-foot line allowed the last note to be held, and a breath taken to start the next line. The second stanza opens with an irregular foot; we would normally stress "deep," but the meter's push to shift the stress to "in" is very strong. Similarly, in the second to last line, the meter nudges us to read "god IS" instead of "GOD is." It's easy to miss these irregularities if you let the meter draw you in like a ticking clock.

4. In the first poem, there are irregular feet in this line: NOthing beSIDE reMAINS. ROUND the deCAY…" Two of the feet are trochees. In line 3, "stands in the desert" presents a similar problem, but it's the only irregular foot so the mind is nudged to just say "stands IN the DESert" as a sort-of acceptable reading. But in the line ending "decay," two irregular feet make it harder, so the line feels rough.

   In "Mutability," the word "streaking" is a trochee in a line of iambs. The rest of the poem is very regular, though it's also worth noting that "quiver" and "ever" in the first stanza are feminine endings; so are "sorrow" and "morrow" in the fourth. Skipping the "v" in "never" reduces it to one syllable, which permits the syllable count to remain at 10, as it should be in iambic pentameter. In the last line, the meter prompts us to say "nought MAY enDURE," where a natural intonation would probably stress "nought." This is interesting because it brings emphasis on "may," as if to stress that endurance of other conditions is not possible.

5. Ten sample lines of Hamlet: feminine line endings are in italics, and a foot is in brackets [ ] if it's not a regular iamb. In the first line, it's arguable that the foot "that is" should indeed be read as an iamb, "that IS," rather than the usual "THAT is," because not only does this fit the meter, it also implies that it's settling an argument. In the 5th line, the word "them" is extraneous to the meter, as it adds an unstressed syllable right next to another, in "to DIE." The irregularities of the meter, in such a speech, protect it from sounding too artificial.

   To be, or not to be—[that is] the *question:*
   [Whether] 'tis nobler in the mind to *suffer*
   The slings and arrows of outrageous *fortune*
   [Or to] take arms against a sea of *troubles*
   And by opposing end [them.] To die, to sleep—
   No more—and by a sleep to say we end
   The heartache, and the thousand natural shocks
   That flesh is heir to. 'Tis a consum*mation*
   Devoutly to be wished. To die, to sleep—
   To sleep—perchance to dream: ay, there's the rub…

Similarly, in "Paradise Lost," Milton's opening lines shift the iambic stress to "THAT" forbidden tree. When "that" is stressed, it draws attention to the item: THAT tree, not the others. In the poem's context, the iambic stress is appropriate. In many places, Milton has used apostrophes to adapt words to the number of syllables he has to fit them into (usually one). In his century, it was still normal to add the ending -est to the "thou" form of a verb: thou madest, thou knowest; but that created two syllables, and the meter demanded only one. After we see the lengths the poet went to alter words for a smooth regular meter, it's surprising to see a central line that stumbles: "And chiefly thou, O Spirit, that dost prefer." Like "And by opposing end them. To die, to sleep," it has an extra unstressed syllable. It's possible that Milton's dialect spelled "spirit" but pronounced "sprite," which would make it regular.

6.
   a) dactyls; "the Lads in their Hundreds" always ends the line on a strong beat (da da DUM), whereas here, the lines typically end with unstressed syllables (DUM da da). There are two feet per line; it is dactylic dimeter. The meter is very regular, with one interesting exception:

   HALF a league, HALF a league,

   HALF a league ONward,

   ALL in the VALLey of [DEATH]

   RODE the six HUNdred.

   If we skipped the word "death," the meter would be perfectly regular; later, when the line reads "into the jaws of Death," it's regular again. But here, at the start, each time "death" appears, it is an extra strong beat that disrupts the meter's patter. Did Tennyson do this intentionally?

Review 1

1. Art made with words.

2. pentameter: 5;

   tetrameter: 4;

   heptameter: 7;

   dimeter: 2;

   trimeter: 3;

   hexameter: 6;

   Alexandrine: 6;

   Fourteener: 7.

3. b

4. c

5.
   a) trochee;
   b) iambic;
   c) spondaic;

    d) anapest;
    e) dactylic

6.
    a) Austrian: dactyl;
    b) Finland: trochee;
    c) Japanese: anapest;
    d) Brazil: iamb;
    e) Ecuador: dactyl;
    f) Hong Kong: spondee

7.

Iamb	Trochee	Dactyl	Spondee
Taiwan	Norway	Hungary	Mumbai
Peru	Sweden	Canada	Shanghai
Ukraine	Yemen	Latvia	Cape Town
Vientam	Turkey	Pakistan	San Juan
Sudan	China	Germany	Key West

8. A is end-stopped; B is enjambed; C is a caesura; D is enjambed; E is end-stopped.

9.
    a) double-dactyl;
    b) limerick;
    c) accentual verse;
    d) blank verse

10.
    a) Frost;
    b) Tennyson;
    c) Poe;
    d) Blake;
    e) Browning

Lesson Six

Review:
a) Gíve it báck to me! = coúnterfáctual; Whén can you téll me? = ábracadábra; It's júst my síze = incárceráte

b) Sít and wátch by her síde an hóur; While the óne elúdes, must the óther pursúe; I cróssed a moór, with a náme of its ówn. Lines are from poems by Robert Browning; I've lightly marked stressed syllables to help make the accentual patterns clear.

c) Blank verse is unrhymed iambic pentameter.

1.
- a) Austen; Sensibility.
- b) taken; face.
- c) drowning; meant.
- d) Third; blunder.
- e) Hitler; occurring.
- f) Dickens; sheep.
- g) jelly; Prince.
- h) ninety-three.
- i) Hermit; First Crusade.
- j) gravy; sodium.

2.
- a) Perfect rhyme: go, show
- b) slant rhymes: abroad, understood; door, everywhere; hay, sea.
- c) intended slant rhymes: field, cloud; blew, sky. The first pair I can accept, and the nearby word "hard" seems to fit with them. The second pair doesn't sound to my ear like rhyme at all, though Dickinson could have argued that they're both vowels. What do you think?
- d) I understand "its" to refer to the sun.

3.
- a) same sound different spellings: known, alone, groan; heart, part, art; prayer, there, care; "I am," d—n (that is, "damn"); parallel, hell, well;
- b) double rhymes: exceeded, she did; copy, shop he; fine as, Inez; problem, ennoble 'em; calculation, education, personification; covers, lovers, discovers; surpass her, Macassar;
- c) triple rhymes: mathematical, Attic all, what I call; magnanimity, sublimity, dimity; homily, Romilly, anomaly; vanity, insanity; comparison, garrison, Harrison;
- d) rhymes that cross word boundaries: exceeded, she did; mathematical, Attic all, what I call; problem, ennoble 'em; surpass her, Macassar;
- e) rhymes that feel forced (your opinion may differ): muslin, puzzling; problem, ennoble 'em; tongue, song, wrong; lecture, director;
- f) Lopé is rhymed with copy; Inez is rhymed with fine as.

4.
- a) Third stanza: thrilled me, filled me; Fifth stanza, the repeat of "dream" may count as rhyme. But mostly the 2nd line does not have internal rhyme. (Looking past the first 5 stanzas, in stanzas 9 and 10, words are repeated as in 5, and in 10, "soul" and "pour" form a slant rhyme.)
- b) what is repeated and what varies, in lines 4 and 5, by stanza:

    4: "tapping" is repeated, nothing else.

    5: "the word Lenore;" and "whispered" appears in both lines.

    6: "Let me/my" and "and this mystery explore"

7: "perched" is in each of 3 lines; "above my chamber door"

8: "Night's [Plutonian] shore" and "Nightly shore" are almost the same, but vary

9: "bird...above his chamber door" in the second case other phrases come between to vary it

10: "have flown before"

11: "followed fast and followed faster" and "till his ____ bore," words in the middle vary.

12: "fancy" "what this..." "ominous bird of yore"

13: "velvet lining" and "velvet-violet lining" and "what/that the lamp-light gloated o'er"

14: four words get repeated: respite, nepenthe, quaff, Lenore. But each appears in a varying phrase.

15: "is there—-is there?" and "tell me truly I implore" and "tell me tell me I implore" almost the same.

16: "clasp...maiden whom the angels name Lenore" but the words between vary

17: "take thy ___ from out/off"

18: "shadow...on the floor" but the other words vary

- c) to me, lines without internal rhyme do feel like they stretch longer; for line 5 in stanza 5, I don't hear "-ered" as a rhyme, rather I notice the repeated word "whispered." What do you think?

- d) stanza 6: lattice, that is, thereat is; stanza 7: made he, stayed he, lady; If I read these out loud, I feel like they do work as rhymes. Stanza 15: I see but don't really "hear" the match of "Tempter sent, or"; Stanza 18: pallid/Pallas does strike me as a rhyme, perhaps because they are not right on top of each other. What do you think? It's sort of a slant double rhyme.

- e) When he calls the bird a prophet of evil the second time, he may be reacting to its just having told him that there is no balm in Gilead, which seems an "evil" message. What do you think? About its artistry: your thoughts.

Lesson Seven

Review:
a) perfect rhyme: he, tea. Slant rhyme: tea, Nineveh. Double rhyme: appearance, year hence. Dactyl rhyme: Acropolis, Constantinople is

b) iambic pentameter; the iambic but feminine ending places a strong stress on "year" (like yéar'nce) which emphasizes its double rhyme with "appearance." Otherwise, we might read it as a spondee: year hence, with equal weight; or even put more stress on "hence."

c) Who's sáil'd where pícturésque Constántinóple's (apostrophes show where syllables must be merged)

d) timBUCtoo

1.
- a) any word that rhymes with "that"; iambic pentameter; tercet; a word that rhymes with "dime"
- b) any word that rhymes with "slow"; trochaic tetrameter, 4 feet, 3 feet, 4 feet, 3 feet; bonus: hymn or ballad form; the new form would be a quintet, XAXAA.
- c) for the B rhyme, any three syllables that rhyme with "prize," such as "exercise," bake some pies," or "bad disguise"; for the A rhyme, any four syllables that rhyme with "disunity," such as "community," "immunity," "identity," or "repent said he." dactylic tetrameter; sestet; your personal answers: were you able to find 3 and 4 syllables that stayed in dactyls? and does your A

word rhyme with -y (single rhyme), -ity (double rhyme) or -unity (triple rhyme)? The new rhyme scheme, with ostriches, would be ABABCC.

2.
- a) ABBABCCDD
- b) ABCBB
- c.) AABCCB
- d.) ABAAB
- e.) ABABCCDDE, FGFGHHIIE

3. ABABCCDDXD; or is it ABABCCDDEED, with "drop drop drop drop" mentally divided into two lines, "drop drop/drop drop"?

4. "If you were coming in the fall": XAXA, hymn/ballad form (iambic tetrameter/trimeter, quatrains)

   "When You Are Old": ABBA, iambic pentameter quatrains.

   "I To My Perils": ABBCABBC, or, in the second stanza ABBCXDDC; octaves of accentual dimeter; this poem uses double rhymes wherever the lines are adjacent: "charmer/armour," "believe her/deceiver," "fleeting/meeting," "steady/ready."

5.
- b) A rhymes, more/store/restore; B, abroad/road/abroad/load; C, pine/wine; D, suit/fruit/dispute; E, thorn/corn; F, drown it/crown it; G, me/thee/see; H, blasted/wasted; I, hands/sands; J, age/cage; K, draw/law; L, heed/need; M, fears/forbears; N, wild/Child; O, word/Lord.
- c) iambic; Herbert's use of enjambed lines gives the speaker a frantic tone, and then at times the sudden end-stopped lines, which may be short, feel like shouting or ranting. All blasted? All wasted?
- d) your own thoughts.

Lesson Eight

Review:
a) The rhyme scheme is a poem's pattern of rhymes.
b) octave; iambic
c) "poetry"; slant rhyme; "more"; the A rhyme has the first end-rhyme and the last, so it binds the end to the beginning with similar sound.

1. Circe turned Odysseus' men to swine;
   and something in the story as it's told
   proves our resemblance to the men of old.
   Our daily business, like the poisoned wine
   un-humans us; and everything that's fine
   or noble in our nature slips our hold,
   leaving a chattel to be bought and sold—
   our hoped-for vintage dying on the vine.

> The hero lives forever in the song—
> or lives as long as human eyes can see.
> We, anyway, will never live so long,
> as mortal beings, so our pride must be
> in things of transient beauty said or done,
> like water-droplets, blazing in the sun.

2. Sidney's sonnet for Stella: (a) it's rhymed ABBAABBACDDCEE. (b) the first two quatrains end with periods, closing each thought. The sestet is rhymed like a quatrain and couplet, but its thought is unified through all six lines.

   Shakespeare's Sonnet CXXX: (a) it's rhymed ABABCDCDEFEFGG. (b) each quatrain has a complete thought, with the couplet set apart as a conclusion.

   (c) your personal thoughts on how they compare and contrast

3. Shakespeare's Sonnet LXIII: (a) it's rhymed ABABCDCDEFEFGG. (b) each quatrain has a complete thought, with the couplet set apart as a conclusion.

   Milton's "How Soon Hath Time": (a) ABBAABBACDEDCE (notice anomaly DCE). "even" and "heaven" are not perfect rhymes in modern English, but probably they were in his time. (b) The octave's two quatrains each present a complete thought; there is a shift in the sestet, introduced by "Yet." The sestet presents a thought to balance the octave.

   Keats' "When I Have Fears": (a) ABABCDCDEFEFGG, like Shakespeare. (b) Each quatrain begins "When I" and presents another way in which he fears an early death. But the couplet isn't set apart as clearly; its first line is a continuation of the sentence from the previous quatrain. The last line is the continuation of the sentence, but it does stand on its own.

   (c) your personal thoughts on how they compare and contrast

4. Shakespeare's LXIV: (a) ABABCDCDEFEFGG as always. (b) His quatrains present four situations in which he can observe time decaying something, with two of them presented in the first quatrain. The second and third quatrains each present one, with "When I" as the opening foot. The couplet's thought is a separate conclusion.

   Blunt's "If I Could Live":

   a) ABABCDCDEFEFGG, but the C rhyme is also the B rhyme, so you could also say ABABBCBCDEDEFF. The 6th line opens with a trochee, not an iamb. The couplet features a double rhyme.

   b) His quatrains are full sentences, with end-stopped lines. The second quatrain develops the idea of the first, then the third introduces a contrary idea. The couplet is made of two short statements that hold together thematically and presents the logical conclusion.

   c) Shakespeare presents Time as all powerful by detailing the many things that get ruined over time, then concludes that such a powerful force can also take his love away, and that thought itself is like a death. Blunt presents Time has something that would be better ignored; it is a barrier to watching nature and feeling happy. However, in the end he too acknowledges Time's power, but for him, it's about his own death. Time will take him away, not just his love.

5. Shakespeare's LXXI: (a) ABABCDCDEFEFGG as always. (b) punctuation closes each of the first two quatrains, and each begins with "No" or "Nay." The third quatrain, which begins "O," does not close with a period or colon, but its comma does break up the thought with a clear transition to a conclusion idea in the couplet. So I'd say the ideas do follow the quatrains and couplet structure here.

Browning's "How Do I Love Thee?": (a) ABBAABBACDCDCD. Some of her A rhymes are creative: praise, Grace, everyday's, and ways. The D rhymes are a little bit slant: faith, breath, death. (b) Browning's ideas respect the quatrains and couplet for the most part, but her phrases tend to be shorter than a quatrain, so sometimes there is a new idea in each line. On the other hand, the third quatrain's close just flows into the couplet with an enjambed list "breath, /Smiles, tears…" She does not keep the couplet's idea as separate as Shakespeare typically did.

Millay's "Only Until This Cigarette": (a) ABBAABBACDCDCD, like Browning. (b) The octave contains one full idea, closed by a period. The first line of the sestet is a true transition, saying literally "adieu, farewell" to the love described in the octave. Its idea is in contrast to the love suggested in the first 8, saying "yours is a face I can forget."

(c) your personal thoughts on how they compare and contrast; what do you think of Millay's kind of love?

6. Owen's "Anthem for Doomed Youth": (a) ABABCDCDEFEFGG, like Shakespeare. His rhyme pairings support the theme, that choirs and anthems have nothing to do with this type of death from "monstrous anger." Like "guns" and "orisons," an antique word for prayers, and "shells" and "bells." (b) His punctuation respects the quatrains and line endings, but the ideas of the third quatrain flow into the couplet, with a list of what will have to stand in for good-byes, flowers, and white palls (cloths draped on the coffin).

McKay's "If We Must Die": (a) ABABCDCDEFEFGG, like Shakespeare. (b) McKay uses the quatrains and couplet to organize his ideas. In the first quatrain, he presents the image of hogs being hunted by dogs; in the second, he states directly that they should die nobly; in the third, he defines "we" by addressing "O kinsmen!" In the couplet, he answers the first image: no, not like hogs, but like men who fight back.

(c) your personal thoughts on how they compare and contrast.

7. Wordsworth's "Composed Upon Westminister Bridge": (a) ABBAABBACDCDCD. (b) The octave is a long sentence, separated by colons, ended by a period. It describes the city as wearing the morning like a garment, with details of buildings and light. The sestet is similarly one long sentence with three opening exclamations of "Never!" or "Dear God!" that separate the sestet into three parts.

McKay's "The Tired Worker": (a) ABABCDCDEFEFGG, like Shakespeare. The rhymes in the couplet particularly catch my attention: pity and city, especially in context "Have pity!" and "the ugly city." They reinforce the poem's pain, especially after the gentle words that form the earlier quatrains: noon/moon, soft/aloft, night/invite, sheet/feet. (b) The first quatrain describes the relief of day darkening into evening, the second depicts the night as soothing and compassionate. The third quatrain starts in the same vein, but its last line interrupts the feeling, "O dawn! O dreaded dawn! O let me rest!" This plea continues into the couplet.

(c) your personal thoughts on how they compare and contrast.

8. Your opinion.

Review 2

1. A is end-stopped.
2. B is enjambed.
3. C is a caesura.
4. iamb
5. five, pentameter
6. D is "sonnet"
7. the third option, ABAB-CDDC-EFEF-GG, captures an anomaly in Burns' rhyme scheme.
8. switch lines 5 and 6, or 7 and 8.

9. quatrain
10. couplet
11. English. The CDDC quatrain suggests the Italian sonnet, but it seems to be an anomaly, not a pattern.
12. Shakespeare
13. slant
14. internal
15. double
16. ballad and hymn are both correct answers
17. accentual
18. blank
19. tercet
20. triple

Lesson Nine

Review:
a) -old, oans.
b) same as the first four.
c) CDECDE
d) -ay, -ate.
e) No.
f) four lines plus a couplet.

1. "that darn autocorrect!" for "The Raven"

Alliteration	Assonance	No sound repetition
Wan/weak	Steamy/dreary	serious/more
Quiet/quaint	hoard/lore	never/vainly
Vanguard/volume	blogged/nodded	
Called/came	Napping/laughing	
Gingerly/gently	padding, rapping	
Church/chamber	sweet/bleak	
Vagabond/visitor	mile/dying	
Daily/distinctly	popped/wrought	
Robot/remember	kissed/wished	
Sooty/separate	soft/lost	
Gamble/ghost	vain/rare	
Matron/morrow	lady/maiden	
Banks/books	steel/here	
Random/radiant		
Attendants/angels		

2.
   a) 345: alliteration of vowels: "oft the ear the open"
   b) 347: he uses all one-syllable words for the ten syllables of iambic pentameter

- c) 348-9: alliteration of R's "ring round" "returns" "rhymes"
- d) 356-7: he mentions the Alexandrine seven-foot line and then likens it to a wounded snake, and the snake's line has that extra foot after "length" ("along")
- e) 360: "and praise the easy vigor of a line," compared to the "ten low words" at 345, is visibly shorter but fills up the five iambic feet; it doesn't feel like it stretches too long or tries too hard, because of those two simple two-syllable words, "easy vigor."
- f) 362-2: Pope makes his point here with a clever analogy, written elegantly. This is the kind of ease in writing you only get through much reading and practice—-just like dancing well.
- g) 366-7: when he talks about the wind, he uses many S and Z sounds to simulate its whispering sound.
- h) 368-9: speaking of a storm, he uses many contrasting sounds. There's alliteration, but he repeats whole sequences of contrasting sound: "the loud surges lash the sounding shore," L-s-r-ge/sh. Soft "g" and "sh" aren't the same sound, but they are similar. Next, "hoarse, rough" begins with a breathy H and open O's, followed by the evocative verb "roar" with another open O.
- i) 371: to evoke the sense of lifting something very heavy, in line 370 Pope uses consonant clusters that are hard to say quickly together ("Ajax strives"). In 371, he uses short words with alliteration.
- j) 373: Camilla's swift running is meant to be evoked by S and F sounds, with an ellipsis in a word, o'er, as though there isn't time to say the V.

3.

- a) "This is how the wind shifts" rewritten to have identical repetitive structure; I've put the repetitions in italics:

    This is how the wind shifts:

    Like the thoughts of an old human,

    Who still thinks eagerly and despairingly.

    This is how the wind shifts:

    Like the thoughts of a human without illusions,

    Who still feels irrational things within her.

    This is how the wind shifts:

    Like the thoughts of humans approaching proudly,

    Who still approach angrily.

    This is how the wind shifts:

    Like the thoughts of a human, heavy and heavy,

    Who still does not care.

    The new altered poem is made of four tercets beginning "this is how the wind shifts," then "like" and "who still." Compare it to the original version. I think the original is much superior to this simplified one. Its variations make the words' music interesting, not repetitive, while the repetition shows that as mysterious as the poem is, it's definitely developing four aspects of one idea.

- b) "Carnet de Voyage III" is in iambic dimeter, though the first two lines don't fit. The repetition of the opening lines, at the end, feels to me like a wide-angle picture, then a zoom up close to the fishes and their many colors, then a zoom-out again, now that you know what's in the stream, to see the wide picture again.

4. Instead of presenting answers for a, b, and c, I present my observations for each poem.

   "God's Grandeur" observations: **bold** for alliterative repetition; || for caesura; <u>underline</u> for repeated or almost-repeated words; [R] for internal rhymes; *italics* for assonance.

   There's so much here it's hard to mark it all. Notice the caesura after "ooze of oil /crushed." It stops the flow of thought, which at first appeared to be a hymn about God's greatness. After the caesura, one-syllable words tap out a question: why do men not obey God?

   It turns out then that the poem is about pollution, all the ways we have used up and dirtied the world. That's the full thought in the octave. The sestet opens a new idea of hope: God's spirit assists nature to keep refreshing the dirty world. I feel that the repeated words when talking about pollution support a sense of weariness and things being worn out. There are three lines that either repeat or nearly repeat phrases; they also use internal rhyme. Especially when "have trod" is repeated without variation, it sounds tired. Then "seared with trade" is followed by "smeared with toil," so the sounds are repeated but with variation; similarly, "man's smudge" and "man's smell" repeat and vary.

   The sestet uses evocative exclamations like "oh" and "ah!" with its sets of alliterative clusters. Look at the meter of the last line, how the iambs bring out "broods," "warm," "ah!" and "wings." The last four lines have a general alternation of "w" words with "b" or "br." "west went…brown brink," then "world broods," "warm breast," and at last the order reversed, "bright wings." I find this particularly beautiful, so that its sound supports the message of hope. I often think of this poem when I worry about pollution. Hopkins' last word on it is his cry of delight "ah!" on recognizing the bright wings, which rise with the sun above our dirt.

   The world is charged with the *grandeur* of <u>G</u>od.
   It will **f**lame out, like **sh**ining from **sh**ook **f**oil;
   It gathers to a greatness, like the <u>oo</u>ze of <u>oi</u>l
   Crushed. || Why do men [R] then [R] <u>n</u>ow <u>n</u>ot <u>r</u>eck his <u>r</u>od?
   Generations <u>have trod</u>, <u>have trod</u>, <u>have trod</u>;
   And all is <u>seared [R] with trade</u>; bleared [R], <u>smeared [R] with toil</u>;
   And wears [R] <u>man's smudge</u> and shares [R] <u>man's smell</u>: the soil
   Is bare <u>n</u>ow, <u>n</u>or can **f**oot **f**ee**l**, **b**eing shod.

   And for all this, **n**ature is **n**ever spent;
   There lives the **d**earest freshness **d**eep **d**own things;
   And **th**ough **th**e last lights off **th**e **b**lack **W**est **w**ent
   Oh, morning, at the **br**own **br**ink eastward, springs—
   Because the H**o**ly Gh**o**st **o**ver the bent
   World **br**oods **w**ith **w**arm **br**east and **w**ith ah! **br**ight **w**ings.

   "No Worst" observations: **bold** for alliterative repetition; || for caesura; <u>underline</u> for repeated or almost-repeated words; [R] for internal rhymes; *italics* for assonance.

   I've counted as alliteration a few sounds that aren't in initial position, because they sound connected in a cluster with ones that are. Lines 3 and 4 use repetition of word and phrase: comforter/comforting, "where, where," then "where is your" paralleled in line 4 "where is your." In each case, the second repeat is varied.

   To put his meaning in prose, he is saying that in clinical depression, what seems very bad can always get worse, and it feels like there is no relief. The only relief from being pounded on an age-old anvil is a lull, not really an improvement. In the sestet, he compares depression to hanging on a cliff in your mind, and says you can only "hold them cheap," that is, think that they're not so bad, if you haven't experienced it. Again, he says, relief comes as a lull: with small (en)durance, we fall asleep. Night is compared to a death, but in this case, not a tragic one, instead an absence of pain that is a comfort.

I think his use of sound supports his meaning with a frantic chaos of alliteration; in "God's Grandeur," he used many pairs of alliterating words, but here he strings them together at length and without much pattern. When he quotes Fury, he is especially creative; Fury's speech is set off by caesuras before, during and after. Fury enjambs a line by breaking up a word awkwardly. It's all exclamation points and sudden stops, held together by alliterative l's and f's (the central word, "fell," has both).

There are at least eight caesuras in this sonnet, chopping the flow of thought into parcels. It seems to imitate the speech of someone in great pain, gasping out phrases. Some of the alliteration sequences do this too, like the p's in the opening lines, the string of panting h's in the middle, or the d's in the closing.

> <u>No</u> worst, there is <u>no</u>ne. || <u>P</u>itched <u>p</u>ast <u>p</u>itch of grief,
> More <u>p</u>angs will, schooled at fo<u>re</u>pangs, wilde<u>r</u> w<u>r</u>ing.
> <u>Comforter, where, where</u> is you<u>r</u> <u>comforting</u>?
> <u>Ma</u>ry, <u>mo</u>the<u>r</u> of us, whe<u>re</u> is your <u>r</u>elief?
> <u>My</u> cries <u>h</u>eave, <u>h</u>erds-long; <u>h</u>uddle in a <u>m</u>ain, a chief
> Woe, wórld-sorrow; on an áge-old anvil wince and sing—
> <u>Then lull, then leave</u> off. || <u>F</u>ury had sh<u>rie</u>ked "No <u>l</u>ing-
> ering! || <u>L</u>et me be <u>fell</u>: || <u>f</u>orce I must be b<u>rief</u>."
>
> O the <u>mind, mind</u> has <u>m</u>ountains; c<u>l</u>iffs of <u>f</u>all
> <u>F</u>rightful, sheer, no-<u>m</u>an-<u>f</u>athomed. || <u>H</u>old <u>th</u>em cheap
> May who ne'er <u>h</u>ung <u>th</u>ere. || Nor <u>d</u>oes long our small
> <u>D</u>urance <u>dea</u>l with that st<u>ee</u>p [R] or <u>d</u>eep [R]. || Here! creep [R],
> Wretch, <u>u</u>nder a <u>c</u>omfort serves in a whirlwind: || a<u>ll</u>
> <u>L</u>ife <u>d</u>eath <u>d</u>oes end <u>a</u>nd <u>ea</u>ch <u>d</u>ay <u>d</u>ies with s<u>l</u>eep.

5. "Dover Beach" is iambic, but the lines vary between 3 and 5 feet. Most end sounds have a rhyme within the next five lines, sometimes more. "The grating roar" is not rhymed until two stanzas later, so is it an X line or does it fit with them? I see it as an X line that foreshadows "roar" being used again, this time to rhyme with "shore." The last stanza, "Ah love, let us be true!" uses rhyme in a more sonnet-like way: ABBACDDCC. This brings a sense of closure and resolution.

Alliteration: full/fair, gleams/gone/glimmering, coast/cliffs, long line/land/Listen, Faith/full/folds/furled, [with] drawing/roar/retreating, night/naked, lie/like/land, love/light, peace/pain/plain,

Assonance: fair/straits, sea meets/hear, blanched land, Sophocles long ago, now/only/long/roar, wind/shingles,

Consonance: cadence/sadness, misery/this distant, girdle/furled, melancholy/long, darkling/alarms/armies

Repetition of syntax: so various, so beautiful, so new; neither/nor (5x)

"Melancholy, long, withdrawing roar" lists 8 syllables of description before the verb, so it feels long; there are also four open O sounds (I count "aw") to echo the "roar."

What else do you see and hear?

Lesson Ten

Review:
a) blinder/broke; Alfred/against; gripped/ground/grasped; staggered/strove/stand

b) than/land; broke/strove

c) folk, broke; land/and

d) sea-folk, sea; repeats of "and"

e) and gripped the ground/and grasped the air

f) "sea" has no end-rhyme here, so it is X

1. the Pantoum:

    a) iambic pentameter

    b) ABAB, BCBC, CDCD, DEDE, EAEA

    c) The second and fourth lines in one stanza become the first and third lines in the next.

    d) The poem closes by using the first stanza's 1 and 3 lines again.

    e) Each stanza breaks in half, thematically, and all of the first halves, and all of the second halves, must be unified. In this poem, the first two lines always talk about the town by the sea, while the second two lines always depict the bagpiper. The contrast of these two themes develops the meaning.

2.

    a) Both ballades are in accentual meter, four beats per line. Both are rhymed ABABBCBC, with the same A, B and C rhymes for all three stanzas.

    b) "Ballade for Dead Actors" repeats the last (8th) line, while "The Ballade of the Automobile" repeats not only the last line, but also the 4th line.

    c) your thoughts

3. Hardy's triolet: a. "Around the house the flakes fly faster" is repeated with "Around the house" stopped by a period. "The flakes fly faster" is also varied, in the middle case 'faster' is grouped with a following phase, with "the flakes fly" set on its own by an exclamation point. "And all the berries now are gone" appears the same in both uses. b. The meaning isn't developed much in Hardy's triolet, since it's mainly descriptive. We learn during the middle repetition that "faster" can also apply to shutting indoors a "crumb-outcaster" (a child?), but otherwise it means pretty much the same at the end as at the start.

    Bridges' triolet: a. "When first we met we did not guess" is only varied in the third repetition, where it's split by a question mark, "When first we met?" leaving "We did not guess" to begin a new sentence. "That love would prove so hard a master" is varied only by personification—-capital L—-in the first use. b. The repeated lines in Bridges' triolet tell a story, a bit more unfolding with each repetition. "When first we met" is literal in line 1, explaining the situation when they first met: innocence, naiveté, no premonitions of trouble. The second appearance clarifies this by using "when first we met" to describe their having no inkling about more than common friendliness. "Love" is theoretical, not yet applying to them. The turning point is midway with the new lines: "Who could foretell this sore distress/ this irretrievable disaster/when first we met?" It's no longer a potential disaster and distress, it's "this" one, the one they have now. Falling in love worked out so badly that their initial friendship can't be retrieved. I find the line "this irretrievable disaster" one of the most elegant uses of a five-syllable word in poetry: it dominates the triolet, where there's so little new information permitted in those lines, but "irretrievable" tells us the story in one word. And it has internal sound repetition: eer-ree-tree, three short wails of grief. It must be pronounced carefully to be understood, so it forces the reader to linger over it. When we see the repeated lines again, it's a commentary on the past, a sad head-shake: "We did not guess that love would be so hard a master." Now they know, as they didn't in line 1.

4.
- a) Henley's rondeau "What is to Come" is in iambic pentameter. As he repeats "what is to come," he does not alter the punctuation or word use much; all three settings are about what we can know or not know of the future. In imagining potential good or bad futures, he sketches in some content to "what is to come" before setting it aside as irrelevant: we don't need to care about this, because the past matters more.

- b) "In Flanders Fields" is in iambic tetrameter. The uses of the half-line are "In Flanders Fields poppies grow," "we lie in Flanders Fields," and "we shall not sleep in Flanders Fields." Speaking in the voice of the recent dead, he moves from the literal field of graves to the idea of what they died for. If the war is lost through giving up, the Flanders Fields should be a memorial to their resentment.

- c) Dunbar's "We Wear the Mask" is in iambic tetrameter. The uses of the half-line are "We wear the mask that grins and lies," "let them only see us while we wear the mask," and "let the world dream otherwise while we wear the mask." He develops the idea of hidden pain; in the first line, the "mask" by nature hides things, but there's only a hint in "grins and lies." A grin is not necessarily a *happy* smile, it's rather a conscious one for others to see. In the second stanza, he pretends to defend the world's need to believe that they're happy, which is the reason they wear the mask. In the third stanza, he articulates the dimensions of the hidden pain: cries from tortured souls, clay under feet for many miles. His defense of the world's need for them to hid pain serves to accuse the world for its contentment not to wonder about pain that should be obvious when it's so lightly covered. Of the three rondeaux, I think this one develops its half-line idea the most.

5. Robinson's "The House on the Hill"
- a) The first line is irregular, but otherwise the lines seem to be iambic trimeter. The first line might fit in an accentual-meter way: "they're ALL GONE aWAY."

- b) "They are all gone away" comments on wind going through the house, and poses the question "why are you here?" in its repeated appearances. "There is nothing more to say" in its second appearance comments on the people being so thoroughly gone that nobody can even say something bad about them; then it remarks on the futility of the children's words in the wind. (or: your thoughts!)

- c) The details provided in the stanzas fill out the meaning of the repeated lines, so that when they close the poem, they stand for everything from the sunken door sill to the total silence when the children go away. The statement is comprehensive and final, an epitaph.

- d) Robinson's "Cortège"

    The poem isn't a villanelle, but it uses repetition in the same way. "Four o'clock this afternoon" and "best for them they go today" are roughly the repeated lines, but the exact words vary, and they are in different places. "Four o'clock this afternoon" appears in the first line three times, and twice in the third line. Its phrasing doesn't alter, just its position; its regularity and identical repetition are like a clock's chime. "Best for them they go today" varies a lot, with "best" sometimes in a different line, and once with "the grave" as the "best" he can recommend.

    Two other phrases are repeated: "X will hide them," and the distance 'Fifteen hundred miles away."

    The repetition and variation are pleasing: "Earth will hide them far away" and "Love will hide them deep, they say." The distance, like the time, chimes identically in each appearance.

Exercises Eleven

Review:
a) It's okay because the meter is accentual, not qualitative.
b) line 1: alliteration and assonance; line 2: alliteration; 3: consonance (laughter and perfect, central F sound)
c) They are not sight rhymes, they are different sounds that happen to have the same spelling.
d) Lines 3, 4, 7 and 8 are end-stopped; lines 1 and 2 are enjambed, though the phrasing pause coincides with the line's end, but lines 5 and 6 are also enjambed; in line 8, "Then ho!" forms a caesura. If you counted line 5's commas setting off "automobiling" as caesuras, that answer is acceptable too.

1. As an example, I did b), editing "Cones." Did my edits improve it? Probably not really.

   After rain has stopped
   blue mist in empty spaces
   Fills all the trees, wet.

   Behind the houses
   Shaking gold spire of leaves as
   Sun touches poplars.

   A branch sways in sight
   Here, but there in sound twitters
   A sudden sparrow.

   Curtain flutters, its
   Rose-broidered hem half reveals
   A red chimney pot.
   Quiet in the room
   Patiently bears a footfall
   on the rainy street.

2.
   a) alliteration: huddled/haggard/hunger/haunted; blue burst; long lake; sun/spray/storm

      assonance: huddled/ugly/hunger; lake waves breaking/spray; veering/wheeling/free

      Internal rhyme: lake/breaking

      Walls/gulls: I think it's coincidental, not meant to be any sort of rhyme. There are no other examples of rhyme apart from the one internal rhyme.
   b) All of the h-words have sad, pinched connotations and even the breathy h connotes effort, panting, or being out of breath. They make the passage dark and sad. The phrase "huddled and ugly walls" is repeated in identical form.
   c) In the second half, ee's and ay's predominate, open vowels that feel both cheerful and unrestricted. The descriptors include 3 colors and active verbs (breaking, fluttering, flying, veering, wheeling). What else do you observe?
   d) first pattern: blue burst of lake; spray-flung curve of shore; fluttering storm of gulls; masses of

great gray wings. Second pattern: long lake waves; great gray wings; flying white bellies.

- e) Sandburg's lines tend to end where a thought pauses, often with punctuation. He doesn't break up phrases like "on a blue burst" or "under the sun."
- f) Humans are associated with the first half, in which the tone and diction steadily connote grief, insufficiency (hunger), and ugliness. The second half uses tone and diction connoting openness, freedom, plenty (masses), and beauty.

3.
- a) I can't find any role for repetition-type sound elements or meter; Pound's word sounds are distinctly different each from the other. That's its own kind of beauty, but not in the ways we've been studying.
- b) time: "when my hair was still cut straight," "at fourteen," "at fifteen," "at sixteen," and "by the gate now" with a change to present-tense verbs.
- c) Like Sandburg, Pound here makes the line breaks match completion of phrase or thought, not breaking up phrases like "playing with blue plums."
- d) Outside of the context, the details are mixed. Monkeys chattering—-usually heard as cheerful, not sorrowful; deep moss——probably neutral; falling leaves—-often used to connote sorrow or loss, as here; paired butterflies—-usually seen as beautiful and cheerful, not a marker of passing time when they cannot mate like the butterflies.
- e) "forever" is repeated 3 times. The meaning doesn't change in a dictionary sense, but when a word like this is repeated, the effect is to convey overwhelming emotion. It sounds like a child or a teenager who feels that piling more words up will make a bigger impression.

4.
- a) The poet regularly breaks up thoughts, phrases and words. He breaks "mud-luscious" so that the line appears to say "the world is mud" and we see this in other places, where he wants the last word to stand out. He also breaks up parallel phrases differently: "eddieandbill come/ running," whereas he writes that "bettyandisbel come dancing;" "running from marbles and/ piraces" versus "from hop-scotch and jump-rope and."
- b) "the little lame balloonman whistles far and wee" is repeated, but with variations: "the queer old balloonman," then "the goat-footed balloonMan."
- c) "spring" opens the poem, perhaps part of the phrase "in Just-spring," but it's not clear. After that, it appears in the phrase "and it's spring," but once, the placement has it close a stanza instead of opening; the other time, the placement is in the middle, in lines with lots of white space and single words.
- d) Variations in "far and wee" may be meant to convey that sometimes the sound is from farther away, other times it's quieter (wee). It can be "far [white space] and wee," or "far [white space] and [white space] wee," or "far/and/wee." The last one might suggest the balloonman going actually farther away, into the distance. About the change from "balloonman" to "balloonMan," I notice that when the adjective "goat-footed" suggests a mythical faun, Man is emphasized with a capital letter. Does that contradict the suggestion of a faun, or emphasize it? I don't know. What do you see?
- e) When I read, I do pause for both white space and line breaks. The phrases come out in bits and gasps, separately. It does seem a good imitation of the constant motion of children playing; children sometimes even literally start a sentence, jump across a puddle, and then say the last

word. The poem embodies that kind of movement.

5.
- a) Inside the house, where we keep all of our valuables dry, is "worldly" compared to the unworldliness of rain outside.
- b) rain's chief trait here is that it falls equally on any object that isn't protecting itself. He seems to be saying that love, too, will fall on all of us and invade the spaces we wall off.
- c) "you" seems to address a personification of Love, though it could also be God or a person whose love is being showered on him.
- d) your thoughts.

6.
- a) Stevens does use some parallel phrasing and lightly repeated words, such as in 4 with "are one," and 5 with the "Or" phrases. I don't observe use of sound elements otherwise; he uses contrasting, not repeating, sounds and words.
- b) 1—snowy; 3—autumn; 6—icicles and shadows, it is daytime in winter; 10—a green light, suggests summertime; 11—shadows, so it's daytime; 13—snowing and evening. The other stanzas don't seem to have any connection to time or seasonal setting.
- c) 1—eye; 3—wings; 5—beak whistling; 6—the bird's whole body but in silhouette; 7—its feet; 10—bodies and wings, flying; 13—the blackbird's whole body, sitting still.
- d) 2—"like a tree in which there are 3 blackbirds;" 4—the blackbird idea forms a unity with men and women somehow; 5—the blackbird's whistle is here, but so is the silence afterward, which is a lack of whistling, an "innuendo" of the sound; 6—the blackbird's shadow is here, but so is an idea of mysterious causation; 7—the blackbird is here walking, but it's also compared to imaginary golden birds that the "thin men" prefer; 8—the blackbird seems to stand in for something that unifies human thoughts; 9—the blackbird's absence marks the edge of an imaginary circle in the air; 11—a man is afraid of the blackbird's shadow and mistakes part of his own shadow for it (the bird is not actually there, even in shadow—it's just his fears); 12—the stanza draws a strange logical conclusion that if the river is moving, the blackbird must be flying, as though all movement in nature is connected. The blackbird is a unifying thread in our being, thoughts, knowledge, fears, and imaginings; it is real in a way that golden birds and invisible circles are not.
- e) Stevens uses line breaks most often as the conclusion of a phrase or thought, arranging phrases to be parallel or words to appear twice in similar positions. Some line breaks are end-stopped. Although his lines are short like Cummings' lines, his line breaks are more like Pound's and Sandburg's here, since they coincide with completed phrases.

REVIEW 3

1. alliteration (a's, q's, l's)
2. word repetition
3. assonance (-a-)
4. consonance (-nd-)
5. word repetition
6. couplet
7. alliteration and assonance

8. slant rhyme (and, in 14, "sleek")
9. internal rhyme
10. double rhyme
11. ballade
12. rondeau
13. triolet
14. villanelle
15. sestina
16. envoi
17. 5-7-5
18. free verse
19. it is not part of Provençal troubadour poetry, but it is part of the other three: free verse, French verse, Arabic verse.
20. free verse
21. pantoum (bonus)

Lesson Twelve

Review:
a) AABBCC...
b) iambic meter; in the central "pillar" each line is two feet; the "top" has two lines that are five feet, then two of four feet; the "base" of the altar has two lines of four feet, then of five.
c) "cemented" must be read "CE-men-TED" to fit the iambic meter.
d) calligram; also correct would be "concrete poem," although I don't use the term in this text

1. your own answers.
2.
   a) Colors: I see green (grassy holms), blue, yellow (ragwort) and "bronzed" for the evening sky; Land features: falls, fords, shallows, holms (river islands), mountains, towers of a ruined castle, terrace, mill-race, sandy fields, groves of flowers, rocks; Proper nouns: Derwent, ragwort, Skiddaw; the main implied sound is the running water that could always be heard from his garden and terrace, even from the windows, while the implied motion is, again, the running water. There's also the suggested motion of the little boy jumping in and out of the water on a summer day.
   b) Nature breathes calmness into our hearts, when we are caught up in the "fretfulness" of the city. In the last image, the child Wordsworth is like a Native American whose life is mainly lived outdoors; in childhood, he is a picture of morally innocent mankind in a state of Nature, as some philosophers of his time were discussing.
   c) Your answers.

3.
   a) "Spring Storm"—daylight but the end of day, and there are gutters, so it's in a town; colors: black, green. "Summer"—there seem to be three settings; one has a privet flower: an English hedge?

The next is at a gravel quarry, the last in a city garden at sunset. Colors: black, scarlet, white; crimson, rose. "New England Landscape"—it's a rural setting, probably fall because of the colors. Colors: sepia, orange, black, white, chrome, red, lilac, blue. "Autumn"—an English country road, as probably the hedge is real, not just part of the analogy. And, at night. Colors: red, white. "Blizzard"—probably in country, not town, because of the "solitude," though "alleys" of trees suggests a town with actual alleys. Colors: yellow, blue, implied "white".

b) "Spring Storm" uses some repeated words. "Summer" doesn't seem to use any of the patterned sound elements. "New England Landscape" uses rhyme irregularly. "Autumn" has three prominent words beginning with R. "Blizzard" has one line with assonance, "deeper and deeper for three."

c) In "Spring Storm," the sky has been bitter, in "Autumn" the stars are "wistful," in "Blizzard" the snow is made of anger, and maybe of idleness. These touches seem to integrate the human writing words about them, by projecting onto them some feelings that he has or imagines. The speaker/viewer doesn't appear in the poem, but we see through his eyes and so things are tainted by human feeling and thought. "Spring Storm" also becomes more directly descriptive after the opening statement that the "sky has given over its bitterness." In "Summer," there is no emotional projection at all, just three images described in a photographic way. Similarly, in "New England Landscape," there is little to no human attribution. The birches "stencil" a design, the stones "find" a bed, and the cloud "unwinds" its skein, but these are just actions.

d) Richard Aldington's line breaks also coincide with complete phrases or thoughts, so that some line breaks change the subject as if there were punctuation. There is no semi-colon here, but the break seems to make one: "Fantastically cut by dark chimneys/ Candles winking in the windows." The pale sky is what's fantastically cut, while "candles winking" is really a separate thought. T. E. Hulme, too, uses line breaks where thoughts and phrases come to rest, with or without punctuation. "ruddy moon lean over a hedge" and "like a red-faced farmer" are divided by a line break, permitting each phrase to be complete. DuBose Heyward, too, uses line breaks where phrases end; his one clear anomaly is the line "the pines," but he may have placed this line break to highlight the rhyme with "lines." William Carlos Williams, on the other hand, tends to break things up more. Direct objects may be on a different line from their verbs ("given over/its bitterness," "snow keeps/its hold,"), while conjunctions and prepositions may also be separated from the words they govern ("nor/ bitten by the sun," "drunk with/the swirl," "of/yellow and blue flakes"). Some line breaks work with punctuation, not against it. In "Blizzard," the poet gives us a colon at the first word, with a line break almost like a title, then mid-poem there are two caesuras caused by working against the punctuation: "…eh? Then/the sun! a clutter…"

e) your answers.

4.

a) the Alph River starts with a geyser or artesian spring, then wanders five miles in a place level enough to create meandering loops, then pours into a crack or cave to go underground again. It's not realistic! Coleridge describes the pleasure ground's ten (square?) miles of forest, gardens, flowering trees, and sunny spots. The only kind of flora or fauna he specifically mentions is an "incense-bearing tree." Then he depicts a steep valley of cedars and the geyser or spring. He appears to describe the "pleasure dome with caves of ice" but he doesn't present a coherent picture.

b) Coleridge seems to be describing his subjective experience of exaltation when he was dreaming about Xanadu. If he could recall that feeling, he would be like someone enchanted. His descriptive energy depicts the wild state of his emotion and how shocked everyone around would be when they saw it.

c) Rhyme: I'm starting over at A for each new stanza: ABAABCCDEDE; ABAABCCDDEEFFGHHDII;

ABABCC; AABBACDCD, ABAABCDDC. (Note: in British dialect, "dulcimer" would rhyme with "saw," since they would not pronounce the final R.) There's a rhyme scheme that Coleridge almost uses at the start of each stanza: ABABCC, with either (or both) A or B rhyme repeated, and with variations on "CC." Stanza 3 gives the pattern in its clearest form; if you look at other stanzas in its light, you can see that one or the other rhyme, or both, repeats just to linger over the sound for a moment longer before giving us "CC." Do you see other patterns?

Meter: The first seven lines have four feet, then five feet until it reverts to four again in the 3rd stanza. The shorter lines feel more like song, since they return us to the rhymes faster; it also feels like song because four feet are the ballad/hymn pattern.

d) Coleridge uses repeated sounds (rhyme, alliteration (measureless to man), consonance (fertile, girdled)), and some repeated words: "caverns measureless to man," "sunny dome," "caves of ice." He uses patterned word stress, in his iambic tetrameter and pentameter lines. I see, too, exclamations to give the words an emotional tone of exultation. What else do you observe?

5.
a) Meter: iambic pentameter; Rhyme scheme: ABABCDECDE; Sound elements: alliteration, word repetition (happy, for ever), and variation of sound (note the contrasting sounds in the first two lines).

The tone is formal, lofty, and consciously ornate; Keats uses the older pronoun and verb forms (thou canst) that were no longer current even in his time.

b) The first scene has musical instruments and a singer; it may be the same scene with the Bold Lover trying to kiss a girl under leafy trees. The second scene is a religious procession: a priest leads a heifer with flower garlands, while people follow.

c) Art is immortal because there can be no change in the images. Actions shown halfway complete cannot be completed, since there is no motion or time. People do not age; the heifer will never be sacrificed; love cannot be disappointed. I'm reminded of the Elizabethan sonnets that spoke of memorializing the beloved in the poem. Keats' point also clarifies why we always use the present tense when we speak of literature. A poet wrote these lines at some point in time, past tense; but in the poem, he speaks eternally just as his images are permanent. He may die, but we say his poem "speaks," not spoke. Coleridge's poem is eternally waking from a dream, while Keats' ode forever contemplates beauty.

d) Keats' words "Beauty is truth, truth [is] beauty" get quoted frequently, sometimes alone and sometimes with the added "all ye need to know" comment. When the urn "says" this, it is stating that its truth is beauty, because beautiful images are all it has. The urn doesn't have time, motion, causation, logic, or even morality, since there are no actions. So in its most restricted sense, Keats' words tell us that the truth of art is beauty; art can't participate in other kinds of factual or logical truth. Keats implies that he agrees with the urn, that he sees the truth of art as a supreme kind of truth. His statement is still pretty limited, since he is making art (with words) as he says it. What do you think?

Lesson Thirteen

Review:
a) It was a miracle of rare device, /A sunny pleasure dome with caves of ice.

Have known the evenings, mornings, afternoons, /I have measured out my life with coffee spoons;

b) "It was a miracle of rare device" has 5 feet but 25 letters; "From the fountain and the caves" has 4 feet but 26 letters.

"I know the voices dying with a dying fall" has 6 feet but 33 letters; "I have measured out my life with coffee spoons" has 5 feet but 38 letters.

c) the pattern ABCABC is used by neither of the samples.

1.
- a) done as example
- b) The language of the sea and its tides is applied to religious faith in its times of greater or lesser popularity. A simile would compare sea and tides with the church's up and down times. Simile in my words: In one generation the church would be full, in the next generation it would have empty pews, just like a beach with the tide coming in and out.
- c) The language of birds is applied to hope. A simile would compare birds habits and traits of hope. Simile in my words: Hope gathers its own energy, like a wild bird gathering seeds in the woods.
- d) The language of fruit trees is applied to anger and hatred. A simile would compare fruit trees and anger. Simile in my words: My anger grew like a tree, with tears as water and false smiles as sunshine.
- e) done as example
- f) The simile compares men (living and) dying with the process of hunting a wild pig with many men and dogs. A metaphor would apply the language of hunting hogs to the deaths (or lives, or hardships) of men. To make this into a metaphor, I want to avoid talking about a man's literal death in the language of hunting hogs, unless the man's death was not much like the hogs in a literal sense. I'll make my metaphor about the death of a man's reputation, instead: His good name went down in the mud as the hounds trampled and growled. Or about the death of a culture: Traditional folk arts ran and hid, but the baying dogs of pop music and television ran them down.
- g) The simile compares the sad time of a lover's absence and winter's bleak cold. A metaphor would apply the language of winter to my sorrow at someone's absence. Metaphor in my words: I shivered in the solitude and rubbed my heart to keep it from frostbite.
- h) The simile compares the city's morning beauty with wearing clothes. A metaphor would apply the language of clothes/getting dressed to the city's morning beauty. Metaphor in my words: The city slid into the morning, zipping up its traffic and buttoning its dawn-reflecting windows.
- i) Bonus: It's already a metaphor that applies the language of ropes and cages to rules and regulations.

    Simile in my words: The rules tie me tightly like a kidnapper's ropes.

    Metaphor in my words: They locked the law's door and tied the regulations tight.

2.
- a) Keats' metaphor compares poetry to a geographical area. States and kingdoms might be kinds of poetry, or poetry in different languages or from different time periods. Islands might be kinds of poetry that are unusual or from farther away (or longer ago). Poets are medieval lords sworn to serve King Apollo, the Greek god of poetry. b. Keats compares himself to an astronomer who charts a new planet, then to an explorer who finds a new place. c. In Keats' telling, Cortez and his men have just reached the top of a mountain range in Central America, and they can see blue ocean stretching to the western horizon. They are silent because they're suddenly realizing that it might not be a lake, they might actually have discovered a sea that isn't on the map yet. That's the "wild surmise." Keats is commemorating a feeling of being overwhelmed at his new

discovery of a body of poetry previously inaccessible. d. "Silent upon a peak in Darien" begins with a trochee, SI-lent, while the rest of the line forms iambs: upON a PEAK in DArIEN. However, because it's the last line and the iambic rhythm is so well-established, it's hard not to read it as siLENT. The effect is to make the word into a spondee, SI-LENT, giving it greater emphasis. I always want to pause after that word: Silent! …upon a peak in Darien.

3. a) Fire is desire (envy, covetousness, greed) while ice is hatred. The end of the world might mean the end of an important human relationship, like a marriage, or a society falling into civil war. b) It's in iambic tetrameter, with three lines of only two feet. The rhyme scheme is ABAABCBCB. To my ear, the short lines interrupt the regular rhythm of the ballad meter as a way of imitating the way destructive emotions interrupt the regular rhythm of normal life. What do you think?

4. These are my thoughts; yours may differ.

    a) Tears are coins because at some micro level, they reflect the other person's face, like a coin, and it's the grief over the loved one's face that causes his tears to form, so in two senses they are "minted" from her face. Tears are globes for the same reason, since a globe is a ball with images laid on it; also, two people's tears mixed will fill the ocean on a globe, causing a flood. His beloved is more than moon because her presence draws tears—his sea—toward herself, as the moon's gravity draws the ocean nearer. Tears are seawater here, and sighs are storm winds. Grief will stir up dangerous storms.

    b) Tears as coins are dangerous because they only reflect the person's face when they are forming. When they fall, the image is destroyed, so that in some spiritual sense, "thou and I are nothing". Tears as globes are dangerous because as they mingle they will fill the ocean and create flooding. Tears as storms and high tides are dangerous because he fears literal storms and shipwreck, so he implies that if they both stay calm and don't cry, they'll have contributed toward calm seas and safety. Or, at least, they'll have minimized the "death" either will find in grief of absence.

    c) AS-ee-AH, to fit the iambic meter

5. These are my thoughts; yours may differ.

    a) Light means his ability to do things, since seeing is a primary way of responding to the world. Without light, we usually stand still. Blindness creates literal darkness, but also the helplessness of a newly-blind man is like the way sudden loss of light paralyzes our actions.

    b) The talent is whatever ability he had to do things, and his blindness buries it the way the man in Jesus' story buried his silver. Buried silver can't create a profit; blindness is like burial of money, no return on investment.

    c) The yoke is what oxen wore so that carts or plows could be attached to their strength. Here, the work he might have done is part of his yoke, but so too is the affliction—-blindness—-he now must carry. Additionally, Jesus told his followers to wear his (Jesus's) yoke because they would find it mild or easy; this refers to a spiritual state or attitude about what is most important. While the yoke that Milton now wears feels cruel to him, he is referring to it as "mild" perhaps because the real task is not to keep doing the things he had done when he could see (which would be too heavy), but to serve God in this new state, whatever that means.

    d) Milton is the servant, as are all other people. They are sent on journeys or they fight in wars, but Milton now has to sit or stand still. His blindness enforces the role of waiter, not ambassador or general.

6. These are my thoughts; yours may differ, and ultimately it's not clear what E.B.B. meant.

   a) When people strive for right, they have to put aside lesser considerations.

   b) When people turn from praise, it shows that they do not expect to receive any reward for what they do. Love like this would persist even when it's not rewarded.

Lesson Fourteen

Review:

a) It's a metaphor because the boundary between "my life" and the coffee is blurred by implying that the spoons can measure out life directly.

b) The analogy is between an insect pinned on a board for scientific study, and himself; the pins are other people's eyes, and their "formulated phrases" are what paralyze him to be pinned. It's not a simile because he applies the language of insect-pinning directly to himself, not keeping them separated by "like."

c) Some phrases are repeated: "known them all already, known them all" is repeated both later in the first set of lines, and at the start of the second set of lines. It's varied there by "known the eyes already." The closing line "So how should I presume?" is repeated, too. Both sets also have the same A rhyme, "-all." On the other hand, not only are some of the words varied, but the rhyme scheme is different. The first stanza is ABBACC, while the second is ABCACB+ repeated line with rhyme from previous set. They feel like they match, but they don't. What else do you observe?

1. There are no wrong answers, since it's asking your personal thoughts. Feel free to compare your ideas with the results of internet searches for symbolism.

2.
   a) When the rose was uncut, perhaps in a sheltered place, it was like the shy girl who prefers not to be seen.

   b) as a cut-flower gift, it is like the girl when she can be seen and praised, as she praises this flower.

   c) when it dies, it will be like her beauty that remains unseen as she ages and gradually loses it. The Rose seems to symbolize beauty that can be seen, rather than hidden beauty; it may also symbolize generosity of sharing joy with others. As a cultural symbol, the rose means beauty, so the two symbols—-general and particular—-are close in sense. Waller is clearly working with the cultural meaning, expecting it to be imported.

3.
   a) "my spirit wails," "when I wake, alone," "impotent of parts, of fevered brain."

   b) water is something that can refresh his spirit, like love or freedom. You may have other ideas.

   c) New York City was literally hot and dry, but it was also spiritually unbearable since McKay had grown up in relative freedom and equality in Jamaica, so his thirst might be for that sense of freedom and self-respect. His images of water seem drawn from the country, probably where he grew up.

   d) the archetypal meanings of water range from "life" to "the unconscious" to references to Christian baptism. The meaning of "life" could enhance the symbolism. What do you think?

4. The autumn leaves symbolize aging and death in all life, including human life, including her own. Hopkins suggests that Margaret is not consciously aware of the symbolism, but that some inborn archetypal ideas of life and death are causing her to weep. Margaret feels the tie of life with life so strongly that she can't see the leaves as playthings, as children usually do. When she is older, she will have mastered it as a conscious idea, so that she won't grieve for leaves that are just renewed each year. Instead, she will grieve for deaths of individuals who cannot grow back.

   In line 9, the iambic meter forces us to emphasize the verb in an unusual way; we'd normally say YOU will WEEP, but here we must say "and YET you WILL weep AND know WHY." It's a strong prediction, almost a command. She has no alternative: she will weep, and she will know.

5.
   a) the Jar is gray, which suggests it's a simple ceramic jar, not glass. It is tall and round, with a wide mouth. It is "bare" and does not have anything living in or on it.
   b) The wilderness is "slovenly," which means unkempt, that is, uncombed. Nobody has neatened it up into rows of trees nor raked the grass. In contrast to the jar, it is full of living things. The jar alters the context of the wilderness by adding this man-made, symmetrical, non-living "thing" in its picture. To the poet, this makes the wilderness no longer wild. The jar seems to symbolize civilization and the works of man, which (to our eyes) become dominant in a scene with wild things.

6.
   a) It's late fall and everything is cold and dying; moreover, there has been a drought so it's extra dry and dead. Suddenly, a cotton flower blooms out of season.
   b) Toomer suggests that the flower "eyes" show "not a trace of fear," a beauty that is unexpected and out of place. I wonder if his meaning has reference to how racial segregation made black people (who also had "brown eyes") in Georgia feel afraid, so that it would be a rare and striking thing to have someone who felt no fear. What do you think?
   c) the poem has 14 lines like a sonnet, but it is rhymed AABBCC straight through, without any interlocking rhymes, unlike sonnets.

7. My thoughts: Roberts depicts a "Celtic" garden that is all in cool gray, blue and silver. The other flowers are associated with words like "sorrow" and "bitter." The tiger lily is tall, "regal," and brave. It may symbolize something like courage in difficult circumstances, courage when we don't expect it. What do you think?

Lesson Fifteen

Review:
a) Each short line has two or three accentual beats, but they don't fall into a pattern like a nursery rhyme. It almost feels unmetered, but not quite.
b) ABBA,CDC,EDE
c) The coat image is a metaphor for his poetry, because the attributes of the coat are transferred to the poetry (or is it the other way around?), blurring the images. The coat he describes is heavily embroidered from top to toe, covering the whole person, with images from mythology. In Yeats' case, it was Irish mythology that he used. Yeats was irritated by his many imitators; in these lines, he reminds himself that wearing the naked core of poetry is better than having just the style.

1. Achilles   5

Aeneas	8
Ajax	9
Apollo	2
Athena	10
Bacchus/Dionysus	1
Circe	4
Delphi	7
Elysian Fields	3
(F) Philomela	6
Gorgon	17
Helen	14
Icarus	11
Jason	18
Lethe	20
Muses	15
Narcissus	19
Orpheus	13
Pandora	12
Penelope	16
Persephone	29
Pluto/Hades	26
(Q) Cupid/Eros	28
Romulus and Remus	22
Sisyphus	30
Troy	21
Ulysses/Odysseus	24
Venus/Aphrodite	25
(X) Styx	27
Zeus/Jupiter	23

2.
  a) The stanza here is ten lines, all iambic pentameter except for the 8th, which has only 3 feet. It is rhymed ABABCDECDE. This is the same stanza form as in "Ode on a Grecian Urn" except that its lines are all regular pentameter.

  b) the Hippocrene was a spring on Mt. Helicon that was believed to give inspiration to poets. Lethe was the river of forgetfulness in the underworld. Flora was a Roman goddess of flowers and spring; dryads were nymphs (divine spirits) of the trees. The nightingale is a dryad to Keats because it "animates" the tree with its song.

c) the bird will not know: weariness, fever, anxiety, palsy of old age, wasting illness in the young, sorrow and despair.

d) Bacchus is the god of wine; it's a Greek name but comes from the Roman mythology.

e) In the Book of Ruth, the young widow Ruth goes out to gather stray grain from the harvest, which was the right of widows and orphans. Keats depicts her not as happily and busily gathering grain, but as working through tears of homesickness because even the type of wheat was alien to her. He speculates that a nightingale might have been singing nearby for Ruth to hear.

3.
a) wise men: skill, laws, highest Cause, knowledge; they bring "studied vows."

b) shepherds: harmless will, humble, Life, love, walking, wonder; they bring tears and sighs about their frailty.

c) The wise men represent the intellectual side of human nature, which tries to figure things out; the shepherds represent the emotional side, which feels awe, fear, love, and other emotions.

d) knowledge of science leads to wonder at its marvels, while simple ignorance "is wonder's seed," because then everything is a marvel.

e) Godolphin's moral for us is to use our intellect to know our frailty, and have our emotions sanctified by "the object," that is, being offered to God.

4.
a) the rhyme scheme is ABABBCBCC; the meter is iambic pentameter, but the 9th line has six feet, hexameter (or an "Alexandrine" line). In the first line, the first foot is a trochee: "COURage he SAID, as he POINTed TO the LAND…" This first foot makes it sound like it's going to be a trochaic poem, and the extra unstressed beat ("as he") makes it stumble a bit more, before it becomes regular in later lines. I feel that this line brings out the captain's shout of "Courage!" more clearly, and the irregular meter points up their desperation to find land.

b) here are three mountains inland, from which rivers flow to the sea, and at the beach the streams fall over tall cliffs. In the valleys between, palm trees and galingale (a spice) grow.

c) The poem states that it seemed to be afternoon, but it also cites a red sunset that lingers and lingers. The moon is in the sky at the same time, and both sun and moon seem to stand still.

5.
a) His canoe apparently moves on its own power; the magician has a charmed armor of wampum (sea shells strung together); the woodpecker can talk; the magician has an unguarded spot on his head.

b) Longfellow is telling the Iroquois legend of how the woodpecker got his red crest.

6.
a) the serpent is "wise and lovely" because it gave us knowledge, in this poem. This view is the opposite of the archetypal image of the serpent as evil and dangerous, but it's a deliberately chosen opposite to make her point.

b) Seiffert's Eve doesn't really appear in the poem directly, that is, we don't have a description of her or any spoken words. Coatsworth's Demeter is briefly described in the gesture of wiping sweat from her brow, and then her words fill the poem. If Seiffert's Eve spoke, she would have to give us the viewpoint of the modern generation that isn't interested in "knowledge of good and evil" but wants to use "common sense" instead. The poem as it is presents only Seiffert's narrative voice talking about this modern attitude.

  c) Seiffert's sonnet complains that today they are not interested in feeling reverence for good and evil, or in making decisions based on anything but pragmatic common sense.

  d) Demeter's reapers must have been complaining about all of the weeds they had to pick through to get the wheat. If we didn't know the speaker was Demeter, we wouldn't understand that she has a special authority and personal connection regarding grain and harvests, so her rebuke might sound peevish. What do you think? At base, Coatsworth is complaining about the modern attitude of farming at greater volume and speed, disregarding nature's beauty, looking only for maximum gain from minimum work.

LAST REVIEW

1. Short answer: Poetry is art made with words. Long answer: It is made to commemorate an insight or feeling; it is made of sound elements and images.
2-4 in any order: Rhythm, rhyme, and repetition.
5. trochaic tetrameter
6. iambic pentameter
7. no meter at all
8. iambic trimeter
9. iambic tetrameter
10. accentual tetrameter
11. dactylic hexameter
12. accentual dimeter
13. metaphor
14. Bible reference, so "myth"; for second answer, accept either symbol or metaphor
15. simile
16. simile; metaphor
17. metaphor ("simile" could be accepted if the reader was focusing on "tis something *like* a house")
18. symbol; simile
19. Bible reference: "myth"
20. sonnet; it is unusual because it splits the 12 lines into four tercets (not three quatrains) rhymed ABA, BCB, CDC, DED, plus the couplet. The rhyme scheme is also called terza rima.

Bonus: The image of the night is used as a symbol.

Lessons 16 and 17 do not have answer keys.

INDEX

Page reference is boldface for the location of a complete poem (or an excerpt 10 lines or more).

A

Accentual meter 26, 29, 30, 86, 256, 288

African poetry 9, 287

Akala 289

Aldington, Richard 183, 188

Alliteration: in daily speech 14; in poetry 118-9, 122-3, 285, 288; in Japanese verse 155

"Amicus Curiae" **201-2**

Amoretti 114

Analogy 195-202

Anapest 38-40

Anatomy of Criticism 227

"Anecdote of the Jar" **224-5**

"Anthem for Doomed Youth" **111**

"April Rain" **137-8**

Apollinaire, Guillaume 158

Arabic poetry 158

Archetype 213-7, 218-9, 227

Arnold, Matthew 130-1, 199, 230, 233, 250, 282

"Around the House" **145**

Art: why we make 10-1; poetry as 11-5, 159, 176, 195, 213, 217, 280; repetition as tool in 118; in Asian poetry 154-6, 172; ekphrasis 181-3; human voice as 280-4, 285-9

"Art of Losing, The" 138

Assonance 119-21, 123, 288

Astrophel and Stella, stanza IX **106**, 114

Atlantic Monthly, The 236

Auden, W. H. 140, 182-3, 235-6, 250

Austen, Jane 176

"Autumn" **190**, 197

"Avenge, O Lord, thy slaughtered saints" **101**

B

Ballad form 86-7, 132

Ballad of the White Horse, The 141, **259-60**

Ballade 132, 141, 143-5

"Ballade of Dead Actors" **143-4**

"Ballade of the Automobile, The" **144-5**, 162

Ballades, Rondeaus, Chants Royal, Sestinas, Villanelles and etc. 150

"Bantams in Pine-Woods" **131**

Beat poetry 288

"Before the Mirror" **181-2**

"Belshazzar had a letter" **252**

Beowulf 26-7

Bentley, E. Clerihew 70

Berryman, John 104, 105, 114, 260

Bible, The 213, 228, 232

"Binsey Poplars" **173**

Biography for Beginners 70

Bishop, Elizabeth 138, 140-1

Blake, William 16, 41, 44-5, 66, 80, 81, 85, 223

Blank verse 54, 176, 258

Blixen, Karen 9

"Blizzard" **190**

Blunt, Wilfrid Scawen 113-4

Boccaccio 88, 255

Book of Practical Cats, The 25, 79

Bowers, Faubion 172

Bradley, Adam 288

"Break, Break, Break" **33**, 87

Breughel, Pieter 182-3

Bridges, Robert 146

"Broken Altar, A" **186**

Brontë, Emily 83-4

Browning, Elizabeth Barrett 110-1, 114, 208-9

Browning, Robert 26, 34-5, 259, 281-2

Buller, A. H. Reginald 49

Burns, Robert 115, 176

Butler, Ellis Parker 144-5

Byron, Lord (George Gordon) 67, 72-4, 82-3, 88, 89, 189

C

"Caedmon's Hymn" 27

Caesura 53

"Caliban Upon Setebos" **282**

Calligram 158, 162

Campbell, Joseph 227

Canterbury Tales 38, 67, **255**

Canzoniere 114

"Cape Breton" **141-3**

"Carnet de Voyage, III" **128**

Carol 132

Cathay 155

Caudate sonnet 103

"Charge of the Light Brigade, The" **60-2**, 288

Chaucer, Geoffrey 38, 67, 255

Chesterton, G. K. 141, 259-60

"Chicago" **153-4**

"Childhood and School-time" **187-8**

Chinese poetry 151, 155, 172

"Circe turned Odysseus' men to swine" **105**, 231-2

Classic Tradition of Haiku: An Anthology, The 172

Clerihew 70-1

"Coat, The" **238**

Coatsworth, Elizabeth J. 249-50

Cockney rhyming slang 12

Coleridge, Samuel Taylor 176, 191-2, 203, 261-79

"Collar, The" **94-5**, 119-20, 196, 199, 218

"Complaint for Absolute Divorce" 139

"Composed Upon Westminster Bridge" **112-3**

"Cones" **163**

Congo and Other Poems, The 286

Consonance 119-21

"Corona, La" 100

"Cortège" **149**

Couplet 82-4, 89, 99-101

Cowper, William 56-7, 83, 178-9, 183, 185, 194

Crown of sonnets 100

Crutchfield, Robert 105, 231-2

Cummings, E. E. 104, 113-4, 166-7

"Cupid, I Hate Thee" **230**

Curtal sonnet 103

D

Dactyl 38-40, 68, 257

Dactyl rhyme 66-7, 70

Dante 85, 114, 138

"Death Be Not Proud" **100-1**

Decameron 255

Deejay 287

Defoe, Daniel 256

"Demeter" 249-50

"Detail" 282

Dickinson, Emily 68, 71-2, 80, 87, 92-3, 196, 197, 199, 252-4

Dinesen, Isak *see* Karen Blixen

Divine Comedy 85

Djeli *see* Griot

"Do Not Go Gentle" 138

"Don Juan" 67, **72-4**, 82-3, 88, 89

Donne, John 100-1, 206-7, 210, 230

Doolittle, Hilda 183

Double rhyme 66, 70

Double-dactyl 49

"Dover Beach" **130-1**, 199, 282

Dunbar, Paul Laurence 147-8, 217-8, 287

E

"Eagle, The" **16**, 66, 80, 196

"Easter Wings" **157**

Educated Imagination, The 227

Eiffel Tower calligram **158**

Ekphrasis 181-3

"El Dorado" **31-2**, 87

"Elegy for a Woman Unknown" **159-61**

"Elegy for Jane" 209

Eliot, T. S. 17, 25, 69, 79, 81-2, 156, 197, 203, 220, 230, 280, 282-4

Elizabethan sonnet *see* English sonnet

End-stopped: line 53; rhyme (also *end rhyme*) 68, 70

Endymion 180

English sonnet 99-100, 104

Enjambed line 53, 104

Envoi 140, 141

Essay on Criticism, An **125-7**

Evangeline 52, **257**

Excavating English 26

Eye rhyme *see* Sight rhyme

F

Faerie Queen, The 99, 244

"Fall of Rome, The" 235-6, 250

"Fall, Leaves, Fall" **83-4**

"Fan-Piece, for her Imperial Lord" **156**

Fellowship of the Ring 37

"Figlia Chè Piange, La" **17**, 69, **81-2**, 197-8

Finnegans Wake 260

"Fire and Ice" **205-6**

Flint, F. S. 163

Flow 288

Foot 38

"Fourteen" **115**

"Fra Lippo Lippi" **281**

Free verse 151-62, 163-70

French poetry 38, 132, 151, 158-9

"Fresh Prince of Bel-Air, The" 28

"From Cocoon Forth a Butterfly" **71-2**, 196

Frost, Robert 35-6, 47-8, 52-3, 70, 87, 205-6, 211-2, 218, 232, 250 254, 288

Frye, Northrop 227

Fungi from Yuggoth 114

G

Gawain and the Green Knight 255

"General William Booth Enters Into Heaven" **285**

Ginsberg, Alan 154, 287

"Go, Lovely Rose" **222-3**, 232

Godolphin, Sidney 243-4

"God's Grandeur" **128-9**

"Good Friday" **212-3**, 232

"Good Night" 185

"Gratitude" **199-200**, 210

Griot 287

H

Haiku 154-7, 162-4, 170

Half rhyme *see* Slant rhyme

Hall, Donald 151

"Hamlet's Soliloquy" **59**

"Harbor, The" **164**

Hardy, Thomas 86, 96, 145

Harlem Renaissance 147, 287

Harrington, Anthony 49

"He ate and drank the precious words" **252**

"Heavy Bear, The" 209

Henley, William Ernest 143-4, 146

Herbert, George 94-5, 119-20, 157, 186, 196, 199, 218

Hero with a Thousand Faces, The 227

Heroic couplets 83, 255

Heyward, Dubose 189-90

"Higgeldy-piggeldy T. Intermedia" **49**

"Higgeldy-piggeldy Thomas A. Edison" **49**

Hip-hop 13, 23, 28, 286-7

"Hip-hop and Shakespeare?" 289

"Hokku" **163-4**

Hollander, John 49, 79

"Homage to Mistress Bradstreet" 105, 260

"Home Thoughts From Abroad" **35**

Homer 38, 181-2

"Hope is the Thing with Feathers" **68**, 86-7, 199

Hopkins, Gerard Manley 103, 128-30, 171, 199, 224

House of Life, The 114

"House on the Hill, The" **148**

"House That Jack Built, The" **30-1**

Housman, A. E. 43, 88, 94, 97

"How Clear, How Lovely Bright" 88, **97**

"How do I love thee? Let me count the ways" (Sonnet XLIII) **111**, 208-9

"How Soon Hath Time" **108**

Howe, Julia Ward 148

"Howl" 154

Hugo, Victor 141

Hulme, T. E. 190, 197

Hymn form 86-7

Hyperion **177**, 194

I

"I have been one acquainted with the night" **254**

"I To My Perils" **94**

Iamb 38-40

Iambic pentameter 51, 54, 86, 99, 137, 255

Ideas of Good and Evil 285

Idylls of the King, The **257-9**

"If I Could Live" **109**

"If I Should Have a Daughter" 289

"If You Were Coming in the Fall" **92-3**, 197

"If We Must Die" **111-2**, 151

Iliad, The 181-3, 194, 231

Images: in daily speech 14; in free verse 152, ; in haiku 155; in plain descriptions 174-8, 179-81; in Imagism 183-5; in analogies 195; as symbols 210-3

Imagism 154, 157, 183-5, 188-90

"In a Station of the Metro" **155**

"In Flanders Fields" **147**, 176

"In Just" **166-7**

Internal rhyme 69, 70

"It is the Harvest Moon!" **222**

Italian sonnet 100-2, 104

J

Jam *see* Slam

Japanese poetry 38, 151, 154-5, 170

"John Brown" **286-7**

Johnston, Ruth 17-8, 55, 84, 134, 136, 137-8, 142-3, 199-200, 201-2, 234-5

Jonson, Ben 55-6, 91-2, 231

Joyce, James 260

Jung, Carl 227

K

Kay, Sarah 289

Keats, John 107-9, 177, 178, 182, 193-4, 205, 210, 228, 240-2

Kenner, Hugh 172

"Kermess, The" 182

"Kubla Khan" **191-2**, 203

L

"Lads in their Hundreds, The" **43**, 52

Lake poets 102, 176

"Landscape with the Fall of Icarus" (painting) 182-1, 183

"Landscape with the Fall of Icarus" (poem) 183

Lawrence, D. H. 214-7, 219, 262

Lear, Edward 49

Leaves of Grass **151-2**

"life is more true than reason will deceive" **104**

"Light Shining Out of Darkness" **56-7**, 84, 86

Limerick 49, 87

Lindsay, Vachel 285-7, 288

Lines: feminine 52, 54; masculine 52, 54; metrical types of 50-1, 54; and punctuation 53

"Lines composed a few miles above Tintern Abbey" **180**

"Little over Jordan, A" **254**

"Locust Tree in Flower, The" **184**

Longfellow, Henry Wadsworth 40, 45-6, 52, 87, 220-1, 236-7, 246-9, 250, 256-7

"Lord, when the wise men came from far" **243-4**

"Lotos Eaters, The" **244-6**, 282

Lovecraft, H. P. 114

"Love-Song of J. Alfred Prufrock, The" 203, 220

M

"Magi, The" **244**

Malaysian poetry 141-3

Mallarmé, Stéphane 159

Man and His Symbols 227

Markham, Edwin 219

Masculine line 52

"Maud" 29-30

McCrae, John 147

McKay, Claude 103, 111-4, 223-4, 287

Mechanic Muse, The 170

"Mending Wall" **47-8**, 51, 52-3, 54, 70

Meredith, George 114

Metamorphoses 228, 230

Metaphor 198-202

Meter: qualitative or quantitative 38, 41; types of feet in 38, 41, 54; identifying 39-41; irregularity of 41

Millay, Edna St. Vincent 103, 110-1

Milton, John 54, 60, 101, 102, 107-8, 207-8, 232

"Miracle for Breakfast, A" 140-1

Modern Love 114

Moll Flanders 256

Mongol chants 13

Monroe, Harriet 286

Moore, Clement Clarke 238, 250

"Morning Lyric" **17-8**, 85

"Musée des Beaux Arts" 182-3

"Mutability" **57-8**, 86, 120-1, 122, 196

"My Father's Watch" **210-1**, 217

"My Last Duchess" 281

"My mistress' eyes are nothing like the sun" (Sonnet CXXX) **107**, 196

"My Picture Left Behind in Scotland" **55-6**

"My sonnet is" **113-4**

Myth: definitions 228; Greek 228-32; poetry creates 236-8

N

Narrative verse 254-61

Near rhyme *see* Slant rhyme

"Neutral Tones" 86, **95-6**

"New England Landscape" **189-90**

"New Eve, The" 249

"Nightingale, The" 230, 250

"No longer mourn for me when I am dead" (Sonnet LXXI) **110**

"No worst, there is none" **129-30**, 176, 199

Noguchi, Yone 163-4

Nothing by Design 139

"November Cotton Flower" **225-6**

Nursery rhymes 28

O

"O Captain" 152

Octave 88, 89, 100, 102, 133

"Ode on a Grecian Urn" 181, **193-4**

"Ode to a Nightingale" 240-2

"Ode to the West Wind" **85**

Odyssey, The 231-3

Off rhyme *see* Slant rhyme

Old English (or Anglo-Saxon) verse 26-7, 118-9, 154

"Old King Cole" **28**

"On First Looking Into Chapman's Homer" **205**, 228

"On His Blindness" **207-8**, 232

"One day I wrote her name upon the strand" **99-100**

"Only Until This Cigarette" **111**, 151

Onomatopoeia 119, 123

Ottava rima 88

Out of Africa 9

"Outwitted" 219

"Oven-bird, The" **211-2**

Ovid 228, 230

Owen, Wilfrid 111-2

"Ozymandias" **57-8**, **102-3**

P

Pantoum 141-3

Paradise Lost 54, **60**

"Paul Revere's Ride" **236**, 250, **256**

"Paysage Moralisé" 140

Pemantle, Robin 49

"Perception" **124**

Perfect rhyme 66

Performance poetry *see* Spoken word poetry

"Persephone" **234-5**

Petrarch, Francesco 98, 102, 114

Petrarchan sonnet *see* Italian sonnet

"Philomela" 230, **233**, 250

Pictures from Breughel 182

"Pied Beauty" **103**

"Pippa's Song" **34**

Poe, Edgar Allen 31-2, 69, 74-9, 80, 87, 218, 230-2

Poetry magazine 155, 172, 181, 285

"Poison Tree, A" **16**, 80, 81, 85

Pope, Alexander 125-6, 181, 183, 194

"Portrait of a Lady" **280**

"Portraits are to daily faces" **252**

Pound, Ezra 151, 154-7, 165, 181-3

Power of Mythology, The 227

"Prayer for Moving Day" **84**

Prelude, The 180, **185-6**

Provençal poetry 132-3, 151, 154

"Provide, Provide" 232, 250

"Psyche" **235**

Purchas, Samuel 191

Q

Quatrain 85-6, 89, 100, 133

Quintet 87, 89, 135

R

"Rain" **167-9**

Rap 286-7; *see also* Hip-hop

"Raven, The" 69, **74-9**, 80, 133-40, 218, 230, 232

"Red Wheelbarrow, The" **157**

"Remembrance has a rear and front" **253**

Re-Modeling the Mind: Personality in Balance 214, 227

Renaissance poetry 98

Repetition: of sounds 118-21, 288; of words 121-3, 139-41, 288; of lines 132-9; in rap 288

Rhyme: in daily speech 12-3; types of 66-8, 70, 288; in line placement 68-70; schemes 80-9, 99, 100, 102-4, 133-9; as repetition 118; in rap 288; in spoken word poetry 288-9

Rhyme's Reason 49, 79

Rhythm: in daily speech, 13; in Imagism 181; in spoken poetry 288, 288-9

"Rime of the Ancient Mariner, The" 216, **261-79**

Ring and the Book, The **259**

"River Merchant's Wife, The" **165**

"Road Not Taken, The" **36**, 87, 211, 218, 288

Roberts, Walter Adolphe 226-7

Robinson Crusoe 256

Robinson, Edward Arlington 148-9

Roethke, Theodore 138, 209

Romantic poetry 29-30, 102, 177-80

Rondeau 135-6, 141, 146-8

Rossetti, Christina 212-3, 232

Rossetti, Dante Gabriel 114, 194

S

Salter, Mary Jo 139

Salter, William G. 210-1, 217

Sandburg, Carl 153-4, 164

Schwartz, Delmore 209

Seasons, The 177-8

"Seaweed" **45-6**, 52, 87

Seiffert, Marjorie Allen 249

"Separation on the River Kiang" **156**

Septet 87-8, 89

Sestet 87, 89, 100, 102, 140

Sestina 139-41

Seuss, Dr. 62

Shakespeare, William 54, 59, 99, 107, 108, 109, 110, 196, 198-9, 282

"Shall I compare thee to a summer's day" (Sonnet XVIII) **99**, 196

Shelley, Percy Bysshe 57-8, 85, 86, 102-3, 120-1, 122, 196

Sidney, Sir Philip 106-7, 114, 230, 250

"Shield of Achilles, The" 181, 183

"Sick Rose, The" **223**

Sight rhyme 67, 70, 101

Simile 195-8

Slam 289

Slant rhyme 67-8, 70, 103, 104

"Slow, Slow, Fresh Fount" **91-2**, 231

"Snake" **214-6**, 218, 262

"So Much Is Love" **135**

Song of Hiawatha, The 237, **246-9**, 250, 257

"Song of Myself" **152**

Song of Roland, The 255

Songs and Sonnets 98

Sonnet: history 98, 132; English (Shakespearean) form 99, 104-5; cycles of 99-100, 105; variations 102-5; Italian (Petrarchan) form 100-1, 104-5; collections of, 114; examples of in homework 105-14, 115, 128-9, 205, 208-9, 221, 223-4, 225-6, 249, 254

Sonnets for Chris 114

Sonnets from the Portuguese 114

Spenser, Edmund 99-100, 102, 114, 244

"Splendour Falls, The" **34**, 123

Spoken word poetry 288-9

Spondee 38

"Spring and Fall" **224**

"Spring Storm" **188**

Stanza: definition 25, 29, 84; kinds of 84-8, 89; rhyming in 80-1; haiku as 155

Stevens, Wallace 128, 131, 157, 170-2, 198, 219, 224-5

"Summer" **189**

"Surprised by Joy, Impatient as the Wind" **102**, 196

Swahili verse 9

"Sweet and Low" **33**

Swinburne, Algernon Charles 181-2, 183

Syllables 19-21, 28-30, 38-42, 52, 54, 66-7, 120-1, 155, 288

Symbol: as real objects 208-11; archetypes as 211-5, 218; interpreting 215-8

"Sympathy" **217-8**

"Symphony in White, No. 2" 181-2

T

Tennyson, Alfred 16, 26, 29-30, 32-4, 80, 87, 123, 233-4, 244-6, 250 257-9, 282, 288

Tercet 84-5, 89, 135, 136, 140

Terza rima 85, 138

"Terzanelle in Blonde" **138-9**

Task, The 177, 181, 194

Tempest, The 282

"There was a young lady named Bright" **49**

"There was an Old Man with a beard" **49**

"That time of year thou mayst in me behold" (Sonnet LXIII) **107**, 198-9

"There is no frigate like a book" **253**

"There's a certain slant of light" **253**

"They Flee From Me" 88, **96-7**

"Thirst" **223-4**

"Thirteen Ways of Looking at a Blackbird" **170-2**, 219

Thomas, Dylan 138

Thomson, James 177-8

"Tiger Lily" 226-7

"Tired Worker, The" **113-4**, 151

"Tirocinium" **83**

"To Helen" **231**

"To Market, To Market" 28

Toasting 287

Tolkien, J. R. R. 27, 37

Toomer, Jean 225-6

"To Waken an Old Lady" **209**

Triolet 133-5, 141, 145-6

"Triolet for Tishe" **134**

Triple rhyme 66-7

Trochee 38-40, 237, 257

Troubadours: history of 132-3; verse forms of 132-40

"Tyger, The" **44-5**, 51, 85

U

"Ulysses" **233**, 250

V

"Valediction: of Weeping, A" **205-6**

Variation 118, 122, 123, 139

Vers libre 151

Villanelle 136-9, 141, 148-9

"Visit from St. Nicholas, A" **237-8**, 250

Vita Nuova, La 114

Visual rhyme *see* Sight Rhyme

Voice 280-4

W

"Waking, The" 138

Waller, Edmund 222-3, 232

"Wasteland, The" 230, **282-4**

"We Wear the Mask" **147-8**

"What is to come" **146**

"When first we met" **146**

"When I have fears that I may cease to be" **108**

"When I have seen by Time's fell hand defaced" (Sonnet LXIV) **109**

"When You Are Old" 86, **93**

Whistler, James 181

White, Gleeson 150

White space 159-61

Whitman, Walt 151, 152-3

Williams, William Carlos 157, 167-9, 182-5, 188-90, 209, 282

"Willow Poem" **187-8**

"Wind Shifts, The" **127**, 198

Wolanskyj, Lidia 159-61

Word stress: in English, 19; patterns in syllables 19-20; patterns in phrases 20-2, 39-41; in accentual meter 26-7; in qualitative meter 38-41

Wordsworth, William 102, 112-3, 176-8, 187-8, 194

Wyatt, Thomas 88, 96-7, 98

Y

Yeats, William Butler 86, 93, 238, 244, 285-6

Yost, Chryss 138-9

"You should be gone in winter" (Sonnet 73) **104**

About the Author

Ruth A. Johnston is an independent scholar and student of languages. Her three sons were homeschooled between 1991 and 2009; during those years she founded a Scripps-Howard Homeschool Spelling Bee in Schenectady, NY (1994) and taught AP English Literature for the Pennsylvania Homeschoolers AP Online program (between 1996 and 2003). On retiring from homeschooling, she began writing books.

Greenwood Press published *A Companion to Beowulf* in 2005, and *All Things Medieval* (an encyclopedia of material "things") in 2011. Ellen McHenry's Basement Workshop published *Excavating English*, a middle/high school work/text about the history of the English language and spelling, in 2013. Johnston created Pannebaker Press to issue *A Companion to Beowulf* in an affordable paperback edition in 2010. In 2015, Pannebaker Press also published her treatise on human personality, *Re-Modeling the Mind: Personality in Balance*. Her poetry has appeared in *Measure* and *Modern Age* and her collected poems can be found as *Rain in Season*, which is available as an e-book at www.ruthjohnston.com. This personal website also offers a blog, *All Things Medieval*, where she writes about the medieval world. Johnston's most recent book, *Speak Like Rain*, is published by Pannebaker Press in conjunction with Ellen McHenry's Basement Workshop and is available both as a paperback via major booksellers like Amazon, and as a digital book directly through www.ellenjmchenry.com.

www.ingramcontent.com/pod-product-compliance
Lightning Source LLC
Chambersburg PA
CBHW060508300426
44112CB00017B/2581